Gloria T
702 869-27

A GUIDE TO JEWISH PRAYER

ISRAEL INSTITUTE FOR TALMUDIC PUBLICATIONS

Translator
Rebecca Toueg

Production Manager
Ditsa Shabtai

Chief Editor
Rabbi Jonathan Chipman

Editors
Rabbi Jonathan Chipman
Elana Schachter
Esther Hershkowitz
Jessica Bonn

A Guide to *JEWISH PRAYER*

Rabbi Adin Steinsaltz

SCHOCKEN BOOKS · NEW YORK

Published in the United States by Schocken Books, a division of Random House, Inc., New York, and simultaneously in Canada by Random House of Canada Limited, Toronto.

Originally published in Israel in two separate volumes as *Ha-siddur Veha-tefillah* by Miskal Publishing Ltd., Tel Aviv, in 1994.

This book was published with the assistance of the Israel Ministry of Religious Affairs.

Library of Congress Cataloging-in-Publication Data

Even-Israel, Adin.
[Sidur veha-tefilah. English]
A guide to Jewish prayer / Adin Steinsaltz.
p. cm.
Translation of: ha-Sidur veha-tefilah / 'Adin Even-Yisra'el.
Includes bibliographical references and index.
ISBN 0-8052-4174-4
1. Prayer—Judaism. 2. Judaism—Liturgy—History. I. Title.

BM660.E92513 2000 296.4'5—dc21 00-022605

www.schocken.com

Book design by Trina Stahl

Printed in the United States of America
First American Edition
2 4 6 8 9 7 5 3 1

Dedicated by the Beker and Grundman families
in loving memory of

Rhoda and Irwin Grundman
Beloved parents and grandparents

Founders of the Orthodox Jewish community of
Teaneck, New Jersey

They discovered the light of ha-Shem
in the words of the Siddur

משפחות בקר וגרונדמן
מקדישות ספר זה באהבה לזכרם של

שושנה בת יצחק חיים ויצחק בן צבי גרונדמן
הורים וסבים אהובים

מייסדי הקהילה האורתודוקסית
בעיר טינק, ניו ג'רסי

הם גילו את אור ה'
במילות הסידור

CONTENTS

PART TWO ❧ *History*

PART THREE ❧ *The Order of Prayer Services*

PART FOUR *The Synagogue and Communal Prayer*

Appendices

INTRODUCTION

THIS BOOK IS intended to open the gates of Jewish prayer for those who want to know and comprehend both its essence and its structure, and the numerous details concerning the various prayer services.

The book is designed for both those who know very little and for those well versed in prayer, as well as for those who take only an occasional interest in it. For those with little knowledge, it may serve as a guidebook, to assist them in understanding what is going on in the synagogue during prayers, to acquaint them with the contents of the Siddur (Jewish prayer book) they are holding, and to help them to know what they should do and say during the service. For those already knowledgeable, it will shed new light upon the significance of various elements of prayer, explain the structure and order of the prayer services, clarify details, and provide further information about the history and development both of the various prayers and of the prayer customs followed in Jewish communities throughout the world.

The book is not meant to be read all at once. Rather, it is arranged in several sections, each with its own specific purpose and corresponding style of writing. Some parts will demand additional study and reflection, some are intended for continuous reading, while others are meant for reference whenever a reader wishes to clarify a specific issue.

PART ONE: PRAYER (Chapters 1–5), explores general issues concerning the essential nature of Jewish prayer.

PART TWO: HISTORY (Chapters 6–7), presents a history of the Siddur itself, how it developed over the generations, and of the way in which the various prayer rites and customs were created.

PART THREE: THE ORDER OF PRAYER SERVICES (Chapters 8–13), presents a detailed survey of the order of prayer services conducted throughout the course of the Jewish year. This section also contains a chapter about public Torah readings, the manner in which the objects used are made, and the laws and customs that apply to them.

PART FOUR: THE SYNAGOGUE AND COMMUNAL PRAYER (Chapters 14–17), explains various matters regarding the synagogue, communal prayer, artifacts used in prayer, and customs that are not an essential part of prayer itself. This section is largely descriptive, but also clarifies certain aspects of prayer.

At the end of the book, there are four appendices: a short glossary of terms, biographies of the prominent sages mentioned in this book, short bibliographical notes about the books cited, and the names of the Jewish months and the festivals and special days that occur in each of them. These are followed by an index.

On the Style and Use of This Book

Glossary entries are indicated by an asterisk (*); in most cases they are transliterated Hebrew words and are therefore in italics. Names listed in the biographical section are indicated by the "at" sign (@), and references to the bibliographical notes by the number sign (#).

The book contains many discussions of halakhic (Jewish legal) matters; it should be noted that these are intended here for general explanation and guidance only. Due to both the considerable differences among the various prayer rites, and the smaller variations among communities and congregations even within the same prayer rite, as well as other considerations based on the particular circumstances of the worshipper, what is stated here should not be taken as halakhically (legally) binding; rather, whenever there is a need to clarify matters of actual religious practice, one should consult local rabbinic authorities.

The discussion of the prayers is based mainly upon the Sepharad (Ḥassidic) prayer rite, with note being taken of significant differences in the Ashkenazic rite. However, as there is no single, universally accepted version of the Sepharad prayer book, the version used here may not be identical in every detail with versions used in other prayer books.

None of the other major rites (namely, Oriental, Italian, Yemenite, Ḥabad, and Vilna Gaon rites) are discussed here.

Frequent reference is made in this book to the names of famous Jewish personalities. For the sake of brevity, no titles are used except those of "Rabbi" or "Rav," nor are the usual epithets customary for the deceased, such as "of blessed memory," or for the living, such as "may he live for long and good days," except in those cases where the epithet has become an integral part of the name. Sages known in Hebrew by the initials of their names are referred to by their more widely known name in English; e.g., the Saintly Ari—Rabbi Isaac Luria@; Hagra—the Vilna Gaon@; Rabbi Moshe ben Maimon (Rambam)—Maimonides@; Rabbi Moshe ben Nahman (Ramban)—Naḥmanides@; but the Maharsha,@ which stands for Morenu ha-Rav Shmuel Eideles, is referred to as Maharsha; Rabbi Moshe Isserles, as Rema@; etc.

The material in this book was culled from a wide variety of sources. In order not to encumber the reader, footnotes are given only when of special importance.

Quotation marks are used to indicate citations from the original text.

Biblical references indicate book, chapter, and verse. Mishnah* references give chapter and number of the passage. For the Babylonian Talmud, tractate and page are indicated; for the Jerusalem Talmud, tractate, chapter, and section; for Midrash* quotes, according to the accepted convention. Quotations from Maimonides refer to the book, section, chapter, and subsection of *Yad ha-Ḥazakah*,# and citations from the *Shulḥan Arukh*,# to section, chapter, and paragraph.

Special features of the transliteration of Hebrew words are:

ח = ḥ

כּ = k

כ = kh

צ = tz

The basic English translation used throughout this book, with minor deviations, is the Ḥabad translation of the Siddur.

ALTHOUGH THE SIDDUR is relatively small in size, it is a constantly flowing spring. Everything contained in this guidebook is merely a beginning, from which "Let the wise man hear and increase his instruction" (Proverbs 1:5).

PART ONE

PRAYER

CHAPTER ONE *The Prayer Book*

Among the basic texts of Jewish religious literature, the prayer book, or Siddur, occupies a modest place. It lays no claim to original thought or lofty inspiration like the Bible, nor to the breadth and profundity of the Talmud, nor does it give us the mystic insights and spiritual exaltation of the *Zohar*.# Alongside these great and voluminous works, the Siddur seems to occupy a side niche. These other works are constantly studied, elucidated, and pondered with deep interest by the eminent sages of each generation, who write learned commentaries that their students labor to comprehend; while the little Siddur, the common prayer book so familiar to all, is used for prayer and then put aside until the next prayer service.

Yet no book is closer to the heart of the Jew than the Siddur, and none has had such a profound influence. Though other books may be more highly valued and admired, none has been so well loved and so uniquely able to penetrate to the very depths of the soul as the Siddur.

For generations, the Siddur was the first book the Jewish child learned to read, and through the struggle to grasp the combination of its letters, he repeated and learned to recite its phrases by heart. Children who for various reasons might have been unable to progress further in their studies, at least learned how to read the Siddur—even if they did not understand the meaning of the words.

This bond with the prayer book engendered a great intimacy between the Jew and the Siddur in both the emotional and intellectual spheres. The sentences and phrases of the prayer book became part of Jewish consciousness, and over the years were gradually incorporated into the everyday speech of Jews the world over.

But the bond is not only a primary, intimate one; it is an ongoing, lifelong process. From the moment he is first introduced to the Siddur, the Jewish child never ceases to use it. While other books are used only as study texts which, once mastered, need not be read again, or are reread only after a long period, the Siddur accompanies the Jew throughout life. He prays at first, as a young child, haltingly, stumbling over the words; he goes on reciting them as an adult, and continues to repeat the words even when he has become an old man who knows them by heart.

One aspect of the bond with the Siddur lies in its being a book that unites the entire Jewish people. Other books have limited appeal, being meant only for those able to study them and interested in doing so; but every Jewish person uses the Siddur. Even if not all of the "People of the Book" were familiar with the Bible, or never studied the Talmud, the Siddur was known to all. On the other hand, even the greatest and most erudite scholars and sages still related to the Siddur, using it in the same way as did their fellow Jews.

Another aspect of this deep and intimate bond arises from the very essence and nature of Jewish prayer. The Siddur is not merely a book containing the liturgy of the synagogue, but a comprehensive collection of prayers and benedictions relating to every aspect of Jewish life. Not only may a person occasionally pray at home, just as he would in the synagogue, but there is an entire cycle of benedictions and prayers that are by their nature unrelated to the synagogue service—from the prayers recited on rising in the morning, through those that accompany a person throughout the day, until the recitation of the *Shema** upon retiring to bed.

Moreover, the order of prayers relates not only to the weekdays and festivals, but to the entire life cycle: from birth until death, upon reaching maturity and entering marriage, the Jew is accompanied by prayers and benedictions. Nearly every sorrowful or joyous event, of everyday life or of special occasions, is reflected in the prayer book, since the Siddur is the book of Jewish life, in which everyone is involved and to which everyone relates.

But the Siddur's influence is derived not only from its use and from the connection to it but also from its contents. No other Jewish book contains, as does the Siddur, the entirety of Judaism. The Siddur is like a garland, intertwining all the strands of Judaism and encompassing all fields of Jewish creativity in all their variegated forms. It includes sections that reflect the fundamentals of the Jewish faith, and those relating to the field of religious law. There are some that describe a world outlook, and others that recount the central events in Jewish history. The Siddur contains sections of exalted poetry, and matters of ritual procedure. There are prayers that deal with the most intimate details of individual needs and problems, supplications reflecting the sorrows and aspirations of the entire nation, and prayers that touch upon the entire cosmos. It contains texts based upon profound philosophical thought, and numerous others rooted in kabbalistic mysticism. There are selections taken from the Torah, the Prophets and the Writings (Hagiographa), from the Mishnah and Talmud, from the Midrash* and kabbalistic works, from the stylized and complex poetry of medieval times, and from the private, personal prayers of Jewish sages.

In the same way as the Siddur represents the entire expanse of Judaism, it also reflects it through the dimension of time, in the generations of Jewish creativity. Some passages, taken from the Torah and other books of the Bible, hearken back to the earliest history of the Jewish people. Other formulations date to early Second Temple times, while there are prayers and benedictions composed during the mishnaic and talmudic eras. It includes *Piyyutim** (liturgical poems) of the Middle Ages, sections composed long centuries ago, and prayer formulations created in our very own times.

The Siddur is not a finished work produced by the efforts of a particular author, but rather a kind of treasury in which the people of Israel, generation after generation, have deposited things of exquisite beauty. Each generation chooses its own pearls of wisdom and emotion, stringing them together to form verses of prayer.

Yet the Siddur is not merely a depository for precious objects. By its very nature and the manner of its use, the Siddur has a distinctive power of its own. By the very fact of their incorporation within its framework, the various chapters and passages, poems and meditations included acquire a new meaning, in which Torah becomes prayer, abstract thought acquires emotional weight, and matters of significance in their own right become part of the dialogue between man and his Creator. And at any time, whether daily or on special days during the year, a Jew may enter this treasure-house and draw from it the tears and hopes, exaltation and simple words, that he needs in turning to his Creator.

An aggadic* (literary, or nonlegal) passage in the Talmud (*Ḥagigah* 13b) relates that there is an angel on high who "fashions crowns for the Almighty from the prayers of Israel." This saying stresses not only the significance of prayer, far above and beyond its subjective, human aspect, but also the autonomous value of its content, in which words of prayer are seen as elements from which crowns of glory are fashioned.

This conception gives an added dimension to the Siddur, not necessarily on the part of the individual worshipper, but primarily on the part of the great sages and leaders of the nation. "Reflection" or "Devotion in Prayer"—whose "fruits are enjoyed in this world, while the principal remains to be enjoyed in the world to come" (Jerusalem Talmud, *Pe'ah* 1:1)—is the attempt to comprehend and extract the full meaning of prayer, both on the level of actual experience during prayer and on the intellectual level of study and preparation for prayer. A close examination of the language used in the Siddur, the understanding of its structure, and the search for hidden meanings within it, is already evident in the Talmud; like the Siddur itself, such intellectual activity has continued to develop ever since.

But there are many aspects to devotion in prayer, and it has shades of meaning that change and develop over the generations and through the differing intellectual moods of the thinkers who have reflected on it. There is a rich exegetical literature on the prayer book, with commentary applying to every aspect of the Siddur. From earliest times, there have been linguistic commentaries and halakhic studies, exegeses on the structure and form of prayer. Just as there have been, from the very first, studies on the composition of the Siddur, there have also been sages who counted and expounded the number of words, and even of letters, contained in various prayers.

Philosophical discourses have been based on the Siddur, as well as *Kavvanot** derived from kabbalistic ideas. The Siddur may be portrayed as both a reservoir and a summation of Jewish creativity throughout the generations, as it is a source and inspiration for fresh Jewish creativity.

Being without doubt the most frequently used Jewish book, the Siddur is also the one most widely distributed. Prayer books were among the first Hebrew printed books (the first appeared in 1475), and since that time the Siddur has been printed in an enormous number of editions. There are thousands of editions and imprints of the Siddur, but to date there is no complete bibliography of printed Siddurim (plural for Siddur) listing all the editions and places of publication. In our day, not a single year passes without the printing of hundreds of Siddur editions.

Siddurim are published in all sizes and in a great variety of forms—from large folio tomes to tiny palm-sized booklets. Some Siddurim are comprehensive, including prayers for the entire year; others are limited to prayers for a particular festival or group of festivals *(Maḥzor*)*, while still others are confined to the regular weekday services or some part of them. There are Siddurim with numerous commentaries and instructions, including various appendices, and others with no addition whatsoever. Some are printed on cheap paper and in simple print, while others are elaborately bound editions with decorative bindings.

There have been, and still are, Siddurim with such extensive commentary and explanations that the actual prayer text is almost completely buried within its own commentary, while others contain the prayers in a condensed and abbreviated form. Alongside those in the original Hebrew, each generation had its Siddurim with explanations in various languages, or even with full translations of the prayers. There is no way of knowing how many Siddurim have been printed, but the editions published over the centuries must number many millions—far more than any other Jewish text.

In contrast with the "ancient mountain-tops" (Deuteronomy 33:15) of the Bible, the "sea" of the Talmud, or the Clouds of Glory of the mystic wisdom of the Kabbalah,* the Siddur is a wellspring carrying the essence of all of the other sources. Sometimes its waters flow gently, providing words for the mouths of babes and simple folk, while at others they gush strongly into a "wide stream"[1] with all the expanse and depth that the sages have found it to possess. Yet the Siddur will forever remain a "fountain of living waters" (Jeremiah 2:13), quenching the thirsty soul, and revivifying and nourishing the hearts of the people of Israel at all times and in all places.

---

[1] Genesis 36:37, used as a kabbalistic metaphor for the Divine plenum.

CHAPTER TWO *The Essence of Prayer*

PRAYER IS THE salient expression of religious emotion in man and of his relationship with his Creator. There are, of course, many other forms by which people may express their religious feelings—from those fixed ceremonial rites that in themselves constitute a religious ritual, to those acts which man performs in order to obey the will of God, or from which he may refrain because they negate the Creator's will and command.

While these aspects are to be found in every person possessing religious feeling, they are to be found even more so in the Jew, whose life is filled with positive and negative commandments, traditions and customs, and Jewish ways of expression and thought.

Yet there are various influences that are prone to obscure or conceal the inherent purpose of those acts that a person might perform in order to express a relationship with God. Habit and routine may cause a person to cease being aware of the reason for the performance of a given action. It often happens that a person living in a society that shares his faith and behaves in a similar fashion will perform these acts because they seem the normal mode of behavior, without attention to their actual content.

Even when a person performs a ritual ceremony, there is no assurance that the meaning of this performance will be fully realized, as every act involves an external, technical aspect. By punctilious insistence upon performing it in a precise and particular manner, and in assuring that all the objects required are in proper condition, a person is liable to forget its main purpose.

By contrast, prayer is a direct and unequivocal act of relating to God. In whatever way it is performed, and in whatever manner it is uttered, prayer is essentially one thing: an explicit addressing by the human "I" to the Divine "Thou." In the most essential sense, prayer is direct speech, in which man confronts and addresses his Creator.

Such speech may be of many kinds: request, supplication, thanksgiving, complaint, or even simple conversation. All these can be found in prayer, and each one of them can be expressed by personal, individual prayer. The prayers that may be found in the books of the Bible—particularly in the Book of Psalms, which is basically a compendium of individual and public prayers—represent all of the kinds and varieties of prayer with which the individual or public may address God the Creator. The wide range of prayers and benedictions found in the Siddur likewise include the entire spectrum of ways in which a man may address his Maker.

Many prayers are requests or pleas in which man addresses God and asks for something—be it life, health, or success, deliverance from disaster or from poverty. Man may appeal on behalf of himself or for others, whether near and dear or distant acquaintances. On the other hand, there may be requests of an entirely different sort, in which a person asks God to consider the shame he has suffered, or voices his desire to be avenged, to have his enemies punished.

There are still other prayers that are a way of saying "Thank you," whether in general—for all the good things in life, or for the existence of something beautiful or pleasurable—or for some personal, private matter—recovery from illness, deliverance from danger, or in acknowledgement of some special event.

On the other hand, there may be prayer that is an expression of questioning, of wonder, or even of complaint, such as the bold words of criticism uttered by Abraham: "Far be it from You to do so, to slay the righteous with the wicked. . . . Shall not the Judge of all the earth do right?" (Genesis 18:25); or the complaint that also indicates supplication and submission: "Righteous are You, O Lord, when I complain to You; yet I would plead my case before You. Wherefore does the way of the wicked prosper?" (Jeremiah 12:1).

There are yet other prayers that have no clear, definite form of address, but are merely a kind of conversation or outpouring of the heart before God. At times, this confession is a declaration of love and yearning such as "My soul thirsts for You, my flesh longs for You" (Psalm 63:1); at others, it expresses a sense of distance, in which the person bares his heart before God, asking nothing, yet expressing his grief at his material or spiritual loss.

On yet other occasions, a person may wish to "tell" God about his good deeds, and to say with a sense of satisfaction, "Remember this, O my Lord, for my good" (Nehemiah 5:19), or may wish to confess his sins, both overt and covert. All these types, and many others, may be expressed in personal prayer, and are thus to be found in the Siddur, formulated as it is for both personal and public use.

This aspect of prayer—of direct speech addressed to God—is essentially very intimate in character. Not only when a person is alone in the darkness of night, pouring out heart and soul, but even when standing in the midst of a large congregation, with everyone reciting the same words aloud, a close, intimate relationship with God is being expressed. This address in the form of conversation, of direct speech of the human "I" to the divine "Thou," even when expressed by the entire congregation, is based on the simple assumption that such dialogue is possible.

But whether plea or praise, prayer is always speech addressed to God, and such speech is only possible when a person knows that "Verily God has heard me and attended to the voice of my prayer" (Psalm 66:19). This realization that "You hear the prayer of every mouth"[2] is what directs man to pray and to confide in God all those secret, personal matters—needs, anxieties, requests, and heartfelt desires.

But in order to pray in this manner, to "pour out his complaint before the Lord" (Psalm 102:1), one needs to feel a sense of intimate closeness to God, as "Our Merciful Father."[3] The child standing before his father feels he can tell him everything in his heart: to plead, to complain, to thank, or to simply tell him about things.

At every such moment of baring of the heart, in times of distress or joy, prayer takes place with the same feeling of affinity as that reflected in one of the *Piyyutim** recited during the Days of Awe,* "For we are Your sons, and You are our Father" or, in a more profound and even mystical manner, "We are Your beloved and You our Lover."[4]

But in contrast to this approach to prayer, there is another aspect, deriving from a totally different point of view. There is a different mode of relationship to God—that expressed by the prophet: "For who is this that has ventured to approach Me, says the Lord"

---

[2] From the *Amidah** prayer.

[3] From the benediction preceding the *Shema*.*

[4] From the Yom Kippur* prayer.

(Jeremiah 30:21); or, expressed differently, "For I am a great King, says the Lord of Hosts, and My Name is awesome before the nations" (Malachi 1:14).

This sense of awed reverence, of standing before the exalted Divinity, is rooted in the recognition of the distance separating Man from God. As Maimonides@ says, "When he [i.e., man] considers such matters as they really are, he immediately retreats in fear, knowing he is a small, lowly creature standing light-mindedly before the Omniscient God."[5]

Once a person adopts such a point of view, intimate conversation is impossible, and prayer acquires an entirely different character. Confronted by "the Great King," one can only offer the rituals of sacred service. That is, given such a conception, prayer itself is no longer a spontaneous form of speech, but becomes a kind of ritual, sacrificial act. When prayer assumes this aspect of holy service, each part fulfills a particular function in the ritual, and every word fits into its context in a precise and specified manner. This ritual requires that one wear special clothing, and every movement of the body has its own meaning and significance. Prayer then becomes a kind of royal audience, composed entirely of ceremonial grandeur, each word and phrase having its specific place within the ceremony.

Such a ceremony may be held in the "Royal Temple," a site symbolizing the dwelling place of the King of the Universe. Yet by the same token it may be held anywhere, as there is no single "place" for the Omnipresent God, and hence no need for any special building. Unlike prayer, the "temple" or "palace" has a physical reality—but in essence entry to them is identical. When praying, one is as if standing at the gates of a spiritual temple, and every step taken—in the spiritual sense—is a passage from one chamber into another, until one ultimately stands before the Presence of the Almighty.

Such a feeling is not one of fear, but essentially of awe, of the sense of standing before the sublime, "For God is in heaven and you upon earth, therefore let your words be few" (Ecclesiastes 5:1). The emphasis here is not on the fewness of one's words, but on the consciousness of the qualitative distance between Man and God. When such a real-

---

[5] *Sefer ha-Madda, Hilkhot Yesodei ha-Torah*, chap. 2, *halakhah* 12.

ization occurs, man cannot simply say whatever he pleases. Every word uttered must be weighed and counted, and every gesture must be considered and measured. Such feelings need not imply fear or melancholy; on the contrary: they are always accompanied by a sense of privilege that "the King has brought me into His chambers" (Song of Songs 1:4). But in any event, and whatever the content of prayer, it is always a ceremonial occasion, of worship and ritual.

Both these conceptions—God as father, close and intimate, and God as exalted and majestic Being—which seem to be at opposing poles of religious experience, are united in the world of Judaism. Indeed, their combined presence is in itself a fundamental principle in the Jewish worldview. As the poet says, "Further than any distance and nearer than any nearness,"[6] or, "Wherever I find You, You are concealed and evanescent, and wherever I do not find You, Your Glory fills the earth."[7]

This dual conception, known in philosophy as the combination of the transcendental and immanent view of the Divine, and referred to in the Kabbalah* as the tension between the aspects of God as "surrounding all worlds" and "permeating all worlds," is an essential element of the inner truth of Judaism, and constitutes a central issue in every work of Jewish thought. Any examination of Jewish faith relates to this issue, either directly or indirectly.

The kabbalistic appellation of God—"the Infinite, blessed be He"—in itself reflects this double aspect of the Divine, combining an abstract, distancing term alongside one of nearness and human concern.

But such ideas are not confined to the theoretical concerns of sages and philosophers, but are expressed in the very nature of prayer itself. In fact, prayer can only be understood as combining both of these conceptions. Already in one of the most ancient prayers, we find the opening phrase conveying this attitude, "Our Father, Our King" *(Avinu Malkenu*)*. The inner tension of our relationship toward the Creator—"whether as sons or as servants"[8]—runs through the entire

---

[6] *Shir ha-Yiḥud.**

[7] Ibid.

[8] From the Rosh ha-Shanah* prayers.

order of prayer services. Sometimes one prayer may express the sense of standing before an exalted Being, while the very next prayer may be a petulant complaint uttered in extreme intimacy.

Sometimes the formulation of one benediction, such as that of *Hashkivenu** in the Sephardic rite, may delicately interweave both conceptions, "Lay us down, our Father, to sleep . . . and raise us up, O King, to life and to peace." When a person goes to sleep, it is as if he reposes in the arms of his Father, while when he arises from bed he is ready to serve and obey the King, his Master.

These two formulations also find expression in the rabbinic dispute as to whether "Prayer was instituted by the Patriarchs" or "Prayer was instituted corresponding to the sacrifices" (*Berakhot* 26b). This inner tension is also reflected in the prayers of various communities and congregations: some tend to stress the ritualistic aspect, while in others, the more personal, private element is predominant. Yet everywhere and for everyone, both aspects always coexist.

This dual view is essentially based on the very mystery that surrounds our attitude, understanding, and perception of the Master of the Universe *(Adon Olam*)*, who is at the same time "the Merciful Father" *(Av ha-Raḥaman)*. Our Siddur encompasses and combines together both these appellations of God as a whole, thereby allowing us to alternate in word and thought from one conception to the other.

CHAPTER THREE

Individual and Communal Prayer

JEWISH PRAYER, as represented in the Siddur, is essentially the prayer of the community and of the people as a whole. In principle, its structure, contents, and wording are geared to the needs, hopes, and sense of gratitude of the community, so that even the individual praying does so as part of the whole community.

Communal prayer has very ancient roots, derived from two complementary sources. On the one hand, we know that from earliest times, whenever great trouble and suffering befell the community—warfare, plague, or drought—everyone would assemble together to pray, crying out to God to deliver them from their distress. As the prophet describes it, "Sanctify a fast, call a solemn assembly, gather the elders and all the inhabitants of the land into the house of the Lord your God, and cry unto the Lord" (Joel 1:14).

This quotation describes how the people used to pray in times of trouble, elaborating in greater detail upon what is said on the same subject in the dedication ceremony of the Temple by King Solomon (see I Kings 8). Similarly, albeit in a somewhat different vein, II Chronicles 20 describes the offering to God of public thanksgiving for the victory and salvation granted to the people.

At times, communal prayer may be the soul-suffering cry of the entire population, while at other times it expresses itself in the words of supplication or thanksgiving of an individual, offering prayers on behalf of the general public. The Song of the Sea,* beginning with the words "Then sang Moses and the Children of Israel" (Exodus 15:2), was initially a hymn sung by one person, Moses, in his own particular style, in which the people as a whole participated and responded.[9]

The other source of communal prayer is found in the sacred

[9] *Ibid.*, vv. 20–21, describe how the women play and sing a refrain of this song.

hymns connected with Temple rites and rituals. From the very beginning of the Temple period, the sacrificial rites performed by the priests *(Kohanim*)* were accompanied by songs and prayers performed by the Levite choirs. This genre—the weekday psalm, and those for Shabbat and festivals—is found in many of the Psalms, which are clearly sacred hymns sung in the Temple; in addition to personal prayers, this book also contains choral songs and special public recitations. From the very start, Temple worship included "hearkening unto the song and the prayer" (I Kings 8:28).

An even more detailed description of the order of service and song exists for the Second Temple period, when Temple worship was an integration of sacrifice, song, and prayer.

These two sources of communal prayer are interconnected. The hymns of the Temple, as reflected in many of the Psalms, intended for choir and public recitation, consisted not only of songs of praise for divine service, but also incorporated occasional prayer—prayers and supplications in times of trouble, as well as thanksgiving and benedictions for victory and salvation. Just as the Temple worship incorporated sacrifices on behalf of both the community and the individual, it also combined individual and communal prayer.

Thus, once the synagogue was instituted as a gathering place for public worship outside the confines of the Temple, whether in the Land of Israel, outside it, or even in the city of Jerusalem itself, it assumed the character of a *Mikdash Me'at* ("little Temple")—a place set aside for the worship of God and as a venue for communal prayer. Moreover, the basic model for prayer, with regard to both the setting of fixed times and procedures for prayer, and even the actual wording of the prayers to be recited, drew upon and imitated the Temple service.

The Nature of Communal Prayer

The difference between individual and public prayer does not necessarily depend on the number of participants, but rather on the different character and essential nature of each type of prayer.

The individual worshipper may express himself fully, saying those things that seem appropriate to him, in his own personal style and manner.

By contrast, the community—in prayer as in all other activities—is not merely a collection of individuals, but must of necessity create a common ground of sentiment shared among all. This common denominator necessarily blurs some of the individual perspectives, just as it may highlight or lay special emphasis upon other aspects to which a given individual might not respond with the same degree of emotional involvement as another. The community is concerned with those matters shared by the majority of its members, while the feelings and personality of its individual members are absorbed into and obscured by those of the general public; whereas the public cannot relate to the personal problems of the individual, to his private joys or sorrows.

Moreover, even when there is a general feeling common to all the congregants, each individual has his own personal response toward any particular matter, which is not fully expressed through the communal response. For that reason, even though communal prayer can give voice to general sentiments, it cannot express the finer sensibilities of the unique individual. This holds true even when public prayer is held for some specific situation or occasion, and all the more so when it is conducted in accordance with a fixed order and text. Thus, while communal prayer does not fully render what each participant would wish to say, at times it might draw and direct him toward matters that he would not have been personally inclined to consider.

There is another, more inner aspect of communal prayer. When a congregation is deeply absorbed in prayer, a new entity is created—no longer a collection of individuals, but a *Kahal Kadosh* ("Holy Congregation"), praying in unison. Each worshipper then becomes part of a greater unit, drawing strength from the other worshippers, and giving a part of himself in return. Whether consciously or unconsciously, a new set of experiences is created through these interrelated communal components.

The depth and intensity of this awareness largely depends upon the individual and the particular congregation in which he prays, on the spiritual sensitivity and degree of involvement of the individual with the community in which he finds himself. On occasion, a strong and unified congregation may have such a powerful influence upon the individual that he feels completely encompassed by it, so that not only his words and external actions, but even his thoughts and emotions work in unison with the congregants and are fused with those of the communal body. Thus, even though each individual still prays by himself, he no longer prays for himself alone. His prayer is transformed from an isolated component existing alongside others into an element within the unified whole, that only has meaning and significance as an integral part of the entire community.

Even though this sense of communal unity does not necessarily take place each time a Jew prays with a congregation, prayer as such aims to achieve such unity. The main prayers are not only intended to be recited within the framework of public worship, with a "congregation" of at least ten members; each community also prays as part of the greater totality—the people of Israel as a whole.

Apart from the petitions and pleas formulating the needs of the individuals within the community in a collective sense, prayer also contains requests relating to the nation as a whole, with all its sufferings and hopes. When a person prays for livelihood or for good health, he is doing so for himself or for other individuals; but when he prays for redemption or for the restoration of the House of David, he does so for the entire people of Israel as a collective entity. In this way, prayer reaches far beyond the limited framework of the lives and desires of the individuals, or even of the specific congregation, to voice the yearnings and needs of *Knesset Yisrael**—the entirety of the Jewish people.

The same holds true even for private prayer. Even though the person praying alone is not present at that particular moment within a congregation, in a certain sense he nevertheless functions not as an individual, but as part of an absent, invisible congregation. This receives concrete expression in the worshipper's physical orientation during prayer services: while worshipping, all Jews face, not in a particular direction, but toward one specific point—the Temple site in Jerusalem. Thus, even if the worshippers are not gathered together in one place, they nevertheless all belong to a series of concentric circles extending throughout the world, all of which have a common center turning them into a single congregation, bonded together by a mystic unity. In this way, even the person worshipping by himself—wherever he might be—is bound up with the entire congregation of worshippers around the world, through both the prayer text, the time, and the orientation of prayer.

The Communality of Prayer

The communal character of Jewish prayer as the prayer of the entire Jewish people is reflected in many of its aspects: in terms of place, time, number of participants, prayer text and contents, the manner of speech, and the accompanying *Kavvanah** (see Chapter 5).

Although a Jew may (and should) pray anywhere, the synagogue, whose Hebrew name *(Beit ha-Knesset)* means "the place where the community assembles," is the place specifically designated for prayer. Our sages have stipulated (*Berakhot* 6a) that even one who prays alone should preferably do so in the synagogue. Apart from the concept of the holiness of the synagogue as the place set aside for and sanctified for prayers, the insistence upon praying there indicates that even the individual worshipper ought to create a link between himself and the community, by at least worshipping at the location of communal prayer. As the Talmud *(ibid.)* says, "Man's prayer is heard only in the synagogue."

The same applies also to the set times for prayer. It is true that the halakhic considerations determining the fixed time for each prayer relate to the diurnal cycle itself—sunrise, noon, sunset—and to the times established for sacrifical offerings in the Temple. The latter is reflected in the names given to some of the prayers—e.g., *Minḥah** ("afternoon offering"), *Musaf** ("additional offering"). However, the setting of fixed times for prayer also creates a sense of unity among the members of the community, who are engaged in worship wherever they might be. The sages said (*Berakhot* 7b and 8a) that one should pray at a "propitious hour," described as "the hour of communal prayer"—i.e., even if one is not present among a congregation in the place of worship.

The importance of communal prayer is even more evident in the fact that various major sections of the order of prayer may only be recited in the presence of a congregation. It is not only that the individual worshipper does not recite certain things that are, by their very nature, related to public prayer (e.g., the repetition* of the *Amidah** by the *Shaliaḥ Tzibbur**), but that other parts of the prayer service, such as the reading of the Torah or the recitation of the *Kaddish*,* can only be performed when there is a minimal quorum of ten—a *Minyan.** That is, the full order of prayer was composed and intended in principle for communal use, while the individual worshipper recites only portions of this full text.

Even the wording of prayer is likewise formulated, in nearly all cases, in the plural rather than in the singular. At times, biblical quotations that originally appeared in the singular form are altered to the plural when adapted as prayer texts. This occurs not only in those prayers dealing with matters of public concern, but even in those cases that would seem to be highly personal and private. Thus, the *Vidduy** ("Confession of Sins") is recited in the plural form.

This also applies to the contents included in the standard prayer book. The prayers and supplications, and even the words of praise and thanksgiving, relate primarily to national matters. Memories of the past, thanksgiving for present acts of kindness, and hopes for the future commonly refer to the entire world or, more specifically, to the people of Israel as a whole.

This emphasis on the communal and comprehensive aspect of prayer is sometimes found even in the very wording of prayer, which insists that the prayer being uttered is not only for us here, in this particular community or congregation, but for all the people of Israel, wherever they might be. Communal responsibility is also highlighted in certain formulations related to *Kavvanah*, such as *le-Shem Yiḥud,** in which a person performing a given commandment proclaims that he does so "in the name of all Israel."

Individual Prayer

The Siddur is essentially a book designed for the prayer of the Jewish people, of the community. Given that, what place can there be for the prayer of the individual? An individual, who might still feel the desire to offer up a personal prayer for himself alone, whether because he is suffering from some private sorrow or pain, because he feels the need to utter personal words of thanks, or simply because he wishes to pour out his heart in praise and adoration.

In fact, the existence of the institution of public prayer does not at all negate or contradict individual prayer. The individual can and may offer his own private prayers in addition to the public order of service. It should be noted that the fixed prayer texts are intended primarily as an aid to prayer, providing clearly formulated words and thoughts to articulate the feelings of the heart that the individual cannot always adequately express, whether because of lack of knowledge or poverty of language. But if a person wishes to pray by and for himself, he may do so, and the fact that there are fixed forms of prayer need not prevent or constrain him.

Individual prayer may itself assume various forms, some related to general or public prayer, and others completely dissociated from it. Already in talmudic times, various sages used to add some brief personal supplications at the end of the fixed prayer text, or would recite a brief private prayer of their own, whether regularly or on special occasions. Some of these were later introduced into the regular prayer services and became part of communal prayer, while others are preserved only in the Talmud or in other texts. Moreover, the composition of personal, private prayer never completely ceased, and in each generation there have been those who have either written or recited special words of prayer that they, members of their family, or their disciples, used on occasion.

Indeed, even the fixed communal prayer text leaves room for pertinent additions to the general petitions and benedictions. For example, one concerned about a relative suffering ill health may pray for him by mentioning his name in the general benediction for healing, while a person in need of a livelihood or with other financial worries can utter a personal plea while reciting the benediction relating to economic welfare. Even those requests for which no particular benediction is formulated may be included under the rubric of the general blessing concerning prayer. Such additions are not only permitted, but are even desirable, because they enable the individual to express himself about whatever affects him personally and for whatever he feels the need to pray.

Some prayer books include certain texts for the most frequently needed private prayers. These formulae are likewise designed to assist the worshipper who finds difficulty in finding suitable words or phrases for the ideas he wishes to express. But these are in no way intended to curtail the freedom given the worshipper to utter what is in his heart in whatever form or manner he chooses. The worshipper who pronounces the regular text of the *Amidah* benediction for the forgiveness of sins, or the standard version of the *Vidduy*, may add other confessions, personal pleas, and expressions of remorse, just as the one in need of health or economic sustenance may and should add words concerning the private troubles that weigh upon him at that particular time.

Moreover, individual prayer need not be closely linked to the standard prayers or to its text. A person may offer a prayer at any time and in any way he pleases. For many generations, down to our own day, people have felt the need to give voice to their own particular anguish. Men and women frequently come to the synagogue, open the Holy Ark, and pray to God—in their own way and their own language—about matters that trouble them.

Furthermore, individual prayer is not necessarily connected to the synagogue or to some sacred site. A person might feel a special sense of holiness or of closeness to God in these places, but prayer is not specifically dependent upon such locations. Many people have been known to go out—be it at regular intervals or on special occasions—to an isolated location, a field or forest, in order to commune with God in their own private way. Others might engage in words or thoughts of prayer in any place—while walking or traveling, while sitting by themselves engaged in deep, contemplative thought, or lying in bed.

As a rule, such prayers do not consist of any fixed terminology, but are uttered or thought in the language that the worshipper naturally uses. They follow no strict linguistic rules, and are often the result of a momentary emotional impulse. These individual prayers, alongside statutory communal prayer, are of great value, and have considerable significance and influence: from Moses' brief prayer on behalf of his sister Miriam, "O Lord, I beseech You to heal her!" (Numbers 12:13), to the personal prayers of simple folk or small children, offered in their own language and fashion. Such prayers, despite their awkward style, may often be preferable to formal prayers recited with strict care for linguistic and halakhic precision.

The Meaning of Communal Prayer

Since individual prayer is neither forbidden nor rejected, what is the function of regular, fixed, mandatory communal prayer?

There are a number of reasons underlying the manner in which our prayers are formulated in the Siddur as they are: first and foremost, because prayer is itself a form of holy service. Those prayers that have a specific, delineated formulation, and are pronounced by all worshippers without exception, in themselves constitute an act of ritual worship corresponding to the public sacrifices offered in the Temple.

The notion that prayer corresponds to sacrifice is already mentioned in several ancient sources, and finds expression in the verse "So let us render calves by our lips" (Hosea 14:3). The wish to perform an act of divine worship as though it were being conducted in the Temple is not associated with the memory of its destruction; it is connected rather with the fact that even while the Temple was still standing, many people who lived a long distance away from that holy site, or who were not Temple priests, wished to perform an act of worship wherever they were residing. Communal prayer, with its fixed formulations and regulated ceremonials, served as a means of active participation in holy service.

Another aspect of communal prayer, already noted, is its expression of the problems and wishes of the entire nation, going beyond the limitations of individual needs. The individual person usually lives his life within rather narrow parameters; his troubles and sufferings, desires and dreams, relate mainly to his own life or to that of his immediate family. Only on occasion is he able to turn his attention to the pains and aspirations of the general community. For that reason, communal prayer supplements private, personal prayer, leading the individual to reflect upon and express matters that affect the nation as a whole, to think about exile and redemption, to recall the past history of the nation and its hopes for the future.

Moreover, private prayer by its very nature is based upon the "I." True, this "I" is confronting the divine "Thou," yet even so it still retains a considerable amount of egotism. "I need something," "I want," "I request," and sometimes even "I thank," are all different expressions of the "I" as the center of all else. Communal prayer blurs this egotistic attitude by making the communal collectivity the subject offering up prayer, in which the individual is merely one component.

Moreover, the very fact that communal prayer includes such a large variety of requests and supplications, which by their nature do not express the immediate needs of the worshipper himself, in itself makes him more conscious of the problems of others. One who is not ill is reminded of others suffering from illness, while one who is unconcerned with rain becomes conscious of those for whom rainfall is a vital necessity. This very sharing of concerns with others adds another dimension to prayer—the link with and relationship to other people.

The fixed prayer text admittedly restricts self-expression. But for most people the problem lies not in the limitations imposed by the prayer text but, on the contrary, in the difficulty of finding a channel for expressing their innermost thoughts. A person surely does not need flowery phrases or a grand style to address God; "God wants the heart"[10] rather than polished rhetoric. The main issue, therefore, is not the formulation of words, but the definition and clarification of concepts. What prevents man from expressing himself properly in prayer is not the lack of beautiful words and well-turned phrases, but the lack of words altogether. The fixed prayer text thus serves as a means of expressing thoughts that man cannot think clearly for himself, or of feelings that are so blurred and confused that they do not even assume the form of thought.

In addition, the regular repetition of the same well-coined phrases has an educational and didactic significance. The range of thinking of the individual, which is likely to be limited in scope and compass, can receive both breadth and height as a result of praying from the Siddur. But for new ideas to be absorbed by the mind, rather than remaining subjects of chance encounter, they must be constantly repeated. Only through recurrent repetition of the enormous range of thought and emotion found in the Siddur can a person begin to absorb and internalize the significance of the various prayers. It is impossible for a person to absorb everything all at once with the same degree of clarity, for which reason the constant repetition entailed in prayer constantly

---

[10] *Sanhedrin* 106b.

reveals new aspects each time, creating in the worshipper feelings and thoughts that he might never have reached on his own, so that he not only utters the words of the Siddur, but they spring from his own mind and heart.

Individual Prayer Within Communal Prayer

The person praying from the Siddur in a congregation is in a state of constant tension, which itself becomes a significant and positive component of the prayer. This tension is created by three factors involved in communal prayer. First, the worshipper himself, when truly praying and not merely reading or mouthing the words, feels and thinks his own emotion and thoughts; even when he does not bring to his prayers all those personal concerns that have occupied him throughout the day, there are certain matters that he wishes to express and reflect upon in prayer. On the other hand, fixed prayer provides a train of thoughts, themes, and concepts imposed upon the individual from without, from the prayer to the worshipper. Yet a third component is the praying congregation itself, which, both as a whole and as a collection of individuals, affects each particular worshipper.

Each of these three factors diverts and draws prayer in different directions, to a greater or lesser extent, making the prayer of each person the result of the interweaving of these various factors. On the one hand, the worshipper recites the words written in the Siddur, tries to understand them and to focus his heart and mind upon them. But even when he succeeds in doing so properly, his own thoughts and feelings add a further dimension of meaning to the words on the page before him. And all this is affected, whether consciously or not, by the assembled congregation within which he is praying, by the voices of the *Ḥazzan** and the congregation, by the mood of the congregants and the fabric of personal relationships he has with them.

The prayer of the individual worshipping with the congregation may be compared to a musical performance. The score in front of the musician indicates the music that he must play, the sequence of notes and the general mood in which it should be rendered. Yet it is the musician himself who gives to the composition as a whole his own personal interpretation, the manner in which he understands and feels the music, and the particular accent related to his own personality. The orchestra around him also constructs and gives tone to the piece, contributing its own musical virtuosity to both the work and to the musician. That is, the same fixed and written score changes its character and expression in every performance. Sometimes, depending upon the musician's abilities, the music is simply a mechanical repetition of the notes, while at others it rises to the very heights. Notwithstanding the fixed notation, it expresses the musician as much as it does the composer.

Similarly, the individual worshipper prays according to what is written in the Siddur, but at the same time his thoughts and words give to each phrase his own unique interpretation, while his personality as a whole lends a range of personal and private overtones to the fixed prayer texts. His very essence as a human being, as well as his particular mood at that moment, find expression despite the rigid adherence to the written text. Finally, the community in which he prays adds its own contribution, whether of harmony or discord, elevating or diminishing the spirit of each individual worshipper praying within the congregation.

CHAPTER FOUR ❧ *Men and Women*

The Commandment to Pray Applies to All

The commandment to engage in prayer, which is in principle a Torah-based law, is defined as a general injunction to worship God with one's heart and to turn to Him in all times of distress. This commandment is not confined to any specific time period, and is mandatory for all members of the Jewish faith, both men and women.

Even after the sages introduced regular times and texts for prayer, they nevertheless did not consider prayer as one of the time-dependent commandments (from which women are usually exempted), but as one that in principle is not linked to any specific time, and as such is incumbent upon everyone. For that reason, the sages, from earliest mishnaic and talmudic times[11] down to the most recent halakhic decisors,[12] have consistently maintained that women are obligated to pray. Nevertheless, various factors—including both internal, substantive reasons and external, historical causes—have led to certain differences in the way in which men and women conduct their prayers.

Differences in the Concept of Prayer

One such factor is a fundamental difference in the concept and definition of prayer for men and for women. The prayer of men consists of two aspects: that of "service of the heart"[13] and that of ceremonial ritual, corresponding to the dual concept of prayer as private

[11] *Berakhot* 20b.

[12] See *Shulḥan Arukh, Oraḥ Ḥayyim* 106:1.

[13] *Ta'anit* 2a.

converse with God by the individual, and the creation by a group of individuals of a new entity—a community—which, as such, engages in ceremonial acts of prayer as a "congregation."

The prayer of women consists of only one of these aspects—namely, the "service of the heart," the direct personal relationship to God—while the public, ceremonial aspect does not exist at all. This distinction is consistent with a more general division between the sexes in the performance of Divine commandments, in which for women the more spiritual aspects are stressed, whereas the ritualistic aspects are played down.

This distinction has weighty implications for the act of prayer. Women's prayer is not communal prayer; they cannot combine into a *Minyan**; and hence all those sections of prayer that are parallel to or derived from the Temple service are not to be found in it. As a result, a woman has no need for a *Minyan*, nor for most of the ceremonial rites usually performed in the synagogue, in order to pray. It is true that women have been known to attend synagogue services since mishnaic times; however, this was not based upon any obligation, but stemmed from the simple desire to participate in the ceremonial and ritualistic forms of communal worship.

Prayer as such has no fixed venue; it is a direct "I–Thou" relationship with God. There is no need of assistants or intermediaries in order to pray, for "God seeks the heart"[14] and hearkens to the prayer of everyone. The same does not hold true, however, regarding the ceremonial and ritualistic aspect of prayer, which is not incumbent upon all, and which is carried out in a prescribed manner at a specific place. For that reason, many communities had no women's gallery at all in their synagogue, because the women in those communities did not feel it necessary to come especially to the synagogue in order to pray. In other communities, it was customary for unmarried women not to attend synagogue prayers, except on rare occasions.

Over time, the fact that women have no obligation to participate in communal prayer led to various changes in the way women pray. On the one hand, it resulted in the fact that only a very small number of women regularly recited all the daily prayers, even privately. Many

---

[14] *Sanhedrin* 106b.

women sufficed with reciting only one prayer, and even this often in highly abbreviated form. There always was, of course, a small number of unusual women who regularly recited all the daily prayers, including *Tikkun Ḥatzot,** but these were always a small minority. On the other hand, women developed their own style of praying, with more intimate prayer texts relevant to their immediate life concerns, which they might recite whenever they had time or were in a suitable frame of mind.

Such prayers were recited on numerous different occasions, such as the lighting of candles at the beginning of Shabbat, at the conclusion of the Shabbat, upon visiting the cemetery, and so on. Sometimes there would be an accepted text in which each woman could insert her own variations, while at others the prayer would be entirely spontaneous and free, dictated by personal feeling and immediate need. There were also certain more regular, stylized prayers, such as the *Teḥinnot,** composed by learned women and written in the vernacular, which were as widely known and recited by women as were the prayers in the Siddurim.

Historical Causes

In addition to these innate, substantive factors, there were also certain external reasons, related to environment and life circumstances, that created differences between the prayer habits of men and women.

The first, and most basic and constant one, is that women have generally been occupied as housewives. Men have generally been occupied, whether in the home or outside it, in work that has definite time limits, beginning and ending at a fixed hour, whereas the work of a housewife, and especially that of a mother of children, cannot be limited to fixed hours. Even when a woman's work does not involve a greater amount of time, the exigencies of her life make participation in fixed public prayer, or the demands of reciting a lengthy sequence of prayers, unfeasible, if not impossible. The needs of the home and children frequently create minor or major disruptions and, even if these are not a matter of life and death, they cannot be easily postponed or neglected.

Thus, even though the obligation of prayer for women was

never formally suspended, the sages realized that the strict imposition of obligatory prayers would be excessively burdensome for them. A woman who takes care of her household needs, and even more so—of the upbringing and education of her children—may be considered to be performing an ongoing commandment and therefore—like all those occupied in the performance of one commandment—are exempt from others.[15] Moreover, the importance of the commandments in which she is engaged is often far greater,[16] for which reason the sages were not overly concerned as to whether women recited all the daily prayers. Indeed, they urged women not to neglect important matters to which they were obliged to attend, in their zeal to perform the commandments meticulously. For that reason, very few women, both in the past and the present, have recited all three daily prayers in full. Many women recite only one prayer daily; some may also recite *Minḥah;** while the majority do not recite *Ma'ariv** at all.

Consequently, even in those places where women do attend synagogue, they generally do so only on Shabbat and festival days, when household needs are prepared in advance. Those women who do frequent the synagogue constantly are mostly older women, who no longer have small children to care for, and can more easily arrange their work schedule to facilitate participation in communal prayer.

There were other historical reasons for women's non-participation in regular communal prayer. For centuries, little attention was given to the education of girls, and there were many countries, especially in the Orient, in which women were completely illiterate. Even in those countries where an attempt was made to provide every child, boy and girl, with at least some minimal reading ability in Hebrew, this did not ensure a knowledge of the language itself. Most women (as well as many men who, for financial and other reasons, did not receive more advanced education) were only taught how to read the prayers from the Siddur, but did not understand what they were saying. In many synagogues, there was, therefore, a *Maggidah* ("reciter")—a learned woman who acted as a kind of prayer leader in the women's gallery, who would read out, and at times also explain, sections of the prayers to the women present.

---

[15] *Sukkah* 26a.

[16] See also *Sotah* 22a.

Among those women who did not know how to read at all, or found it difficult to do so, only a few somehow managed to learn the prayers by heart. Yet even they did not usually recite the prayers according to the fixed order of service but, as was the custom among Jews of old, in their own language and to the best of their ability. As, according to Torah law, prayer does not have a fixed structure, some halakhic authorities ruled that it is sufficient for women to recite the *Birkhot ha-Shaḥar** (morning benedictions), or *Modah Ani** (the prayer on awakening), or even Grace After Meals,* to fulfill their obligation to pray.

And just as there was totally spontaneous prayer, there were also various prayer formulae composed in the vernacular and recited with great devotion by women—e.g., *Gott fun Avrohom* ("God of Abraham") recited by many women before the conclusion of the Shabbat.

Women's Prayer Texts

Nevertheless, certain changes were made in the women's prayer text for various reasons, mostly in small details. Prayer in general is composed in the plural form, making no distinction between men and women. This is particularly so because communal prayer was originally formulated to encompass the needs of the entire community, including those individuals to whom specific parts of one prayer or another might not directly apply. Thus, certain things that neither obligate nor are connected with women—such as the phrase in the Grace After Meals, "and Your covenant which You have sealed in our flesh," referring to the circumcision—remain unchanged for women,[17] because they are praying for the people of Israel as a whole. Since Hebrew contains no neutral gender, the masculine form is generally used for indeterminate references. However, in instances of personal prayer women would, of course, use the feminine form (as is indicated in some of the more carefully edited Siddurim).

However, those texts relating to commandments from which women are altogether exempt, such as the donning of *Tzitzit** or

[17] See *Shulḥan Arukh, Oraḥ Ḥayyim* 187:4, and *Magen Avraham,*# *ibid.*

*Tefillin,** or those prayers that by their very nature pertain to men alone, are not recited by women altogether.[18]

In *Birkhot ha-Shaḥar,** women use the feminine form in the blessings "who has not made me a [female] Gentile," and "who has not made me a bondswoman," while, regarding the blessing made by men—"who has not made me a woman"—the sages ruled that a woman should replace this with another blessing of praise: "who has made me according to His will." Certain commentators have explained that this blessing indicates the unique standing of a woman, upon whom the human world depends for its continued existence, for which she here expresses her profound gratitude.

The Women's Gallery *(Ezrat Nashim)*

The most ancient synagogues already had a certain section set apart for women, the *Ezrat Nashim* ("women's gallery"). The term *Ezrat Nashim* also refers to a section of the Temple, but there is no similarity between the two senses of the term. The *Ezrat Nashim* in the Temple was the large central courtyard, in which both men and women could congregate together. Only on special occasions, such as *Simḥat Beit ha-Shoevah,** celebrated during Sukkot* with dancing and unusual expressions of joy, a raised wooden gallery was temporarily set up, where the women could sit and watch.

Furthermore, by very definition, there was a difference between the experience of visiting the Temple and that of attending the synagogue. Those who visited the Temple were festival pilgrims, or people who came to offer sacrifices. The Temple was a place not for communal prayer but of sacrificial offerings, in which those who stood in the courtyards mostly watched the priests perform the sacrificial rites. Naturally, those who came to the Temple also prayed there, but this was a purely personal kind of prayer, each person addressing God on his own behalf, in his own way and with his own words, saying what was in his heart. The synagogue is, on the other hand, a place of com-

[18] Halakhic authorities differ in their views concerning specific prayers and benedictions to be omitted by women.

munal prayer, where people pray as a unified group, a "congregation," albeit composed of many different individuals.

Since the synagogue is the place where the community needs to pray "as one man and with one heart,"[19] it was necessary to prevent the intrusion of other factors that might interfere with prayer in one way or another. Whenever men and women are present together, a certain psychological atmosphere is created that is difficult to ignore. Even if everyone is dressed suitably and behaves in a thoroughly modest and respectable manner, this element is still present and plays an active role. Under different circumstances, such as in work or in business transactions, or even in neutral social gatherings, this element may not be so important or conspicuous; but during prayer, when a person has to deepen and refine his inner sensibilities, any extraneous spiritual element has an exceptionally strong impact.

The need to remove all other thoughts from the mind during prayer does not specifically refer to "sinful thoughts": even feelings of family warmth can mar the perfect communion of prayer. There are, of course, occasions when a family acts together as a single social and emotional entity in the service of God—for instance, during the Shabbat meal (see Chapter 9), or even more so during the Passover *Seder** (see Chapter 10). But there is no place for such things in the synagogue, where they can even become an obstruction. Because of this, our sages have ruled that a person may not kiss his little children while he is in the synagogue, so as not to mingle other forms of love with the love of God.[20]

In a certain sense, the soul's direction in prayer is in principle a "vertical" one, from below to above, whereas the "horizontal" relationship between man and his fellow men—which is present in all prayer, and especially in communal prayer—is of secondary importance, its function being only to help and direct the worshipper to elevate himself through prayer. Hence, any emotional direction that is not germane to the basic purpose of prayer, to the attempt to merge oneself with the entire congregation in order to rise together to a higher state of mind and heart, would only disrupt the inner experience of

---

[19] See Rashi's® commentary on Exodus 19:2.

[20] *Shulḥan Arukh, Oraḥ Ḥayyim* 98:1.

prayer. Just as the sages have applied this ruling to negative emotions—e.g., if one hates another person in the congregation, for whatever reason, he ought to pray in a different synagogue—they likewise applied it to positive emotions such as love, affection, or mutual interest, when these distract the worshipper from the feelings he should be experiencing in prayer.

Hence, the women's gallery is built as a separate section of the synagogue, in order to reduce any admixture of emotions and sensitivities of another kind in the duration of the prayer. Obviously, partitions as such cannot prevent a person from thinking about anything, but they can at least minimize those thoughts that are stimulated by sight. As our sages said, "the eye sees and the heart ponders."[21] And the sages of Israel have always been consistent in their effort to structure prayer and to design the house of prayer in a way as to assist the worshipper to direct his heart toward God—and God alone.

---

[21] Midrash,[#] *Numbers Rabbah*, 10:2.

CHAPTER FIVE ❧ *Kavvanah*

The Importance of *Kavvanah*

There is a well-known dictum stressing the importance of *Kavvanah**:[22] "Prayer without *Kavvanah* is like a body without a soul."[23] This means that prayer, which is the speech addressed by man to his Creator, loses its essential quality when it becomes solely the recitation of words, without inward attention to the meaning of the words being spoken.

Obviously, spontaneous, personal prayer, uttered in time of need, is expressed with *Kavvanah*, because it springs entirely from the heart of the worshipper at that particular moment; such words of prayer (if they are in fact articulated verbally, and the one praying does not suffice with thought alone) are an expression of earnest intention. The problem arises when there is a fixed order of prayer, recited from the Siddur or learned by rote, so that one may reach a stage where the words are recited almost mechanically, without thinking about their real meaning or significance.

The problem is not a new one; the sages of the Mishnah (*Berakhot* 4:4) already referred to it by stating that "one who makes his prayer a fixed routine, his prayer is not considered a supplication." Some of the greatest teachers of mishnaic and talmudic times (Jerusalem Talmud, *Berakhot* 2:4) complained of difficulty in maintaining a level of inner concentration during prayer. In later generations, it was even conceded that, in general, "at no time are we ever sufficiently concen-

---

[22] In the plural, *Kavvanot*. The Hebrew term *Kavvanah* is a complex one that means, among other things, intention, attention, purpose, devotion, and concentration of thought during prayer or in the performance of religious commandments.

[23] This saying was first mentioned in the book *Yeshu'ot Meshiḥo*, by Rabbi Isaac Abravanel.®

trated,"[24] as a result of which certain practical guidelines regarding prayer were proposed.[25]

Nevertheless, *Kavvanah* in prayer is not only a spiritual desideratum for the worshipper: it is also a binding halakhic requirement. The following is the formulation of the *Shulḥan Arukh*,# which generally deals with the formal halakhic details of Jewish religious life:

> *The worshipper must inwardly intend the meaning of the words uttered by his lips, and imagine himself to be in the presence of the* Shekhinah,* *and should remove any disturbing thoughts, until his mind and heart are pure for prayer. He should think that, were he standing before a king of flesh and blood, he would prepare his words carefully and address them well in order not to fail in his attempt. All the more so when he is standing before the King of Kings, blessed be He, who searches our innermost thoughts. For this reason, pious and worthy men of old used to seclude themselves and concentrate their minds in prayer until they were able to transcend their physical being and strengthen the power of their intellect so as to attain a level close to prophecy.*[26]

While not everyone is required, or can even be expected, to attain such a high level, it certainly sets a certain standard in regard to *Kavvanah*, and even those unable to reach such heights should not remain satisfied with being merely "like a twittering bird"—in the derogatory words used by certain sages[27]—or like a parrot repeating sounds that have no meaning for it.

Levels of *Kavvanah*

There are, in fact, various levels of *Kavvanah*, each one higher than the other.

The lowest level is one that is nearly passive: simple understanding of the words being recited. This basic level of *Kavvanah*—to "direct

---

[24] *Tosafot*,* *Berakhot* 17b.

[25] See *Shulḥan Arukh, Oraḥ Ḥayyim* 70:3, and elsewhere.

[26] *Ibid.*, 98:1.

[27] See the *Kuzari*# by Rabbi Yehudah Halevi,@ art. II, par. 24.

his heart to the meaning of the words which he utters"[28]—is a basic requirement pertaining to any act of reading or recitation: to at least comprehend what is being uttered. Admittedly, throughout the ages, there have always been Jews who never managed to learn Hebrew, and who never understood the meaning of the prayers, but merely recited them by rote. Yet these unlettered folk would often pray with a fervor that had its own significance and holiness. Thus, they really prayed, because in their prayers they were conscious of standing before the Creator, and felt the sense of communion with Him. Even if their thoughts were not always related to the words they uttered, "their hearts cried out to God" (Lamentations 2:18).

Our sages taught that such prayer should not be disdained. They spoke of its great value, and even stated that it would be received with far more grace than the more highly articulate, but indifferent, prayer of others. But in an age when deep religious emotion is not very common, the recitation of prayer with sufficient comprehension of its meaning is a basic level of *Kavvanah* in prayer.

This initial level of *Kavvanah* is characterized by varying degrees of intensity, depending upon the spiritual abilities of the worshipper and the amount of time and concentration invested in prayer. This stage of mere comprehension may consist simply of plain, literal understanding of each separate word or phrase, or may involve a greater penetration into the form, contents, and related aspects of prayer. This kind of reading with comprehension creates, at least, some sort of relationship, and, if strengthened and deepened, may also lead to a certain exaltation of spirit.

The next level of *Kavvanah* goes beyond that of simple reading and understanding, to the identification of the worshipper with the prayers recited. The prayers in the Siddur are no longer seen as an external text, but are an expression of inward feeling and experiences. The emotions of the worshipper go hand in hand with the words written in the Siddur, so that he himself experiences the feelings of thanksgiving and joy, recollection and contemplation, reflected therein.

Such a degree of identification is not impossible to attain, as many people feel it in other contexts. People listen to music and feel in total unity with the emotion expressed therein, or they read a story and

---

[28] *Shulḥan Arukh, Oraḥ Ḥayyim* 98.

identify wholeheartedly with the characters and events portrayed. *Kavvanah* in prayer is very much like this, in that it calls for the same kind of identification with the words uttered during prayer.

There are various degrees of this second level of *Kavvanah* as well, corresponding with the depth and intensity of identification. For some, the words in the Siddur are a general guide for the inner emotions that run parallel to them. At a higher degree of identification, words and worshipper fuse together, with every word and phrase of prayer becoming his very own thoughts and feelings.

This kind of identification, when it reaches its highest degree of intensity, is no longer mere verbal communication, but creates a concrete, cosmic connection. The Talmud (*Ta'anit* 24a) relates that when certain sages recited the words "He lets the winds blow," the winds instantly began to blow; and when they said "and the rain to fall,"[29] rain fell. Such prayer is no longer the subjective appeal of the worshipper, but is an actual, objective encounter with the Creator and with the world He created.

Another form of *Kavvanah* is derived from mystical and esoteric teachings. Here, too, there are different levels. There are general *Kavvanot* that explain or stress the meaning of prayer as a whole, or of particular words and expressions. At times, such *Kavvanot* are printed in regular prayer books, especially those of the Oriental communities, and are in principle an additional, more profound way of interpreting the words uttered in prayer.

There are yet deeper kinds of *Kavvanot*, that are not only more complex, but which demand that the worshipper enter into a different mode of prayer. The *Mekhavnim*—as those praying in this manner are sometimes called—are said to actually experience what they fix their minds upon. One who directs his prayer toward higher worlds not only knows the "address" of a particular phrase within a prayer, but is able to raise himself to that level. In theory, a person might practice such *Kavvanot* in the same manner as he does any other skill; but this would deprive such *Kavvanah* of its unique quality. Prayer books that provide these detailed *Kavvanot* can only serve as a guide, while the actual act of inner concentration and spiritual elevation can be attained only by the worshipper himself, if he is indeed worthy and able of doing so.

---

29 From the second benediction of the *Amidah*.*

In earlier generations, there were those who opposed such *Kavvanot*, not only because they were unsuitable for all, but also because they were no more than technical charts. They claimed that prayer itself, if only performed in the right manner, could reach these same heights even without this kind of esoteric knowledge. As one of the Tosaphists said, "I pray with the mind of a little child"[30]—that is, with the absolute simplicity and innocence of a child. Since talmudic times, eminent sages have always asserted that prayer that comes from the depths of the heart, with earnest inward desire, reaches a higher level than that attained through the most sophisticated *Kavvanah*.[31]

In any event, this type of *Kavvanot* remains the path of a select number of people who have prepared themselves adequately, through their personal being, thought, and action, to rise to those spiritual heights.

Kavvanah and the Regularity of Prayer

The main reason for a person failing to be fully attentive during prayer (even in the lowest, simplest sense)—i.e., at least as much so as he would be while reading a letter—lies in the regularity of prayer. This regularity involves two aspects, both of which tend to diminish *Kavvanah:* the fixed time set for prayer, and the fixed text.

The obligation to pray at certain fixed times often compels people to pray on occasions that might not be conducive for concentration. One who has had a sleepless night, even if spent on Torah study or in charitable work, is usually too exhausted to concentrate during the morning prayer of the following day. Likewise, one rushing to attend to some emergency will be too hurried to focus his mind on prayer, while one preoccupied with various matters will find it hard to dismiss them and fix his attention on prayer.

With regard to the fixed text, a person who prays regularly over a long period of time becomes increasingly familiar with the prayer texts, and sometimes may even know them all by heart. This familiarity may

[30] Rabbi Shimshon of Chinon; see *Responsa of the Ribash* 157.

[31] See Tractate *Ta'anit*, chap. 3, in both the Jerusalem and Babylonian Talmuds.

lead one to lose interest in them, and even to boredom; and, since the words and sentences seem to flow almost by themselves, there seems hardly any need for any mental activity on the part of the worshipper reciting them; his mind drifts away to other things, his eyes rove about, his ears listen to things irrelevant to prayer—and all these serve to distract him from the meaning of the words of prayer, which are recited mechanically. It is not uncommon for a person who has been praying since childhood to reach a point where he says precisely everything that he is supposed to say—standing, sitting, or bowing at the appropriate times—without being at all aware of the prayer that he is praying, even to the extent of forgetting that he has prayed at all!

The problem of fixed prayer was already well known in the past, and in earlier generations the expectations of fixity in prayer were more flexible, so as to allow greater opportunity for inward concentration, which is the very heart of prayer. In later generations, however, greater fixity was introduced into the format and times for prayer,[32] based largely upon the argument that, since most people do not concentrate very well anyway, it is preferable to at least retain the regular aspects of prayer.

This regularity is not maintained for formal reasons alone, but embraces other positive aspects. The fixity of prayer is in itself an expression of a particular aspect of prayer, especially that of public prayer—namely, its being a form of "service," a ritual act. Even if the only sacrifice offered in prayer is the sacrifice of the time alloted to it, and the only meal offering we bring is one of words, these still represent an act of real giving. And even though it may not be a perfect offering of the heart, it is still a form of holy service.

Psychologically speaking, too, this is not at all simple or straightforward. While reducing novelty and spontaneity, regularity in prayer has other values—e.g., the sense of commitment, of an ongoing, constant connection with God. Just as there are people who have a deep religious awareness and an inward need to "converse" with God, there are others who would rarely do so of their own accord, if at all. Regular prayer provides even those who by nature are distant from spirituality with a reminder and incentive to create a relationship with God. External and formal as it may be, this relationship nevertheless exists

[32] According to the *Tosafot*,* mainly in medieval times, and in certain instances even later.

and functions. Despite its being repeated in a routine manner, the very regularity and frequency of fixed prayer can well generate moments of real communication that would never have otherwise occurred.

Achieving *Kavvanah*

"The service of prayer," as it is called by the sages of Israel, is not a particularly easy task. The greatest difficulty is not that of its regular performance and the recitation of its words, but that of achieving the necessary inward *Kavvanah*. For such service to be properly carried out, there is need of what one Ḥassidic teacher called "the effort of the spirit and effort of the flesh." Only a small number of people are privileged to experience continuous renewal and spiritual arousal. For the ordinary person, the effort and labor involved in achieving this is a heavy burden that cannot always be borne.

But even though there is no "magic formula" that applies to everyone, there are ways to achieve *Kavvanah*. Each person's soul is a unique world unto itself, and what works for one person is not necessarily effective for another. Nevertheless, there are some pieces of advice that are likely to be useful, to some extent, for most people.

First, there are certain external measures that can be taken to at least prevent disturbances during public prayer. The sages, from earliest time down to the present, warn against any kind of conversation in the synagogue unrelated to the prayers, even if the subject is neither trivial nor prohibited. The *Zohar*[#33] states that conversing in the synagogue is contemptuous and arrogant behavior toward the presence of the *Shekhinah* (the form in which God is ever-present in the world), which abides there. Many sages have stated that it even entails "profanation of God's name," with all that this serious transgression implies. One of the great sages, Rabbi Yom Tov Heller,[@] composed a special *Mi she-Berakh** prayer for those who refrain from conversing during prayers.

Shenei Luḥot ha-Berit[#34] cites a ruling against bringing small children to the synagogue if they have not yet learned how to behave there

[33] *Zohar*, Exodus 131b.

[34] By Rabbi Isaiah ben Abraham Halevi Hurwitz, better known as the Holy Shelah.

with due respect. The presence of small children, who innocently play or disturb their parents and other worshippers, can be a source of serious distraction during worship. However important it may be, educationally, for children to visit the synagogue and to feel a sense of identification with it, care must be taken that this be done in such a way as to inculcate a proper attitude of respect. When the worshipper in the synagogue is forced, for family reasons, to act also as a baby-sitter, he becomes a hindrance to both himself and others. An awareness of the dignity of the synagogue and an attitude of an inner feeling of "Temple-like awe"[35] toward it are in themselves an important means of attaining a closer, heartfelt relationship with God through the prayer recited in the synagogue.

But beyond that, *Kavvanah* can be attained by inner effort. The first step is the simple awareness that entering into prayer is, in fact, stepping into another kind of reality, in which a person undertakes the maximal effort to detach his mind from all those mundane matters with which he is usually surrounded. Our sages have described the hour of prayer as the "Shabbat" within each day, a period of time set aside for sacred matters, during which a person leaves the sphere of his regular activities and turns his mind away from the matters that surround him constantly.

Of course, this cannot always be done simply by expressing a wish to do so; however, people do constantly do similar things: when taking a holiday or going out to enjoy themselves, they manage quite well to forget their troubles and to place themselves on a different plane. Indeed, if personal problems and preoccupations are really so serious that one cannot tear his mind away from them, this fact in itself should be a reason for prayer. Thus, instead of worrying about one's troubles during that time, or considering various possible plans and possibilities for dealing with them, one should pray about them—whether they concern finance, health, or any other matter that weighs upon one. Prayer should not be divorced from daily life, but rather be a means of elevating it. When one pours out one's sorrows and troubles before his Creator—such is true prayer. The very transference of a problem from the arena of human effort and capability to that of entreaty and earnest

---

[35] Leviticus 19:30; *Yevamot* 6b.

supplication before God alters, in itself, one's mental attitude and behavior.

Another step in achieving *Kavvanah* is the deliberate effort to concentrate upon what is being recited. Such concentration, even in a brief prayer, is not always successful; but in this, as in many other areas of life, one should not adopt an extremist, either/or position. Even if one becomes distracted at certain times or in certain passages, one must always consider the other side—namely, those times or portions of the prayer during which one did succeed in attaining concentration and in achieving some degree of *Kavvanah*. Moreover, over time and with consistent, sustained effort, concentration of thought becomes easier. Concentration of any kind does not come easily to everyone, but with time and with regular practice, people learn how to concentrate on matters that they are studying or are involved with.

There are other ways in which people may help themselves to attain concentration and *Kavvanah*. Some people are able to concentrate better when they recite things aloud and accentuate them, so as to make it clear to themselves what they are saying. (Of course, this is not easily done in public worship, although there are some congregations in which it is customary for everyone to pray aloud, so that no one disturbs the other.)

Some people manage to attain more perfect *Kavvanah* when they sing the words, or introduce some special melody in prayer. Not all music is suitable for this purpose, and at times the singing may become more important than the content of prayer. But there are certain melodies that were composed so as to induce meditation and concentration of thought, and through which one may enter into an atmosphere of worship.

There are also various techniques to prepare oneself for prayer. It is said in the Mishnah (*Berakhot* 5:1) that "in former times, pious people used to wait for an hour and then pray." Such waiting was a way of preparing one's heart to enter into the right mode for prayer. In later times, Ḥassidim would spend several hours prior to prayer in order to reach a stage of contemplation. Some do this through meditation alone, while others devote this time to the study of subjects that stir the heart and prepare it for prayer.

There are no strict rules for this; rather, each person finds some means that is effective in arousing his feelings in the direction of prayer. Of course, not everyone can regularly allow himself such lengthy preparation; but even if some period of time is occasionally set aside for this purpose, the benefit of such preparation is enjoyed not only during the prayer that immediately follows but also for a long while afterward.

The external environment is also an important factor. For generations, Jews have refrained from decorating synagogues or prayer books with illustrations, so as not to distract the mind from the prayer itself. Our sages did recommend having windows in the place of prayer; these, however, were not set overlooking the noise and tumult of the street—which would cause distraction—but were facing skyward, which not only causes no distraction, but also elicits greater *Kavvanah* from the heart. Even the most beautifully decorated synagogues were usually ornamented only with objects that arouse holy thoughts. Our sages have also recommended that one should pray facing a place in which there are no objects (and, if possible, even no other people) liable to divert one's attention from prayer.

There is also the human environment, the congregation in which a person prays. When one prays with people with whom one feels no spiritual kinship, then psychologically speaking, one is praying alone. If he dislikes all, or some, of his fellow worshippers, this may become a serious impediment to prayer. One must remember that prayer is essentially an entry into a state of high emotional sensitivity. True, in prayer a person exposes himself mainly before God; yet while in this state, one becomes more keenly aware of subtle matters, such as the feelings and experiences of others. During the course of everyday life, a person learns how to shield one's soul with protective devices, by whose means one may continue to function even when the human and physical environment provides abundant stimuli, which may either attract or repel. But during prayer the worshipper is required not only to concentrate his thoughts but to show a readiness and an openness to emotional experience. Yet precisely by doing so, one becomes more vulnerable to external disturbances as well.

From one point of view, the worshipper is always alone and isolated, even when praying among a large group of people: the focal point of his prayer is the relationship between the human "I" and the divine "Thou" of God as He reveals Himself at that particular moment. Even though prayer is mostly formulated in the plural form, uniting the individual with the nation as a whole, in essence it is a private expression and personal attachment. Just as one cannot be nourished by the food eaten by another, so he cannot pray except by himself.

But from another point of view, a person praying by himself does not do so only as a separate individual. The prayer of every Jew is always, in truth, in the "name of all Israel." The individual standing alone in prayer carries with him his environment, the people to whom he is connected in various ways, and even the inanimate objects that surround him.

For this reason, when praying in public, a person should always seek a congregation that will be supportive of his prayer, rather than the contrary. In a praying congregation, the prayer of each person strengthens and encourages the prayer of every other individual. At moments of emotional weakness or dullness of the heart, one may participate in, and be swept along by, the praying congregation.

The congregation acts like a circle of dancers giving constant support to one another, helping the individual to overcome weariness and continue further than each one might do alone. The Ba'al Shem Tov[@] explains this by means of a parable: In order to reach the heights, the worshippers create a kind of human ladder, each one standing on the shoulders of the next, thus enabling the individual to climb up high. Anyone who leaves this ladder not only removes a rung, but destroys the entire ladder. On the other hand, one who finds a congregation suited to his prayers is invigorated and elevated through it and by his participation in it.

PART TWO

HISTORY

CHAPTER SIX

The History of the Siddur

THE ESSENCE OF PRAYER—man's turning to his Creator in supplication and gratitude, with praise and petition—is a quintessential part of man's relationship with God, and as old as man's existence on earth. This elemental form of prayer, however, has no fixed pattern; rather, it springs from the innermost emotions of the human heart, or from the social cohesion that occurs when a group of individuals join together as a congregation to express their sense of faith and devotion to God.

Even in the Torah, whose central concern is the creation of frameworks and pathways by which the Jew can relate to God, there is no fixed or sharply defined structural pattern prescribed for prayer. Some sages hold that the Torah obligates a person to turn to God daily to offer Him this "service of the heart," while others think that the Torah requires a person to pray only in times of distress. All concur that the biblical commandment of prayer does not impose specific times for worship, and certainly not any fixed formulation.

However, since earliest times there have been individuals who set aside regular periods of the day for offering God this service of the heart, which the *Zohar*#[36] calls "the Service of Love." In the words of King David, "Evening and morning and noon will I pray and cry aloud, and He shall hear my voice" (Psalm 55:17). Later, we find fixed times for prayer recounted in Daniel, "His windows being open in his chamber towards Jerusalem, he kneeled upon his knees three times a day, and prayed and gave thanks before his God" (Daniel 6:10).

But the maintaining of fixed hours for worship was the custom of only a few individuals, who felt an inner need to address themselves to their Creator at regular intervals. The majority of the people prayed whenever the need arose, whether in response to their inner emotions,

---

[36] *Zohar*, Leviticus 68a.

or in times of distress, or when they had some special petition to make to God.

The Creation of Standard Prayer Texts

At the beginning of the Second Temple period, this situation was radically altered by the Sages of the Great Assembly, the leaders of the people at that time. As the result of exile and oppression, a large part of the Jewish people in both the Land of Israel and in other countries had lost the sense of continuity with their heritage. Familiar traditions that had been observed during the First Temple period were forgotten or became confused, while even the Hebrew language became adulterated with foreign words and idioms. People found it difficult to express themselves in any form of speech, and particularly so in their own language, the Holy Tongue. In addition to the immense effort, undertaken by the religious leaders of Israel—beginning with Ezra the Scribe—of reeducating the people, it was necessary to set down clear and specific guidelines that might be learned and transmitted from one generation to another.

One of the things the Sages of the Great Assembly managed to accomplish was to fix and regularize the text of the prayers. In order to do so, they coined a standard version (*Matbe'a;* literally, "coin") of the basic prayers and benedictions. The free but incoherent expression of individuals was thus replaced by well-defined formulae, which rendered, in simple and lucid language, brief yet eloquent, a complete framework of prayers and blessings. In this way, the basic formulae for the principal blessings were created, and a standard pattern of prayer created for all Jewry.

The Sages of the Great Assembly were a group of mostly unknown scholars who acted in ancient times (fifth to third century B.C.E.) as a unified entity with a common purpose. During that period, while the scriptural canon was being closed, great care was taken that the Oral Law, which included both the inherited traditions and the regulations that had been instituted in the course of time, should continue to be transmitted orally and not be written down. For this reason, we do not have any specific knowledge of the detailed formulations set down by the Sages of the Great Assembly.

In addition to the outlines for the major blessings—whether those pronounced by individual worshippers, in public worship, or for Temple rites—they established the basic structure for what was initially known simply as *Tefillah* ("the Prayer"), and later came to be known as the *Amidah* ("Standing Prayer") or *Shemoneh Esreh** ("Eighteen Benedictions"). The *Amidah* has a well-defined structure, which has been retained almost intact from that time till today, consisting of three opening benedictions, which are primarily words of praise and glorification, and three closing benedictions, containing thanksgiving and general supplication. In between these benedictions—which serve as a framework, and remain fixed and unchanged in all the prayers throughout the annual cycle—they instituted twelve petitionary benedictions which are recited on ordinary weekdays, dealing with both the personal needs of every individual and the general concerns of the Jewish people as a whole. In this way the basic pattern of the *Amidah*, which became the central core of Jewish prayer, was created.

On Shabbat and festival days, rather than these twelve petitionary benedictions, only one benediction is recited, dealing with the sanctity of the day (be it Shabbat, a festival day, or Yom Kippur—the Day of Atonement). For the New Year festival, in which the blowing of the *Shofar** plays a central role, they composed three benedictions in a lofty, majestic style, referring to the Kingdom of God on earth, the day of judgment, and the future Redemption (see Chapter 11). For the major public fasts (see Chapter 12), which were held in times of trouble or distress without any fixed dates, with public prayers being conducted everywhere, particularly near the Temple area, six special petitionary benedictions were added to the *Amidah*, making twenty-four in all.

In addition to instituting the basic prayer formulations, the Sages of the Great Assembly introduced fixed times and orders for the prayer services. As the established order of prayer, with its fixed formulations, gives powerful expression to the praying community, the holy congregation that gives vent to its general and particular supplications, these prayer services—"the service of the heart"—were linked to the time periods fixed for the public sacrifices offered in the Temple. Thus, *Shaḥarit,** the Morning Service, is held parallel to the time for the morning daily *(Tamid)* sacrifice; *Minḥah,** with that of the afternoon *Tamid* offering; while *Ma'ariv** (or *Arvit*)* coincides with the conclusion of the Temple rites at night. On festive days throughout the year, extra public sacrifices *(Musaf)* were offered in the Temple in addition to the regular ones, corresponding to which an additional prayer service called *Musaf** was instituted for those days (namely, Shabbat, *Rosh Ḥodesh*—see Chapter 12—and festival days), in which the central benediction of the *Amidah* prayer depicts the sanctity of the day and its special sacrifices. On major fast days (of which we nowadays observe only Yom Kippur—see Chapter 11), a closing prayer service was added close to nightfall, *Ne'ilah,** for final supplications and spiritual awakening.

In those days, the Temple services and the inner service of prayer were considered as two parallel systems. In the Temple itself, only the *Shema** and a few benedictions were publicly recited, while whoever wished to pray in the Temple did so in his own language and style; whereas outside the Temple precincts, synagogues were established, where the community could gather for public prayer as well as for study and public meetings.

Such synagogues were to be found everywhere, both in the Land of Israel—such as the one on Masada, the only surviving synagogue from the Second Temple period—as well as in the Diaspora. Synagogues also existed in Jerusalem, including one adjoining the Temple, on the Temple Mount itself. The regular public prayers were recited in this Temple synagogue; we know of certain sages who used to go first to the Temple, to view the offering of the sacrifices, and proceeded from there to the synagogue to recite the prayer corresponding to that sacrifice.

Insofar as it is possible to reconstruct the prayer customs of that period, it would seem that the morning service began with a number of hymns, mainly from the Book of Psalms, preceded and followed by *Birkhot ha-Shir** ("benedictions of the song"). Then came the reading of the *Shema*, with the relevant benedictions before and after, followed by the *Amidah* prayer. The Afternoon Service consisted of the *Amidah* alone, while the Evening Prayers contained both the *Shema* and the *Amidah*. This basic structure has remained throughout the generations, albeit in the course of time it has become expanded and far more elaborate in form.

The basic manner of conducting prayer originates from the same period. Public prayer, as prayer of the whole community, is always performed in a "holy congregation"—i.e., with a *Minyan** of ten or more men. As the standard formulation of the prayers was still transmitted orally at that time, there was need for a *Shaliaḥ Tzibbur** ("prayer leader") to recite the prayers aloud, while part or all of the congregants, who did not know the text by heart, prayed with him.

During the period, standard formulations were also composed for many privately performed ceremonies, such as the benedictions for the opening and conclusion of holy days—i.e., the *Kiddush** and *Havdalah** for Shabbat and festival days; the *Haggadah** for Pesaḥ (whose text still reflects the period during which it was recited together with the eating of the paschal offering in Jerusalem); and the various blessings of praise and thanksgiving (see *Birkhot ha-Nehenin**).

Prayer in Mishnaic and Talmudic Times

Even though the principal prayers and benedictions were composed by the Sages of the Great Assembly and their disciples during the Second Temple period, they did not receive their final form at that time. Even the order and formulation of the benedictions remained loose, and many discrepancies arose among the customs practiced in different locales and according to different schools of halakhic thought. Even the fixed nature of prayer was not established definitively: questions arose whether this or that prayer should be said daily, or only on occasion; whether one needed to recite the entire text or only a shortened form of it; and even the status of the *Ma'ariv* service, which did not correspond to any specific public sacrifice as such, was unclear.

The need for more definitive rulings became acute after the Destruction of the Temple in 70 C.E. This national tragedy generated an enormous spiritual upheaval, demanding not only new definitions of the place and status of prayer, but changes in their very formulation.

When the Sanhedrin, the highest religious authority for the Jewish people, sat in the town of Yavneh following the Destruction of the Temple, it laid down many regulations, including the form and order of the benedictions of the *Amidah*. These were fixed according to the School of Hillel,* thereby resolving many disputes; indeed, the very existence of a single central authority led to a general uniformity of the prayer formulation.

At Yavneh, an additional benediction was inserted into the Eighteen Benedictions of the *Amidah* prayer, one which was actually an imprecation and curse against the various deviant sects and against informers. This benediction was intended to emphasize and strengthen the barriers, and to prevent the penetration of heretical views into the Jewish community. It was finally decided at that time that the fixed daily prayer would be obligatory for all, and that only two prayer services—*Shaḥarit* in the morning and *Minḥah* in the afternoon—would be considered as fully mandatory. Only in relatively later times did *Ma'ariv*, the Evening Prayer, also become obligatory.

Although there remained the theoretical possibility, in certain cases, of reciting a truncated version of the prayers or to omit a prayer entirely under certain circumstances, the dominant tendency was to fix the time and version of the prayer once and for all. During this period, and particularly later, following the failure of the Bar Kokhba revolt in 135 C.E., the Sanhedrin introduced changes into the prayer text, so as to adapt it to the situation in which the Temple no longer existed and the people of Israel ceased to be politically independent. Additional passages were hence inserted into the text of the *Amidah*, as well as of other benedictions, referring to the destruction of the Temple and the yearning for redemption and national restoration.

During the generations of the *Tannaim** (sages of the Mishnah) and the *Amoraim** (sages of the Talmud) in the Land of Israel and in Babylonia, there was an ongoing tendency to expand and refine the prayer liturgy. Further additions were made to some of the briefer benedictions in classic Hebrew style—a combination of biblical and mishnaic language—and many ancient prayers received their final formulation. Thus, for example, the essential formulation of the prayer *Nishmat Kol Ḥai,** recited on Shabbat and festival days—whose original, ancient version was embellished with additional sections—was the work of the sages in the Land of Israel. But the grand style of the prayers for the Days of Awe, particularly of Rosh ha-Shanah (the New Year, see Chapter 11), derives from the Talmudic academies of the early Babylonian *Amoraim.* The basic structure of the *Shema* benedictions and the prayers for Shabbat and festival days were also evidently fixed during this period.

Gradually, prayers and benedictions formulated by individual sages became part of the general prayers: e.g., *Elohai Netzor** ("O Lord, guard my tongue"), recited at the end of the *Amidah* prayer; or *Modim* *de-Rabbanan,** which is a conglomerate of prayers by different sages, recited during the repetition of the *Amidah*. Some rabbis integrated various prayer texts into more complex and complete units. What characterizes all these prayers is the lucidity of language and the absence of external forms, such as rhyme or rigid metrical patterns, beyond their intrinsic poetic quality.

A further innovation of those generations was the introduction of psalms and of other biblical passages as an integral part of standard prayer. At the beginning of the amoraic period, the recitation of Psalm 145—now known as *Ashrei**—as a hymn repeated three times daily, was introduced. Later, more such psalms were added, until the collection to be recited during the *Shaḥarit* service, known as *Pesukei de-Zimrah,** taken entirely from biblical sources, took shape. One may thus state that the basic pattern of the prayer services in common use until the present day had already taken shape by the end of the amoraic period. Although this liturgy was not completely fixed, the main prayer formulae had already become standard practice, and the order and customs of prayer were accepted by all.

Liturgical Poets and Devotional Poetry *(Piyyut)*

At the end of the talmudic period, a new era began for the prayer book—the age of the liturgical poets and of their devotional poetry *(Piyyutim*)*. In the broadest sense of the term, one may include under this rubric the entire body of religious poetry intended to serve as part of public prayer. In a narrower sense, it refers to the devotional poetry composed by poets in the Land of Israel and their disciples during the talmudic era and immediately thereafter.

The forebears of such poetry are to be found in the biblical psalms, many of which were sung as part of the holy service while sacrifices were being offered in the Temple, in addition to being included in the prayer formulations of the Great Assembly. The creation of *Piyyutim* apparently began already in the days of the Mishnah,* but only after many generations did the *Piyyut* become a creative genre with its own unique style, gradually gaining in variety and quantity.

The *Piyyut,* or devotional poem, functions as a lyrical interlude; it does not form an integral part of the prayer benediction but is supplementary to it. Notwithstanding its belonging to a specific prayer or benediction, it stands as an independent entity in its own right.

The earliest *Piyyutim* were written in the language of the prayers—in the clear, lucid style of mishnaic Hebrew, which is both simple and sublime. An example of this kind of *Piyyut,* which is found in all the prayer texts, is the lyrical sequence of the *Kedushah** within the benediction *Yotzer Or,** which precedes the recitation of the *Shema.*

The early *Piyyutim* have a poetic cadence similar to that of biblical poetry, but do not conform to any defined metrical pattern, nor are they rhymed. However, even in early times, many *Piyyutim* were alphabetically arranged, as are a number of biblical psalms. The *Piyyutim,* composed by anonymous poets, were meant to supplement the general prayers, particularly on Shabbat and festival days, yet once introduced into the main body of prayers, they became an inseparable part of it.

At a later time, near the close of the Jerusalem Talmud period (around the fourth century C.E.), these *Piyyutim* began to grow in number. They now had both alphabetical arrangement and verse rhyme, but no fixed metrical pattern. During this period, some *Piyyutim* began to be composed with an acrostic, forming the author's name by the first letters of each line, rhyme or verse, so that we get to know at least the names of some of their authors. Such, for example, are the *Piyyutim* describing the service of the High Priest on Yom Kippur (see *Seder ha-Avodah**), many of the *Hosha'not** for the Sukkot* festival and *Hosha'na Rabbah,** some of the *Seliḥot** for the Ten Days of Repentance,* and many other *Piyyutim* for special occasions throughout the year.

A further advance took place when the *Piyyutim* began to draw upon the corpus of aggadic Midrash* (rabbinic legends and tales—each called a *midrash,* referred to in the plural as *midrashim*), which was then in the process of being collected and arranged and which often contains great poetic compositions as well. But these *midrashim,* which originated in homilies delivered in the synagogues by the sages in prose form, were here adapted by the liturgical poets into verse form.

In this way, many unique structural forms of the *Piyyut* were created, containing not only acrostic patterns and rhymes, but also a wealth of newly coined linguistic forms. Their authors took complete poetic license, creating for their literary purposes a multitude of linguistic forms that had never existed before. They composed poetry of a highly complex form, richly embellished with intricately woven midrashic lore. Sometimes the midrashic references were explicitly stated, but generally they appeared in subtle, tortuous allusions, almost as in a riddle, which only a well-versed scholar could recognize and comprehend.

In this manner, an enormous number of *Piyyutim* were created—*Kerovot,** *Yotzerot,** *Geulot,** *Ofanim,** *Reshut**—and appended to various prayers, to be recited or chanted within the formulae of the various benedictions, which provided a kind of framework and conclusion to the sections of *Piyyut.* It would seem that the synagogues were constantly revising and changing these *Piyyutim,* every Shabbat or festival day, and so thousands of *Piyyutim* were composed, either by request or by spontaneous improvisation, though only a small number of them were incorporated in the various texts of the Siddur.

Since it was difficult to pray at length on weekdays, most of the *Piyyutim* were created for Shabbat and festival days, or for special occasions. There are thus cycles of *Piyyutim,* not only for the Shabbat in general, but also for particular Sabbaths during the year, in which the poets refer to the themes of the approaching festival or of the Torah portion to be read that week. There are also cycles of *Piyyutim* for the festivals themselves and, in particular, for the Days of Awe.*

In addition, there were poems, written in the same style, which were not meant to be linked to the prayer liturgy but rather to be recited independently—as communal singing on Shabbat and festival days (*Zemirot** or *Bakkashot**), or on special occasions in the life of the community or the individual, such as weddings, circumcisions, and days of mourning.

Many of the *Piyyutim* written in this style were composed by poets and sages of the Land of Israel, one of the best known of whom was Rabbi Eleazar ha-Kallir.@ But poets in various Diaspora lands also began to partake in this poetic creativity, each community adopting for itself a different set of *Piyyutim,* whether from those composed in the Land of Israel or by poets of their own community.

By the end of the Geonic period (ca. eleventh century C.E.), two distinctive styles of *Piyyutim* began to emerge. The former, characteristic of the Land of Israel and which spread to those countries directly or indirectly influenced by it, continued the style of the liturgical poets of the Land of Israel. This style appeared in the poetic compositions of the Jewish poets and sages of Italy, and later also of France and Germany, albeit the latter's style was less complex, with a smaller number of new words and literary coinages and far fewer midrashic allusions. Many of these poets were among the greatest sages of their generation, including such luminaries as Rabbenu Gershom Meor ha-Golah[@] and Rashi,[@] whose *Piyyutim* were at times preserved in the prayer book thanks to their authors' eminent standing. It was this poetic style, developed over a period of generations and from so many sources, that was finally introduced into the prayer book and shaped the prayer version of the Western countries—the Ashkenazic rite, in all its variations, including the Ḥassidic Sepharad rite (See Chapter 7).

A completely different poetic style developed in those countries under Islamic rule and under the influence of Arabic poetry and culture—Babylonia, North Africa, and, to a greater extent, Spain. In these countries, *Piyyutim* were likewise composed as additions and supplements to the fixed texts of the prayers and benedictions, but their authors drew mostly on the language of the Bible, with its rich lexicon and distinctive grammatical style, and tended not to coin new words or use unfamiliar neologisms. Unlike the allusive, elliptical language of the *Piyyut* of the Land of Israel, these *Piyyutim* were of far greater clarity both in form and content. Although most of the poets retained the traditional acrostic pattern and use of biblical idioms and poetic closures, their meters were based largely on those of Spanish poetry, which borrowed in turn from Arabic poetry. But in their sacred verse they made lesser use of complicated metrical patterns and created poetry both simpler in form and more lyrical in expression. Some of these *Piyyutim*, which were probably written at the request of the community by such eminent sages and poets as Rabbi Solomon ibn Gabirol,[@] Rabbis Moshe and Avraham ibn Ezra,[@] and Rabbi Yehudah Halevi,[@] represent the heights of sublime religious poetry, profound in content and superbly beautiful in form.

The poems composed in southern France (Provence) and later in Italy belong to the same literary genre. These *Piyyutim* were introduced into the various prayer texts of those countries, some of them being found to this day in the Siddurim and *Maḥzorim*[*] of the standard Oriental liturgy, while others became part of the prayer rite of other communities.

This period of poetic creativity ended in approximately the fourteenth century C.E., when the various prayer rites became more or less fixed. But the composition of religious poetry did not cease entirely, and various poetic works continued to be composed during the centuries that followed, mainly in the Eastern countries and in Yemen, and some of them were even introduced into the various liturgies. Yet these can in no way be compared to the far greater number of earlier *Piyyutim*, nor do they hold such a central position in the liturgy.

Siddurim and *Maḥzorim*

Although some texts of prayers and benedictions were already written down during talmudic times, this was done mainly by individuals and was generally frowned upon. During the posttalmudic period, prayers began to be recorded, but evidently, these still were, mostly, notations by private individuals and did not have any official status or authority.

With the increasing dispersion of Jewish communities in the world—many of which were lacking in substantial local Torah leadership—and with the growing number of *Piyyutim* and other accretions to prayer services, an enormous number of customs and prayer liturgies were created. Many of these were, of course, merely additions or embellishments to suit the local taste; but there were also many aberrations, as well as fundamental errors, both in what was said and in the manner in which the prayers were conducted. Many of the questions sent to eminent rabbinic leaders in the major Torah centers—particularly, during the Geonic period, to the *Geonim*,* who headed the *Yeshivot** in Babylonia—related to issues concerning prayer and its customs. As a result, they felt it necessary to lay down general guidelines and to create standardized prayer texts.

The first known Siddur written by a major authority with the aim of establishing a fixed liturgy was that composed by Rav Amram ben Sheshna Gaon (d. ca. 875 C.E.), in response to a request by the Jews of Barcelona, Spain. It included a main prayer text, supplemented by the laws and customs of prayer. Rav Amram Gaon's Siddur thus became a classic source for the creation of a single prayer liturgy in many Jewish communities around the world.

A more detailed Siddur was written by Rav Sa'adia Gaon,@ consisting of a standard prayer text, with the addition of *Piyyutim* (many composed by himself), and laws of prayer written in Arabic. Twelfth-century Europe produced both the *Siddur of Rashi*,# composed by Rashi's disciples, and the *Maḥzor Vitry*,# which was likewise a product of the school of Rashi, both of which contain the laws of prayer and well-defined liturgies. Maimonides'@ law code, the *Mishneh Torah*,# also incorporates basic prayer texts of the Siddur.

There are a number of extant manuscripts of a variety of versions of Siddurim and *Maḥzorim* from the late medieval period. Generally speaking, the term Siddur was used for the prayer texts of the regular order of services held during weekdays and Shabbat, while the term *Maḥzor* was reserved for the liturgies of the three major festivals and the Days of Awe (the High Holy Days), which include many *Piyyutim* and other additions. But the distinction between these two terms is not rigid, and they are often used interchangeably. In addition, it was customary to write, and later to print, separate collections for the *Seliḥot** recited prior to Rosh ha-Shanah and during the Ten Days of Repentance, the *Kinot** for the Ninth of Av (see Chapter 12), and the Passover *Haggadah*.*

So long as books were handwritten, and hence their distribution very limited, there was a large variety of prayer texts for the different communities. With the invention of printing, prayer rites gradually became more uniform; and although they never achieved complete conformity (see Chapter 7), common formulations and prayer customs were established for large groups within the Jewish people around the world.

The Influence of the Kabbalah

The Kabbalah, the mystical doctrine of Judaism, is the "inner" teachings concerning the significance and secret meanings of the Torah, which goes hand in hand with the revealed Torah. The earliest rudiments of these mystical teachings seem to have been systematically taught at the centers of study for the disciples of the prophets

[37] II Kings 2:3, and elsewhere.

(known as "Sons of the Prophets").[37] Such teachings were naturally available only to the choice few who wished, and were able, to comprehend them.

We know that, since Second Temple times, the study of the hidden mysteries of the Torah has been considered the highest level of Torah teaching, and was conducted in the framework of the story of creation *(Ma'aseh Bereshit*[38]*)* and the story of the Divine Chariot *(Ma'aseh Merkavah*[39]*)*. As the contents of these teachings were kept secret, we know only how they influenced the formulation of prayer, both in the Temple and outside it, from certain hints. It is quite clear, however, that the sages who composed the prayers encoded within them concepts and key words derived from the realm of hidden, mystic thought.

Only centuries later, in the late Middle Ages, did books begin to appear on these subjects, originating from two different schools: *Ḥassidei Ashkenaz* ("the Pious Ones of Franco-Germany") and *Ḥakhmei Sepharad* ("the Sages of Spain"). Even in those days, such study was limited to a few small, closed groups, albeit it is possible to trace the influence of mystic thought on the prayer liturgy. One indication of this influence is found in the various *Piyyutim* composed by these pious sages, such as *Shir ha-Kavod** and *Shir ha-Yiḥud*.* But its influence was felt primarily in emendations and revisions of the prayer text. Various esoteric traditions relating to the number of words, or even the number of letters, in certain prayers and benedictions, as well as stylistic and linguistic details, were all directed by the mystic tradition and introduced into the fixed liturgical texts.

From the period following the Expulsion from Spain (beginning with the sixteenth century C.E.), study of the Kabbalah became more widespread, making what had once been the heritage of a few small groups an inseparable part of general Torah study. The major center in the city of Safed—which served as a kind of spiritual center for the Jewish people in those days—was the home of some of the greatest halakhic scholars, who also engaged in kabbalistic study, as well as of many great Kabbalists and poets.

---

[38] Genesis 1.

[39] Ezekiel 1.

The influence of kabbalistic learning spread from there throughout the Jewish world, creating significant changes in the Siddur. Many new sections were added to the Siddur, such as *Kabbalat Shabbat,* * *Tikkun Ḥatzot,* * prayers for *Yom Kippur Katan,* * *Tikkun Leil Shavu'ot,* * and others. Some of these customs were accepted in all communities and prayer rites, while others took root only among certain especially pious groups.

Likewise, many additions were made to existing prayer sequences, such as the recitation of *Yehi Ratzon,* * *le-Shem Yiḥud,* * *Berikh Shemeih,* * and others. Nearly every religious ceremony acquired complex patterns and forms derived from kabbalistic sources. This phenomenon is most prominent in such rituals as *Kiddush Levanah** and the Counting of the *Omer,* * but is also quite evident in such commonplace rites as putting on *Tefillin** or the *Kiddush* for Shabbat.

Even details in the existing prayer texts were altered in various ways, by the addition or deletion of words or changes in their order, in accordance with kabbalistic notions. This influence may be observed in all of the prayer rites used today, althogh it is less strongly felt in the Ashkenazic and Italian liturgies, and is far more pronounced in the Ḥassidic *Nusaḥ Sepharad,* and to an even greater extent in the Sephardic, or Oriental, rite (see Chapter 7).

Although the major kabbalistic patterns and additions were already present in all rites by the seventeenth century, religious creativity in the kabbalistic spirit has continued during subsequent generations as well. Kabbalistically inspired words of prayer and song were added to prayer books compiled by various eminent sages, and some have become commonly accepted custom in many communities.

The Ḥassidic movement not only introduced a special prayer rite based upon the Kabbalah, known as *Nusaḥ Sepharad,* but also composed new prayers and introduced new prayer customs. Among many Oriental communities, a wealth of prayers and songs were added to the prayer book, reaching its height in the creative compositions of Rabbi Yosef Ḥayyim of Baghdad@ (the Ben Ish Ḥai), which have become an integral part of the Oriental rite.

Recent Generations

Creativity and change in the Siddur and prayer customs have continued in recent generations as well. Voluntary or forced migrations from one country to another have led to a certain blurring and obscuring of local customs and prayer liturgies. In addition, the publication of editions of the Siddur that are widely distributed has led to a growing unification among prayer customs. There is a definite tendency to delete many of the *Piyyutim*, or at least to allow them to fall into disuse. These include not only those composed for Shabbat, which hardly anyone still recites, but also those recited for the Days of Awe, which in most places have been somewhat reduced in number.

Today many congregations and communities, which were previously completely separate geographically, find themselves in the same place—particularly in Israel—resulting in a certain amount of cross-fertilization regarding prayer rites as well. Notwithstanding the failure of attempts to create a single, "unified prayer version" *(Nusaḥ Aḥid)*, there are mutual borrowings, such as the inclusion of *u-Netanneh Tokef** in some of the Oriental *Maḥzorim* for the Days of Awe, as well as other cross-influences in the style and melodies of prayer.

The composition of songs and *Piyyutim* continues even today, primarily among the Oriental communities, some gaining wide distribution and being included in the Siddurim. Historical events and realia, which were reflected in the prayers of every generation, find expression in our generation as well: from the composition of a special prayer to be recited by airplane travelers to dirges about the Holocaust, or, on the other hand, a special order of service instituted for Israel Independence Day and for Jerusalem Reunification Day. As in earlier generations, some of these innovations remain confined to specific places or communities, while others have spread beyond their places of origin. Some will doubtless remain in use for only a short while, while others will remain for generations to come.

CHAPTER SEVEN ❧ *Prayer Rites*

The order of prayer services is essentially the same among all Jewish communities throughout the world. Despite the dispersion of Jews to every corner of the world, the overall framework of worship, as well as the language and content of the main prayers, has been retained. However, over the course of time, several prayer rites *(Nusḥaot*; singular: *Nusaḥ*)* have developed, differing from one another in many details.

The different prayer rites are parallel to, but not identical with, the customs of the various communities and congregations. In some cases, members of communities widely separated geographically and linguistically, and observing different customs, may use the same prayer rite. In contrast, there are members of communities living in close proximity and observing the same halakhic customs who nevertheless differ from one another in their respective prayer rites.

In our times, the main rites in use are common to a large number of communities and congregations. However, residents of different countries, and at times even communities from different cities—or groups who have remained loyal to the custom of their previous place of residence—may zealously retain their own local customs, including their prayer rites. But these variations in custom, based upon the same basic prayer rite, are generally minor, consisting simply of omissions and/or additions.

Prayer rites differ from one another in various ways, including the order of some of the prayers, the language of specific texts, and the selection of *Piyyutim** (see Chapter 6), which are often unique for each congregation. As a rule, the more ancient the prayer, the fewer and slighter the variations (mainly an occasional change in word, or even in vowel point). There are often more substantial differences in the later prayers, entailing the absence or inclusion of specific prayers, particularly in the case of the *Piyyutim*, only a few of which are common to all rites.

Along with the universal tendency to create innovations in prayers and customs, there is a converse phenomenon—a general tendency to unify or standardize the various rites. These influences originate in one or more of several factors, such as the Kabbalah (Jewish mysticism), the proximity of communities, and improved levels of communication among different communities.

Antiquity of the Prayer Rites

The evidence for the existence of variations in prayer rites is very ancient. We know, for example, of certain differences existing even in mishnaic times (at the end of the Second Temple period) and at the beginning of the talmudic period (third century C.E.). There are several reasons for this. First of all, it is clear from our sources that from the earliest days, no special care was taken regarding the exact text of any particular prayer. It is true that the sages declared that "whoever changes the wording of a benediction fixed by the sages does not fulfill his obligation [in reciting it]" (*Berakhot* 40b), but this dictum only applied to the primary contents of each blessing—namely, the primary subject matter or key words to be uttered, its opening and ending words, and whether or not the name of God was to be mentioned in it.

With regard to the more detailed formulations, however, such fixed rules were not laid down. Both individuals and cantors (see *Ḥazzan**) used to recite the words in their own manner—shortening, elaborating, or making changes as they wished. Moreover, there was a definite tendency to improvise, tradition even relating that some sages would constantly compose their own prayers. In those days, written versions of prayer were unknown; indeed, there was even a rabbinic adage that "those who write down the benedictions are as those who burn the scrolls of the Torah" (*Shabbat* 115b). At those times, people were accustomed to learning everything by heart with great accuracy. Nevertheless, the lack of a written formulation inevitably contributed to the creation of different prayer structures and texts.

The circumstances that followed from the Destruction of the Temple were another factor contributing to these variations: on the one hand, the need to change much of the wording of prayers; on the other, the disappearance of the one unifying center where the people could gather. Moreover, political events—revolts against Roman domination and the Roman-Persian wars—weakened the ability of the leadership in the Land of Israel to resolve the problems of world Jewry, including the issue of the correct composition of the prayers. At the same time, Babylonian Jewry was gaining in spiritual power and creating its own centers of Torah study. It is therefore not surprising that different prayer formulations emerged under such circumstances.

Indeed, in the Mishnah and Talmud, various customs and versions of the benedictions and prayers are compared and discussed; clear rulings are also set down, showing preference for a particular text over another, or for the combination of different texts into a single unified one. Yet many issues remained vague and unresolved, with communities continuing to pray in their old customary ways.

The differences between the new Torah centers in Babylonia and those in the Land of Israel became increasingly marked, and Jewish communities in other countries either followed the lead of one of them completely, or were influenced by both together.

The combination of all these influences, together with original creativity in the areas of religious poetry and prayer, variety in ethnic custom, and the development of several different sources and centers of authority, ultimately led to the earliest formulation of prayer rites. As it became customary to record the Oral Law in general, and formulations of prayers and blessings in particular, prayer rites began to become more regularized. Thus, communities that were close to one another, or subject to mutual influence, began to create a more or less unified prayer rite for an entire region, one that was to last for generations.

Justification for the Different Prayer Rites

The existence of different prayer liturgies is analogous to the existence of variations in halakhic practice. Not only did the sages of Israel not attempt to abolish or discard various customs, but they even granted them obligatory status. Every person is to practice the customs of his forefathers, or those endemic to the place where he lives. These customs are of course subject to the authority of the Halakhah, and when, on occasion, a given custom deviated from Halakhah, it was eradicated; but so long as the various customs are within the ken of the Halakhah, they are entitled to an independent existence.

Prayer rites likewise fall under the general rubric of religious customs which, so long as they are halakhically acceptable, are incumbent upon the members of the particular community. In each generation, there were sages who examined details of their local prayer rite, at times altering them on the basis of halakhic, theological, or linguistic reasons. In principle, however, each rite has been maintained, retaining its own unique character.

Rabbi Isaac Luria[@] is quoted as expounding a deeper and more intrinsic justification for the existence of numerous prayer rites. As described in Ezekiel's eschatological prophecy (Ezekiel 48:30–35), there will be twelve gates to Jerusalem, one for each of the tribes of Israel; so, too, in the "Heavenly Jerusalem," "the City of our God" (Psalm 48:2,9), there are twelve gates, each one intended for one of the tribes. The twelve prayer rites correspond to these gates—each belonging to a different tribe—through which the people of Israel may enter the City of God. The different prayer rites are thus not simply equally valid ways to reach the Divine, but even more so: each tribe of the Jewish people has its own intended gateway, which is the best one for its souls to pass through.

However, Rabbi Isaac Luria is also quoted as saying that there exists a thirteenth gate, a "general gate" encompassing all the tribes, and that the prayer rites that he preferred (which later became the model for certain rites, and for changes in others) were in fact part of this thirteenth gateway.[40]

To put it in other, nonkabbalistic terminology: the various prayer rites are the perfect vessels of expression for the various parts ("tribes") of the people of Israel. Thus, each rite is both the way in which each

---

[40] The main points of this idea are given in a number of books: *Magen Avraham*,[#] on sec. 68 in the *Shulḥan Arukh, Oraḥ Ḥayyim; Ma'avar Yabbok*[#]; and *Likkutei Amarim* ("Collected Sayings") of the Maggid of Mezeritz.[@]

tribe of Israel may express its form of spiritual existence, and the best path for a member of that tribe to reach the "City of God."

Prayer Rites Today

There were far more prayer rites in the past than exist today. Several of the older rites lapsed for various reasons. At times, this was the result of an entire community being expelled from its native locality, its members dispersed in different directions and adopting the ways of the community they joined (as occurred, for example, among the French communities, especially those of Provence). In other cases, members of several dispersed communities, originally distant from one another, ultimately settled in the same place, where they created a common prayer rite (as did, for example, the various Spanish communities that settled in Turkey). In yet other cases, a particular prayer rite that had been in use in one specific small Jewish community was lost with the disappearance of that community (as happened to the Asti-Fossano-Moncalvo rite in Italy). Many other local prayer rites fell into disuse when overwhelmed by a more scholarly, dominant wave of newcomers, who brought with them their own customs and liturgies, assimilating local custom and rite to themselves (as was the case, for example, when the Jews from Spain settled in the Land of Israel).

Today, there are five major prayer rites in use. Three of them—*Nusaḥ Ashkenaz*, the Ḥassidic *Nusaḥ Sepharad*, and *Nusaḥ ha-Sephara-dim* (i.e., the rite of Oriental Jewry)—are used all over the world, while the remaining two, the Yemenite and the Italian, are more localized.

Nusaḥ Ashkenaz—The Ashkenazic Rite

This rite, like the others, is based on the order of service laid down by Rav Amram Gaon (see Chapter 6) and the other Babylonian *Geonim*,* and was originally strongly influenced by the traditions and customs of the Land of Israel. It would appear that the original core of Ashkenazic Jewry was made up of people from the Land of Israel who migrated from Israel to Italy, and from there to France, Franco-Germany (*Ashkenaz*), and Eastern Europe. The influence of the Land of Israel is evident in many of the customs (and possibly also in the pronunciation of the Hebrew), and even more so, in the adoption of the liturgical poetry of the Land of Israel, which was later to be further developed independently by Ashkenazic Jewry.

The origins of the Ashkenazic rite began in France, which during the twelfth century was the major center of West European Jewry (Spain, at that time, belonging to an entirely different cultural and political sphere). But its formulation into a well-defined version—which, in many details, was considerably different from the official French version—occurred in Germany during the generations that followed the *Tosafot*.* The sages of Franco-Germany gave this prayer rite its distinctive character, which persists to this day; tradition has it that they even composed the basic melodies for the prayers. While many changes and additions have been introduced over the generations (largely under kabbalistic influences), the main body of the texts has not undergone any noticeable alteration.

The differences between the various prayer rites can be discerned in nearly every section of the prayers, but in most cases these are merely variations in the formulation of the same basic ideas.

Distinctive features of the Ashkenazic rite include:

- In the Morning Service, the prayer *Barukh she-Amar** precedes *Hodu**.
- At the conclusion of that service, the Song of the Day* is recited after *Aleinu**.
- In most Ashkenazic Siddurim, the portion of the *Ketoret** (incense) is recited neither at the end of the Morning Service nor prior to the Afternoon Service *(Minḥah*)*.
- The *Kaddish** does not include the phrase *ve-Yatzmaḥ Purkaneih*.

The more obvious distinctions are in the *Piyyutim*. It is customary in the Ashkenazic rite to include liturgical poems within the services for the three pilgrim festivals and the Days of Awe (see Chapters 10 and 11), as well as adding *Yotzerot** on special Shabbats during the year. These supplementary *Piyyutim* are distinctive both for their number (no other rite has as many *Piyyutim* as the Ashkenazic one), as well as their language. While most are derived from the liturgical poetry of the Land of Israel, some of them are early poems from Italy, or works of the sages of France or Germany, and were composed by such well-known rabbinic and scholarly figures as Rabbenu Gershom@ and Rashi.@ A number of the *Zemirot** and *Kinot** come from other sources as well, but these are the exception.

The influence of the Kabbalah is evident in the Ashkenazic version, as in all the others, particularly in such sections as *Tikkun Ḥatzot** or *Kabbalat Shabbat,** as well as in various prayers and supplications based upon Jewish mystical notions. Even though there were some Ashkenazic Siddurim in which the kabbalistic element is conspicuous, it is as a rule far less conspicuous in the Ashkenazic rite than in all other rites (many Siddurim of this rite exclude the mystical introductions to the blessings, *le-Shem Yiḥud,** while even the *Yehi Ratzon** supplications do not stress the kabbalistic aspect).

Originally, the Ashkenazic rite was used by all Ashkenazic Jewry, in both Eastern and Western Europe and wherever else they migrated to as entire communities. However, with the spread of Ḥassidism in the eighteenth and nineteenth centuries, most of East European Jewry accepted the Ḥassidic *Nusaḥ Sepharad,* and the original Ashkenazic rite was retained primarily in Germany, among the Ashkenazic communities of Holland, in most of Lithuania, in many areas of Hungary, and in scattered areas (or even parts of communities) in Poland.

Notwithstanding its enormous geographical dispersion and the large numbers of worshippers, the Ashkenazic rite has generally been retained as a single, unified rite. There were, withal, minor regional variations, including those introduced to commemorate specific events in different locations. One may mention, for example, the custom of reciting *Seliḥot** on the 20th of Sivan, in memory of the victims of the pogroms in 1648, when entire communities were destroyed by the Cossacks. Prayers were likewise instituted to recall catastrophes that occurred in the Rhineland communities during Crusader times and afterward. In addition, at one time separate *Maḥzorim** (festival prayer books) existed for the German, Bohemian, and Great Poland rites, respectively, and there were minor textual differences in the order of service by the Lithuanian and Polish communities for the *Seliḥot* and some other prayers.

A special place is held within the Ashkenazic rite by the prayer rite of the Vilna Gaon.@ By virtue of his great religious authority, he renewed and modified some customs, altered some of the wordings and forms, and ordered the deletion of certain additions to prayer that he felt were not sufficiently justified, or for which there was no halakhic reason. Many of the Vilna Gaon's disciples came together to the Land of Israel; hence, it is mostly there that synagogues wherein services are held according to these emendations are to be found.

Nusaḥ Sepharad—The Sephardic (Ḥassidic) Rite

The favored liturgy of the Ḥassidim, the disciples and followers of the Ba'al Shem Tov,@ is the "Sephardic rite," *Nusaḥ Sepharad*. It is based on the Ashkenazic rite, albeit with significant alterations in the order of service, and with several additions and deletions made under the influence of Lurianic Kabbalah.*

As no complete Siddur with the exact version of Rabbi Isaac Luria's prayer text has ever been produced, the numerous Siddurim bearing his name are actually based on the directives found in the book *Peri Etz Ḥayyim*,# and in several Siddurim containing orders of prayer based upon his special regulations and comments.

Nusaḥ Sepharad, which was created by superimposing Rabbi Luria's instructions upon the Ashkenazic rite, is thus a hybrid, which is in some ways a mixture of the Ashkenazic and Sephardic (Oriental) rites.

Even though *Nusaḥ Sepharad* is essentially one rite, with the same general order of service followed by everyone using it, it is nevertheless not based upon one commonly accepted, agreed text. For this reason, various different Hassidic groups have their own slight variations in wording for many of the prayers and benedictions.

One of the prominent features of *Nusaḥ Sepharad* is the large number of double formulations. The compilers and editors of this version were hesitant to delete phrases from the Ashkenazic rite which they had before them, simply augmenting it instead with Rabbi Luria's emendations. There were even some eminent sages, such as Rabbi Avraham David of Buczacz,@ who deliberately ruled in favor of reciting both versions of the same benediction, so long as this repetition did not confuse or obscure the meaning.

Initially, this transition from the Ashkenazic to the Sephardic rite aroused great halakhic controversy. On the one hand, Rabbi Moshe Sofer@ expressed the view that *Nusaḥ Sepharad* was only suitable to exceptional individuals, while other sages were of the opinion that everyone should shift to this version. In point of fact, people gradually adopted this rite wherever the Ḥassidic movement spread, until it was finally accepted in most regions of Eastern Europe, becoming the dominant liturgy in Poland, Ukraine, White Russia, and in many areas of Hungary and Rumania. To this day, it is the most prevalent prayer rite.

The distinctive features of this rite are:

- The recitation of *Hodu* before *Barukh she-Amar*.
- The recitation of *Parashat ha-Ketoret* three times daily.
- Addition of the words *ve-Yatzmaḥ Purkaneih vi-Yekarev Meshiḥeih* in the *Kaddish.**
- The *Kedushah** begins with the phrase *Nakdishakh ve-Na'aritzakh*, and in the *Musaf** prayers, with *Keter Yitnu Lekha.*

In addition, there are hundreds of other variations, major and minor, in the wording of other prayers. As a rule, the *Nusaḥ Sepharad* version makes less extensive use of *Piyyutim*, and those few that remained in the Siddur or *Maḥzor* are, in many communities, generally ignored. There is extensive kabbalistic influence, as exemplified by the frequent use of the *Yehi Ratzon* and *le-Shem Yiḥud* formulae prior to many prayers and benedictions, and the recitation of sections from the *Zohar*# (such as *Kegavna** on Friday evenings) within the regular prayer services. *Nusaḥ Sepharad* also has a few additions peculiar to the Ḥassidim alone, such as the recitation of *Hodu* (Psalm 107) on Shabbat eve.

As already stated, *Nusaḥ Sepharad* is not an absolutely uniform liturgy, but is marked by minor variations between one Siddur and another. In some communities, it is closer to the Ashkenazic rite, while others (such as the Kvidanov-Slonim *Nusaḥ*) contain formulations that exist only in the Oriental rite.

A special place among the *Nusaḥ Sepharad* texts is held by the Siddur of Rabbi Schneur Zalman of Lyady.@ This version, used mainly by Ḥabad Ḥassidim, is referred to by its users as *Nusaḥ ha-Ari* ("the

Lurianic rite"). It was meticulously edited by Rabbi Schneur Zalman himself, and is in fact one of the few *Nusaḥ Sepharad* versions to have undergone scrupulous editing by a prominent sage. Its language and grammar is very accurate, it has none of the duplications found in the usual *Nusaḥ Sepharad*, and many of its formulations closely resemble those of the Oriental (Sephardic) rite. This Siddur also omits many prayers and formulations that are halakhically doubtful (resembling in this, as in other details, the version of the Vilna Gaon; see above). It contains almost none of the *le-Shem Yiḥud* and *Yehi Ratzon* formulae, as well as none of the *Piyyutim*—with the exception of those for the Days of Awe,* and even many of these are deleted or shortened. This Siddur is used by Ḥabad Ḥassidim throughout the world, as well as by individuals from other communities.

The Oriental (Sephardic) Rite

This rite is derived from that used by Spanish Jewry before their expulsion. As in many other facets of Jewish life, the cultural origin of the Jews of Spain was Babylonia, and Babylonian influence was sustained through constant contact with the *Geonim*,* either directly or via North African Jewry. The "Golden Age" of Spanish Jewry (around the eleventh century C.E.) yielded a wealth of religious poetry of the highest literary and intellectual quality. Even when the Spanish poets leaned on the traditional models of the earlier liturgical poets (see Chapter 6), they gave their writing new form in terms of both language and usage, and many of their works became an integral part of the standard prayer services. Many of these poems were in fact *Piyyutim* originally written for the synagogue.

At the time, Spain was not a unified political entity, and the Jewish communities there also differed from each other in their customs and prayers, albeit these differences were expressed mainly in their choice of *Piyyutim* for special occasions. After their expulsion from Spain, the Jews migrated primarily to countries of the Ottoman Empire, which was then at its height. Almost everywhere they went, the Spanish Jews succeeded, by dint of their superior Torah learning and spiritual qualities, in molding the local customs to their own style. In many of these places, the local prayer rite was quite similar to their own, having been likewise influenced by the Babylonian practice, and thus easily adaptable to that of Spanish Jewry.

The growing influence of the Kabbalah on the generations following the expulsion from Spain led to greater uniformity in the liturgy, as well as dissemination of the liturgy among communities not reached by the Spanish exiles themselves, such as Iraq and Persia. The Lurianic *Kavvanot* (see Chapter 5) were based mainly upon the Spanish custom, and under the influence of Rabbi Isaac Luria and his disciples, certain changes were also made in the Sephardic rite. Rabbi Isaac Luria did not greatly value the *Piyyutim* composed in Spain, and preferred those of the Ashkenazim, which he considered to be closer to mystical thought. For these reasons, as well as for halakhic considerations (e.g., unnecessary interruption in the course of the prayer), most of these *Piyyutim* were omitted. The poetry of Spain, as well as those *Piyyutim* composed elsewhere or in later generations, can be found mainly in those prayers that are not part of the regular services, such as the *Seliḥot*, the *Kinot*, *Zemirot* for Shabbat and festivals, and various petitionary prayers and *Bakkashot*.*

The influence of the Kabbalah was augmented wherever the rite of the Sephardim was used; consequently, numerous *le-Shem Yiḥud* and *Yehi Ratzon* passages and selections from the *Zohar*# are to be found in it. Allusions to mystical thought (such as the writing of God's name intertwined with other appellations of the Divinity) are found there even in Siddurim in general use, and not only those used by kabbalistic sages.

In later generations, the Oriental rite came under the strong influence of Rabbi Yosef Ḥayyim of Baghdad@ (known as the Ben Ish Ḥai). By virtue of his great Torah learning, his authority has been accepted by Jews throughout the Orient. The prayers and benedictions he composed, as well as services he introduced for special occasions, have become part of the regular order of prayer of the Sephardim.

In our times, the Oriental rite is used not only by the descendants of the Spanish exiles (both in the separate congregations they created in Oriental countries and in their congregations in Holland and in certain cities in Germany), but is also in regular use among nearly all the Jews of Islamic countries (except for Yemen), including the Jews of Iraq, Persia, and Central Asia (Bukhara, Georgia, etc.), as well as all those Jewish communities that were at one time under Ottoman rule.

This rite is, accordingly, the predominant one among the Jews of the Balkan countries: Greece, Bulgaria, and other places. Although there are certain differences among the various communities and congregations, on the whole the Oriental version has remained quite uniform, apart from small variations resulting from local custom, or, on occasion, the choice of special *Piyyutim*.

The overall order of prayers in the Oriental rite is duplicated in *Nusaḥ Sepharad*, together with its basic formulation. However, the version of the Sephardim does contain a number of distinctive formulations and expressions. Some of these are the result of using the basic Babylonian version, while others are the result of the fact that the Oriental rite did not undergo changes forced upon it by censorship, as was the common practice in countries under Christian rule.

The most striking difference between the Oriental rite and other rites is in the *Shemoneh Esreh*,* especially in *Birkat ha-Shanim* ("the Blessing of the Seasons"), for which the Oriental rite has two separate formulations: one for the summer months and another for the rainy season. This liturgy also has a different version of *Taḥanun*,* while the *Minḥah** service commences with Psalm 84. These distinctions are also found in the Yemenite version. In the *Kaddish*,* the paragraph beginning *Yehei Shelama Rabba* includes a lengthy additional phrase.

The Yemenite Rite

Jews have been living in Yemen since ancient times. According to some traditions, Jews arrived there during the First Temple period, and there is evidence that an important Jewish settlement existed there at the end of the Second Temple period. On the one hand, the Yemenite Jews were geographically isolated from the great centers of Jewish life, and thus their customs and prayer liturgy were unique. On the other hand, throughout the centuries they maintained close spiritual ties with other communities, and were influenced by them.

The uniqueness of the Yemenite prayer rite reflects the duality of their Jewish culture. Yemenite Jewry was, and has remained, under the powerful influence of Maimonides.@ He was highly esteemed in Yemen already during his lifetime, and continued to be thought of by this community as its supreme rabbinical authority even after his death.

His halakhic works served as the source texts for their legal rulings, and his text of the prayer liturgy forms the basis for the Yemenite rite to this day.

Another, even earlier influence on Yemenite Jewry was the works of Rav Sa'adiah Gaon.@ Not only was his Arabic translation of the Torah preserved and revered there, but his prayer formulations and many of the *Piyyutim* that he composed have become part of the Yemenite rite.

In addition to the *Piyyutim* of Rav Sa'adiah Gaon, the collection of *Piyyutim* retained by Yemenite Jews includes some early ones from the Land of Israel, many others composed by the great Spanish poets, and a large number written in Yemen itself. Not only was the poetry of Rabbi Shalom Shabbazi@ held sacred in Yemen; more recently written hymns have also won their place in the community's rich compilation of *Zemirot* and *Bakkashot*, and have become part of the regular prayer services. Nor did the influence of the Kabbalah bypass Yemen, being easily recognized in many of the prayers and formulations.

Being the custom of an isolated community, the Yemenite liturgy contains traditional customs and idiomatic expressions peculiar to itself. On the one hand, many ancient customs and prayers that were discarded or altered elsewhere remain unchanged in the Yemenite tradition (such as the practice of reading the Aramaic translation of the Torah along with the regular Torah reading; the truncated version of *Avinu Malkenu**; etc.). On the other hand, the Yemenite rite contains elements that were created in Yemen itself, and were not transmitted to other places.

Special elements found in the Yemenite rite include:

- Recital of the *Piyyut* called *Adon ha-Olamim* at the beginning of prayer.
- Reading of Rabbi Zeira's halakhah after *Birkat ha-Torah** (as required by the Talmud, *Berakhot* 31a).
- *Hodu* is not recited on weekdays.
- Certain psalms (found in other Siddurim at the beginning of *Pesukei de-Zimrah*) are recited prior to *Birkhot ha-Shaḥar*.*
- The Song of the Sea* is followed by the Song of Miriam until

the end of this passage in the book of Exodus, with the addition of other verses.
- Certain Torah sections, which in other places are recited daily, such as the *Ketoret*, are added in the Shabbat prayers.
- In the *Kaddish de-Rabbanan** the Yemenites include, in accordance with Maimonides' instructions, the formulation *de-Hu Atid Leḥadeta*, which in other rites is only recited on rare occasions.

And, as might be expected, in regard to *Piyyutim* and benedictions that are not an integral part of the basic liturgy, the Yemenite version includes an entirely different set of *Piyyutim*, unique to it.

The Yemenite rite includes certain secondary versions, the most important distinction being that between the rite used in the central city of San'a and that of the peripheral cities and towns (Baladi). In general, this rite was customary only in Yemen and in the neighboring provinces of Aden and Hadramaut. With the emigration of the vast majority of Yemenite Jews to Israel, there has been increasing influence of other rites on the Yemenite rite, both in the elimination of certain elements (such as shortening the reading of the Aramaic translation in Torah readings), and in the addition of others, such as different *Piyyutim* and prayer formulae.

The Italian Rite

The settlement of Jews in Italy began already in the Second Temple period, and Jewish communities have existed in that country ever since. True, as a result of persecutions and expulsions, the Jewish centers in Italy moved from one city to another; but in general, Jews have lived there uninterruptedly for more than two thousand years.

Due to its geographical location, Italy also served as a land of transit and was influenced by other countries and Jewish centers. The Italian communities in turn influenced them to an extent far greater than was warranted by their size. For hundreds of years, three distinct prayer rites have been in use in Italy: the Ashkenazic rite—by Jews who arrived from Germany and Poland; the Oriental rite—by the descendants of the Spanish exiles and immigrants from North Africa; and the local Italian rite—by the historically indigenous Jewish population and their descendants.

This local version was itself not unified, with many communities in Italy using totally different liturgies. With the decrease in Jewish population, and the decline in the level of Jewish culture, only a few centers remain today where the original Italian rite (known as *Minhag Roma* or *Minhag Lo'azim*) still exists in practice.

The Italian rite is a very ancient one, which had basically taken shape by medieval times. Although, like the other *nusḥaot*, it, too, was affected by the Kabbalah (therefore including such prayers as *Kabbalat Shabbat* and the like), this did not happen to the same extent as in other rites; generally speaking, the Italian rite retained its own uniqueness and specific features. Similarly, many of the hymns and prayers introduced later into the Siddur in other popular liturgies are not found in the Italian rite.

From the structural point of view, the Italian rite may be described as standing midway between the Ashkenazic and Sephardic rites, as well as containing elements derived from the Siddur of Rav Amram Gaon (see Chapter 6). This rite also contains phrases and wordings not found anywhere else.

The *Piyyutim* in the Italian version originated from various sources. Many are from the Land of Israel and from Franco-Germany, but there are also a significant number from Spain, as well as several composed in Italy itself.

Some of the unique features of this version are:

- The *Yehi Ratzon* prayer following *Birkhot ha-Shaḥar* contains a lengthy passage with many biblical verses.
- The *Ketoret* section is not recited; instead, the first *mishnah* and the beginning of the Talmud* of Tractate *Berakhot* are read.
- *Vidduy** is recited before the prayer.
- There is a fixed formulation for *Hatavat Ḥalom**: seventy-two verses, followed by Psalm 29.
- In the *Pesukei de-Zimrah*, Psalm 33 is recited daily, as is Psalm 99.
- An additional prayer and a *Piyyut* follow the end of the Song of the Sea.

- There are special, shorter versions of *Taḥanun* for Monday and for Thursday (which differ from one another).
- In the *Pesukei de-Zimrah* for Shabbat and festivals, the only additions are Psalms 92 and 93.
- There is a special formulation for *Birkat ha-Ḥodesh** (the New Moon benediction).
- There is a Hebrew version of the *Kol Nidrei** for Yom Kippur eve.
- In addition, of course, there are special *Piyyutim* for *Seliḥot*, *Kinot*, and other occasions.

Nowadays the Italian rite is used only among a few congregations still intent on the preservation of this ancient rite, with its distinctive language and customs.

Extinct Prayer Rites

In addition to the above-described liturgies, which are still in use today, there are other rites that have became extinct, as there are no longer any communities that pray according to them. Fragments of these still survive, however, in the local customs of various congregations.

Possibly the oldest prayer rite in Europe was *Nusaḥ Romania* (the so-called Romanian Rite)—that of the Jews of Greece and of European Turkey. Several of these communities were among the earliest to be established in the Diaspora, there being some evidence of Jewish settlement in these regions already during the First Temple period. These Jews were known elsewhere as the "Grigush" (i.e., Greeks), as was their liturgy.

This rite has in practice been obsolete for many generations, although at the beginning of the seventeenth century a "*Nusaḥ Romania*" *Maḥzor* did appear in print. The disappearance of this rite is probably due to the influx into the Ottoman Empire, following the Expulsion from Spain, of an overwhelming number of Spanish Jews, who came to dominate these communities, their customs and prayers being eventually adopted by the local Jewish communities.

Ancient Jewish settlements were also founded in France, which reached their spiritual peak in the eleventh and twelfth centuries (at the time of Rashi,[@] the *Tosafot*,[@] and others). Here, too, there were several local prayer rites, which fell into disuse with the expulsion of Jews during the thirteenth and fourteenth centuries. For centuries, there was no ongoing Jewish presence in France; centuries later, upon their return, they brought with them different customs and prayer rites.

Of the indigenous French traditions and customs, there remains the *Maḥzor Vitry*,[#] which contains the ancient version of prayer from the days of Rashi's disciples. Most of those expelled from France settled in Germany and adopted the local customs, but there were a few isolated communities where the remaining worshippers preserved the French rite.

In the Middle Ages, the regions of Provence and Languedoc in southern France constituted an independent state with a flourishing Jewish culture of its own. This area served as a bridge between the Jewish communities of northern France and those of Spain. The Provençal Jews had their own special prayer rite, but their settlement was destroyed with their expulsion from the region. However, some of these Jews, who resided in the papal state, remained and even published their own prayer book. Likewise extant are two distinctive *Maḥzorim*, one from Avignon and the other from Carpentras, as well as a rare prayer book, in manuscript form, containing the rite of the Montpellier community. These rites contain not only many of the Ashkenazic and Spanish *Piyyutim*, but also the *Piyyutim* and prayers composed by the sages of Provence. However, the Jews living in the papal state (the *Arba Kehillot*—"four communities") gradually decreased in number until they disappeared, together with their customs and prayer rite.

The Piedmont region of northern Italy also had its unique local rite, *Minhag AFM (*Asti-Fossano-Moncalvo*)*, now extinct.

The ancient Jewish settlement in Spain had several different customs and prayer rites. Just as Spain during the Middle Ages was divided into several states, so did the Jews in each state have their own rite. Even after their expulsion, these ancient communities continued to preserve their own separate customs. In Turkey, for example, entire communities with their own specific traditions continued to exist for a very long time. We thus have extant prayer books and *Maḥzorim* according to the rites of Catalonia (*Nusaḥ Barcelona)*, Aragon, and so on. Only several generations later did the barriers come down and these congregations merge to form one "rite of the Sephardim."

The Jews from Islamic countries, who today follow the Oriental prayer rite, likewise used to have distinct prayer customs and rites that differed from country to country, and even from region to region in the same country. In North Africa, where important Jewish centers existed from Second Temple times, a rich Jewish culture developed, maintaining particularly close ties with the Babylonian *Geonim*. The different communities there possessed their own customs and prayer rites. *Maḥzorim* for the Algerian rite were printed, as well as for the special rite of Oran (Vaharan), of the Jews of Tunis, and also of Libya—the "Tripolitan" version. These rites contained many *Piyyutim* by Spanish poets, as well as some composed by the local sages of those countries.

In Egypt, too, there was a special rite, greatly influenced by Maimonides[@]; and in Syria, a *Maḥzor* according to the rite of Aleppo *(Minhag Aram Tzova)*, an important center for Torah study and Jewish culture, appeared in print. The Jewish settlements in Iraq, where Jews lived ever since the Babylonian captivity (after the destruction of the First Temple), were the world center of Jewish culture for hundreds of years. Their prayer customs were already established during the Geonic period* and were to a large extent incorporated into the Oriental rite, albeit members of various communities still preserved remnants of ancient rites.

The Land of Israel had a unique prayer rite that exerted considerable influence on all other rites, but the persecution and expulsion of the Jews during the Crusader period drastically reduced the numbers of those who still followed this rite. During the days of Maimonides, and perhaps even later, there was still a "Land of Israel" community in Egypt that preserved its own unique prayer customs. But this community, too, gradually decreased in number, and its remnants (called the *Mista'arvim*) were absorbed by the waves of immigrants from Spain.

As a rule, one may say that in times past there were a far greater number of prayer rites, differing at times from one community to the other. Over the course of time, with the appearance of printed editions and easier means of communication, customs and prayer rites gradually merged into larger units.

PART THREE

THE ORDER OF PRAYER SERVICES

CHAPTER EIGHT

Weekday Prayer Services

Prayer and the Life Cycle

The Siddur closely reflects the Jewish cycle of life. On the one hand, the Siddur embraces the entire human life cycle, by its inclusion of prayers, benedictions, and ceremonial rites for every event in the life of the Jew—from rising in the morning till bedtime at night, from birth till death, in times of sorrow and in times of joy, in the small, ordinary events of everyday life and on special occasions. On the other hand, and to an even greater extent, the Siddur relates to the cyclical changes of time itself. The fixed prayers are constantly adjusted in accordance with the progression of time, each change in time being reflected in the order of prayer services. All the major and minor time changes have a fixed expression and place in some special prayer or in an appropriate variation in the regular order of service.

The order of prayer services relates to four cycles of time: the day—through the specific prayers recited at different times of the day; the week—with the minor and major changes between the weekday prayers and those for Shabbat; the month—with the *Rosh Ḥodesh** prayers (see Chapter 9), *Birkat ha-Ḥodesh** (the blessings for the new month), and the benedictions and prayers relating to the lunar month; and the year—with its unique festivals and special dates. Even though there is a complex system for defining the relative importance of different days in the year, the general rule is that the larger the time cycle to which a given day belongs, the more clearly does it define the order of prayer services. Thus, the daily prayer service is altered every Shabbat, while the Shabbat prayer service in turn assumes the special character of festivals that occur on it.

The Daily Prayers

There are five fixed orders of prayer services daily, to which certain additions are made on special days—Shabbat, festivals, *Rosh Ḥodesh* and other holidays—while maintaining their basic underlying pattern. Three of these services—*Shaḥarit,** *Minḥah** and *Ma'ariv**—center around the *Amidah* prayer, while the other two do not include this prayer.

The three fixed daily prayers are based on the biblical verse "Evening and morning and at noon will I pray and cry aloud, and He shall hear my voice" (Psalm 55:17). These prayers are connected to the visible changes that occur every day: *Shaḥarit* at the beginning of the day, with the rising sun; *Minḥah* in the afternoon, when the sun turns toward setting; and *Ma'ariv* in the evening, once darkness falls.

These three prayers also correspond to the order of sacrifices in the Temple: *Shaḥarit* corresponds to the daily offering *(Tamid)* brought in the morning; *Minḥah* to the *Tamid* offering brought toward dusk; and *Ma'ariv* to the flesh of sacrifices burnt on the altar during the night hours. The three prayer services likewise correspond to the three Patriarchs: *Shaḥarit* is linked with Abraham, *Minḥah* with Isaac, and *Ma'ariv* with Jacob (*Berakhot* 26b).

These correspondences are not merely homiletic interpretations, but are proscriptive for the manner in which each prayer service should be conducted: regarding both the halakhic rules about the time for the prayers, their obligatory nature, etc., and the inner meaning, content, and purpose of these prayers.

In addition to the three major prayer services, there are two other fixed orders of prayer: *Tikkun Ḥatzot,** recited during the night hours preceding *Shaḥarit;* and the *Shema* Upon Retiring to Bed,* recited just before a person goes to sleep.

Tikkun Ḥatzot

Tikkun Ḥatzot (which is the practice of individuals, albeit part of the fixed order of prayers), is a series of supplications and psalms that it is customary to recite every night, summer and winter, from midnight onward. Some people recite it just before midnight, from midnight onward engaging in Torah study. Some rise at night to recite the *Tikkun Ḥatzot* only from the 15th of Av to the 15th of Iyyar, while others also recite it at midday during the three weeks of *Bein ha-Meitzarim** (see Chapter 9).

The central theme of *Tikkun Ḥatzot* is lamentation for the Destruction of the Temple and for the exile, and a plea for complete redemption. There are indications in early sources that pious men used to rise at midnight to study the Torah and to pray, in accordance with the verse "At midnight will I rise to give thanks unto You for Your righteous laws" (Psalm 119:62), a practice also hinted at in the Talmud (*Berakhot* 3a). Rav Sherira Gaon@ and Rav Hai Gaon@ report that it was a fixed custom to rise and recite supplications from midnight on. But the main support for this custom appears in the *Zohar*# (Genesis, portion *Lekh Lekha*), which refers to this as a mandatory obligation upon all; indeed, Kabbalists have always greatly extolled the observance of this practice. It was they, and particularly the disciples of Rabbi Isaac Luria,@ who established the definitive structure for *Tikkun Ḥatzot.*

As stated above, throughout the generations, *Tikkun Ḥatzot* has been a practice of individuals, and was not made a part of the fixed order of prayers. However, in certain locales it was so widely practiced that groups of people used to gather together to recite it, despite the criticism that it should be done in a private manner. It is nevertheless not considered an actual obligation, and is not observed by most people. Only scholars and pious men make a regular practice of reciting it, and then go on studying Torah until it is time for the *Shaḥarit* prayer. However, *Tikkun Ḥatzot* can be found in most prayer books, especially those of the Oriental rite, because there are people who do recite it on occasion.

The essential idea of *Tikkun Ḥatzot* is based upon the Talmudic statement that God Himself weeps over the destruction of the Temple and the exile, and that at the time of *Tikkun Ḥatzot* the people of Israel share in His grief. Exile is thus perceived not merely as a historical event concerning the Jewish people but as a cosmic upheaval, a flaw in the cosmos as a whole, that we are obliged to try to repair (hence the term *Tikkun*, "repair").

The *Tikkun* of the *Shekhinah** appears in two forms: in sorrow

("Rachel weeping over her children"; Jeremiah 31:14) and in hope (Leah, the "happy mother of sons"; Psalm 113:9). Corresponding to this, there are two basic components in *Tikkun Ḥatzot*. The former consists of weeping and lamentation *(Tikkun Rachel)*; some worshippers behave during its recitation as on Tish'ah be-Av (see Chapter 9)—placing ashes on their heads and reciting the dirges while sitting upon the ground. (Some, however, do not recite the lamentations of *Tikkun Rachel* at all, but only its psalms and prayers.) In the latter part, *Tikkun Leah*, everyone rises to recite the petitions and expressions of hope for redemption.

The *Shaḥarit* Service

The *Shaḥarit* (Morning) Service is the longest and most complex of all the daily prayers. The most basic reason for its length and complexity is that this is the prayer with which one begins the new day before turning to the daily occupations (it is forbidden to even eat before praying, and no labor or journey should be begun until the recitation of the prayers is completed).

During the course of the day, a person is generally preoccupied with work or with attending to one's affairs, a fact that leads one to ignore, or to be insufficiently conscious of, one's relationship with God. It is therefore particularly important that there be a time devoted to spiritual elevation and to maintaining and strengthening one's connection to God at the very beginning of the day. A relationship is thereby established between man and his Creator, between man and the surrounding world, and between man and himself—as a result of which, the Morning Service influences a person throughout the day.

Various additions have been made to the Morning Service, both preceding and following it, many of which can be found in most prayer books. Some of these have become a fixed part of the communal prayer, while others remain as private, individual prayers.

The fixed sections of *Shaḥarit* are arranged in a subtle manner, creating a complex structure imbued with significance and perfect rhythm. The essential structure is composed of seven elements, although on most days it includes eight or even nine distinct sections.

This structure may best be seen as a path of ascent and descent, or of entry and exit. Prayer may be seen, not only metaphorically but in essence, as a kind of spiritual ladder by which one ascends toward Heaven[41] or, to use a different but analogous image, as a path ascending the Temple Mount. The Temple in Jerusalem was built as a series of structures: each successive structure, set on a higher level, was of greater holiness than the previous one, with stairways both separating the levels and leading from one to another. Upon leaving the Temple, the same stages were traversed in the opposite direction, but along a different path.

The main sections of *Shaḥarit* thus correspond to the parts of the Temple and to those of the higher worlds, together forming the Heavenly Temple. Between each section there are "steps"—the reciting of the *Kaddish**—seen as a way of climbing from one world to another. (Some prayer books refer to these divisions in the headings of the different sections of prayer, while others, such as the *Siddur of Ya'avetz*# by Rabbi Yaakov Emden [Ya'avetz], have an even more detailed division, corresponding with the structural sections of the Temple.)

The opening section of the service is the series of benedictions and Torah study *(Korbanot*)*, which form an introduction and entry to the world of prayer. This corresponds to the *Ezrat Nashim*, the Women's Courtyard in the Temple, or to the World of Action, the first of the four worlds described in kabbalistic lore.[42] This is followed by *Pesukei de-Zimrah*,* corresponding to *Ezrat Yisrael*, the Men's Courtyard in the Temple, or to the World of Formation (the World of the Angels). From there, one turns to the reading of the *Shema** and its benedictions, corresponding to the *Ezrat ha-Kohanim*—the priestly courtyard—and the Holy Place in the Temple, as well as to the World of Creation (the Divine Throne and Chariot). One then enters into the *Amidah*,* corresponding to the Holy of Holies, and to the World of Emanation.

---

[41] See Genesis 29:12.

[42] The four worlds are: The World of Action (*Olam ha-Assiyah;* our world); the World of Formation (*Olam ha-Yetzirah;* the World of the Angels); the World of Creation *(Olam ha-Beriah);* the World of Emanation *(Olam ha-Atzilut)*. See *The Thirteen Petalled Rose* by Rabbi Adin Steinsaltz (Northvale, N. J.: Jason Aronson, 1992), chap. 1.

This is followed by additional sections of prayer—*Taḥanun** and Torah reading.* Then come *Ashrei** and *u-Va le-Zion Go'el,**—which may be seen as parallel to the *Shema* reading and its benedictions; a selection of psalms and the Song of the Day,* which parallel *Pesukei de-Zimrah**; and, finally, the section including the *Ketoret** and *Aleinu,** parallel to the section of *Korbanot* and benedictions at the very beginning of *Shaḥarit.*

THE FIRST SECTION OF *SHAḤARIT*. This belongs to the World of Action in every sense, serving as a means of preparation for reaching the higher levels. It contains benedictions of thanksgiving relating to everyday matters *(Birkhot ha-Shaḥar*)*, words of meditation (on the one hand the Chapter of the Binding of Isaac (the *Akedah*) and, on the other, the midrashic passage *(Tanna de-Vei Eliyahu Rabbah,#* chapter 21, *le-Olam Yehe Adam*)*; and, primarily, selections from the Bible and the Talmud concerning the Divine service conducted at the Temple during the morning hours: the *Kiyyor* (water basin), *Deshen* (ashes), *Tamid* (daily sacrifices), and *Ketoret* (incense). To these are added a précis of the order of the Temple service, and a summary of all the sacrifices offered therein.

This entire section was not originally systematically arranged, and for that reason there are many variations in the different prayer customs and practices (even within the same overall prayer rite) as to what comes first and what thereafter. Likewise, some rites lengthen this section, and others shorten it during weekdays.

In general, the main purpose of this section is to begin the day and to enter into prayer by reading words of Torah. There is little here for spiritual elevation as such; it is mostly a means of preparation for prayer. The Mishnah* records that in olden times, pious men used to spend an hour before worship in preparing their hearts for prayer (see Mishnah, *Berakhot* 5:1). In similar spirit, our sages have said in the Talmud that "one does not stand up to pray either in a mood of sadness, laziness, or mirth . . . nor in trivial occupation, but only in a state of joy in performing a *mitzvah**" and also "only after [studying] words of settled halakhah."[43] For that reason, we recite these particular

[43] But not through study of a complex halakhic argumentation, which may unsettle the heart; *Berakhot* 31a.

passages, i.e., passages concerning the fulfillment of *mitzvot*, because they correspond to work performed in our world, the world of human action, in order to ascend from this starting point to higher levels.

This section concludes, in light of all that has been said thus far, with "May it be Your will . . . that the Temple be speedily rebuilt," followed by the recitation of *Kaddish de-Rabbanan** for the Torah study in which we have just engaged. This Kaddish serves in turn as entry into the next section, which also constitutes another spiritual world: *Pesukei de-Zimrah*.

PESUKEI DE-ZIMRAH. This section, corresponding to the World of Formation or the World of Angels, is meant to arouse the spirit. *Pesukei de-Zimrah* (literally, "verses of song") is a collection of psalms and other biblical passages describing the greatness of God, which are preceded and followed by the benedictions of *Barukh she-Amar** at the beginning, and *Yishtabbaḥ** at the end. In all prayer rites, a portion of the *Pesukei de-Zimrah* is actually recited before *Barukh she-Amar;* these are seen, however, as introductory to the section as such. Halakhically, the fixed order of the *Shaḥarit* service begins with this opening benediction.

The Talmud does not elaborate upon this section of prayer, which would appear not to have always contained the same selection of psalms and verses (except for *Ashrei**). Yet notwithstanding the differences among the various liturgies, all versions of *Pesukei de-Zimrah* may be seen as made up of two main parts: the first consists of praise and glorification of God's work in the world, based mainly on the Psalms (particularly Psalms 145–150); the second part involves praise for His redemptive acts in history, and for the loving-kindness shown to our forefathers. This includes a brief summary of the early days of Israel's history (taken from the books of Chronicles and Nehemiah), and concludes with the Song of the Sea,* the climax of the redemption from Egypt.

All of *Pesukei de-Zimrah* are words of poetry that appeal mainly to the emotions. Beyond their descriptive contents, they are hymns of praise for all of God's Creation and for His loving-kindness to Israel. The recital of these passages is meant to sweep the worshipper into also participating in this song of thanksgiving, as in the wording of the opening benediction, "We will extol You, Lord our God, with praises and songs; exalt, laud and glorify You."

Shema. From the *Pesukei de-Zimrah*, we proceed immediately to the Reading of the *Shema* and its benedictions. The transition from the world of *Pesukei de-Zimrah* to the Throne World of the *Shema* reading is accomplished through the recitation of the half *Kaddish** by the *Shaliaḥ Tzibbur*.* It is otherwise forbidden[44] to pause between the benediction of *Yishtabbaḥ* and that of *Yotzer Or*,* the opening benediction of the *Shema*.[45]

Before reciting these benedictions, the *Shaliaḥ Tzibbur* says *Barekhu*,* which serves as the ceremonial opening of the benedictions as well as the commencement of the main section of communal prayer. In the simplest terms, this is a call to the congregation to join together, with one heart, in prayer. Until this point, the prayer had more of an individual nature, being based on emotional appeals to personal feelings and sentiments. From here on, the congregation prays as a single unified community. Indeed, in terms of the content of the first benediction, the "hosts of the Lord" below stand in array opposite the "heavenly hosts" above to bless and praise God.

This section of the service is related to the World of Creation, and indicates the entry into the sphere of holiness itself. Although this section, too, contains many elements that uplift the heart in love and awe, these have one defined purpose, being always directed toward contemplative thought, beyond the mere feelings of the heart. In terms of the ascent to higher worlds, this is a taking hold of the World of the Throne, of the Divine Chariot. Not only does this section of the *Yotzer Or* benediction contain a description of the Divine Chariot (the *Seraphim*, holy *Ḥayyot* and *Ophanim*),[46] but the very essence of prayer in this section is contemplation of God's "Throne of Glory." This does not yet express a full relationship of the human "I" facing God; what there is is an acceptance of the yoke of Heaven, compliance with the commandments, and communion with the Divine. It might be said that at this point in the prayer, the worshipper strives to become part of the

---

[44] See *Tur*,# *Oraḥ Ḥayyim* 51, in the name of the Jerusalem Talmud.

[45] See also *Shulḥan Arukh*, *Oraḥ Ḥayyim* 54:3.

[46] Names of various kinds of angels.

Divine Chariot, to unite with the larger whole of the universe, which acknowledges its Creator and clings to Him.

THE *AMIDAH.* At this juncture, we reach the high point of the prayer service—the *Amidah* prayer (also known as *Shemoneh Esreh,** or Eighteen Benedictions). The worshipper has, so to speak, ascended from world to world, entering from one room to another until he reaches the innermost sanctum, standing now face-to-face with the Utmost Holiness itself. This is the moment for direct communion—to plead and give thanks, to praise and to make supplication. The *Amidah* is thus the meeting point at which man stands before his Divine Father, Creator, and Ruler. Like most prayers of the Siddur, this is formulated in the plural form, because each person is praying not only for oneself as an individual but as part of the entire congregation of Israel. Even one who recites the *Amidah* alone, in a room by oneself, is still included within the praying community of Israel. Likewise, even the private, personal request inserted into his prayer becomes part of the anguish of *Knesset Yisrael.** Through one's prayer, each individual becomes a microcosm, reflecting and representing the macrocosm outside.

Communally, the *Amidah* is first recited in a quiet whisper, and then repeated aloud by the *Shaliaḥ Tzibbur*. This silent recitation, even when conducted within a congregation and at a time when all are praying together, is a personal prayer in still another sense. Not only may the worshipper insert into various benedictions private requests concerning himself alone; the entire prayer is a private one. Whether one prays from a Siddur or with one's eyes closed, whether entirely enwrapped in a *Tallit** or not wearing one at all—one stands before God on one's own behalf. The worshipper is like a person admitted into a royal audience; thus, even when surrounded by a large entourage of people, one addresses the king in one's own words, and the king addresses him alone with his private, personal reply. For this reason, the prayer is recited in a whisper (despite one's knowing that everyone is saying exactly the same words), because it is like a private conversation, a whispered exchange. Two people may use the same words, yet each one says them for and from oneself alone. Thus, even within a community and congregation there may be privacy and solitude.

The ensuing repetition* of the *Amidah* by the *Shaliaḥ Tzibbur* is not only recited aloud but has a different inner quality of the prayer. When the *Shaliaḥ Tzibbur* prays, he does so not as an individual, but as a representative of the community, and the congregation that participates with him in the repetition feels things in a completely different way—as a community, as a congregation. All the changes made in the repetition reflect this concept: that it is a public prayer, for the sake of, and in the name of, the public (for more, see Chapter 15).

On most weekdays, following the conclusion of the repetition, there are the *Vidduy** ("confession") and the *Taḥanun** prayer, with the recitation of the Thirteen Attributes of Mercy,* followed by *Nefilat Appayyim** ("prostration"). This section, in which there are many variations among and within the different prayer rites, is not completely fixed, as there are many days of the year on which the *Taḥanun* is not recited at all (see Chapter 12). Moreover, on Mondays and Thursdays* there are additional supplications (which vary among the prayer rites). These, too, are omitted, or only a small part retained (see *El Erekh Appayyim**), on those days on which *Taḥanun* is not recited.

The recitation of *Taḥanun* in this section of *Shaḥarit*, with its various components, should be seen as the direct continuation of the *Amidah*.[47]

Even though there are now more or less fixed formulations for the *Vidduy*, *Taḥanun*, and even for the words spoken during *Nefilat Appayyim*, all these are, by their very nature, highly private. A person's sins are a matter of intimate secrecy between him and his Creator alone.[48] Similarly, *Nefilat Appayyim*, in which a person covers his face and prostrates himself before God (although today it is not generally done in this way, but only in a symbolic fashion, by laying the head on the hand), is a manner in which a person expresses extremely personal and private matters—be it thanks to God from the depths of one's heart,[49] or voicing inwardly some request or earnest supplication.[50]

---

[47] In those prayer books where the sections of prayer are marked in mystical terms, this is called *She'erit ha-Atzilut* ("the remainder of Emanation").

[48] The Talmud, *Berakhot* 34b, says that anyone who publicizes his sins—even in the context of repentance—is considered insolent.

[49] See Genesis 17:17.

[50] See Deuteronomy 9:18.

The placing of the *Vidduy* and *Taḥanun* prayers immediately after the *Amidah* makes them a more private, personal continuation of the previous prayer. It is as though, having stood in prayer and being admitted into the "king's chambers" (Song of Songs 1:4), one finds oneself in the inner sanctum, and takes the opportunity to add a few things of a more private nature, like a whispered secret in a moment of intimacy.

The arrangement of the various parts within this section (as they appear in most prayer rites) should hence be understood in these terms: following the spiritual elevation and intimacy of the *Amidah* prayer, one senses more deeply one's own sins and faults. Having spoken words of praise to God and made many requests to Him together with the entire congregation, there is an inner need to say, "Yet we and our fathers have sinned." The question then arises: in light of all this guilt and betrayal, how can one come and make requests? The answer appears in the form of the communal recitation of the Thirteen Attributes, which serves as a form of encouragement and strengthening, as if to say that, on the highest of levels, there is Divine mercy accorded to all, which has the power not only to grant forgiveness and pardon, but also to serve as a pretext for us to make requests.

After reciting the Thirteen Attributes, which represents the highest, most sublime level of revelation, and which prompts one to make requests,[51] the worshipper prostrates himself and says whatever is in his heart. One then goes on to make further supplications, both personal and collective (see also *ve-Hu Raḥum,* El Erekh Appayyim*). At this particular moment, then, when about to leave the king's inner chamber, one dares to say whatever one could not say before.

Normally, there is a regular Torah reading on Mondays and Thursdays. The reading of the Torah on weekdays is a very ancient tradition whose purpose is to assure that no Jew will remain without Torah study (even in some small measure) during the weekdays, which for most people are also days of preoccupation in worldly affairs. (For details regarding the Monday and Thursday readings, see Chapter 13).

According to the Ashkenazic rite, the Torah scroll is returned to

---

[51] Cf. Moses' requests after God revealed to him the Thirteen Attributes—Exodus 34:8–9.

the Ark at this point, while in *Nusaḥ Sepharad* it is only returned after reciting *u-Va le-Zion Go'el.**

Descent to the World of Creation. Having completed this section of prayer, the rest of the service is a kind of egress from the realm of holiness, a gradual descent from the supernal world of encounter between the human and the Divine back to the World of Creation—parallel to the route of ascent, but in the opposite direction. There is a marked contrast between the length of the sections following the *Amidah* prayer as compared with those that preceded it. This makes sense, for the entry into holiness, the ascent from one world to the next, demands intense effort and work. It is difficult to extricate oneself from ordinary human existence and attain a level of devotion. For most people, the descent is far easier. Nevertheless, this is not done abruptly, in a rapid fall from the sublime spiritual heights to mundane affairs, but gradually, level by level, to return us once again to the reality of our world.

From this point on, the prayer is call *Seder ha-Yom*—the order of the day.[52] The first section contains *Ashrei* (Psalm 145), Psalm 20,* followed by *u-Va le-Zion Go'el.* In terms of its inner significance, the recitation of *Kedushah* (Kedushah de-Sidra*)* within *u-Va le-Zion Go'el* corresponds to the benedictions of *Shema*, which also contains *Kedushah*. The other contents of *u-Va le-Zion Go'el* are likewise similar to those of the *Shema* benedictions: thanks to God for having separated us for His service, the acceptance of His rule, and gratitude for having been given the Torah.

This section of the *Shaḥarit* prayer concludes with *Kaddish Titkabbal,** marking the end of the main section of the communal prayer (again paralleling, in reverse, the *Shema* benedictions in the first half of the prayer). As mentioned earlier, according to *Nusaḥ Sepharad*, the Torah scroll is returned to its place at this point.

Descent to the World of Formation. The next section of prayer is parallel to *Pesukei de-Zimrah* (this is true of the Sephardic and Oriental rites, which are constructed according to the Kabbalah. In other prayer rites, the order is different). This section, too, is brief,

---

[52] This term is still used in the Yemenite prayer rite.

composed of psalms and scriptural verses, like *Pesukei de-Zimrah*. It includes (in *Nusaḥ Sepharad* and some other rites) Psalm 86 (omitted on days when *Taḥanun* is not recited), followed by a selection of verses from the Prophets (Isaiah 2:5; Micah 4:5; I Kings 8:57–60), and by Psalm 124 (which is also not recited on days of exceptional joy, when *El Erekh Appayyim* is also omitted). This is followed by the Song of the Day and other psalms to mark certain days, such as Psalm 27,* which is recited during the month of Elul, and other psalms, depending on the custom of each congregation. *Kaddish Yatom** follows, dividing this section from the next one—the one corresponding to the World of Action and paralleling the first section of the *Shaḥarit* prayer service.

DESCENT TO THE WORLD OF ACTION. This section, too, is extremely short, including elements similar to those found in the first section of the service, thus returning us to the reality of our world. In this section, there are recited three verses (Psalm 27:4; I Samuel 2:2; Psalm 18:32); the brief *Piyyut* called *Ein ke-Eloheinu**; the *Ketoret* section (generally recited only in part); and an aggadic dictum in praise of those who study Halakhah every day (*Megillah* 28b) and praise for Torah scholars (*Berakhot* 64a), as well as a few other verses in praise of the Torah. *Kaddish de-Rabbanan** is then recited as a conclusion to the Torah study just engaged in. In *Nusaḥ Sepharad*, *Barekhu* is recited, followed by *Aleinu* and *Kaddisḥ Yatom*.

In the Ashkenazic rite, this order is reversed: they recite only *Aleinu*, *Kaddish Yatom*, and the Song of the Day (many do not recite the *Ketoret* section, for fear of omitting one of its ingredients).

This concludes the fixed, communal order of *Shaḥarit*. From this point on, any additions are a matter for individual choice—the reading of various passages from the Torah, Psalms, or the study of set texts. In some places, almost the entire congregation participates in such readings, and therefore end their study with *Kaddish de-Rabbanan*.

It is customary nearly everywhere to recite the *Shesh* (Six) *Zekhirot*, and in many congregations worshippers recite *Parashat ha-Yir'ah*,* *Parashat ha-Teshuvah*,* *Parashat ha-Man*,* and the Thirteen Principles of Faith (see *Yigdal**), among other selections. It is common practice to have a daily study session or read Psalms. The *Ma'amadot** are recited mainly in Ashkenazic congregations, and it has become a widespread custom to study the book *Ḥok le-Yisrael*.* Those who are less pressed for time often extend these study selections even further, and for many it is tantamount to a mandatory practice. But in principle, these are voluntary additions and not part of the regular order of prayer services.

The *Minḥah* Prayer

Minḥah is the second obligatory daily prayer. The *Minḥah* service was established to correspond to the *Tamid* (daily) sacrifice offered at dusk; in Scripture, this time period is referred to as *Minḥat Erev* ("evening offering"; see Psalm 141:2; Ezra 9:4–5), for which reason the period allowed for reciting it corresponds to the time set for this sacrifice—*Bein ha-Arbayyim*, i.e., from the time when the sun begins to decline in the west until nightfall. This period is calculated as beginning half an astronomical hour* after astronomical high noon* (when the sun is at its zenith) and extends till sunset. At times, in emergency situations, this may even be extended until the appearance of the stars, especially if the *Minḥah* prayer had begun earlier. It is best to pray during the latter half of this period *(Minḥah Ketanah*)*, and there are places where, either for convenience—namely, in order to link the *Minḥah* and *Ma'ariv* prayers in the synagogue—or for other reasons,[53] the *Minḥah* prayer is recited very close to the end of its permitted period (as the Talmud puts it, "with the fading of the sun"—*Berakhot* 29b).

In praise of this prayer, the sages say, "One should always be careful concerning the *Minḥah* prayer" (*Berakhot* 6b), because of its importance. This has been explained[54] as follows: whereas *Shaḥarit* is recited before a person begins his daily round, and *Ma'ariv* is said after he finishes working, *Minḥah* is generally recited while one is in the midst of one's occupations and worries, and needs to make time and free one's mind in order to pray. One must therefore be careful both not to forget it and not to be distracted by anything during this prayer. On the other hand, if one manages to pray properly, one's reward is far greater.[55]

---

[53] See Psalm 72:5.

[54] *Tur*, *Oraḥ Ḥayyim* 232.

[55] See *Zohar*,# Genesis 230a.

The structure of the *Minḥah* prayer consists of only a few parts. Some begin with *Parashat ha-Tamid** and related readings of *Korbanot*, followed by *Ashrei;* the Ashkenazic rite begins with *Ashrei*, followed by half *Kaddish*, the *Amidah* (in the Ashkenazic liturgy the *Amidah* is preceded by Deuteronomy 32:3), and its repetition by the *Shaliaḥ Tzibbur*, *Vidduy* and *Taḥanun* (the latter are not said after the stars appear, and some do not say them even after sunset). Finally, *Aleinu* and all that usually accompanies it is recited.

The *Amidah* is the same as that of *Shaḥarit*. In the Ashkenazic custom, the individual worshipper adds *Anenu** on fast days within the benediction of *Shome'a Tefillah*.* On Tish'ah be-Av (see Chapter 12), the passage *Naḥem** is added to the *Boneh Yerushalayim** benediction. Some begin the last benediction with the words *Sim Shalom*, while others with *Shalom Rav*.

The repetition by the *Shaliaḥ Tzibbur* is like that of *Shaḥarit*, except that generally the Priestly Blessing* is not even mentioned, in accordance with the ruling of the Talmudic sages not to recite this blessing at *Minḥah*. However, on a public fast day the priestly blessing is mentioned, and in those places and rites where the priestly blessing is ordinarily recited in *Shaḥarit* throughout the year, those *Kohanim** present pronounce the Priestly Blessing at *Minḥah* as well. In addition, the *Shaliaḥ Tzibbur* recites *Anenu* after the benediction of *Go'el Yisrael*, and on Tish'ah be-Av he says *Naḥem* in the benediction *Boneh Yerushalayim*. During the Ten Days of Repentance,* and in many rites also on public fast days, *Avinu Malkenu** is recited at this point.

On those days when *Taḥanun* is recited, this is preceded in the Sephardic rite by *Vidduy* and the Thirteen Attributes. The *Shaliaḥ Tzibbur* then recites *Kaddish Titkabbal* (which on days when there is no *Taḥanun* follows immediately after the repetition of the *Amidah*).

There is a variety of customs regarding the conclusion of the *Minḥah* prayer. The Ashkenazic rite concludes with *Aleinu* and *Kaddish Yatom*. Most of those who follow the *Nusaḥ Sepharad* rite recite Psalm 27 here from the month of Elul until Shemini Atzeret (see Chapter 10). Some do so after *Aleinu* and some before it, and this is again followed again with *Kaddish Yatom*.

Since people sometimes begin reciting *Minḥah* very close to sunset (or the congregation may be pressed for time and cannot stay for long), it is customary in some places to shorten the repetition of the

Amidah. Thus, following *Ashrei*, the *Shaliaḥ Tzibbur* begins reciting the first three blessings of the *Amidah* aloud, and the congregation responds to the *Kedushah* as usual, after which all continue their prayer in silence; the rest of the prayer is concluded in the normal manner.

The *Ma'ariv (Arvit)* Prayer Service

During the mishnaic period, a few years after the destruction of the Temple, the sages debated as to whether or not the *Ma'ariv* prayer is mandatory,[56] it being finally ruled that it was not. Yet over the centuries, the entire people of Israel has accepted this prayer as obligatory, and today it is considered one of the three mandatory daily prayers. Nevertheless, as it is essentially a voluntary prayer, there is no repetition therein of the *Amidah*, except on Shabbat eve, when the *Shaliaḥ Tzibbur* recites a shortened version (see *Me'ein Sheva**).

In practice, the *Ma'ariv* prayer is linked with the evening recitation of *Shema* and, together with the *Amidah*, forms a unified prayer structure.

From the beginning, the time period allotted to this prayer was from the appearance of the stars until midnight. However, one should attempt to pray it as early as possible rather than later; on the other hand, it is permissible to recite this prayer throughout the entire night until dawn* (and, in emergency situations, even until sunrise). In many places, it is customary to begin the *Ma'ariv* prayer while it is still daytime, immediately following the *Minḥah* service, to avoid burdening the community with needing to attend synagogue prayers twice during the evening hours. This custom is widely observed in countries where summer days are very long and the stars appear at a very late hour. Yet even in such places, *Ma'ariv* is recited after *Pelag ha-Minḥah** (the last quarter of the *Minḥah* period); and whoever prays at this hour is required to repeat the reading of the evening *Shema* at its proper time (i.e., after dark).

Ma'ariv is the nighttime prayer, an aspect stressed in its *Shema*

---

[56] *Berakhot* 27b.

benedictions, both with regard to the general course of human life—with everyone completing their daily tasks and preparing for rest and repose—and with regard to the significance of the time of day: i.e., the descent of darkness and the surrounding gloom. In Jewish tradition, darkness symbolizes descent, gloom, the inability to see properly, and is always accompanied to some extent by "fears of the night" (Song of Songs 3:8; cf. Psalm 91).

The realm of night is always threatening, and alludes to God hiding His face from us.[57] The Bible refers to this idea frequently—from the very first mention of darkness and light in the story of creation,[58] in which light is referred to as "good" (Genesis 1:4)—and it naturally follows why it ought to be separated from darkness. Many references to this can also be found in the prophetic and poetic literature.[59]

Night is therefore a time of sinking and reduction of vitality. Moreover, the atmosphere of the Attribute of Justice *(Middat ha-Din)*, already present when the day begins to decline at the time of *Minḥah*, is felt in even greater measure at the hour of *Ma'ariv*. But night has other aspects as well.

Just as night is the end of a day of activity and life, in terms of the reckoning of times, it is also the beginning of the next day. Its darkness is not only a deprivation but also a means of obtaining rest; in this sense, each night is a hopeful prelude to the following day. Hence the spiritual significance of *Ma'ariv* as a mixture of both mercy and judgment, associated with the Patriarch Jacob, to whom it is ascribed. Thus, although darkness exists as the absence of light, there is also faith and hope for the future.

The main components of *Ma'ariv* are the Reading of the *Shema*, with its benedictions preceding and following it, and the *Amidah* prayer; but various additions have been made to this over the generations.

It is customary to recite various verses before the beginning of the prayer. The shortest version, usual in the Ashkenazic rite, is that in which only *ve-Hu Raḥum** ("but He, being full of compassion,

---

[57] See Deuteronomy 31:18.

[58] Genesis 1:1–5.

[59] E.g., Isaiah 60:2; Joel 2:2; Psalm 139:11; Job 15:23, and many more.

forgives . . ."—Psalm 78:38) is recited, which is already mentioned in all the early Siddurim. To this is added the verse "Save, Lord! The King will answer us when we call" (Psalm 20:10), as indicated already in the *Siddur of Rav Amram Gaon.*#

In *Nusaḥ Sepharad*, one first recites Psalm 134 and three further verses (Psalms 46:8; 84:9; 20:10), each of which is repeated three times. Some add other psalm verses as well. Among some communities, it is customary to recite the half *Kaddish* before *ve-Hu Raḥum*, in order to link the *Kaddish* with *Barekhu*.

The actual beginning of the prayer is with the call of *Barekhu*, whose literal meaning is an introduction to the *Shema* and its benedictions (and is therefore recited in both the *Shaḥarit* and *Ma'ariv* prayers); however, this has also been explained in other ways.

Then come the first two benedictions: *ha-Ma'ariv Aravim** and *Ahavat Olam*,* followed by the three sections of the *Shema* and concluding with the last two benedictions: *Emet ve-Emunah*,* and *Hashkivenu*.* Various prayer rites in the Diaspora include the prayer *Barukh ha-Shem le-Olam*,* while others omit it entirely.

The *Shaliaḥ Tzibbur* says the half *Kaddish*, and the *Amidah* prayer is recited silently. In principle, the *Amidah* of *Ma'ariv* is the same as that of *Shaḥarit* and *Minḥah*, the only special addition being *Attah Ḥonantanu*,* added to the fourth benediction, *Ḥonen ha-Da'at*,* at the conclusion of Shabbat or festivals.

In some rites, it is customary to say *Shalom Rav* (rather than *Sim Shalom*). In this service, there is no repetition of the *Amidah* by the *Shaliaḥ Tzibbur*. Therefore, after the silent recitation, the *Shaliaḥ Tzibbur* says *Kaddish Titkabbal*.

At the conclusion of the Shabbat, it is customary to add certain things after the prayer (see Chapter 9). On the intervening days between Pesaḥ and Shavu'ot, there is the Counting of the *Omer*.* According to *Nusaḥ Sepharad*, one then recites Psalm 121, followed by *Kaddish Yatom* and *Barekhu*.

In the Ashkenazic rite, the prayer concludes with *Kaddish Yatom* and (in the Land of Israel) *Barekhu*, concluding the prayer in similar style. At the suitable season, Psalm 27 is recited at this point in the Ashkenazic rite (and not in *Minḥah*, as in *Nusaḥ Sepharad*), as is Psalm 49, recited in houses of mourning.

Shema Upon Retiring to Bed

The recitation of *Shema* at bedtime is one of the five fixed daily orders of prayer; yet, far from being a communal form of prayer, it is a highly personal one, meant for the individual while alone with himself. The origin of reading the *Shema* at bedtime (i.e., immediately before going to sleep, some reciting it while actually lying in bed) is in the Talmud,[60] which states that it was instituted mainly for purposes of safety and defense. In the literal sense, it is supposed to guard a person from all kinds of danger that might come upon one during the night, when asleep and defenseless. But in a deeper sense, it is intended to guard the soul from all kinds of spiritual harm that might occur while one is lying in bed.

The night hours are a time of darkness that correspond, in the inner spiritual sense, to a period in which all kinds of evil powers predominate: "You make darkness, and it is night; wherein all the beasts of the forest creep forth" (Psalm 104:20).[61] The activities of all daytime life forms—human beings, birds, plants, etc.—gradually decrease, and the lack of illumination indicates, whether physically or spiritually, concealment and a waning vitality. Together with this change in the world in general, another major change occurs in the state of human existence—sleep. Sleep is the withdrawal of conscious spirit, and the level of vital energy is lowered not only in terms of general activity but also in the bodily functions of heartbeat and breathing. For this reason, our sages have said that sleep is a "mini death," "a sixtieth part of death" (*Berakhot* 57b). Wherever light and life vanish, they are replaced by twilight beings and forces of impurity (this is one reason for the washing of the hands as soon as one rises in the morning; see *Netilat Yadayyim**). Therefore, sleep, especially during the night, requires protection.

Another explanation for reading the *Shema* at bedtime is to ensure that one goes to sleep with the words of the Torah in mind (some peo-

---

[60] *Berakhot* 4b and 60a.

[61] See also *Bava Metzi'a* 83b.

ple were even accustomed to repeat certain phrases over and over until they fell asleep). In this way, one not only prevents one's mind from dwelling on trivial or impious thoughts, but engages in sacred matters. Falling asleep in this manner, even one's sleep and dreams will be affected by this worthy occupation.

There is yet another aspect to all this. Since during sleep a person is no longer conscious of one's thoughts and deeds, sleep constitutes a temporary cessation of conscious life, between the time one goes to bed and the time one wakens in the morning. Although our sages have mentioned the renewal that comes after sleep,[62] there is also a direct line of continuity in activity and thought between the end of one day and the beginning of the next one. When one prepares oneself for sleep, the conscious continuity of one's life follows that same line of thought and experience. As one sage has caustically expressed it, "Whoever goes to sleep like a dog cannot rise like a lion." Thus, suitable preparation for sleep—through reading the *Shema* at bedtime—is not merely a conclusion to the day but also the beginning of a new one.

As the bedtime reading of the *Shema* is not a communal prayer, and is recited in complete privacy, a large variety of formulations have been created, differing not only between one rite and another but even within the same rite itself, or even among members of the same congregation. The most essential components of this reading (retained in the minimalist bedtime *Shema* recited on Passover eve) are the reading of the biblical portion of *Shema* and the benediction *ha-Mappil.** The numerous additions to this are of two main types: requests and protective formulations (various prayers and verses), and confessions and words of remorse. Such confession before sleep has a double meaning. On the one hand, a person going to sleep is, in some way, like someone who is about to die. It is a little death only, but nevertheless involves a conscious foregoing of one's full vitality, and its entrustment to God (indeed, in many rites the prayer concludes with the words "I entrust my spirit into Your hands"—Psalm 31:6), while waking up each morning is seen as a recurring grace of resurrection. It is therefore appropriate for a person to make confession before yielding up the soul, as one does at the point of death.

On the other hand, as this *Shema* reading is the last act done at the

---

[62] See *Midrash Genesis Rabbah*# 14:9.

end of the day, it is appropriate that it include a summation of the day's activities. Throughout the day, a person undergoes many things; one might, for example, have been hurt by someone, and might need to say, for one's own peace of mind and for that of other people, a prayer to pardon those who have sinned against one. There is also room for self-accounting, if one has sinned against others. Such a summing up might reveal that, during the course of the day, one might have committed various sins, either intentionally or by accident. Some may notice only things that are evident and clear-cut, while others might be able to discover also more tenuous matters. Yet at all times and for all people, it is necessary to examine the gap between capability, expectation, and actual realization. The recital of the *Shema* at bedtime can be seen as an act of cleansing and purification, with a clear mind and a plea for atonement. Only once this has been done, and all the accounts have been completed, can one sleep peacefully.

CHAPTER NINE ❧ *Shabbat*

JUST AS THE Shabbat is set apart from all the other days in its sanctity, so has it been singled out and distinguished in its prayers. Shabbat was given to us "for sanctity and rest" (as it says in the blessings of the *Haftarah**) and, in the words of the Prophet (Isaiah 58:13), "Call the Shabbat 'delight,' the day made holy by the Lord, 'honored.' " Sanctity and rest on Shabbat are not two opposing poles, but rather one unit of meaning: a sanctity of rest, a repose of holiness.

Indeed, it is this special combination that defines Shabbat prayers and sets them apart from the weekday prayers. On the one hand, we refrain from mentioning any mundane matters in the Shabbat prayers; we make no requests relating to them, nor do we discuss concrete problems, serious or trivial, encountered during the six weekdays. Thus we uphold "and you honor it [Shabbat] by not following your customary ways, refraining from pursuing your [ordinary] affairs and from speaking [profane] words" *(ibid.)*. On Shabbat, one should distance oneself from life's tribulations, both material and psychological. Therefore, in the Shabbat prayers we do not mention our sins and transgressions, nor ask for pardon and forgiveness for them.

On the other hand, since Shabbat was given to us for holy respite, and since on that day there is no pressure of work or the fear of losing work hours, Shabbat prayers are more extensive, and make reference to matters not expressed during weekdays—either because of an objective shortage of time, or due to an inner sense of stress and hurry. The Shabbat leisure enables us to prolong contemplation and study, as well as to devote ample time to praise and thanksgiving, and to readings from the Torah and the Prophets.[63]

---

[63] The scholars of the Halakhah* ask why, on Shabbat and festivals, our sages did not rule that we should recite all the eighteen blessings of the weekday *Amidah*.* Their con-

The Order of the Shabbat Day

Shabbat can, in a certain sense, be viewed as one unified whole. The Midrash* says that the all-encompassing light that burst forth on the first day of Creation became increasingly bright in the course of the First Shabbat. Thus, Shabbat can be described as a day in which there is no darkness, only light. Therefore, on Shabbat people do not greet each other with "Good evening" or "Good morning," as ordinarily, but rather with "*Shabbat Shalom*" ("A good Shabbat," or "A Shabbat of peace").

Another aspect of Shabbat is, as written (Exodus 16:5), "and it shall be twice as much as they gather daily"; to which the sages comment (*Pesikta Zutrati,*# *be-Shalaḥ* 16, 29), "All Shabbat matters are twofold: a double [portion of] bread, a double sacrifice, a double punishment, a double reward." Moreover, on Shabbat an "additional soul" is added to our everyday soul (*Beitzah* 16a); and the Shabbat customs emphasize this doubleness: two candles are lit at the beginning of Shabbat; there are two loaves of bread in each Shabbat meal, two prayers on Shabbat mornings (*Shaḥarit** and *Musaf**), two Torah readings (in *Shaḥarit* and *Minḥah**), and so forth.

At the same time, however, there are some changes of essence within the Shabbat, corresponding to the various hours of the day, which on Shabbat have an entirely different character than on weekdays. These alterations find their expression in the Shabbat prayers, as well as in the Shabbat meals and in other customs.

The Shabbat eve is a night of brightness (as symbolized by the candlelighting at the beginning of Shabbat); and in the Kabbalah* it is conceived of as Divine revelation in the aspect of *Shekhinah,** of the bride decked out in all her finery. On Shabbat in the daytime, the light intensifies even further; therefore, "the honor of the day" surpasses

---

clusion was that the sages wanted to make things easier for the Jews on Shabbat, both by not encumbering them with lengthy benedictions and by not reminding them of the troubles and tribulations of the weekdays. However, since the weekday prayer was not totally suspended, the ruling is that whoever starts, inadvertently, to recite the weekday benedictions, and at some point remembers that it is Shabbat, should complete whatever blessing he is currently saying and then go on with the regular Shabbat prayer.

that of the night (*Rosh ha-Shanah* 27a), and this should be expressed by the garments worn during the day, and by the Shabbat morning meal. In Jewish mystical thought, Shabbat morning is considered a supreme revelation of the aspect of *Keter Elyon* ("Supreme Crown"; *Attika Kaddisha*, "the Ancient One"). It reaches culmination at twilight. On weekdays, twilight is a time of descent and of waning vitality, whereas on Shabbat it is the opposite: [the light] "glows ever more brightly, until the day dawns" (Proverbs 4:18). Moreover, it is a time of stronger illumination (called, in kabbalistic terms, *Ze'eir Anpin*), which comes about in a way of appeasement and conciliation, "a rest of peace, tranquility, serenity and security."[64]

The light of Shabbat is so strong that we wish it to shine throughout the week, on the days that follow it and those that precede it; indeed, in Hebrew, the weekdays do not have proper names, but are called after the Shabbat, "the first day [of Shabbat]," "the second day," etc. Generally speaking, in all the Shabbat-related laws we have to add a certain amount of time to Shabbat,[65] both before its cosmological beginning and after its end. So, too, in the order of prayers: we attach and add prayers to Shabbat both before its beginning (*Kabbalat Shabbat,** see below) and after its conclusion. Broadly speaking, there is a correlation and a parallelism between the entrance of Shabbat and its exit: almost everything that we do and say at the beginning of Shabbat has its counterpart also at the end of it.

In the course of the Shabbat, four full prayer services (namely, prayers that include the *Amidah*) are offered, besides series of Psalms and invocations, study and recitation texts, before, during, and after the Shabbat day. In addition to the prayers—which are essentially synagogue-related—there are other aspects, in word and in deed, meant to underscore the sanctity of this day.

The course of Shabbat includes: candlelighting; the Friday *Minḥah* prayer; *Kabbalat Shabbat; Ma'ariv** of Shabbat; the Shabbat eve meal (the First Meal) and its concomitant ceremonies; Shabbat *Shaḥarit* prayer; Torah reading; Shabbat *Musaf* prayer; the Shabbat day meal (the Second Meal) and what accompanies it; the Shabbat *Minḥah* prayer; the Third Meal*; the Shabbat afternoon study and recitation

---

[64] From the Shabbat *Minḥah* prayer.

[65] This is called "Shabbat supplement." See *Rosh ha-Shanah* 8b.

texts; preparations for the departure of Shabbat; the *Ma'ariv* prayer on *Motza'ei Shabbat** (the conclusion of Shabbat); *Havdalah** and what accompanies it; and the *Melaveh Malkah** meal.

Each of these items differs—sometimes profoundly so—from what is customary on weekdays, including the special prayers and *Piyyutim** that set the Shabbat apart.

Shabbat Prayer Services

The Friday *Minḥah* Prayer

The Friday *Minḥah* prayer itself is the same as that on regular weekdays, except that *Vidduy** and *Taḥanun** are never recited (not even in *Minḥah Gedolah**).

On Shabbat Eve, more than on other days, the custom is to link together the *Minḥah* and *Ma'ariv* prayers in one continuous time flow, utilizing the interval between them for *Kabbalat Shabbat*.

In most congregations, the Song of Songs* is read (in its entirety, or, by those who cannot say it all, the abbreviated rite); some read it before *Minḥah*, while others do so subsequently. This recitation, however, is not an inseparable part of the public prayer. A number of explanations have been given for this custom; apparently, it is a preparation for ushering in the Shabbat; and in honor of the special revelation of the Shabbat at night—namely, the aspect of "Queen" and "Beloved"—we first read Song of Songs, a book entirely devoted to these aspects.

In the Ḥassidic (Sepharad) rite, Psalm 107 is recited (unless Shabbat eve occurs on a festival day or on *Ḥol ha-Mo'ed.** Then *Pataḥ Eliyahu,** from the *Zohar,*# is recited (although not everywhere), followed by the *Piyyut** *Yedid Nefesh.** Some recite or sing this *Piyyut* after *Minḥah*.

Kabbalat Shabbat—The Reception of Shabbat

The custom of *Kabbalat Shabbat* as part of the public prayer service is relatively recent. It originated with the sages of Kabbalah in Safed, in the second half of the seventeenth century C.E.. Because it comes from a single source and began not too many generations ago, it is essentially uniform. Moreover, because *Kabbalat Shabbat* comprises only Psalms and *Piyyutim*, in some congregations boys under Bar Mitzvah* age are allowed to be the cantors for this prayer.

Kabbalat Shabbat is made up of six psalms: Psalms 95 through 99 and Psalm 29, recited with elevated spirit and joyful enthusiasm (in some places, the recitation of these psalms was accompanied by musical instruments; however, halakhic authorities ruled to abolish this custom). According to some sources, each of these six psalms corresponds to one of the weekdays and is intended to elevate it to a state of completion and perfection; it was also pointed out that the numerical value of the first letters of these six psalms is equal to the numerical value of the Hebrew word *nefesh*, "soul," alluding to the "additional soul" of Shabbat.

In many Ashkenazic congregations (those that follow the Sepharad rite), on a Shabbat that falls during *Ḥol ha-Mo'ed*, on a festival day, or on the day right after a festival day, only Psalm 29 is recited. This psalm is then followed by *Ana be-Khoaḥ.** Then the *Piyyut* of *Lekhah Dodi** is either recited or sung.

LEKHAH DODI. The hymn *Lekhah Dodi*, composed by Rabbi Shelomo Alkabez,[66] is regarded as one of the pearls of Jewish religious poetry. Its simplicity of form and linguistic charm serve to highlight the beauty and richness of its spiritual message.

The hymn is composed of ten[67] stanzas, the first of which is the shortest of all, and serves also as a refrain. The initial letters of the eight middle stanzas form an acrostic for the author's first name. The language of the hymn is based on biblical phrases and is full of allusions to talmudic and other sources, with only very few additions by the poet himself. However, all of that combines to form a complete and very original, lyrical composition.

An essential aspect of the hymn's beauty lies in a seemingly puz-

---

[66] Ca. 1505–1584; Talmudic scholar, biblical commentator, Kabbalist, and poet; member of one of the families expelled from Spain who settled in Safed.

[67] The number ten has special meaning and significance in Judaism, and particularly in kabbalistic thought.

zling aspect of it: who is the "bride" spoken about? In certain verses, it is clearly the Shabbat, while in others it seems to be the people of Israel, or the city of Jerusalem. The meaning of "beloved," too, keeps shifting accordingly: in certain stanzas it is the people of Israel, going out to meet the Shabbat Queen; and in others, it is God.

This multifaceted imagery is deeply embedded in the language of the Kabbalah and its mystic concepts. Shabbat, *Knesset Yisrael,** and the City of Jerusalem, are all connected with one comprehensive kabbalistic concept: the *Sefirah** of *Malkhut* ("Kingdom"), which the sages call the *Shekhinah*. Shabbat is often described in rabbinical literature and kabbalistic sources as a "taste" of the World to Come. It is the archetype of the future world, a lesser kind of redemption, the release of the body and, even more so, of the spirit, and its elevation to a higher level. Shabbat and redemption are therefore two aspects of the same notion—the restoration of reality to its pristine state of purity, an emergence from the region of toil and sin to one of total delight. And indeed, the inner core of this poem is this multifaceted concept of redemption: the redemption of the individual and of the nation. The welcoming of the Shabbat is, in itself, a preparation and a call to "the day which is all Shabbat"[68]—the day of the great redemption.

The hymn is, thus, more than just a song of praise for the Shabbat day: it is a song of deep devotion, of the bond of love between man and God. For many of the symbols mentioned, there are additional kabbalistic implications, and it is precisely because these symbols are not made explicit that they contribute to the depth and extent of its significance.

This hymn is well loved by all, and is sung to hundreds of melodies, many of which were composed specially for it.

Then come Psalms 92—"A Psalm, a song for the Shabbat day"—and 93*—"The Lord reigns, He is clothed with majesty." Some say only parts of *Lekhah Dodi*, and others (the Ashkenazic rite) start from Psalm 92. In some congregations, the *Piyyut* of *Bar Yoḥai** is always sung at this point, while in others it is customary to sing it after *Kabbalat Shabbat*, or only on certain occasions.

---

[68] From the Grace After Meals.*

In many congregations, Chapter 2 of the Mishnah, Tractate *Shabbat* (called *ba-Meh Madlikin,** and dealing with candlelighting) is now recited; some say it as part of *Kabbalat Shabbat*, and others, after *Ma'ariv*. This chapter, however, is not read on holidays that fall on Shabbat or on Shabbat eve, and on *Shabbat Ḥol ha-Mo'ed* (some omit it also on the Shabbat of Ḥanukkah; see Chapter 12). The recitation of this chapter is followed by "Rabbi Elazar said in the name of Rabbi Hanina," etc., and by *Kaddish de-Rabbanan.**

The Shabbat *Ma'ariv* Service

In the Sepharad rite, *Ma'ariv* of Shabbat is preceded by the portions *Kegavna** and *Raza de-Shabbat* from the *Zohar*. Then in some places the cantor says half *Kaddish** and *Barekhu**; others say *Barekhu* without the half *Kaddish*. *Ve-Hu Raḥum** is not recited anywhere, and the main part of the prayer begins.

In some congregations (such as in some Ḥassidic groups), the custom is to say this prayer wrapped in a *Tallit.**

The blessings preceding the *Shema,** and the *Shema* itself, are the same as on weekdays (although in some places *Piyyutim* are added on special Sabbaths). In most congregations, the *Emet ve-Emunah** blessing is precisely the same as on weekdays. The *Hashkivenu** blessing, however, is changed everywhere, in honor of Shabbat. In the Sepharad rite, "enemy, pestilence," and all the other calamities are not mentioned, and even in the Ashkenazic rite, the end of the blessing is changed into "spread over us the shelter of Your peace," or "a shelter of mercy [in some versions, "life"], and peace," and it concludes with "Blessed are You Lord, who spreads the shelter of peace over us, over His entire people Israel, and over Jerusalem." The reason for the change is that Shabbat is essentially different from the weekdays, and is "a reflection of the world to come" (*Berakhot* 57b). It forecasts a time that is wholly good; hence the "shelter of peace" that is spread upon everything on Shabbat.[69]

---

[69] See Isaiah 4:6.

Now the verses "Wherefore the children of Israel shall keep the Shabbat," etc. (Exodus 31:16–17), are recited almost everywhere (the exceptions being the rites of the Vilna Gaon@ and Ḥabad).

The Shabbat evening *Amidah** prayer, like all the Shabbat prayers, is comprised of the first three and last three blessings of *Amidah*—which remain unchanged throughout the year—and one middle blessing that is particular to Shabbat. This latter blessing is essentially the same in all the Shabbat prayers, and its most important part is "Our God and God of our fathers, please find favor in our rest . . . Blessed are You Lord, who sanctifies the Shabbat." This blessing is preceded by a *Piyyut*, a different one for each of the Shabbat prayers. The *Piyyut* of *Ma'ariv* begins with "You have consecrated to Your Name the Seventh Day," and continues with "And thus it is written in Your Torah," as well as the entire section of *va-Yekhulu.** Then (except for the Ashkenazic rite) it says, "Those who observe the Shabbat and call it a delight shall rejoice in Your kingship . . . in remembrance of the work of Creation," followed by the main blessing, "Our God and God of our fathers, please find favor in our rest," etc.

Most congregations, in *Ma'ariv* of Shabbat, say (according to Kabbalah), "and may all Israel . . . rest on *her*"; for Shabbat eve is God's revelation in the aspect of *Shekhinah* (see above), and therefore the feminine gender is applied to the Shabbat as well (as is sometimes done also in the Torah itself).

Unlike on weekdays, on which the prayers are recited with closed eyes, many people pray on Shabbat only from a Siddur—both because of the many changes in the Shabbat prayer and because it is a merit and a virtue.

After the conclusion of the *Amidah*, all the congregants rise to their feet and recite *va-Yekhulu* in unison. This is like standing up for testimony, and therefore it is customary for one praying alone not to recite these verses. One unable to join a *Minyan** should attempt to have another individual join him in saying these verses. The cantor then recites the *Me'ein Sheva** ("sevenfold") benediction (a summary of all the seven blessings of the *Amidah*)—unlike in all the other *Ma'ariv* prayers, in which there is no repetition* of the *Amidah*. This repetition was instituted by the sages to extend the Shabbat Evening Service, allowing individuals who pray longer to conclude together with other congregants, and thus not to have to return home alone.[70] Since this sevenfold blessing is a kind of repetition by the *Shaliaḥ Tzibbur,** it is not recited by individuals (or, in some rites, only parts of it are read by individuals, without the blessings). The cantor then says *Kaddish Titkabbal.**

In the Sepharad rite, at this point, Psalm 23* ("The Lord is my shepherd, I shall not want") is recited, followed by half *Kaddish*.

Most congregations now say *Barekhu.** This, too, was instituted for the benefit of those arriving late at the synagogue. The prayer is concluded with *Aleinu.** There is a custom in many congregations to add *Yigdal** or *Adon Olam.**

The *Shaḥarit* Service

It has become accepted not to rise for the *Shaḥarit* of Shabbat as early as on weekdays (although the prayer should begin at such an hour as to ensure recitation of the *Shema** on time).

The first part of *Shaḥarit (Korbanot*)* is very similar to that of weekdays, and it is read in its entirety even in those congregations that during the week abridge it or skip it altogether (due to time limitations and the burden upon the praying individuals). In this, there is a great deal of uniformity among the various prayer rites. However, the *Yehi Ratzons** after the *Korbanot* sections are generally omitted.

In the *Pesukei de-Zimrah** section, various changes are made on Shabbat, mostly additions. Most rites omit Psalm 100* ("A Psalm for the thank offering"), because in the Temple this sacrifice was not brought on Shabbat. Otherwise, most rites are basically similar. In some, a few psalms are added, some of which are connected in one way or another with the Shabbat, and most of them contain praises for which there is insufficient time during daily prayers. These additional psalms are: 19, 33 (except for the Ashkenazic rite), 34, 90, 91; the Sepharad rite also adds Psalm 98, and some of the Songs of Ascents*—namely, Psalms 121, 122, 123, and 124, followed by the Grand *Hallel**—Psalms 135 and 136. In the

---

[70] Especially since synagogues were often situated out of town; see Chapter 14, on the synagogue.

Ashkenazic rite, Psalm 33 is recited here, whereas in the Sepharad rite they recite here *ha-Aderet veha-Emunah*,* followed by *Barukh she-Amar** (which in the Ashkenazic rite is recited, on Shabbat as on weekdays, earlier on).

In all rites, Psalm 92 is now said, along with Psalm 93, and *Yehi Khevod*.* From here until after the Song of the Sea,* the order in each of the rites is precisely the same as on weekdays. Then comes the prayer of *Nishmat Kol Ḥai*.* *Pesukei de-Zimrah* are concluded, as always, with *Yishtabbaḥ*.*

In the blessings before and after the reading of the *Shema*, a number of changes are made in all the rites. In the first blessing, *Yotzer Or*,* the *Piyyut* of *ha-Meir la-Aretz*, which is recited on weekdays, is replaced on Shabbat with *ha-Kol Yodukha* ("All shall praise You"). Then comes the alphabetical *Piyyut* of *El Adon* ("Almighty God is the Master," in place of the weekday *Piyyut* of *El Barukh*), followed by the special Shabbat *Piyyut*—*la-El Asher Shavat** ("To the Almighty God who rested"). Then the prayer proceeds in the usual order, "Be eternally blessed. . . ." In some prayer customs, there are numerous *Piyyutim* for the blessings of the *Shema*.

The *Amidah* of the *Shaḥarit* of Shabbat is similar to that of the Shabbat *Ma'ariv* prayer, except that the middle blessing is preceded by a different *Piyyut*. This ancient *Piyyut*—which appears, with minor variations, in all of the prayer rites, and which begins with "Moses rejoiced in the gift of his portion"—is based on Exodus 16:29 and on the saying of our sages (*Shabbat* 10b), that the gift of the Shabbat was bestowed on Israel through the special mediation of Moses Our Teacher, and it is therefore appropriate to mention him and praise him liberally in this context. In most rites, the *Piyyut* "And You . . . did not give [the Shabbat] to the nations of the world . . ." is said, after which comes the main blessing, "Please find favor in our rest." All rites nowadays say, "May all Israel . . . rest in *him*"—applying the male gender to Shabbat, which, according to the Kabbalah,* is a reference to the Crown of Glory *(Keter Elyon)* revealed on Shabbat morning.

In the repetition of the *Amidah*, the Ashkenazim have a long formulation of the *Kedushah*.* After the repetition, the cantor says *Kaddish Titkabbal*.* In the Sepharad rite, the Song of the Day* is read (on *Rosh Ḥodesh**—Psalm 104, and from the beginning of the month of Elul until Shemini Atzeret*—also Psalm 27*), and *Kaddish Yatom*.*

Torah Reading

Reading from the Torah[71] on Shabbat morning is one of the commandments of Shabbat. The main rites of the ceremony in which the Torah scroll is removed from the Ark,* and the accompanying texts, are similar to those of the weekdays; however, on Shabbat many more items are added, both in honor of the Shabbat and because people have more leisure for these devotions.

Most prayer rites begin with a short formulation of *Attah Horeita** ("Unto you it was shown"—Deuteronomy 4:35), and in the Ashkenazic rite, *Ein Kamokha* ("There is none like You"—Psalm 86:8), followed by *va-Yehi bi-Neso'a ha-Aron,** and *Berikh Shemeih.** All the Ashkenazic rites have here a prayer taken from Tractate *Soferim: Al ha-Kol Yitgaddal* ("May the Name of the Holy One, blessed be He, be exalted . . ."). Then, *Av ha-Raḥamim Hu Yeraḥem* ("May the All-Merciful Father have compassion . . ."). At this point, in some Ashkenazic communities the Torah scroll is raised, to be displayed to the public. Then the Torah reading is begun.

After the reading of the Torah and the *Haftarah,** the custom everywhere is to add special blessings for the congregants and for others. The actual wording of these additions, however, differs greatly from one rite to another. The Ashkenazic communities recite an ancient blessing (which probably originated in Babylon), called *Yekum Purkan,** for all the Jewish leaders and Torah students and another *Yekum Purkan* and special *Mi she-Berakh** for the congregants and those who tend to the local communal needs (these blessings are therefore not recited by individuals who pray in private).

In most congregations, the custom is to memorialize subsequently (so as to "honor the living before the dead") the souls of the departed (usually those the anniversary of whose death is on one of the days of the following week), and there is a short rite of *Hashkavah,** recited in most congregations, in which the names of the deceased are mentioned. The Ashkenazim also add to the short *Hashkavah* a

[71] For a more detailed discussion of Torah readings, see Chapter 13.

general prayer—*Av ha-Raḥamim**—composed during the Crusades. However, neither *Hashkavah* nor *Av ha-Raḥamim* are recited on days on which *Taḥanun* is not said, on Sabbaths on which the blessing for the New Moon *(Kiddush Levanah*)* is recited, on the Sabbaths of the month of Adar on which the *Arba Parshiyyot** are read, and also when a circumcision* ceremony is held, or a bridegroom is present, in the synagogue.

In most prayer rites, on the Shabbat preceding a new month, the Blessing of the Month (or "Declaration of the Month," *Birkhat ha-Ḥodesh*) is recited.Then *Ashrei** is recited and the Torah scroll is put back into the Ark. In the Ashkenazic congregations, the cantor declares, "Let them praise the Name of the Lord, for His Name is sublimely exalted" (Psalm 148:13), and the congregation responds, "His radiance is upon the earth and heavens . . ." etc. (*ibid.*, vv 13–14).

In most congregations, Psalm 29 is recited while the scroll is being brought back to the Ark. The Ashkenazim add a few more verses. Then *Ashrei* is recited.

The *Musaf* Service

As an opening to the *Musaf* prayer, the cantor says half *Kaddish* (and there should not be any interruption between *Ashrei* and this half *Kaddish*). Then the congregation prays *Musaf.*

The *Musaf* of Shabbat, like all the other *Musaf* prayers, is composed of seven blessings: the unchanging first three and last three blessings, and the special middle blessing of this prayer. This middle blessing is made up of several parts. The beginning is a *Piyyut* in which the first letters of the words are in reverse alphabetical order (including the five final letters): *Tikkanta Shabbat Ratzita Korbenoteha* ("You have established the Shabbat, longed for its offerings . . ."). Then comes a request for restoring the Temple sacrifice worship, after which the biblical reference to the additional *(Musaf)* Shabbat offering is quoted. Most rites now have "Those who observe the Shabbat . . . shall rejoice in Your kingship." The middle benediction then concludes with the main Shabbat blessing, "Please find favor in our rest."

In the repetition of the *Amidah*, a different formula of the

Kedushah is recited—*Keter** (which in the Ashkenazic rite begins with the words *Na'aritzakh ve-Nakdisakh*, "We will adore and hallow You"). After the repetition, *Musaf* is concluded with the passages dealing with the *Ketoret* (and in the Ashkenazic rite, also the Song of the Day*), and *Kaddish de-Rabbanan*.* In the Sepharad rite, *Barekhu* is said here, followed by *Aleinu*, and *Kaddish Yatom.**

Some have the custom of reciting the portion about the shewbread (Leviticus 24:5–9) after this prayer, because the shewbread in the Temple was laid out every Shabbat, after the *Musaf* offering. In some congregations, excerpts from books of morals and guidance are read, in cantillation, before *Aleinu*.

Some Ashkenazic congregations say the *Shir ha-Yiḥud** of Shabbat. Many Ashkenazim, including those who pray according to the Sepharad rite, have the custom of rising to their feet, opening the Ark, and reciting, or singing, *Shir ha-Kavod.** Some also say *Yigdal** after the prayer.

The *Minḥah* Service

On weekdays, the afternoon—*Minḥah* time—is considered a time of judgment, and the Afternoon Prayer corresponds to our Patriarch Isaac (stressing "the Fear of Isaac," Genesis 31:42). On Shabbat, however, this is not so; rather, *Minḥah* time on Shabbat is considered the time of *Ra'avah de-Khol Ra'avin*, "the Will of all Wills," and a most supreme revelation (in kabbalistic terms, *Ze'eir Anpin* and *Attik Yomin*). Therefore the atmosphere at that time is one of calm and conciliation, of serenity and complete relaxation, accompanied by spiritual thirst and longing, as the pinnacle of all Shabbat yearnings.

There is, however, another aspect to this time of Shabbat: that of grief over the departure of central figures in Jewish history: Joseph, Moses Our Teacher, and King David—all of whom, according to tradition, passed away at this time. The combination of these two aspects has implications on the formulation of the Shabbat *Minḥah* prayer, as well as on the customs surrounding the Third Meal that follows it (see below).

The Shabbat *Minḥah* prayer begins like the *Minḥah* of weekdays, namely, with the recounting of the *Korbanot*, followed by *Ashrei;* then *u-Va le-Zion Go'el** is recited.

An ancient custom in all rites is to say here the verse "And as to myself, may my prayer to You, Lord, be at a propitious time; God, in Your abounding kindness, answer me with Your true deliverance" (Psalm 69:14), which, on the one hand, contains a reference to the "propitious time," and on the other, emphasizes the uniqueness of the Jew ("and as to myself") who, on the day of his rest and joy, releases himself to prayer. Some repeat this verse once more, right before *Amidah*. Even individuals who are praying alone, or where there is no Torah scroll, say this verse. Then the Torah scroll is taken out of the Ark.

At Shabbat *Minḥah*, three people are always called to the Torah (according to the injunction of Ezra the Scribe@), and read a short section from the Weekly Portion* of the coming week (sometimes totaling no more than the minimum of ten verses). In practice, however, the length of this section, and its internal division among the readers, vary slightly, according to the portion and local custom.

Half *Kaddish* is then recited, yet not after the reading, but after the scroll has been replaced in the Ark, as an introduction to the *Amidah*. Some Ashkenazim say "A Psalm, a song for the Shabbat day" after the Torah reading. In almost all congregations, Psalm 111 is recited in the *Minḥah* of Shabbat, although here, too, there are differences of custom: in most places it is recited at this point (in some congregations, along with Psalm 112).

The *Amidah* prayer, like the other Shabbat prayers, is made up of the first three and last three blessings, and between them the special Shabbat blessing, along with an ancient *Piyyut* that has become an integral part of it, "You are One and Your Name is One." This *Piyyut*, with very slight variations, is found in all rites. It speaks about the gift of Shabbat rest, "Jacob and his sons rest thereon—a rest of love and generosity, a rest of truth and faithfulness," etc. In most rites, the continuation is "a rest of peace, serenity, and security," which, in Hebrew, has the initials of the name Moshe (referring to Moses Our Teacher). This section concludes with "and through their rest they sanctify Your Name."

Everywhere the custom today is to change the formulation of the blessing, according to the Kabbalah,* to say "shall rest on *them*," which hints at the two supreme aspects that are both revealed at this hour. This is done despite the fact that it is grammatically incorrect.[72]

In the repetition of the *Amidah*, the short formulation of the *Kedushah* is recited, as on all weekdays. Then the three verses of *Tzidkatekha** are recited (there are two customs as to the order of these verses), and the cantor says *Kaddish Titkabbal*. The prayer is concluded with *Aleinu* and *Kaddish Yatom*.

After *Minḥah*, the custom everywhere is to study, or recite Psalms (see the section "Study on Shabbat Afternoon" in this chapter).

The *Ma'ariv* Service on *Motza'ei Shabbat* ("The Conclusion of Shabbat")

In the *Ma'ariv* prayer at the conclusion of Shabbat, there are changes both in the prayer itself and in subsequent recitations.

In most congregations, while Shabbat is departing, before *Ma'ariv*, the custom is to recite a few psalms, so as to escort the Shabbat with dignity—as well as to prevent idle talk, which is particularly inappropriate at this hour. Usually, Psalm 144 is recited—which has a traditional tune, apparently known throughout the Jewish world—and Psalm 67; some also say Psalm 29.

The *ve-Hu Raḥum*,* and the *Barekhu* that follows, are normally recited in a slow melody, so as to prolong the transition from the holy to the profane, as well as to show how difficult it is for us to part with Shabbat.

The weekday *Ma'ariv* is then recited, as usual. In the fourth blessing of the *Amidah*, in which we plead for wisdom and insight, a special formulation for the conclusion of Shabbat (and festival days) is added: *Attah Ḥonantanu*.* This formulation, which is in many ways parallel to the reference to Shabbat in the Shabbat eve *Ma'ariv*, is in fact a form

[72] For this reason, Rabbi Schneur Zalman of Lyady® made a slight change in his Siddur, which retains the plural form while making it grammatically correct. This change has also been adopted by some of the Sepharad congregations.

of *Havdalah*, in which we mention the departure of the Shabbat and plead for a week of bounty.

After the *Amidah*, the cantor says half *Kaddish*. *Vi-Yehi No'am** and *u-Va le-Zion Go'el* (from *ve-Attah Kadosh** on) are recited, followed by *Kaddish Titkabbal*. However, neither *vi-Yehi No'am* nor *ve-Attah Kadosh* are recited if one of the days in the following week is going to be a day on which labor is prohibited. The prayer ends, as always, with *Aleinu*, which is preceded by *ve-Yitten Lekha*.*

The Departure of Shabbat

At the end of Shabbat we make *Havdalah* which, in a sense, is parallel to the *Kiddush* with which we usher in the Shabbat.

In essence, the commandment to remember the Shabbat is fulfilled not only on Shabbat, but on each day of the week. Just as our sages instituted the *Kiddush* to fulfill the commandment of "Remember the Shabbat day to make it holy" (Exodus 20:8), so was the *Havdalah* (literally, "separation") instituted for the very same purpose—namely, to underscore the sanctity and uniqueness of the Shabbat by making a distinction and separation between Shabbat and the weekdays.

In the *Havdalah*, as in all the other customs we follow upon the conclusion of Shabbat, we honor the Shabbat by escorting her out, as it were, just as we had come to greet her upon her arrival (in *Kabbalat Shabbat*, see above). This parallelism is expressed both in the details of the customs and in the very structure of the *Havdalah*. In addition to the different halakhic reasons for it, we both greet the Shabbat and bid her farewell with light—the Shabbat candles and the *Havdalah* torch—to fulfill the verse "Glorify the Lord with light" (Isaiah 24:15). The texts, prayers, and songs of the end of Shabbat, as well as the *Melaveh Malkah* meal (see below), all have the same purpose: to escort the Shabbat out with much ceremony, just as we greet her upon her arrival.

The *Havdalah* Ceremony

Although the formulation of *Havdalah* included in the *Ma'ariv* prayer *(Attah Ḥonantanu)* already allows us to work, the sages instituted the *Havdalah* rite expressly over a glass of wine, and forbade us to eat or drink anything prior to the ceremony.[73] This ritual is accompanied by blessings over spices and fire, as will be explained below.

In many congregations outside of the Land of Israel, and a few congregations in Israel as well, *Havdalah* is made in the synagogue right after the *Ma'ariv* prayer, for the sake of those who do not have wine at home; and then everybody goes home to make *Havdalah* for the family members.

This ceremony, which has ancient origins (see *Berakhot* 51b), is mandatory for both men and women. Women are allowed to perform their own ceremony, without the blessing on firelight.

Havdalah is composed of several sections. There is a ceremonial opening, consisting of selected verses from the Torah that are, in a sense, parallel to the verses of *va-Yekhulu* in the *Kiddush* benediction. These verses vary significantly from one rite to another. They are followed by a series of blessings that includes blessings on wine,[74] on aromatic spices, on firelight, and the blessing on the *Havdalah* itself. The *Havdalah* cup should be filled to the brim, till it overflows and a little of its contents spills out. This is intended to serve as a sign of blessing for a good week ahead. The candle should be a taper with more than one wick. In most places, a special kind of candle is prepared for this purpose.[75]

After the ceremonial opening, one says: "*Savri Maranan (ve-Rabbanan)*" ("Attention, Gentlemen [and Masters!]") and then makes the blessing on wine, "who creates the fruit of the vine."[76] It is cus-

---

[73] Indeed, the law is that whoever cannot make *Havdalah* over a cup of wine should avoid eating until he can do so, even if it means fasting.

[74] However, other kinds of locally available drinks may also be used.

[75] One who does not have such a candle, however, may use two regular candles, or even two matches, whose flames are put together so that they burn as one.

[76] In case another drink is used, one makes the appropriate blessing for that drink.

tomary for the one pronouncing the blessing to pass the cup from his right hand to his left, so that he holds the container of spices in his right hand, and then also gazes at his hand in the light.

After that, the blessing on spices is recited. The reason for this blessing is that when the Shabbat ends, the "additional soul," which a person received on that day, departs, and there is a feeling of weakness and lowered vitality. By smelling the spices, then, one is revived—like any person who feels weak and needs to be strengthened. Many use a special, ornamented spice container.

This is followed by the blessing on firelight: "who creates the lights of fire." The main reason for reciting this is that on Shabbat it is forbidden to create fire, and here we make a blessing for its renewed use at the conclusion of Shabbat.[77] In order to make the blessing on the firelight, it must first be enjoyed (*Berakhot* 53b), and it is therefore the custom to look at the fingernails on one's hand, since by means of the light one can distinguish between the nail and the flesh on the finger.[78]

After reciting these blessings, one returns the cup to the right hand and pronounces the *Havdalah* benediction itself. Complex formulations for the *Havdalah* were composed over the generations, in which all the seven kinds of division that God made in the world were enumerated. However, in our time it is customary, in all the rites, to list only three of them (in addition to the one between Shabbat and weekdays):

Blessed are You Lord, who makes a distinction between sacred and profane, between light and darkness, between Israel and the nations, between the Seventh Day and the six work days. Blessed are You Lord, who makes a distinction between sacred and profane.

---

[77] The sages of the Talmud say (*Pesaḥim* 52b) that the first fire made by man was lit at the conclusion of the first Shabbat of creation, when the darkness of the first night began to fall.

[78] There are various customs as to how one should look at the fingernails during this blessing. Some bend the fingers into the palm, so that they can see both fingernails and palm at the same time. Others bend the fingers over the whole hand, and then stretch them out and turn them over to see the back of the hand. There are other explanations for this custom, based on allusions and mystical thought.

The three differentiations mentioned in this benediction derive from biblical sources: Leviticus 10:10, Genesis 1:4, and Leviticus 20:26. Though there are other divisions explicitly stated in other biblical verses as being made by God, it may be said that the three divisions mentioned in this benediction were chosen because the difference between Shabbat and weekdays includes them all.

At the end of the *Havdalah* benediction, either the person who recited it, or one who had intended doing so from the outset, drinks the wine. It is the custom not to give any wine remaining in the *Havdalah* cup to others; it is also customary for women not to drink from it, unless a woman is making *Havdalah* for herself.

Among Jews throughout the world, there is a great variety of customs connected with the *Havdalah* service, showing the special affection for this commandment in a variety of ways. In many communities, the *Havdalah* candle is extinguished with the remaining wine, and some show their love for the commandment by dipping a finger into the spilled wine and touching it to their eyes or clothes.

When the conclusion of the Shabbat falls on the eve of a festival day, the *Havdalah* service is combined with the *Kiddush* service for the festival (see *Yoknehaz**). If the Ninth of Av (see Chapter 9) begins at the conclusion of Shabbat, the *Havdalah* service is not conducted;[79] only the blessing on firelight is recited, and the service is postponed to the following evening when the fast is over, and no blessing on aromatic spices or on firelight is made then.

The *Havdalah* benediction is also recited at the conclusion of a festival day. When a festival day is followed by a weekday, the *Havdalah* service is like that for Shabbat, except that no blessing is made for aromatic spices or for firelight.[80] When the festival occurs on a Friday, no *Havdalah* service is performed, because the sanctity of Shabbat is greater than that of the festival, and the *Kiddush* of Shabbat is a sufficient division.

The *Havdalah* benediction is recited also at the conclusion of Yom Kippur (see Chapter 11); in this case, the blessing for firelight is made,

---

[79] The Ninth of Av being a fast day, no drinking can take place.

[80] On aromatic spices—because there is no "additional soul" on a festival day; and on fire—because it is permitted to use and transfer light on a festival day.

since the use of fire is prohibited on that day. It is preferable to do this on "light that has rested"—namely, a candle that has remained alight throughout Yom Kippur. However, if such a candle is not available, the blessing may be recited over any other candle.

After the *Havdalah*

One aspect of the many rituals at the conclusion of Shabbat is the prayer and petition to begin the new week in a suitable and appropriate manner. Shabbat is a day of spiritual exaltation ("additional soul," see above), which ought to be devoted entirely to lofty and sanctified matters. However, after the Shabbat departs, we each find ourselves where we had been before, and this leads to a certain feeling of dejection (described as "the departure of the additional soul"), apprehension about the coming workdays and their problems, and a desire not to part entirely with Shabbat and its sanctity. Therefore, the ceremonies at the conclusion of Shabbat, which help us make the transition from Shabbat to weekdays, are also intended to draw the light of Shabbat into the profane, so that the weekdays are not entirely gray but have some of the Shabbat light illuminate them.

In all rites, *ve-Yitten Lekha* is recited at the conclusion of Shabbat. There are, however, variations as to when it is said, and its precise formulation. Some say it right after the *Amidah* of *Ma'ariv*, before *Aleinu*. In the Sepharad rite, some say it before *Aleinu*, and some after *Havdalah*. As for the formulation, most of the Ashkenazim (including the Sepharad rite) say a long *ve-Yitten Lekha*, whereas others have a shorter rite. One should strive to do *Kiddush Levanah** at the conclusion of Shabbat.

Most congregations have special *Piyyutim* and *Zemirot** for the conclusion of Shabbat, but these—like the *Zemirot* of Shabbat itself—do not have a fully established order. Some say a larger number, some say fewer, and the texts themselves, too, vary from congregation to congregation; and since these *Zemirot* are recited at home, each family, in fact, has its own customs. Nevertheless, certain elements are found, in varying forms, in all rites. Thus, for instance, everybody mentions Elijah the Prophet at the conclusion of Shabbat; according to our sages (Jerusalem Talmud, *Pesaḥim*, chap. 3, halakhah 6), Elijah will not come on Shabbat; therefore, right at the conclusion of Shabbat we announce that we expect the immediate arrival of Elijah and of the redemption. There are customs to say this already at the end of the *Havdalah;* elsewhere, there is a variety of *Zemirot* that speak about Elijah the prophet in general, and about the hope for his speedy arrival. Some have the kabbalistically founded custom of saying a series of *Zemirot* in which "Elijah the Prophet" is mentioned 130 times.

In addition, all congregations say prayers for the coming week. These prayers have different formulations, yet some formulas (that parallel even textually those recited on Shabbat eve) are to be found, with slight variations, in the great majority of Jewish communities.

In addition, in many places, study texts and special collections of verses are recited, in preparation for the coming week.

Shabbat Meals

The Shabbat meals fulfill an important role in the course and customs of the day—both because they are mandatory, and because they are surrounded by ceremonies of blessings, study, and song.

It is a commandment to eat three meals on Shabbat, in order to fulfill the injunction (which has the absolute halakhic validity of a rabbinically enacted commandment) of "call the Shabbat 'delight' " (Isaiah 58:13). We are called upon to observe the sanctity of Shabbat not only by refraining from work and devoting the day to heavenly matters, but also by honoring it through physical pleasures. Therefore, the pleasures of the body—which on weekdays are merely a permissible option (and one must make sure not to overdo them or get carried away by them)—have, on Shabbat, an aspect of a commandment. This is expressed in many things, even in what is said in the Midrash *(Yalkut Reuveni,*# *va-Etḥanan)*, "Sleep on Shabbat is a pleasure," as well as in eating three meals on Shabbat (given that on weekdays, the custom was to eat only two main meals).

Unlike all other meals, which are meant just for the sustenance of the body, the Shabbat meal is a form of worship. It is like "family sacrifice" (see I Samuel 20:29)—namely, like the festive consumption of a sacrifice offered by a family. This "family sacrifice" combines two elements: the ritual aspect of the sacrificial ceremony, and the warmth and intimacy of the family gathering. Indeed, the Shabbat meal can be compared to the *Seder* meal of Passover (see Chapter 10): not simply a festive meal, but a meal that is, itself, a way of Divine service.

Therefore, the Shabbat meal is accompanied by a great variety of special customs, as well as by words of Torah and prayer that have a connection to it. The actual customs vary largely from place to place. Already at the time of our sages, it was a habit to eat special foods on Shabbat, and so it is to this day. Every community and congregation has its special Shabbat dishes that are inseparably intertwined with the very substance of these meals. However, halakhically speaking there is only one binding law on Shabbat meals: that of the "double-bread"—namely, that at each Shabbat meal there should be at least two loaves of bread, in remembrance of the double portion of manna that came down from Heaven in the desert on Fridays (Exodus 16). According to the Kabbalah, at every Shabbat meal the table should be set with twelve loaves (like the shewbread that was laid, every Shabbat, on the Temple's golden table); however, few actually practice this custom. (Some explain the special shape of the *Ḥallah*—the Shabbat plaited bread—of the Ashkenazic communities as an attempt to create one loaf made up of twelve small loaves.)

The basis of each of the Shabbat meals must be bread, of which at least an olive-size portion (some 30 grams) should be eaten. There are those who follow a talmudically based custom (*Shabbat* 33b) of bringing two bunches of spices and myrtle to each meal and reciting the blessing for fragrances over them. Another ancient custom, also mentioned in the Talmud (*ibid.*, 118b) is to eat fish during Shabbat meals; and special care is taken everywhere to eat (or drink) something warm *(Ḥamin)* on Shabbat, in demonstration against the strictures of the Samaritans and the Karaites, who prohibited this.

In most rites, there is a fixed, defined order to the texts recited in preparation for, and during, the Shabbat meals. This includes Psalm 23* ("The Lord is my shepherd, I shall not want"), a formula of *Atkinu Se'udata* (see below), and one of the three special poems composed by Rabbi Isaac Luria@ for the three Shabbat meals. Then, the *Kiddush* is recited.

The *Kiddush* of Shabbat Eve, and the First Shabbat Meal

The commandment "Remember the Sabbath day to sanctify it" (Exodus 20:8), which is one of the Ten Commandments, is observed by explicitly declaring, in words, that Shabbat has arrived, and that one is taking upon oneself to sanctify it and be sanctified by it. However, our early sages (*Pesaḥim* 106a) instituted an entire festive ceremony—the *Kiddush*—which includes a benediction over a cup of wine.[81] At the conclusion of the Sabbath day, too, there is a commandment to remember the departing Shabbat, which is fulfilled through the *Havdalah* ceremony (see above).

The reason for making *Kiddush* over wine is that this is a way of connecting the benediction, which refers to things abstract—such as Shabbat, festivals, or commandments—with an act that is experienced through all our senses, thus grounding spiritual essences in universally perceived realities.[82] Wine was chosen because of its unique nature, being associated with joy and festivity that reach as deep as one's very soul.[83] Wine is the drink that "cheers God and man" (Judges 9:13), serving both as a component in human delight and as a libation to be poured out over the sacrificial altar. This adds further emphasis: it is a statement that the commandment is performed not only out of obedient acceptance of heaven's yoke, but with willing assent and heartfelt joy.

[81] Linking this benediction on the sanctification of the day to a blessing over wine is not specific to the *Kiddush* ceremony alone, but is done in quite a number of other ceremonial occasions—e.g., weddings, circumcision* ceremonies, drinking four cups of wine during the Passover *Seder*,* etc. A *Kiddush* service is held also on festival days, to mark their sanctification; however, according to most halakhic authorities, this latter *Kiddush* is not a Torah commandment, but a rabbinical ruling.

[82] Therefore, if one is unable, for whatever reason, to make *Kiddush* over wine, then it can also be made over the *Ḥallah* bread (the special Shabbat loaves); see the section "Some of the Laws and Customs of the Kiddush" in this chapter.

[83] See *Sefer ha-Ḥinukh*,# commandment 31.

PREPARATIONS FOR THE *KIDDUSH*

ALTHOUGH THE *KIDDUSH* benediction itself is not very long, it is performed with great ceremony, because it is the most important part in welcoming the Shabbat at home. This ceremoniousness is very ancient in origin (see *Berakhot* 51a). The practices carried out just before the *Kiddush* ceremony are of two distinct kinds: the first category includes routines that are part of welcoming the Shabbat to the home; the other comprises items that, together with the Kiddush itself, form one whole ceremony.

The customs adhered to and the recitations made in welcoming the Shabbat vary among the different rites, and sometimes even from one family to another. However, the general order is as follows.

On returning from the synagogue on the eve of Shabbat, one enters the home and says "*Shabbat Shalom*" (or "Good Shabbos"). Besides the obvious intention to greet the members of the household, there is also the kabbalistic sense of preparing the home to welcome the inspiration of Shabbat sanctity.

It is customary to bless the children on the eve of Shabbat, either after reciting (or singing) *Shalom Aleikhem** or after the *Kiddush* ceremony. The blessing is bestowed by the father's placing his hands over the child's head and saying, for a boy, "May God make you like Ephraim and Menasheh" (Genesis 48:20), and for a girl, "May God make you like Sarah, Rebecca, Rachel, and Leah" (see Ruth 4:11), followed by the verses of the Priestly Blessing.*

After *Shalom Aleikhem*, it is customary for most of the Ashkenazim, and some other communal groups, to pronouce an invocation in honor of Shabbat, which opens with the words "Master of all worlds." One then recites *Eshet Ḥayil** ("Woman of Valor"—Proverbs 31:10-31), which is a multilayered hymn of praise for the homemaker and for the *Sefirah* of *Malkhut*.

Then those present prepare themselves for the Shabbat meal by saying, "Prepare the meal of perfect faith, which is the delight of the holy King; prepare the meal of the King." This formulation is recited before all the Shabbat meals; however, at this particular meal we add, "This is the meal of the holy *Ḥakal Tappuḥin*, and *Ze'eir Anpin* and the holy Ancient One come to join her in the meal." The holy *Ḥakal Tappuḥin* ("field of the holy apples") is the term used in the *Zohar*# for the *Shekhinah*, the *Sefirah* of *Malkhut* ("Kingdom"), which is manifested on Shabbat eve.

In nearly all Jewish communities, it is customary to follow this with the reciting or singing of the *Piyyut* for Shabbat eve composed by Rabbi Isaac Luria,@ called *Azammer bi-Shevaḥin*, which describes the festive Shabbat meal in its entirety. This is then followed by a prayer in Aramaic which begins with "May it be the will of the most holy Ancient One."[84] In many homes, the *Kiddush* ceremony is preceded also by a *le-Shem Yiḥud.** In the Sepharad rite, it is followed by *vi-Yehi No'am*.

Many also recite Psalm 23* before the *Kiddush* (as well as before the other Shabbat meals). This psalm is especially suited to the Shabbat meal, since God is described there as the Shepherd leading his flock into safe and tranquil pastures.

Some of the Laws and Customs of the *Kiddush*

From the time the Shabbat begins until one makes *Kiddush*, it is forbidden to eat or drink anything. The table on which the festive meal is to be served should be prepared while it is still daytime; it is customary to have the two loaves of *Ḥallah* bread on the table, covered over, during the *Kiddush* ceremony. *Kiddush* must be made in the room where the meal is to be eaten. It is highly recommended to make this *Kiddush* over red wine.

Just before the *Kiddush* ceremony, one pours the wine from the bottle into a cup; the pouring of the wine must be with the intention of doing it for the sake of fulfilling the commandment of *Kiddush*. In emergency cases, e.g., when there is no wine available, one may make *Kiddush* over bread, and instead of the blessing "who creates the fruit of the vine," one says, "who brings forth bread from the earth." In such a case, one must ritually wash the hands (see *Netilat Yadayyim**) before making *Kiddush*, so that one can immediately eat of the bread.

[84] From *Sha'ar ha-Kavvanot*# by Rabbi Ḥayyim Vital.@

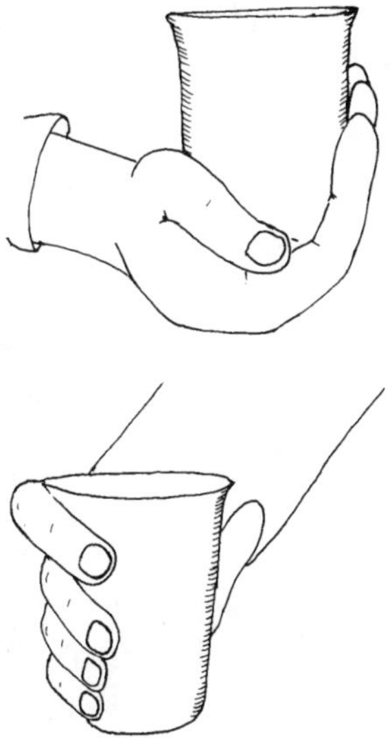

Two ways of holding the *Kiddush* cup

The wine cup must be washed and rinsed both inside and out before the *Kiddush*, even though it is clean, as a sign of respect for the commandment. The wine cup must hold at least a *Revi'it* (86 cc or, according to other opinions, 150 cc) of wine, and must be in perfect condition, without a chip or crack in its brim. It is customary to set aside a specially decorative cup for the *Kiddush* ceremony. The wine is poured so that it fills the cup to the brim, as a sign of blessing and respect for the commandment. Some people pour a little water into the wine, a practice based on talmudic as well as on mystical sources.[85]

Before the *Kiddush* blessing, *va-Yekhulu* is recited, preceded by the words "The sixth day," which are the last words of the previous verse. The reasoning here is that the first letters of these two words (in Hebrew), together with those of the first two words (in Hebrew) of the next verse, form one of God's Names—the Tetragrammaton.[86] In most Jewish communities, strict care is taken to recite the Shabbat eve *Kiddush* with all present standing up, because reciting *va-Yekhulu* is like bearing testimony, and according to Jewish law, witnesses are required to stand while testifying. Also, the *Kiddush* benediction itself is a blessing over a commandment (see *Birkhot ha-Mitzvot**), and it is the custom to stand while reciting such benedictions. Only later, while drinking the wine, do all sit down, so as to make the drinking a part of the meal.[87]

The one who makes the *Kiddush* takes the cup in both hands, and then transfers it to his right hand. The prevailing custom, which is based on the *Zohar*, is for the person making the Kiddush to hold the Kiddush cup on his palm with his fingers encircling the cup from below.

---

[85] *Shulḥan Arukh, Oraḥ Ḥayyim*, 272:5; *Peri Etz Hayyim*,# end of chap. 17.

[86] Some, who do not wish to break a verse in the middle, silently recite the beginning of this verse: "And it was evening and it was morning," and only then say aloud, "the sixth day."

[87] There are, however, those who drink the wine while still standing; some recite *va-Yekhulu* standing, and then sit through the rest of the ceremony; others yet recite even this while seated, after having stood up to recite the opening verse of the *Kiddush*.

The content of *va-Yekhulu* which, as said above, is a form of testimony, whereby a person attests that heaven and earth were created by God, is also the very basis and foundation for the sanctification of the Shabbat and for its observance. As the Torah clearly states elsewhere (Exodus 31:17),

It is a sign between Me and the children of Israel for all time, for in six days the Lord made heaven and earth, and on the seventh day He ceased from work and rested.

Immediately after the *Kiddush*, the person who recited it sits down and drinks from the wine in the cup (or gives it to someone else to drink in his stead). One must drink a significant quantity, and not just a sip.[88] Then the cup is handed around, or the wine in it is poured out for each of the participants.[89] If there are cups already filled with wine in front of them, they may drink from these cups, although it is specially commendable to drink from the cup of blessing. However, one who participates in the ceremony and has listened to the benediction fulfills his obligation even without drinking from the wine.

In most communities, the *Kiddush* is immediately followed by the ritual washing of the hands for the festive meal. Care should be taken not to have too great a lapse of time between the *Kiddush* and the ritual handwashing. Then the Shabbat meal is held.

The Second and Third Shabbat Meals

Prior to the Second Meal of Shabbat (the meal following the *Musaf* prayer), a short *Kiddush (Kiddusha Rabbah*)* is made. Usually, Psalm 23 is recited, followed by selected verses, including "If you turn away your foot because of the Shabbat," (Isaiah 58:13–14), "And the children of Israel shall observe the Shabbat" (Exodus 31:16–17), and "Remember the Shabbat day to sanctify it" (*ibid.*, 20:8–11). The Sepharad rite contains, prior to these verses, the *Atkinu Se'udata* formulation,

---

[88] Some drink at least a mouthful; some drink more than half of the *Revi'it*; others yet drink most of the wine in the cup, even if it is a big one.

[89] More precisely, to those who do not wish to perform their own *Kiddush*.

Prepare the meal of perfect faith, which is the delight of the holy King; prepare the meal of the King. This is the meal of the holy Ancient One, and the holy Ḥakal Tappuḥin Kaddishin *and* Ze'eir Anpin *come to join Him in the meal.*

Then the *Piyyut* of *Asadder li-Se'udata,* by Rabbi Isaac Luria, is recited.

The Third Meal is eaten after the *Minḥah* prayer. During this meal, too, Psalm 23 is read and *Atkinu Se'udata* recited, except that at this time we say, "This is the meal of *Ze'eir Anpin.*" Rabbi Isaac Luria's *Piyyut, Benei Heikhala,* is also recited. Some have the custom of drinking wine with this meal, and even a kind of *Kiddush* was instituted, which is declaimed in the course of the meal.

It is a custom to recite or study (before or during the Shabbat meals) *Tikkunei Shabbat,** which is the reading of eight Mishnah chapters from Tractate *Shabbat* (chapters 1–8 at the First Meal, 9–16 at the Second Meal, and 17–24 at the Third Meal). Another common practice is to recite excerpts from the *Zohar* that deal with the hours at which these meals take place. Some read, prior to the Shabbat morning meal, all of chapter 1 of the Mishnah Tractate *Kelim,* along with the first *mishnah* of chapter 2.

Everywhere there are *Zemirot* sung in honor of Shabbat, either in the course of the meal, or right before or after it. There is no definitive schedule for these *Zemirot,* and although there are *Zemirot* sequences accepted by all, some tend to sing more of them and others fewer, depending upon the time available and the musical talents of the household members. In some places (especially where the Third Meal is shared by a group of people—usually only males, often in the synagogue), there are songs habitually sung in sequence, as well as established tunes and customs; however, these are all local practices, which vary from place to place.

Study on Shabbat Afternoon

In the talmudic and mishnaic periods, the Shabbat afternoon hours were devoted to Torah study. People would gather in the synagogue to hear the homilies of the local sage, which were usually addressed to the general public and contained many aggadic issues along with some specific points of Halakhah. Our sages attached such importance to this custom that they instituted a number of rulings to ensure that it not be abolished. Many of the books of aggadic Midrash* we have today can be traced, in fact, to these Shabbat afternoon sermons. Indeed, in many places this custom has survived to this day (the book *Ben Ish Ḥai*, by Rabbi Yosef Ḥayyim of Baghdad,@ for instance, derives from such homilies). It is the custom among Ḥassidim, who follow the Sepharad rite, to join in a communal Third Meal, and to devote it to issues of Torah and faith. In addition to the sermons given on these occasions, which are adapted in character to the different times and places, it is a widespread custom among the Jewish people to recite *Pirkei Avot** on each of the Sabbaths between Pesaḥ and Shavu'ot, one chapter every Shabbat. In many congregations (mostly those of the Ashkenazim, but also others), *Pirkei Avot* are recited in this order all through the summer, until Rosh ha-Shanah.

As mentioned above, all the Ashkenazim (but for a few congregations) recite certain Psalms during the winter (from Sukkot until *Shabbat ha-Gadol*, see below), as well as Psalm 104* and all the Songs of Ascents.*

Those who follow the custom of reading *Tikkunei Shabbat*, read Chapters 17 through 24 of the Mishnah, Tractate *Shabbat*.

Melaveh Malkah

As early as talmudic times, it was customary to have a special meal after the conclusion of Shabbat (*Shabbat* 119b). This meal is considered the Fourth Shabbat Meal, and in many places is called *Melaveh Malkah** (literally, "escorting the queen"). This meal, too (paralleling the First Meal, that of Shabbat eve), is held in honor of the Shabbat—so as to escort her out with great ceremony and joy, just as we welcome her upon her arrival.

It has been halakhically ruled (*Shulḥan Arukh*, *Oraḥ Ḥayyim*, section 300) that one should prepare for this meal just as for all other Shabbat meals (namely, by setting the table, spreading a tablecloth, etc.), even if one eats only an olive-sized morsel. It is a practice to have two loaves of bread at this meal as well. Another custom is not to eat at this meal only of the foods prepared for Shabbat itself, but to serve a dish made specially for this meal. Many sages have expounded at great length on this meal and the many spiritual benefits bestowed on those who observe it meticulously. There are those who precede this meal with a *le-Shem Yiḥud*. It is also a custom to say, before this meal, *Atkinu Se'udata*, as follows: "Prepare the meal of perfect faith . . . this is the meal of David, the Messiah King." Shabbat clothes are generally not taken off until after this meal. In many places, some of the *Zemirot* for the conclusion of Shabbat are sung during the *Melaveh Malkah* meal.

Special Sabbaths

The fixed orders of Shabbat prayers and customs are sometimes changed, for a number of reasons: sometimes because Shabbat occurs on a day that has its own uniqueness and special significance: a festival day, *Rosh Ḥodesh* (see Chapter 12), or any other special day. The general rule is that the more important the day, the greater its impact on changing the regular course of Shabbat prayers. There are also other events that are part of Shabbat itself but depend on the monthly and yearly cycles, which may also bring about additions to and modifications in the Shabbat prayer; finally, even private events (such as a wedding or a circumcision) may cause certain changes.

Shabbat Mevarkhim

The Shabbat before *Rosh Ḥodesh* is called, in the Ashkenazic congregations, *Shabbat she-Mevarkhim ha-Ḥodesh* (literally, "the Shabbat in which the [new] month is blessed"), for on such a Shabbat the day (or two days) in the week on which the new month will begin is announced. In other congregations, it is called "the Shabbat on which the [new] month is announced" or, simply, "the Shabbat before *Rosh Ḥodesh*."

On such a Shabbat, no changes are made in the regular course of prayers—except for the addition of the Blessing of the New Month *(Birkat ha-Ḥodesh)*. It is a custom everywhere not to say this blessing, or announcement, for the month of Tishrei.

The Ashkenazic custom is to treat this Shabbat like a day on which *Taḥanun* is not recited, and consequently *Av ha-Raḥamim** is omitted.

There are, however, differences in practices in this regard, since some do say *Av ha-Raḥamim* on the Sabbaths on which the months of Tammuz and Av are blessed, because of the calamities that occurred in these months (see Chapter 12); and in most congregations, *Av ha-Raḥamim* is recited on the Shabbat on which the month of Sivan is blessed, because this prayer was composed, and its recitation instituted, following persecutions that occurred during that month.

Shabbat Rosh Ḥodesh

WHEN ONE OF the days of *Rosh Ḥodesh* occurs on Shabbat, there are certain changes in the prayers, as well as in the order of the Torah and *Haftarah* readings.

In the *Amidah* of *Shaḥarit*, *Minḥah*, and *Ma'ariv*, the *Ya'aleh ve-Yavo** prayer for *Rosh Ḥodesh* is added. *Rosh Ḥodesh* is mentioned also in the Grace After Meals.*

Those who recite Psalm 104* on *Rosh Ḥodesh* say it on this Shabbat as well (and those who follow the Vilna Gaon rite say it instead of Psalm 92). In the Sepharad rite, it is recited before the removal of the Torah scroll from the Ark, while in the Ashkenazic rite it is said after *Musaf.* On the *Rosh Ḥodesh* of Elul, Psalm 27 is added.

Shaḥarit is the same as on every Shabbat; but congregations that say *Piyyutim* have special *Yotzerot** for Shabbat *Rosh Ḥodesh*. After the *Amidah* of *Shaḥarit*, half *Hallel** is recited.

For the Torah reading, two scrolls are taken out of the ark; in the first one, the Weekly Portion is read as usual (with seven people called up). After the reading, the two scrolls are laid down on the table together, and half *Kaddish* is recited. The second scroll is used for reading the *Maftir*,* which on *Rosh Ḥodesh* consists of the verses that detail the *Musaf* offerings on Shabbat and *Rosh Ḥodesh* (Numbers 28:9–15). A special *Haftarah* is then read, "The Heaven Is My Throne" (Isaiah 66: 1–24), in which both Shabbat and *Rosh Ḥodesh* are mentioned; the custom is to end with a repetition of the penultimate verse, so as not to conclude with words of doom. (If *Rosh Ḥodesh* Elul falls on Shabbat, some read, as *Haftarah*, Isaiah 54:11–55:5, "O you afflicted, tempest-tossed." If *Rosh Ḥodesh* occurs on a Shabbat of one of the *Arba Parshiyyot*,* the *Haftarah* of the relevant portion is read.) If the following day, too, is *Rosh Ḥodesh*, some have the custom of reading the first and last verses of the *Haftarah* of "Tomorrow is the new moon" (I Samuel, 20:18–42), which is the *Haftarah* read on the eve of *Rosh Ḥodesh*.

Those who say *Av ha-Raḥamim* on regular Sabbaths do not say it on this Shabbat, for it is a day in which *Taḥanun* is not recited.

After the return of the Torah scrolls to the Ark comes the *Musaf* prayer, in which there are significant changes in the middle blessing. This blessing has a special *Rosh Ḥodesh* formulation, in which the regular *Piyyut* for the Shabbat *Musaf* prayer—"You have established the Shabbat"—is substituted, in all rites, with the *Piyyut* "You have formed Your world from of old." This *Piyyut* speaks of the choosing of the Jewish people, the gift of the Shabbat, and the declaration of *Rosh Ḥodesh*. In this prayer, there is also mention of the *Rosh Ḥodesh* sacrifices, and a request for the renewal of the Temple worship. In most rites, the Torah verses that speak of the *Musaf* sacrifices of *Shabbat* and *Rosh Ḥodesh* are cited; some say, after the verses of Shabbat and before those of *Musaf*, "This is the Shabbat sacrifice; and the sacrifice of the day, as stated" (as in the *Siddur of Rav Amram Gaon*@; others, however, refrain from doing this, since they consider this an interruption—*Hefsek**). "Those who observe the Shabbat . . . shall rejoice" is now said in all rites, followed by the regular *Rosh Ḥodesh* blessing—with the additional mention of Shabbat.[90] The blessing ends with "Blessed are You Lord who sanctifies the Shabbat, Israel and *Rosh Ḥodesh* days." The reason for this order is that the sanctity of *Rosh Ḥodesh* (as that of all festival days) depends on the sanctity of the Jewish people, for it is they who sanctify the new months (and consequently, also decide when the festival days will be)—unlike the sanctity of Shabbat, which is intrinsic and independent of the sanctity of the Jews. Therefore, the sanctity of Shabbat is mentioned first, followed by that of the Jews and of the new months.

The conclusion of the prayer is the same as on every Shabbat.

In the *Minḥah* of such Sabbaths, *Tzidkatekha** is not recited (just as it is omitted on a Shabbat that falls on the eve of *Rosh Ḥodesh*). For *Shabbat Rosh Ḥodesh Ḥanukkah*, and *Shabbat Rosh Ḥodesh* during the *Arba Parshiyyot*, see below.

---

[90] And see *Shulḥan Arukh, Oraḥ Ḥayyim*, 425:2.

Shabbat That Falls on Festival Days

When one of the festival days mentioned in the Torah (the three pilgrimage festivals, Rosh ha-Shanah, and Yom Kippur) occurs on Shabbat, all of the prayers are essentially those of the festival days (see Chapters 10 and 11); but in each of them, Shabbat is mentioned in its proper place. The festival day, however, does not override the Shabbat, and all the commandments of Shabbat remain valid. The Shabbat, as it were, remains as is, except that it is attired in festival day garments.

Kabbalat Shabbat is the same as on every Shabbat, but Ashkenazic congregations shorten it. The Sepharad rite begins with Psalm 29, and omits some of the verses of *Lekhah Dodi*, while the Ashkenazic one begins with Psalm 92; and everywhere, *ba-Meh Madlikin** is not recited. Before the *Amidah*, both the verses of Shabbat and the special verse pertaining to the specific festival day are recited. Then comes the *Amidah* of the festival day, in which there is also a mention of the Shabbat; the formula is "Blessed are You Lord who sanctifies the Shabbat, Israel and the Times." After the prayer, *va-Yekhulu* is recited, along with the *Me'ein Sheva** blessing (except for the first day of Passover; see Chapter 10).

The "welcoming" of Shabbat at home is as usual, except that the *Kiddush* recited is that of the festival day, interspersed with phrases pertaining to Shabbat. In the Grace After Meals, *Retzeh ve-Haḥalitzenu** is recited as on every Shabbat, complemented by *Ya'aleh ve-Yavo.**

Shaḥarit is as it is on every Shabbat, but the *Amidah* is that of the festival day (with Shabbat-related additions), followed, on the three pilgrimage festivals, by *Hallel* or half *Hallel.*

Because of the sanctity of the Shabbat, our sages decreed that the blessing on the *Lulav** not be recited, and the *Shofar** not be blown, and that there should not be *Hakkafot** of the *Hosha'not** (even in those places in which *Hosha'not* are recited on Shabbat).

During the removal of the Torah scroll from the Ark, the Thirteen Attributes* and the *Ribbono Shel Olam** prayer that follows—which the Ashkenazim recite on the festival days—are generally omitted (though some do say them).

The Torah reading is the one established for the festival days, except that on Shabbat it is divided among seven men. The *Maftir* and the *Haftarah* are those of the festival day (and in the blessing of the *Haftarah*, Shabbat is mentioned as well).

The *Musaf* prayer is the festival day *Musaf*, with a reference to the Shabbat *Musaf* sacrifice, and the concluding blessing also mentions Shabbat.

Minḥah is just like that of every festival day, with the addition of the Torah reading, as on every Shabbat. This latter reading is according to the order of the Weekly Portions. Then a Third Meal is held, as on every Shabbat.

Shabbat Ḥol ha-Mo'ed

When Shabbat falls on one of the days of *Ḥol ha-Mo'ed** (see Chapter 12), the order of prayers parallels that of all the other days of *Ḥol ha-Mo'ed;* namely, the basic prayers are the regular Shabbat prayers (with slight modifications), with the addition of the *Hallel* and the festival day *Musaf.*

The Ashkenazim shorten *Kabbalat Shabbat* on *Ḥol ha-Mo'ed*, just as they do on Shabbat that is also a festival day. One of the reasons for reciting the six psalms of *Kabbalat Shabbat* is to create a transition between the weekdays, which are entirely profane, and Shabbat; but on *Ḥol ha-Mo'ed*, which is a period of holiness and rest, there is no need for so much preparation. Psalm 107 is not recited (even by those who say it every Shabbat eve), nor are the six psalms of *Kabbalat Shabbat*—as on a festival day that occurs on Shabbat—except for Psalm 29. Some also abbreviate *Lekhah Dodi* in various ways, skipping those verses that speak of exile and enslavement. Some begin with Psalm 92. In none of the rites is *ba-Meh Madlikin* recited. The *Ma'ariv* prayer is the same as on every Shabbat, with the addition of *Ya'aleh ve-Yavo.*

The *Shaḥarit* prayer is, as on every Shabbat, followed by *Hallel* (full *Hallel* throughout Sukkot and half *Hallel* on Pesaḥ). On *Ḥol ha-Mo'ed* of Sukkot, most congregations have special *Hosha'not* for Shabbat (among them one that is found in all of the rites: *Om Netzurah ke-Vavat* "Nation protected like the pupil of the eye"), even though the blessing on the *Lulav* is not made on Shabbat, and therefore it is also customary not to encircle the *Bimah.** Then full *Kaddish* is recited. Most Ashkenazic congregations read, at this point, the book of Ecclesiastes on Sukkot, and the Song of Songs on Pesaḥ, and in most places *Kaddish Yatom* is then said. Some recite here the Song of the Day, which is Psalm 92, and on Sukkot also Psalm 27. Then two Torah scrolls are removed from the Ark. In the first, the portion of the festivals (Exodus 33:12–34:26) is read, in which Shabbat, Sukkot, and Pesaḥ are mentioned. Half *Kaddish* is then recited. The second scroll serves for the reading of the *Maftir*, which on Sukkot consists of the verses dealing with the *Musaf* sacrifice of that day of Sukkot, and on Pesaḥ, the verses about the *Musaf* sacrifice of *Ḥol ha-Mo'ed* of Pesaḥ. The *Maftir* ends the blessings with the words "Who sanctifies the Shabbat, Israel, and the [festive] seasons."

The *Haftarot* of *Ḥol ha-Mo'ed* deal with matters related to the future redemption of the Jewish people. On the Shabbat of *Ḥol ha-Mo'ed* of Sukkot, we read about the War of Gog and Magog (Ezekiel 33:12–34:26), whereas on the Shabbat of *Ḥol ha-Mo'ed* of Pesaḥ we read about the resurrection of the dead (Ezekiel 37:1–14).

After the *Haftarah*, as on every Shabbat, *Yekum Purkan,** *Mi she-Berakh,** and *Ashrei* are recited, but not *Av ha-Raḥamim.* The scrolls are put back in the Ark, and the cantor says half *Kaddish.* Then the festival *Musaf* prayer is recited, as on all the other days of *Ḥol ha-Mo'ed*, except that we add the verses about the *Musaf* of Shabbat to the verses that speak about the festival *Musaf* sacrifice; and some reference to Shabbat is made in the middle blessing (just as is the practice in the *Amidah* prayer of a festival day, when it occurs on Shabbat). After the *Amidah* repetition, the prayer is concluded as on all other Sabbaths.

The *Minḥah* service is conducted as on a normal Shabbat (with the addition of *Ya'aleh ve-Yavo*). The *Minḥah* Torah reading, too, is just like on other Sabbaths—namely, a small segment from the beginning of the coming week's portion (on Sukkot it is always *ve-Zot ha-Berakha*, which is the very last part of Deuteronomy).

At the conclusion of Shabbat, too, prayer is as usual, except that we do not say *vi-Yehi No'am* and *ve-Attah Kadosh*, because of the last day of the festival that will be celebrated in the coming week. *Havdalah* is made as on every Shabbat.

Shabbat of Ḥanukkah

When Shabbat occurs on one of the days of Ḥanukkah (see Chapter 12), there are certain changes in the order of prayers, in the Torah readings, and in the *Haftarah*.

The custom is to start this Shabbat not as early as usual (but still before sunset), so as to allow for the lighting of the Ḥanukkah candles to take place as close to the night as possible.

In the synagogue, the Ḥanukkah candles are lit before *Aleinu* of *Minḥah;* some light them after *Aleinu*, and others even before *Minḥah*. In many congregations, *ba-Meh Madlikin* is omitted.

In all the prayers of this day, as on all the days of Ḥanukkah, *Al ha-Nissim** is added in the *Modim** blessing (as well as in the Grace After Meals). There are also special *Piyyutim* recited on this Shabbat in those congregations that customarily say *Piyyutim*. After the *Amidah* of *Shaḥarit*, full *Hallel* is recited. For the Torah reading, two scrolls are removed from the Ark; in the first one, seven people read from the Weekly Portion; this reading is followed by half *Kaddish*. Then the *Maftir* is called to read from the second scroll, in the portion of the princes that pertains to that particular day of Ḥanukkah (the relevant verses from within Numbers 7:1–83). The *Haftarah* is "Sing and rejoice" (Zechariah 2:14–4:7), which includes Zechariah's vision of the Golden Lamp, which is like the Temple Lamp, and is a symbol of redemption. In the *Minḥah* prayer, *Tzidkadekha* is not recited.

In some years, there are two Sabbaths during Ḥanukkah; in such a case, the order of prayers on the second Shabbat is the same as that on the first (there are also special *Piyyutim* for the second Shabbat of Ḥanukkah), except that a different *Haftarah*—I Kings 1:40–50—is read, which deals with the Temple Lamps.

On Shabbat Ḥanukkah, people try not to conclude the Shabbat late, so as to light the Ḥanukkah candles as soon as possible. In the synagogue, the Ḥanukkah candles are lit before *Havdalah*, whereas at home, *Havdalah* is made first, and only then are the Ḥanukkah candles lit.

Shabbat Rosh Ḥodesh on Ḥanukkah

Once in several years, it happens that *Rosh Ḥodesh* Tevet[91] occurs on Shabbat that is also Shabbat of Ḥanukkah. On that Shabbat, the customs of both Ḥanukkah and *Rosh Ḥodesh* are followed.

This combination is naturally reflected in the prayers of the day, as follows: both *Ya'aleh ve-Yavo* and *Al ha-Nissim* are recited in all the *Amidah* prayers of that Shabbat, as well as in the Grace After Meals (which is, consequently, the longest Grace After Meals, containing three additions: *Retzeh ve-Haḥalitzenu**—because of Shabbat; *Ya'aleh ve-Yavo*—because of *Rosh Ḥodesh*; and *Al ha-Nissim*—because of Ḥanukkah). After the *Amidah* of *Shaḥarit*, the full *Hallel* is recited (because of Ḥanukkah, even though it coincides with *Rosh Ḥodesh*, on which, normally, the half *Hallel* is said). For the Torah reading, which follows immediately, three scrolls are removed from the Ark; in the first, the Weekly Portion is read, with only six people called up; in the second, the seventh person reads the portion that speaks about the *Musaf* sacrifices of Shabbat and *Rosh Ḥodesh*, and half *Kaddish* is recited. The *Maftir* is then called up to read, from the third scroll, the daily portion of Ḥanukkah. The *Haftarah* is, as on all other Sabbaths of Ḥanukkah, "Sing and rejoice" (Zechariah 2:14–4:7).

The *Arba Parshiyyot* ("Four Portions")

The *Arba Parshiyyot*, already mentioned in the Mishnah, are read during the month of Adar (and in leap years—in the second Adar) as study and preparation for the special commandments pertaining to those days.

- The Portion of *Shekalim* (Exodus 30:11–16) is read on the Shabbat prior to *Rosh Ḥodesh* Adar (or on that *Rosh Ḥodesh* itself, when it occurs on Shabbat), as a reminder to prepare the *Shekel* contribution for the Temple, which, when the Temple

---

[91] See Tevet in the appendix "The Jewish Months."

still stood, used to be announced starting from *Rosh Ḥodesh* Adar.

- The Portion of *Zakhor* (Deuteronomy 25:17–19) is read on the Shabbat before Purim (see Chapter 12), as preparation for the commandment to obliterate Amalek, which was fulfilled on Purim.

- The Portion of *Parah* (Numbers 19:1–22) is read on the Shabbat preceding the reading of the portion of *ha-Ḥodesh* (see below), so as to get ready for the need to purify ourselves from every kind of impurity (especially the defilement by a dead body, which requires a seven-day purification process with the ashes of the Red Heifer) in preparation for the Pesaḥ pilgrimage.

- The Portion of *ha-Ḥodesh* (Exodus 12:1–10) is read either on the Shabbat prior to *Rosh Ḥodesh* Nisan, or on *Shabbat Rosh Ḥodesh* Nisan, for it is a preparation for the festival of Pesaḥ

Because these readings are bound to specific dates, they can never take place in four consecutive weeks; an interruption of at least one week—and sometimes two—is necessitated. On such intervening Sabbaths, the Torah readings are as usual.

On the Sabbaths of the *Arba Parshiyyot*, the Torah readings are in the usual order, except that the *Maftir* reads that Shabbat's portion from a second Torah scroll (however, on *Shabbat Shekalim* some read everything from one scroll, because that week's portion and the *Shekalim* portion are adjacent). Each of these Sabbaths has a special *Haftarah*, related to the topic of the portion that is read on that Shabbat.

In addition to the Torah and *Haftarah* readings, there are many series of *Piyyutim* for the *Shaḥarit* and *Musaf* prayers of these Sabbaths (except *Shabbat Zakhor* and *Shabbat Parah*, for which there are no *Yotzerot* for *Musaf*). Some of the more prevalent *Piyyutim* contain a great deal of halakhic material. There are also special *Piyyutim* for the intervening Sabbaths.

An exception is made when *Rosh Ḥodesh* Adar occurs on Shabbat. In such a case, the order of prayers is like that on *Shabbat Rosh Ḥodesh*, but three scrolls are used for the Torah reading: in the first one, six people are called up to read from the Weekly Portion; the seventh person completes the cycle by reading from the second scroll the portion of the Shabbat and *Rosh Ḥodesh Musaf* sacrifices; and the portion of *Shekalim* is read from the third scroll. The *Haftarah* is that of *Shabbat Shekalim.* Similarly, when the portion of *ha-Ḥodesh* is read on a *Rosh Ḥodesh* Nisan that occurs on Shabbat, again three scrolls are taken out of the Ark.

According to some customs, neither *Yizkor** nor *Av ha-Raḥamim* are recited on these Sabbaths; however, at *Minḥah*, *Tzidkatekha* is said.

Shabbat on Days When *Taḥanun* Is Not Recited

When Shabbat occurs on one of the days on which, were it a weekday, *Taḥanun* is not said, the Ashkenazim make slight changes in the prayer. On such days, *Av ha-Raḥamim* is not recited prior to *Musaf*, nor is *Tzidkatekha* prayed at *Minḥah*.

Shabbat ha-Gadol

Shabbat ha-Gadol (literally, "the Great Shabbat") is the name given to the Shabbat right before Pesaḥ. There are several interpretations for this name (found already in medieval literature): that this Shabbat is thus called because on that day, shortly before the exodus from Egypt, great miracles happened to the Israelites; or because it is customary for the local sage ("the great one of the town") to give a public sermon on this Shabbat; etc. But there are some sources that seem to indicate that Sabbaths prior to other festivals, too, used to be called *Shabbat ha-Gadol.*

The order of prayers on this Shabbat is as usual, although there are special *Piyuttim* for this Shabbat; and at the conclusion of Shabbat, *vi-Yehi No'am* is not recited, as is the case on any Shabbat that precedes a festival.

In most congregations, the *Haftarah* is *ve-Arvah* ("Then shall the offering of Judah and Jerusalem be pleasant"—Malachi 3:4–14), both because it mentions the commandment to give tithes (and right before Pesaḥ, there is the duty to "remove" the tithes—namely, to complete all tithing), and because these verses speak about Elijah the Prophet heralding the tidings of the redemption which, according to tradition, will occur in the month of Nisan. Ashkenazim who follow the Vilna Gaon's@ rite, and some of the German Jewish congregations, read *ve-Arvah* only in those years in which *Shabbat ha-Gadol* is not on Pesaḥ eve (for then it would be impossible to "remove" the tithes, and also because, according to tradition, Elijah the Prophet will not come on Shabbat).

A widespread custom in very many communities is for the local rabbi to speak before the public on this Shabbat. The main purpose of the rabbi's talk is simply to teach the laws of Pesaḥ to the public; but in practice, these homilies may take on a different character: scholarly, or moralizing.

After the *Minḥah* of *Shabbat ha-Gadol*, it is a custom to recite a part of the Passover *Haggadah* (up to the words, "to atone for all of our transgressions"), as a kind of preparation for the *Seder* night (see Chapter 10), so that the text will not be unfamiliar and the reader will not commit errors. The Ashkenazic usage is to cease reading, from this Shabbat on, Psalm 104* and the Songs of Ascents (Psalms 120-134), which are ordinarily recited on Shabbat afternoon (see above).

Shabbat Teshuvah (Shuvah)

This is the Shabbat between Rosh ha-Shanah and Yom Kippur. In some communities, it is called *Shabbat Shuvah*, after the special *Haftarah* of that Shabbat that begins with the words *Shuvah Yisrael*—"Return, O Israel, [to the Lord your God]" (Hosea 14:2).

The beginning of this *Haftarah* is the same in all congregations; however, the Ashkenazim add verses from the book of Joel (2:15–27).

This Shabbat, like all of the Ten Days of Repentance* (see Chapters 9 and 12), is suffused by the sense of gravity and the dread of sinning that characterizes these Days of Judgment and Mercy. The custom everywhere, as on *Shabbat ha-Gadol* (see above), is for the local rabbi to deliver a special sermon about matters pertaining to this period of soul-searching.

The special additions to the prayer are the same as on the Ten Days of Repentance, except that *Avinu Malkenu** is not recited; and in the *Me'ein Sheva** blessing, the cantor says, "He is the holy King (instead of the usual 'holy God') like whom there is none." In most congregations, *Birkat ha-Levanah,** although ordinarily performed at the conclusion of the first Shabbat of the month, is postponed till the conclusion of Yom Kippur. However, there are some who do try to sanctify the moon early, so as to have the merit of this commandment as well.

The Sabbaths of Evil Dispensation

The three Sabbaths before the Ninth of Av (namely, in the days of *Bein ha-Meitzarim,** see Chapter 12), are also called *Telata de-Fur'anuta* ("The Three Sabbaths of Calamity"). An ancient custom in most Jewish congregations (referred to already by Maimonides as a widely accepted custom) is to read on these days special *Haftarot* that are not connected to the Weekly Portions, but are, rather, words of rebuke and warning. On the first of these Sabbaths, the *Haftarah* is *Divrei Yirmiyah* ("The words of Jeremiah"—Jeremiah 1:1–2:3); on the second, *Shim'u* ("Hear ye," the main part of which is Jeremiah 2:4–28; but so as not to end on a negative note, additional verses are added—different ones in the various communities); on the third, *Ḥazon Yesha'yahu* ("The vision of Isaiah"—Isaiah 1:1–27).

In some places, these Sabbaths are even called after their respective *Haftarot*, especially the third one, *Shabbat Ḥazon*. In some localities (especially those that follow the Ashkenazic rite), people observe some mourning customs on this Shabbat—e.g., not wearing Shabbat clothes. In other places, *Lekhah Dodi* is chanted in the same mournful tune with which the book of Lamentations is read. However, most Jewish congregations follow the opinions of halakhic decisors and Kabbalists, to the effect that Shabbat is intrinsically holy and blessed, and that of it the verse (Proverbs 10:22) says, "and he adds no sorrow to it"; therefore, they comport themselves even on this Shabbat as on any other Shabbat.

The Sabbaths of Comfort

As against the three Sabbaths of Evil Dispensation, there are the seven Sabbaths of Comfort *(Sheva de-Neḥamata)*—seven Sabbaths in which there is a stress on consolation and the hopes for redemption. This custom prevails almost everywhere.

The main change in these Sabbaths is in the *Haftarot*, which are, again, not connected to the contents of the Weekly Torah Portions, but rather constitute a continuous sequence of messages of comfort.

The *Abudraham*# strings the beginning verses of all of these *Haftarot* into a sort of poetic dialogue between God and the Jewish people. At first, God commands the prophets to say, "Comfort ye, comfort ye, my people" (Isaiah 40:1, the *Haftarah* of Portion *va-Etḥanan*); the Jewish people then replies, complainingly, "Zion said: The Lord has forsaken me" (Isaiah 49:14, the *Haftarah* of Portion *Ekev*)—He is sending messengers to comfort me, but does not do so Himself. Then the prophets come back to God and tell him that the People of Israel is "afflicted, tempest-tossed, and not comforted" (Isaiah 54:11, the *Haftarah* of Portion *Reeh*)—that they refuse to be consoled. Then God Himself says, "I, even I, am He that comforts you" (Isaiah 51:12, the *Haftarah* of *Shoftim*), adding, "Sing, O barren one, you that did not bear" (Isaiah 54:1, the *Haftarah* of *Ki Tetze*), and, "Arise, shine, for your light has come" (Isaiah 60:1, the *Haftarah* of *Ki Tavo*). Finally, the comforted Jewish people replies, "I will greatly rejoice in the Lord" (Isaiah 61:11, the *Haftarah* of *Nitzavim*).

In the Ashkenazic rite, special *Piyyutim a*re added to the prayer, mostly on the first of these Sabbaths—*Shabbat Naḥamu* ("Comfort ye").

Other Sabbaths

In addition to these Sabbaths, in which certain changes are introduced into the order of prayers, Torah reading, or *Haftarah*, there are other Sabbaths throughout the year that have some kind of uniqueness. For instance: there are special *Piyyutim* related to certain Weekly Portions, or for Sabbaths that come before or after a festival. There are also special customs for specific Sabbaths (such as *Shabbat Shirah*, the Shabbat in which the Song of the Sea—Exodus 15—is read). However, these customs are local ones, some of which are observed over wide areas while others are to be found only in individual congregations.

CHAPTER TEN ❧ *Festivals*

Festival Days

THE FESTIVALS—holy days of convocation—called in the Torah *Yamim Tovim,**—"the good days"—have a special order of prayer services. Although there are slight variations for each of the different festivals, the prayer services are essentially the same. From the halakhic viewpoint, Rosh ha-Shanah, and in some respects, Yom Kippur, are also considered *Yamim Tovim;* however, these days are called the Days of Awe,* and have a completely different set of prayer services (see Chapter 11). Prayers for the festival days are, therefore, those for the *Shalosh Regalim**—the three pilgrimage festivals; to be more exact—for the *Yamim Tovim* of those festivals, excluding *Ḥol ha-Mo'ed** (see Chapter 12). In the Land of Israel, these total five days each year, while in the Diaspora, because of the second *Yom Tov* days (see below), they total ten days each year.

Festival	**In the Land of Israel**	**In the Diaspora**
Beginning of Sukkot	First day only	First and second days
End of Sukkot	The eighth day: Shemini Atzeret and Simḥat Torah combined	Two days: the eighth day is Shemini Atzeret, and the ninth day is Simḥat Torah
Beginning of Pesaḥ	First day only	The first and second days
End of Pesaḥ	The seventh day	The seventh and eighth days
Shavu'ot	One day	Two days

The Three Pilgrimage Festivals

The three festivals Pesaḥ, Shavu'ot, and Sukkot are called the pilgrimage festivals because, while the Temple stood, all Jewish men were commanded to go up to Jerusalem to celebrate the festivals there, and to offer special sacrifices, and the public *Musaf** ("additional") sacrifices for each of these festive days.

These three festivals are days of exceptional joy that have a special positive commandment (see *mitzvah**), "and you shall rejoice on your festivals" (Deuteronomy 16:14). In a more spiritual sense, they are celebrations of God's Divine manifestation to His people in the Temple. The festivals were, in this sense, "appointments" between God and Israel, as it is written, "all your males shall appear before the Lord God" (Exodus 23:17).

The order of these three festivals in the Torah is always Pesaḥ, Shavu'ot, and Sukkot. Besides the fact that this is in accordance with the calendar year beginning with Nisan (which also applies to various laws concerning the festivals), there is also an inner significance to this order. On one hand, there is a triad of attributes: Mercy, Strength, and Glory.[92] Mercy is for the Pesaḥ festival, which concerns redemption; Strength is for the Giving of the Torah, which prescribes the laws and edicts; Glory is for Sukkot, which is a total manifestation of joy. In addition, there is the historical significance of the festivals: on Pesaḥ—the first formation of nationhood in the exodus from Egypt; on Shavu'ot—the granting of true meaning and purpose for the redemption by the Giving of the Law; on Sukkot—completion and repose.

There is also the order of the seasons in the year: Pesaḥ is the festival of spring, the time of flowering, when the grain begins to ripen. Shavu'ot is the time when the grain is already harvested, the fruits begin to ripen, and the grape harvest starts. Sukkot is the festival of gathering in and storing all the produce of the fields, when the annual agricultural growth has ended, and there is time to enjoy the fruits of

---

[92] For an explanation, see *The Thirteen Petalled Rose* by Adin Steinsaltz (Northvale, N.J.: Jason Aronson, 1992).

the past year before beginning to plant for the next year. All these aspects are found in these festivals, as well as many more significant elements, which are reflected, overtly or indirectly, in the festival customs and prayers.

The Second Days in the Diaspora

During Temple times, and for centuries after the Temple's destruction, the beginning of the new month was proclaimed and sanctified based on eyewitness testimony. People who saw the new moon appear in the sky would come to the central law court—the Sanhedrin*—located in the Hall of Hewn Stone in the Temple (and after its destruction, to the city or town that was the site of the Sanhedrin in that period). After cross-examination, and acceptance of their testimony, the court would proclaim the new month and sanctify it.

The lunar month is not a set length; there are differences of up to fourteen hours between the times of the new moon in various months. Also, the new moon (which is astronomically the moment just after the moon, sun, and earth are in alignment) sometimes occurs during daytime hours, when it is impossible to detect it, or, in the winter, when the sky is cloudy. Sometimes the witnesses who saw the new moon were unable to arrive quickly enough. If they did arrive in time, the thirtieth day of the previous month was announced as the first day of the new month. If they were delayed, then the sages would declare the thirty-first day to be the first day of the new month. On certain occasions, two days of *Rosh Ḥodesh** were announced.

Knowing when the new month was declared was essential for determining the festival days, since they are dates that are set according to the lunar calendar. For this reason, the announcement of the day declared to be the beginning of the new month was hurriedly transmitted all around the Land of Israel before the festival was due to be celebrated. However, transmitting this information abroad was a problem. For a number of generations, it was done by lighting signal fires on mountaintops, but this practice was discontinued because of various mishaps (some caused by members of the Samaritan sect who tried to create confusion by sending false signals). Then information began to be sent by special emissaries.[93] However, because of the great distances between the Land of Israel and Diaspora communities (such as the large Jewish center in Babylonia, and those even farther away, in Asia Minor or Europe) and because of travel difficulties, some of these messengers could not arrive in time for the festival. In such places, they could not tell whether the *Rosh Ḥodesh* had been proclaimed on the expected day or on the following one.

Because of such doubts, it was decided to celebrate the *Yom Tov* on two consecutive days, to be on the safe side. In this way the "second *Yom Tov* of the Diaspora" was instituted, and it applied to all festival days—except Yom Kippur, because such a rigorous fast could not be imposed on the public for two consecutive days. (However, some individuals in talmudic times would fast for two days, and even down to the present day some people still do.)

In the period immediately following the destruction of the Temple, the Roman authorities began to impose restrictions on the sanctification of the new month and the transmission of the information to the Diaspora. To the political restrictions that hindered consistent contact between the Jews in the Land of Israel and those in the Diaspora, religious restrictions were added after the rise of Christianity, so that it became impossible to sanctify the new month in the customary fashion. According to tradition, in 358 C.E. the president of the Sanhedrin, Hillel II, published a fixed calendar, no longer based on eyewitness evidence, but on astronomical calculations that established the average lengths of the lunar months.

After the introduction of the new calendar, there was a proposal to abolish the "Second *Yom Tov* of the Diaspora," because it was now clear when each of the festivals began. However, the sages of the Land of Israel ruled, with the compliance of the sages in the Diaspora, that those living abroad should "preserve the customs of their forefathers" (*Beitzah* 4b), and continue to observe the second *Yom Tov*. This has remained the practice for all Jewish communities in the Diaspora ever since.

An interesting idea was offered by Rabbi Moshe Sofer,[@] who explained that the second day of *Yom Tov* expresses the unity of the

---

[93] For a detailed account of this, see the Mishnah,* Tractate *Rosh ha-Shana*, chap. 2.

festival everywhere. Since, by the very nature of things, the festival cannot be celebrated everywhere in the world at the same time (being dependent on sunrise and sunset), as a result of the second *Yom Tov*, the festival is being celebrated somewhere in the world for nearly two days. In general, there is no difference between the first and second *Yom Tov*, and all the commandments and prohibitions apply to both (except for some extraordinary cases), as do the main prayer services and benedictions.

The salient differences between the two days of *Yom Tov* are in the Torah and *Haftarah** readings, and in the *Piyyutim*.* In the Torah readings, sometimes a different selection relating to the current festival is read, and sometimes the *Maftir** is also taken from a different section of the Torah. The *Haftarah* selection is always different for each of the two days; and since at times two opinions are expressed in the sources as to which *Haftarah* should be read, this sometimes resolves this problem. In places where *Piyyutim* are recited, it is customary to recite different ones on each of the days.

Residents of other countries who come to visit Israel and intend to return to their home countries must celebrate two days of *Yom Tov* even in Israel. Halakhically, such people should hold their prayer services for the second day discreetly; however, these days it is customary to hold separate services for foreign residents in Israel, and even to hold them publicly. Residents of Israel who are abroad and intend to return home, quietly pray the weekday service and put on *Tefillin** on the second day of *Yom Tov*.

Festival Prayers in General

Although the different festivals each have different laws and appropriate orders of prayer service, there is a fixed pattern of festival prayer services common to all.

The *Ma'ariv* Service

The *Ma'ariv** festival service resembles the weekday service in its structure. In some congregations, the entire service is like the weekday service; all the others change only the last benediction of the *Shema—Hashkivenu** and recite it in the Shabbat formulation. Ashkenazim (especially those who use the *Nusaḥ Ashkenaz*) recite various *Piyyutim* within the benedictions, each festival having its own particular *Piyyutim.*

Before the *Amidah* prayer, it is the general custom to recite a biblical verse relevant to the festivals. In the Ashkenazic rite, they say, "And Moses declared unto the children of Israel the feasts of the Lord" (Leviticus 23:44).

The *Amidah* prayer for the festival has seven benedictions—the standard first three and last three, and the central one, which is special for the festivals. This central benediction is composed of three parts: a brief introductory *Piyyut—Attah Beḥartanu,** followed by *Ya'aleh ve-Yavo,** in which the particular festival day is mentioned, and finally, the main part of the benediction, which opens with the word *ve-Hasienu.* This formulation is essentially the same in all rites, except for some minor variations.

The first section is *Attah Beḥartanu*—"You chose us from among all peoples; You loved and favored us; You exalted us above all tongues and sanctified us with Your commandments. You, our King, drew us near to Your service and called us by Your great and holy name." This emphasis on the election of Israel is especially appropriate for the festival days, because, unlike Shabbat, they were not instituted from the time of Creation but are commemorative days explicitly for the people of Israel. The time of the festivals is set by Israel (according to the religious court's proclamation of *Rosh Ḥodesh**—see above), and they commemorate certain historical events: God's mercy toward Israel during and after the exodus from Egypt. This definition of the election of Israel stresses Israel's essential purpose, "You chose us . . . and sanctified us with Your commandments, and drew us near to Your service," namely, the service of God, as "My servant whom I have chosen" (Isaiah 43:10). This was revealed at the time of the exodus from Egypt—"Let My people go that they may serve Me in the wilderness" (Exodus 7:16).

In the *Amidah* prayer for the festival, the phrase "in joy and gladness" is mentioned several times. The word "joy" *(Simḥah)* refers specifically to the biblical commandment, "and you shall rejoice in your feast" (Deuteronomy 16:14), while the word "gladness" *(Sasson)* is connected with various dates in the Jewish year (see Zechariah 8:19). There is a subtle difference in their meanings: joy is a feeling of the heart that gives a sense of contentment and gratification, while gladness is an outburst of delight, expressed in poetry, song, music, and dance.

The benediction *ve-Hasienu*[94] contains a petition that we may deserve this joy in actuality, and in every possible way. The words of the benediction, based on the biblical verse "He shall receive the blessing from the Lord" (Psalms 24:5), allude to gifts and portions (see Genesis 43:34). The word *Hasienu* suggests that even though we are not yet ready or able to accept the gift of the joy and sanctity of the festival, nevertheless we ask God to "lift us up" to the level at which we will be able to properly receive these gifts.

The benediction for the festival concludes with the words *Mekaddesh Yisrael veha-Zemanim*—"who sanctifies Israel and the festival season." Israel is mentioned first, because the Jewish people sanctify the festival season (*Berakhot* 49a), and then *Zemanim*, "the special times," namely the festival days. The other word for "festivals," *Mo'adim*, also means "times"—days that are dependent on the time of the year and the time of the month, but are sanctified by God's choice and Israel's actions.

When the festival begins at *Motza'ei Shabbat,** a *Havdalah** formulation is recited at the beginning of the central benediction, just after *Attah Beḥartanu.* However, while on ordinary weekdays one says *Attah Ḥonantanu,** on festivals there is a different formulation, *va-Todi'enu.** The wording varies among the different prayer rites, with some longer and some shorter versions, but all contain the basic idea, "You have made a distinction between the holiness of Shabbat and the holiness of the festival, and You have sanctified the Seventh Day above the six working days."

---

[94] This Hebrew word means "to carry," "to receive," "gift," and "to transport" or "to lift up."

The *Shaharit* Service

The first part of the prayer service—the *Korbanot**—is the same as for Shabbat, and the *Pesukei de-Zimrah** are also essentially the same. The *Shema** benedictions vary: the Ashkenazim (including *Nusaḥ Sepharad*) recite the weekday *Yotzer Or** benediction. The *Amidah* prayer for *Shaḥarit** is the same as for *Ma'ariv.* In the repetition, the *Shaliaḥ Tzibbur* recites the same formulation of the *Kedushah** as in the *Shaḥarit* for Shabbat.

Piyyutim are recited in some congregations: *Yotzerot,** or other kinds of *Piyyutim*, within the *Shema* benedictions, and others in the repetition* of the *Amidah* prayer. After this prayer, the *Hallel** is recited. On most festivals, the full *Hallel* is recited, except for the last day (or last two days) of Pesaḥ, when the half *Hallel* is recited.

Wherever the Song of the Day is recited after *Shaḥarit,* it is said on festivals as well; in some rites it is replaced by a special psalm for that festival.

Torah Readings

When taking the Torah scrolls out of the Ark,* the Ashkenazim follow the same procedure as for Shabbat. It is the Ashkenazic custom to recite the Thirteen Attributes* on a *Yom Tov,* though most omit this when the festival falls on Shabbat. In most congregations, this is recited three times, and is followed by a standard prayer for all the festivals. This is a personal prayer in which one mentions one's own name and the names of family members, "Master of the universe. . . . May we have the merit of having Your Divine Presence rest within us. Bestow on us the spirit of wisdom and understanding . . . and one who trusts in the Lord will be surrounded by kindness" (Psalm 32:10). The concluding verses—"May the words of my mouth and the meditation of my heart be acceptable before You," and "May my prayer to You, O Lord, be at a propitious time" (Psalm 69:13)—are repeated three times (for the Torah reading, see Chapter 13).

Most Ashkenazim recite the *Piyyut* of *Yah Eli ve-Goali*, "The Lord, my God and my Redeemer," before beginning the *Ashrei** that precedes the *Musaf** service. In the Diaspora, on those days on which *Yizkor** is recited, this *Piyyut* is omitted. Ashkenazim recite *Yizkor* on the final day of each festival: the seventh (or eighth day, in the Diaspora) of Pesaḥ, Shavu'ot (on the second day, in the Diaspora) and Shemini Atzeret. *Yizkor* is said with great ceremonial solemnity. It is also customary to recite *Av ha-Raḥamim** on this occasion. Ashkenazim omit the *Yekum Purkan** and *Mi she-Berakh.** When the Torah scrolls are returned to the Ark,* those Ashkenazim who recite a psalm now recite Psalm 24, as on weekdays.

The *Musaf* Service

The *Musaf Amidah* prayer has seven benedictions: the standard first three and last three, and a central benediction composed of several sections.

First is *Attah Beḥartanu*, as in the *Shaḥarit* service. Next is *umi-Penei Ḥataeinu*, which says that because of our sins we have been exiled from our land and are unable to offer the sacrifices of the festival. We plead for the redemption of Israel and the rebuilding of the Temple, in which we shall once again be able to offer the special festival sacrifices properly.

In the Ashkenazic and *Nusaḥ Sepharad* versions, the biblical verses about the *Musaf* sacrifices for that day are recited. (If it is Shabbat, the Shabbat *Musaf* sacrifices are mentioned first). This is followed by another prayer for the restoration of the Temple services, "Merciful King, have compassion upon us . . . rebuild Your house as in former times. There we will go up and appear and bow before You. . . ." This concludes with the biblical verses, "Three times a year all your males shall appear . . ." (Deuteronomy 16:16–17). Then the section beginning *ve-Hasienu* (see above) is recited.

In the repetition of the *Amidah* prayer, the *Shaliaḥ Tzibbur* recites the *Keter** *Kedushah** (in the Ashkenazic version they start it with *Na'aritzakh*). On *Yom Tov*, Ashkenazim (including most of those following *Nusaḥ Sepharad*) recite an additional sentence just before the end of the *Kedushah: Adir Adirenu*—"Mighty is our Mighty One, the Lord, our Master. How mighty is Your Name throughout the earth! The Lord will be King over the entire earth; on that day, the Lord shall be One and His Name One."

In Ashkenazic and in some *Nusaḥ Sepharad* congregations, it is customary to recite, within the *Retzeh** benediction, the following formulation, "And may our prayers be pleasing to You as a burnt offering and sacrifice. O Merciful One, through Your great mercies return Your *Shekhinah** to Zion Your city, and the order of the Temple service to Jerusalem." Then comes, "May our eyes behold . . . ," as in all *Retzeh* blessings. The *Shaliaḥ Tzibbur* then concludes with the benediction "Blessed are You, who alone we serve in awe." However, in the Land of Israel, in *Nusaḥ Ashkenaz* and most *Nusaḥ Sepharad* congregations, this benediction concludes, following the opinion of the Vilna Gaon,[@] with the usual formulation "who restores His *Shekhinah* to Zion."

The Ashkenazic custom in the Diaspora is to have the *Kohanim** recite the Priestly Blessing* only in the *Musaf* service for *Yom Tov* (in some places it is customary not to do this when *Yom Tov* falls on Shabbat). For this reason, this blessing is often accompanied by a rich variety of melodies, some of which are extremely ancient. In addition, the congregants recite various biblical verses while the *Kohanim* pronounce the blessing. The *Musaf* service ends as on Shabbat.

The *Minḥah* Service

The *Minḥah** service on festivals is similar in structure to that of weekdays, except that after *Ashrei*, *u-Va le-Zion Go'el** is also recited. The *Amidah* prayer is the same as for the *Ma'ariv* and *Shaḥarit* services, and the *Shaliaḥ Tzibbur* repeats the *Amidah*, and concludes with *Aleinu** as usual. When the *Yom Tov* falls on Shabbat, there is a Torah reading (see Chapter 9).

Conclusion of the Festival

There is no obligation to eat three festive meals on *Yom Tov*, but only to hold one festive meal following the evening *Kiddush*,* and another in the daytime, preceded by the *Kiddusha Rabbah*.* The *Ma'ariv* service at the conclusion of the festival day is like that of weekdays, except for the addition of *Attah Ḥonantanu* in the benediction of *Ḥonen ha-Da'at*.* After the prayers, there is a *Havdalah* ceremony for the conclusion of the festival.

The Pesaḥ Festival

The festival of Pesaḥ is referred to in the Torah and in rabbinic literature by a variety of names, "the Feast of the Passover," "the Feast of Unleavened Bread," "the Season of our Freedom," etc. In the laws of Pesaḥ, the most prominent feature is the Unleavened Bread—the prohibition against the presence and eating of all forms of leavening, and the obligation to eat unleavened bread or *Matzah*. It is a specific Torah commandment to eat *Matzah* on Pesaḥ eve. The *Seder* night highlights the aspect of the Passover—the miraculous salvation of Israel from Egyptian bondage. The festival prayers emphasize the aspect of Liberation—the time when Israel became a nation, and the celebration of the first redemption in the past, which foreshadows the redemption of Israel in the future. The Torah also mentions that this festival occurs in the month of spring, and this finds expression in the Prayer for Dew,* which is recited at the end of the rainy season.

The Beginning of the Pesaḥ Festival

It is customary, after the *Minḥah* service on the eve of Pesaḥ, just before the festival begins, to read the main laws concerning the Passover sacrifice. Some begin with a selection of passages from the Torah on this subject; however, there is no fixed formulation for this, although all basically follow the prescription given by Maimonides@ in his *Mishneh Torah*.#

If the festival falls on Shabbat, the *Kabbalat Shabbat** service is conducted in the same way as for all festivals that occur on Shabbat. The *Ma'ariv* service is the usual one for a festival, and congregations that customarily add *Piyyutim* do so for the *Shema** benedictions.

After the prayer service, most Ashkenazim say the full *Hallel** with its benediction. While saying this benediction, one must have in mind that it will also apply to the *Hallel* recited during the reading of the *Haggadah** on *Seder* night (see below). This practice finds support in the Jerusalem Talmud and in Tractate *Soferim*,# and is considered extremely important by the Kabbalists.

When Pesaḥ falls on Shabbat, *va-Yekhulu** is recited. However, the benediction *Me'ein Sheva*,* normally said on Shabbat, is not recited, because it was originally instituted as a form of protection, and we have God's promise that this night is a night of (Divine) vigil, on which no harm will occur. The service ends in the usual way.

The Pesaḥ *Seder*

The Pesaḥ *Seder* (the festive meal) and the *Haggadah*[95] are among the earliest commandments, originating in Israel's exodus from Egypt, and they have been observed ever since by all the succeeding generations. Thus, the Pesaḥ *Seder* and *Haggadah* retain customs that date back to the days of the First and Second Temples, and other elements that were added during mishnaic and talmudic times and in later generations.

The Pesaḥ *Seder* is essentially a commemoration and perpetuation of the paschal sacrifice observed by the Israelites, from the eve before they left Egypt until the end of the Second Temple era. It is described in the Torah as "a lamb for a household" (Exodus 12:3), a sacrifice eaten within the home and in the company of friends, and is therefore a "family sacrifice" (I Samuel 20:29) in every respect. The eating and drinking at the *Seder* is not merely a festive meal but a religious com-

---

[95] In the literal sense of "telling the story of the exodus from Egypt."

mandment. Eating unleavened bread is a Torah-based obligation; eating bitter herbs is a scribal injunction, and the drinking of four cups of wine was instituted by the sages. The entire order of the paschal sacrifice is a composite unit of ceremony and ritual performed with a sense of close intimacy and love among family members or close friends. The paschal sacrifice is the only one that is eaten only by those who have joined together, in advance, for the purpose of sharing the same sacrifice. For this reason, the *Seder* has an atmosphere of both serious solemnity in its ritual performance, and the pleasurable freedom of a family reunion.

The essential nature of the Pesaḥ *Seder* has remained almost unchanged since the end of the Second Temple period, as it is described in the tenth chapter of Tractate *Pesaḥim.* During the Middle Ages, mnemonic rhymes were composed to indicate the order in which the *Seder* should be conducted, the most famous mnemonic being: *Kaddesh, u-Reḥatz; Karpas, Yaḥatz; Maggid, Raḥtzah; Motzi Matzah; Maror, Korekh; Shulḥan Orekh; Tzafun, Barekh; Hallel, Nirtzah*, as explained in the following table:

	Translation	**Explanation**
Kaddesh	*Kiddush*	Blessing the wine, Israel, and the holiday.
u-Reḥatz	Washing	The hands are ritually washed, but without the usual blessing.
Karpas	Celery (or potato)	Celery (or some other vegetable that is not one of the bitter herbs) is eaten.
Yaḥatz	Dividing in two	The middle *Matzah* is divided in two.
Maggid	Telling	The main part of the *Haggadah* is read.
Raḥtzah	Washing	The hands are ritually washed and the blessing is recited.

	Translation	**Explanation**
Motzi Matzah	Two blessings: over bread and over eating *Matzah*	The blessing for bread is recited together with the one for "eating *Matzah*."
Maror	Bitter herbs	The blessing for the bitter herbs is recited, and they are dipped and eaten.
Korekh	Binding together	The *Matzah* and bitter herbs are wrapped together and eaten.
Shulḥan Orekh	Set table	The festive meal is eaten.
Tzafun	Hidden	The *Afikoman** that was hidden is now eaten.
Barekh	Blessing	Grace After Meals* is recited.
Hallel	Praise	The Grand *Hallel** is sung.
Nirtzah	Accepted	The *Seder* ends.

The main commandment of the day is telling the story of the exodus from Egypt—performed in reading the *Haggadah*—as stated explicitly in the biblical verse "And you shall tell your son on that day, saying, 'it is because of that which the Lord did unto me when I came forth out of Egypt'" (Exodus 13:8). The basic order of the *Haggadah* was already laid down in the Mishnah,* and reflects the arrangement followed during Temple times (and therefore some changes had to be made after the Temple was destroyed). This includes the "four questions" that the son asks the father, as it is written, "And it shall be when your son asks you in time to come" (Exodus 13:14). As a result, the main formulation of the *Haggadah* is the same for all Jews, though each rite adds or alters a few details.

The *Kiddush*, which opens the *Seder*, is the usual festival *Kiddush*. If it is Shabbat, the usual additions are made for festivals that fall on Shabbat, and if it is *Motza'ei Shabbat*, the combined *Kiddush-Havdalah* ceremony for such occasions is performed (see *Yoknehaz**). After this, the *Haggadah* is read, beginning with *ha-Laḥma Anya*—"This is the bread of affliction." The son asks his questions, and the reply is taken from the formulation in the Mishnah, "We were slaves in Egypt . . ."

Next comes a *midrash* about the four sons, each asking a question in his own way, and another, homiletic midrash (from *Sifre*#) on the biblical verses that were to be uttered when the first fruits were offered in the Temple (Deuteronomy 26:5–9). Then the *Hallel* is recited, as it used to be when the paschal sacrifice was eaten (see Isaiah 30:29). Half of the *Hallel* is recited before eating the *Matzah*, ending with the benediction *Asher Gealanu* ("who redeemed us"). After eating the *Matzah* and bitter herbs, and concluding the festive meal with all its benedictions, the recital of the *Hallel* is completed, and the Grand *Hallel* is also recited, ending with *Birkat ha-Shir,** *Nishmat Koi Ḥai** and *Yishtabbaḥ.** During the *Seder*, four cups of wine are drunk as an obligation decreed by the sages in honor of the Pesaḥ *Seder.*

There is a great variety of customs among the diverse Jewish communities regarding the details of the *Seder.* Some of these are derived from the Talmud and accepted by all, such as eating and drinking not in the usual posture but reclining to the left side, as free men or lords used to do. In order to keep the children alert and attentive, and to encourage them to ask questions, everyone makes changes in their conduct and in the serving of food. Some of these customs are particular to a congregation, and some are practiced by individual families.

As stated in the *Haggadah*, it is commendable to recount the story of the exodus from Egypt as extensively as the *Seder* participants wish. However, care must be taken to eat the *Afikoman** before midnight, just as eating the paschal sacrifice had to be completed by midnight. After eating the *Afikoman*, people may continue with Torah study or singing as long as they wish.

The Ashkenazic custom is to conclude the main section of the *Haggadah* with the exclamation "Next year in Jerusalem" (in the Land of Israel, some say "in rebuilt Jerusalem").

In most Ashkenazic communities, various *Piyyutim* are recited (or more often sung, using both traditional and new melodies). These *Piyyutim* were composed by medieval and later poets, some written especially for the *Haggadah*, and others taken from prayer services. In the Diaspora, different *Piyyutim* are recited for each of the two *Seder* nights. Two poems that are like folk songs were added in medieval times: *Eḥad Mi Yode'a* ("Who Knows One"), and *Ḥad Gadya* ("One Kid"). These were initially meant to give a light, cheerful touch to the conclusion of the *Haggadah* (especially for the younger children who find it difficult to stay awake so late at night); however, eminent sages have written commentaries on these folk poems, based on allusions and mystical ideas, even pointing out major principles of faith and fundamental issues implied by them. Although the singing of these *Piyyutim* is an Ashkenazic custom (and is not obligatory), with the growing proximity of congregations, it has gradually became known and practiced by many other Jewish communities as well.

After the *Haggadah* reading is over, it is customary to read the entire Song of Songs, which is interpreted as the love song between God and Israel, with special reference to Israel's redemption from Egypt.

Since the eve of Pesaḥ is a "night of vigil," in which there is no need for protection, the *Shema* Upon Retiring to Bed* is much shorter than usual. Some recite only the first section of the *Shema*, some add the verse "Into Your hand I commit my spirit" (Psalms 31:6) and the benediction *ha-Mappil.**

The *Shaḥarit* Service

After the *Amidah* prayer and its repetition by the *Shaliaḥ Tzibbur*, the full *Hallel* is recited, and in some rites the Song of the Day also. The procedure for taking out the Torah scrolls is the same for every festival. Two scrolls are taken out. Five persons (seven on Shabbat) are called up for the Torah reading from the first scroll, which deals with the festival of Pesaḥ and the exodus from Egypt (Exodus 12:21–51). The *Maftir*, read from the second scroll, is the passage about the *Musaf* sacrifices for the festival (Numbers 28:16–26). The *Haftarah* selection, Joshua 5:2 to 6:1, is about the first Pesaḥ celebrated by the Israelites when they entered the Land of Israel. Some add verses before and after this selection. An ancient custom (mentioned in the *Tosafot** for Tractate *Megillah*, 24b) was to translate this *Haftarah* into the vernacular, so as to further proclaim the miracle by ensuring that everyone indeed understood its content.

The *Musaf* Service

After returning the Torah scrolls to the Ark, the *Musaf* service commences. The *Amidah* prayer includes the Prayer for Dew* (said by some Ashkenazim in the *Amidah* repetition, and by others before it). This prayer marks the beginning of the summer season, and all subsequent *Amidah* prayers use the summer formulation, *Morid ha-Tal** ("Who causes the dew to descend"), as well as the special summertime formulation of the *Birkat ha-Shanim.** The rest of the *Amidah* prayer for *Musaf* is as usual for all festivals, and in most rites the additional sacrifices offered on the festival are mentioned.

The *Minḥah* and *Ma'ariv* Services

The *Amidah* prayer for the festival is recited. If it is Shabbat, there is a Torah reading from the regular Torah portions of the year, as on every other Shabbat. At the conclusion of the festival (in Israel) the *Ma'ariv* service for *Ḥol ha-Mo'ed* is recited (see Chapter 12). Some set the time for this prayer service earlier than usual, in order to ensure that the period of the Counting of the *Omer** will consist of seven "full" weeks (Leviticus 23:15). After the Counting of the *Omer*, the *Havdalah* ceremony is held over a cup of wine.

The Second Day of Pesaḥ (in the Diaspora)

The *Ma'ariv* service is conducted as on the first day of *Yom Tov* (and the *Hallel* is recited wherever it is customary to do so). After the service, the Counting of the *Omer* begins. (Some say it at the end of the *Haggadah* reading, either individually at home or congregating once more in the synagogue to count the *Omer* publicly.)

The second Pesaḥ *Seder* is conducted as on the first day of the festival, but in most places no particular care is taken to eat the *Afikoman* before midnight. Wherever it is customary, the *Omer* is counted during the *Haggadah* reading. For those who are accustomed to sing songs and *Piyyutim* after the *Haggadah* reading, there are special ones for the second *Seder* night.

The *Shaḥarit* service is exactly the same as for the first day. The full *Hallel* is recited, and two Torah scrolls are taken out. Five persons are called up to the first scroll to read the passages about the festivals (Leviticus 22:27–23:44). The passages about the *Musaf* sacrifices are read from the second scroll, as on the first day. The *Haftarah* reading is about the Pesaḥ festival celebrated by King Josiah (in most customs, II Kings 23:1–9 and 21–25).

The *Musaf* and *Minḥah* services are the same as for the first day. At the end of the day, the *Havdalah* ceremony is performed over a cup of wine.

The Seventh Day of Pesaḥ

The seventh day of Pesaḥ is also a festival, a day of holy convocation, decreed in the Torah. Since it is considered the concluding day of the Pesaḥ festival, it is not treated as a new festival in itself but merely as a continuation.

Tradition says that the crossing of the Red Sea (Exodus 14) occurred on the eve of the seventh day of Pesaḥ, and for this reason the Torah reading and other customs reflect this particular aspect of the festival day. The crossing of the Red Sea is not only the final act of the exodus from Egypt, but it is also a time of Divine revelation to the people of Israel (see *Berakhot* 50a and *Mekhilta*,# shira 3).

The *Ma'ariv* service is the usual one for *Yom Tov*,* and the phrase *Zeman Ḥerutenu* ("the season of our freedom") is mentioned in the prayers, as throughout the Pesaḥ festival. If it is Shabbat, references are made to it, as on all festival days that fall on Shabbat.

The *Kiddush* ceremony for the eve of the seventh day of Pesaḥ is a festival *Kiddush*, the only difference being the omission of the *she-Heḥeyanu** blessing.

Some follow the custom of reciting the *Tikkun** for the eve of the seventh day of Pesaḥ, which consists of passages from various biblical sources, selections from the Mishnah, Tractates *Beitzah* and *Ḥagigah*, and discourses from the *Zohar*.# Some also gather at the synagogue and dance through the night in celebration of the Red Sea crossing. Many who live near the seashore go to the beach to recite the Song of the Sea.* In certain places, it is the custom to stay awake throughout this night.

The *Amidah* prayer for the *Shaḥarit* service is the usual one for festivals, followed by the half *Hallel.* Two Torah scrolls are taken out, and five persons are called up (seven on Shabbat) to read from the first scroll. The Torah selection (Exodus 13:17–15:26) is about the parting and crossing of the Red Sea. The description of the *Musaf* sacrifices for this festival is read from the second scroll (Numbers 28:19–26). The *Haftarah* is the Song of David (II Samuel 22:1–51), which, like the Song of the Sea, is a song of praise to God.

If it is Shabbat, most Ashkenazim (and some Oriental communities, too) read the Song of Songs (in the Diaspora they read half of it on this day and the other half on the following day).

The Ashkenazic custom is to hold a *Yizkor** service to commemorate the dead after the Torah reading.

The *Amidah* prayer for the *Musaf* service is the usual one for the festival, and the passages about the *Musaf* sacrifices are also mentioned.

The *Amidah* prayer for the *Minḥah* service is the usual one for the festival, and if it is Shabbat, all the customs for a festival that falls on Shabbat are followed.

The Last Day of Pesaḥ (in the Diaspora)

The order of prayer services is almost identical in detail to that of the previous day, except for changes in the Torah and *Haftarah* readings.

Among other customs for this day, the *Tikkun* is not recited, and Ḥassidim are not strict in observing the additional stringencies regarding food on Pesaḥ (those that are not indicated in talmudic law or in the *Shulḥan Arukh*#) which they take upon themselves on the other days of Pesaḥ. Therefore, even those who do not eat *Gebrochtz* ("soaked *Matzah*," namely, *Matzah* that came in contact with liquids) throughout Pesaḥ, do eat it on the eighth day.

Two scrolls are taken out for the Torah reading, and five persons are called up to read selections about the festivals (Deuteronomy 15:19–16:17). If it is Shabbat, seven people are called up, and the reading begins from Deuteronomy 14:22. In the second scroll, the portion about the *Musaf* sacrifices is read, as on the previous day.

The *Haftarah* reading is Isaiah 10:32 to 12:6, for the simple reason that it contains a reference to the crossing of the Red Sea (Isaiah 11:15–16). It also mentions the fall of King Sennacherib which, according to tradition, occurred during the Pesaḥ festival. Another reason (which finds expression in various ways) is that on this day, the last day to commemorate the deliverance from Egypt, mention is made of the future redemption and the coming of the *Mashiaḥ* (Messiah).

Ashkenazim in the Diaspora conduct on this day a *Yizkor* service in commemoration for the dead.

The *Musaf* and *Minḥah* services are the same as on the previous day.

Some communities conduct a special *Se'udah Shelishit** ("Third Meal") on this last day of Pesaḥ, called *Se'udat Mashiaḥ* ("The Messiah Meal"), during which they discuss the future redemption. (In the Land of Israel, this is done on the seventh day of Pesaḥ).

The Shavu'ot Festival

The festival of Shavu'ot has a few other names, each of which expresses one aspect of the festival's essence. In the Torah, it is generally called *Ḥag ha-Shavu'ot*—"the Festival of Weeks"—because it is held at the end of seven weeks, counting from the second day of Pesaḥ. At the end of the forty-nine days of Counting of the *Omer*, the fiftieth day is designated as the festival day. Another name for this festival is *Yom ha-Bikkurim*—"the Day of the First Fruits"—the day on which that year's "first fruits" of the seven kinds of produce characteristic of the Land of Israel were brought to the Temple. To mark this occasion, a special public sacrifice was offered, of two sheep and two loaves of bread that were brought with the sheep and waved before the altar. The first fruits were not offered on the festival day itself, but from the following day onward, until the festival of Sukkot. The festival is also called *Ḥag ha-Katzir*—"the Harvest Festival"—after the agricultural season in which it occurs.

The sages of the Mishnah* and Talmud* generally call the festival *Atzeret* (*Pesikta*# 30) because the day is a completion, the ending of the

Pesaḥ festival (comparable to the eighth day of Sukkot, which the sages called Shemini Atzeret). They therefore termed it the *Atzeret* of Pesaḥ.* However, the term used in the festival prayers is *Zeman Mattan Toratenu*—"the season of the Giving of our Torah"—because it is the time of the giving of the Torah from Sinai in the presence of all Israel. The actual date of this event is not specified in the Torah, but according to calculations based on the book of Exodus, the giving of the Torah took place on the sixth or seventh day of Sivan (see *Shabbat* 86b–88a).

After the destruction of the Temple, the aspect of the festival as the time of the Giving of the Torah became predominant, as is strongly reflected in the festival prayers, Torah readings, and other customs. In honor of the festival, it is the practice in many places to decorate the synagogue (and sometimes even the home) with greenery and flowers. Some explanations for this are that "on *Atzeret* the fruits of the trees are being judged" (see *Rosh ha-Shanah* 16a), and that it commemorates the joy of the Torah giving, since, according to tradition, Mount Sinai was covered with greenery and flowers during the revelation.[96]

Shavu'ot Prayer Services

The prayer services for the festival are essentially the same as for all the festivals, with this particular festival mentioned in the *Amidah* as "the time of the Giving of our Torah," and in the Grace After Meals as "this festival day of Shavu'ot."

The *Ma'ariv* service is the usual one for the festivals. It is customary to delay the prayers, and to lengthen the recital of the opening word *Barekhu*,* in order to ensure beyond all doubt that the "seven whole weeks" of the *Omer* period are completed. After the prayers, *Kiddush* is made and the first festive meal is eaten.

It is the prevailing custom throughout the Jewish world not to sleep during the night, and to recite the *Tikkun Leil Shavu'ot*.* This is already referred to in the *Zohar*# and has become a universally accepted custom, thanks to the influence of the mystical revelations of Rabbi Yosef Karo@ (author of *Shulḥan Arukh*#) and his disciple Rabbi

---

[96] See the *Levush*# on *Shulḥan Arukh, Oraḥ Ḥayyim* 494.

Shlomo Alkabetz (author of *Lekhah Dodi**). This *Tikkun*, a form of preparation for receiving the Torah, is considered a reparation for the time when the Torah was given at Sinai, because the Israelites were not suitably prepared for it then, since they went to sleep the night before. In addition to reciting the *Tikkun*, many engage in Torah study during the night, each according to his ability. It also commemorates King David, who would stay awake at night and engage in Torah study, and who, according to tradition, was born and died on Shavu'ot.

The *Shaḥarit* service is the usual festival one, and wherever it is the custom to recite *Piyyutim*, there are special ones for Shavu'ot. Many congregations (most of those following *Nusaḥ Sepharad*, and others) recite the *Keter Kedushah*, usually used in *Musaf*, during *Shaḥarit* also.

After the repetition of the *Amidah*, the full *Hallel* is recited. Ashkenazim then read the Book of Ruth (in the Diaspora, on the following day). After this, two Torah scrolls are taken from the Ark, and five persons are called to the first scroll to read the section describing the Giving of the Torah (Exodus 19:1–20:23).

Before the Torah reading, special *Piyyutim* and psalms are recited, according to the various prayer rites. The Ashkenazim recite the *Akdamut*.*

It is a noted custom to call a prominent member of the congregation to the Torah reading of the Ten Commandments. After this, the section about the festival sacrifices (Numbers 28:26–31) is read from the second scroll. The *Haftarah* is the description of the Divine Chariot and the Holy Throne given in Ezekiel 1:1–28 and 3:12. In certain congregations (even some where it is not the custom to read the Aramaic translation of the whole Torah), it is customary to read Yonatan ben Uzziel's@ Aramaic translation of this *Haftarah* selection. Care is taken to call up a person who is a respected Torah scholar for the *Haftarah*, worthy enough to read the story of the Divine Chariot. Many people stand while listening to this *Haftarah*.

Ashkenazic communities in the Land of Israel now recite *Yizkor*. The Torah scrolls are then returned to the Ark. Some recite Psalm 29 while this is being done, as on Shabbat.

After this comes the festival *Musaf* service, and in those places where *Piyyutim* are recited, there are special ones for the *Amidah* repetition. In the Diaspora, the Ashkenazim do the Priestly Blessing during this *Musaf* service. The service concludes as on all festivals. The *Minḥah* service is the usual one for festival days.

The Second Day of Shavu'ot (in the Diaspora)

The order of prayer services is the same as for the first day, but there are a few changes, some of which are a result of the fact that the second day of Shavu'ot can sometimes occur on Shabbat. Customs vary as to the recital of the Shavu'ot *Tikkun* on this night.

Wherever *Piyyutim* are recited, they differ from those of the first day, with each community following its own customs. On the second day as well, two Torah scrolls are taken out. Before the Torah reading, many Ashkenazic communities recite the Aramaic *Piyyut* of *Yatziv Pitgam*, written in praise of the Torah, which ends in words of commendation for Yonatan ben Uzziel,[@] who translated the Prophets into Aramaic.

When this festival falls during the week, five persons are called up to the Torah, to read Deuteronomy 15:19 to 16:17. If it falls on Shabbat, seven persons are called up, and in most customs the Torah reading is Deuteronomy 14:22 to 16:17. In the second Torah scroll, the same *Maftir* is read as on the first day, but the *Haftarah* is from the Prophet Ḥabakkuk (in most customs, from 2:20 through 3:19, and in the Ashkenazic rite, 3:1–19), which mentions the revelation on Mount Sinai. In the Diaspora, Ashkenazim do *Yizkor* after the Torah reading.

The *Musaf* service follows. In a few Ashkenazic congregations, the Priestly Blessing is not recited if the second day of Shavu'ot falls on Shabbat. The *Minḥah* service is conducted as on all other festivals. If it is Shabbat, there is a Torah reading, based on the yearly cycle of Torah readings, as usual for festivals that occur on Shabbat.

The Sukkot Festival

The Sukkot festival, too, has several names given in the Torah and in rabbinic sources. In the Torah, it is sometimes called *Ḥag ha-Sukkot*—"the Feast of Booths"—because of the relevant commandment, and sometimes *Ḥag ha-Asif*—"the Feast of Ingathering,"—

because of the agricultural season in which it occurs. The sages referred to it simply as *he-Ḥag*—"the Festival." In the prayer book, it is referred to as *Zeman Simḥatenu*—"the Season of our Rejoicing."

The festival of Sukkot does not commemorate any specific event, but is a reminder, as it says in the Torah, "that your generations may know that I made the children of Israel dwell in booths, when I brought them out of the land of Egypt" (Leviticus 23:43). Our sages differ about whether this refers to the protective Clouds of Glory that covered the Israelites in the desert (*Mekhilta*# 14:20) or to the actual exodus from Egypt and their wanderings in the wilderness, protected by God against all harm. In any case, according to the deeper interpretations of this question, the festival of Sukkot is not merely a reminder of the past: sitting in the *Sukkah** serves to emphasize, once again, that we are protected under the shelter of God's wings. This is connected with the season of ingathering. At this time, most of the fruits and grains have been harvested and stored safely, yet instead of sitting in our well-built houses, and depending upon our possessions and fortifications, we sit in the *Sukkah*, a "temporary habitation" (*Sukkah* 2a), making God our protection. As it is written, "He shall hide me in His pavilion [the *Sukkah*], in the secret of His tabernacle shall He hide me" (Psalms 27:5).

The festival of Sukkot, which comes after the Days of Awe (see Chapter 11), is a time of reconciliation and joy. The Midrash (*Leviticus Rabbah* 30:2) likens holding the *Lulav** to a triumphal parade, in which we proclaim our certainty that we have been vindicated before God. Of all the festivals, Sukkot best expresses the attributes of compassion and splendor (*Tiferet*)[97]—harmony between Man, Creator, and World. For this reason, the festival is called the "season of our rejoicing," and there is a special commandment to rejoice on this festival more than on the other festivals. Not only does the Torah explicitly say, "and you shall rejoice in your feast" (Deuteronomy 16:14), but there is the additional command, "and you shall only be joyful" (*ibid.*, v. 15). This finds expression in some of the halakhic rulings for the festival, and in the *Simḥat Beit ha-Shoevah*,* the joyous water-drawing ceremony.

---

[97] One of the ten *Sefirot** in Jewish mystical thought. See, e.g., Steinsaltz, *The Thirteen Petalled Rose.*

The Sukkot festival is celebrated, as it says in the Torah, "at the year's end" (Exodus 34:22), namely, very close to the autumnal equinox, indicating the end of the past agricultural year and the beginning of the next one. For this reason, this festival includes references to the rainfall for the coming year, such as the water libation ceremony in the Temple, and, immediately after Sukkot, on Shemini Atzeret, the winter season begins with the Prayer for Rain.*

Sukkot Prayer Services

If the *Yom Tov* falls on Shabbat, the *Kabbalat Shabbat* service is conducted as for all festival days that occur on Shabbat. The *Ma'ariv* service for Sukkot is the usual one for festivals, and in some congregations, *Piyyutim* are added within the *Shema* benedictions.

After prayers, all go to the *Sukkah*, and in many congregations it is the custom to invite on each day the *Ushpizin**—the heavenly guests who come to pay a visit on each of the festival days. It is a widespread custom to recite a special *Yehi Ratzon** prayer, which has various forms, according to the different prayer rites. On the first day of Sukkot, the heavenly guest is the Patriarch Abraham, accompanied by the other six *Ushpizin* (namely, Isaac, Jacob, Moses, Aaron, Joseph, and David). The festival *Kiddush* is recited, followed by the blessing "who has sanctified us with His commandments, and commanded us to dwell in the *Sukkah*" and by the *she-Heḥeyanu* benediction at the end. In the Grace After Meals, the phrase "May the Merciful One restore for us the fallen *Sukkah* of David" is added. (Some do not recite this on the festival itself, but only during *Ḥol ha-Mo'ed*, because it seems like a public form of mourning.) Some also add, "May the Merciful One grant us the merit to be seated in the *Sukkah* of the Leviathan" and "May the Merciful One spread over us His *Sukkah* of Peace." In the reading of the *Shema* at bedtime, some people who sleep in the *Sukkah* omit everything except the first section of the *Shema* (as is done on *Seder* night).

Some rise early, in order to pronounce the blessing on the *Lulav* in the *Sukkah* before going to the synagogue, while others do the *Lulav* blessing after *Shaḥarit*. The *Shaḥarit* service is entirely the same as for all festival days. After the *Amidah* prayer, the full *Hallel* is recited, during which time the *Lulav* is held, and shaken while certain verses are said.

This is the day on which the series of *Hosha'not** prayers begins, either before or after the Torah reading (according to local custom). The *Hosha'not* for the first day are recited.

The procedure for taking out the Torah scrolls is the same one as for all festival days. Two scrolls are brought out, and five people are called up (seven on Shabbat) to read in the first scroll. The selection is Leviticus 22:26 to 23:44, which deals with the order of the festivals. In the second scroll, Numbers 29:12–16 is read, about the *Musaf* festival sacrifices for that day. The *Haftarah** selection concerns the prophecy about the end of days, when all the nations of the world will come to celebrate the festival of Sukkot in Jerusalem (Zechariah 14:1–21). After the Torah and *Haftarah* readings, the *Musaf* service for the festivals begins. In most rites, the verses on the *Musaf* sacrifices are inserted into the *Amidah* prayer.

The *Minḥah* service is the usual one for the festivals, and if it is Shabbat, there is a Torah reading, according to the yearly cycle of Torah portions, which in this case is the very last portion in Deuteronomy. At the conclusion of the day comes the usual *Ma'ariv* service, and, in the Land of Israel, it is followed by *Havdalah* over a cup of wine.

The Second Day of Sukkot (in the Diaspora)

Prayer services on the second day of the festival in the Diaspora are essentially the same as for the first day. The evening *Kiddush* ceremony follows the same pattern as the day before, and the order of blessings is: wine, *Kiddush*, "to dwell in the *Sukkah*," and *she-Heḥeyanu*. Some alter the order of the last two blessings and recite the *she-Heḥeyanu* blessing before "to dwell in the *Sukkah*." In the order of the *Ushpizin*, it is the day for the Patriarch Isaac (accompanied by the other six).

The *Shaḥarit* service is the same as on the first day. The *Hosha'not* recited are those for the second day of the festival. The procedure for taking out the Torah scrolls is the same as for the first day: two scrolls are taken out of the Ark, and five people are called up to read the same selection as on the first day. In the second scroll, the same selection is read as on the first day, about the *Musaf* sacrifices. However, the *Haftarah* is a different one: the biblical account of the Temple dedication in the days of King Solomon, which occurred during the festival of Sukkot (in most places, I Kings 8:2–21).

The *Musaf* and *Minḥah* prayer services are conducted as on the first day of the festival. At the conclusion of the festival day, *Havdalah* is performed over wine.

Shemini Atzeret and Simḥat Torah

The name Shemini Atzeret is derived from the verse "On the eighth *[Shemini]* day you shall have a solemn assembly *[Atzeret]*" (Numbers 29:35; see also Nehemiah 8:18). It is defined by the sages as "a festival in itself" (*Sukkah* 47a), so even though it comes immediately after Sukkot, it is a separate festival in its own right, and its laws and prayers are not related to those of Sukkot.

Our sages see this festival as a private celebration between God and Israel. On the festival of Sukkot, we pray on behalf of the entire world, whereas Shemini Atzeret is like a "small banquet made by the King for His beloved" (Rashi@ on Numbers 28:35). This festival also marks the beginning of the winter season, for on it we begin to pray for the rains of the coming year.

Perhaps because of this special significance, it was decided to connect this festival with the ceremony for completing the yearly cycle of Torah readings and with the festivities for Simḥat Torah—"the Rejoicing in the Law." (This was probably introduced during the Geonic period,* because it is not mentioned in the Talmud.) Both in Israel, where Shemini Atzeret and Simḥat Torah are celebrated on one and the same day, and in the Diaspora, where Shemini Atzeret is celebrated on one day and Simḥat Torah on the next, there is a growing tendency (in customs as well as inward feeling) to have the aspect of Simḥat Torah override the aspect of Shemini Atzeret.

Simḥat Torah is an expression of Israel's joy in having the merit to complete the Torah readings, and of gratitude for having received the gift of the Torah. It is true that we celebrate the Giving of the Torah on the Shavu'ot festival; however, on that occasion the emphasis is on the great event of Divine revelation and its awesome and sublime significance. On Simḥat Torah, there is greater stress on joyful, grateful acknowledgment of the gift of the Torah, and for having merited to receive it and live by it. For this reason, the festival customs express this intense joy, mainly through the *Hakkafot** and the ceremonies for the Torah reading.

Shemini Atzeret (in the Diaspora)

When Shemini Atzeret falls on Shabbat, *Kabbalat Shabbat* is conducted as it is usually done on festivals. In the festival *Ma'ariv* service, "this Eighth Day Feast" (or in a different formulation, "the Eighth Day Feast of Assembly") is mentioned. This festival, too, is called in the prayers *Zeman Simḥatenu*—"the season of our joy."

In various places it was customary to hold *Hakkafot* after the *Amidah* prayer, as on Simḥat Torah. The evening *Kiddush* includes the *she-Heḥeyanu* blessing, because this is a festival unto itself, which deserves a blessing of its own. In the Diaspora, where the additional days express the reminder of doubt regarding the precise calculation of the festival's beginning, this day is also the last day of Sukkot; therefore, it is customary to eat some of the meals in the *Sukkah*. This issue was disputed among the *Rishonim*,* and this led to certain differences in custom. In some places, the evening meal is eaten in the *Sukkah*, and in others, the daytime meal. In either case, however, the blessing for sitting in the *Sukkah* is not recited.

The *Shaḥarit* service is conducted as on every festival, and is followed by the full *Hallel*. Some congregations even hold *Hakkafot*. Taking out the Torah scrolls is done in the same way as on every other festival: two scrolls are taken out and five persons (seven on Shabbat) are called up to the first scroll to read the selection about the festivals. Some always read Deuteronomy 14:22 to 16:1. Others read this only when Shemini Atzeret falls on Shabbat, and when it falls on a weekday they read Deuteronomy 15:19 to 16:17. The *Maftir* is read in the second scroll, about the *Musaf* sacrifices for the festival (Numbers 29:35 to 30:1). The *Haftarah* is about the joyful celebrations at the end of Sukkot and Shemini Atzeret, when the Temple of Solomon was dedicated (I Kings 8:54–66).

Some communities say *Yizkor* on this day. After returning the Torah scrolls to the Ark, the Prayer for Rain* is recited, either before the *Musaf Amidah* or during its repetition by the *Shaliaḥ Tzibbur.* From this time onward, the phrase "who causes the wind to blow and the rain to fall" is included in the benediction of *Meḥayeh ha-Metim**—"who revives the dead" in all *Amidah* prayers. The *Musaf* service for *Yom Tov* is conducted, and in the *Amidah* there is a reference (in most customs) to the verses concerning the *Musaf* sacrifices for this festival.

The *Minḥah* service is the usual one for the festivals, and if it is Shabbat, there is a Torah reading in which a portion of *ve-Zot ha-Berakhah* is read.

Simḥat Torah

If Simḥat Torah falls on Shabbat, in the Land of Israel, *Kabbalat Shabbat* is recited as is usual on festivals. The festival *Ma'ariv* service for *Yom Tov* is conducted. After the *Amidah* prayer (along with the *Me'ein Sheva** blessing on Shabbat), a series of biblical verses is recited, beginning with *Attah Horeita**—"To you it was shown, that you may know it" (Deuteronomy 4:35), and at the same time the Ark is opened and all the Torah scrolls are taken out for the *Hakkafot* ceremony. In this ceremony, all the congregants encircle the *Bimah** seven times, with song and dance, holding the Torah scrolls in their hands, and certain verses and *Piyyutim* are recited at the beginning of each *Hakkafah*.

In some Ashkenazic communities, it is customary to read from a Torah scroll after the *Hakkafot*, so as to take out the scrolls not only for joyful celebration but for reading as well. (Torah reading at night, which is just a custom, is permitted on this occasion alone). Customs differ, with some calling up three persons and some only one person. Some read from the Torah portion *ve-Zot ha-Berakhah*, and some read Isaac's blessing to Jacob (Genesis 27). The scrolls are then returned to the Ark, and the prayer service ends as usual. The *Shaḥarit* service is the usual festival one, with the full *Hallel* recited after the *Amidah* prayer. Then *Attah Horeita* begins, followed by *Hakkafot*.

All Jewish communities have special *Piyyutim* for Simḥat Torah, some having many and some only a few.

After the *Hakkafot*, all the Torah scrolls are returned to the Ark, and three scrolls are taken out again. From the first, the portion of *ve-Zot ha-Berakhah*, which is the very last portion of the Torah, is read. It is a widespread custom among all communities to call up every congregant to the Torah on Simḥat Torah, including children who have not yet reached the age of Bar Mitzvah.* In some places they even call up very small children who do not know how to pronounce the blessings, together with an adult who says the blessings with them (see *Kol ha-Ne'arim**). For this reason, the Torah portion is read and reread until all those present have been called up.

The *Ḥatan Torah**—"the Torah Bridegroom"—is honored by being called up to read the last passages of the Torah. In many communities it is customary to call up the *Ḥatan Torah* and the *Ḥatan Bereshit**—"the Genesis Bridegroom" (see below)—with a poetic style of invitation *(Reshut*)* which probably originated in Geonic times. Some communities spread a *Tallit** canopy over the *Ḥatan Torah* and *Ḥatan Bereshit*, as well as over *Kol ha-Ne'arim* and those standing near them.

In the second scroll, the *Ḥatan Bereshit* reads the opening passages of Genesis (1:1–2:3). This is done to link the end of the Torah back to the beginning, so as not to give the impression that we have finished reading it and do not intend to deal with it again. Instead, we immediately start rereading it from the beginning.

In the third scroll, the *Maftir* is read from the description of the *Musaf* sacrifices for Shemini Atzeret (Numbers 29:35–30:1). The *Haftarah* is from the first chapter of Joshua (Joshua 1:1–18), which is the continuation of the story of Israel's history after Moses' death. Some Ashkenazim hold a *Yizkor* ceremony for the dead after the Torah reading.

After returning the Torah scrolls to the Ark, the usual festival *Musaf* service is recited. The special Prayer for Rain is recited as part of this *Musaf* service, in some congregations before the silent *Amidah*, and in some, in the repetition. However, the phrase *Mashiv ha-Ruaḥ**—"Who causes the wind to blow"—is said in the silent *Amidah*, even in those places where the Prayer for Rain has not yet been said. On Shemini Atzeret and Simḥat Torah, the Priestly Blessing is recited, even among Ashkenazim in the Diaspora, although some refrain from doing so in the *Musaf* service, for fear that the *Kohanim* may have drunk wine during the celebration of the *Hakkafot*.[98]

The *Minḥah* service is like the one for regular festival days, and if it falls on Shabbat there is a Torah reading, just as on every Shabbat.

At the end of the festival, the *Ma'ariv* service for the conclusion of a *Yom Tov* is recited, and the *Havdalah* ceremony is performed over a cup of wine. In some places in the Land of Israel, it is customary to hold "Second *Hakkafot*," in order to participate in the celebrations of Diaspora Jewry who are holding their own *Hakkafot* at that time.

---

[98] In which case, they are barred from making the blessing.

CHAPTER ELEVEN ❧ *Days of Awe*

FOR GENERATIONS, Rosh ha-Shanah, the New Year festival, and Yom Kippur, the Day of Atonement, have been called the Days of Awe. The word "awe" is used here, as in numerous places in the Bible, to express a sense of the sublime, which generates feelings of reverence for God's majesty. Our Patriarch Jacob, in describing the place where he had his vision of the ladder to Heaven, says, "How awesome is this place! This is none other than the house of God, and this is the gate of Heaven" (Genesis 28:17). The word is also mentioned in the Writings, "God is of awesome majesty" (Job 37:22), and in the Song of the Sea,* after the miraculous parting of the Red Sea, "Who is like unto You . . . awesome in praises, doing wonders?" (Exodus 15:11).

Though Rosh ha-Shanah and Yom Kippur differ from each other in liturgy and law, and even in their character and content, they do share many common aspects. Unlike other festival days, which are times of joy and commemoration of the miraculous deeds and gracious favor bestowed on the nation of Israel since its beginning, the Days of Awe are related to the essential nature of man in the present, to his private life and immediate concerns. The Days of Awe are not associated with historical events or agricultural production. On these days, each Jew stands alone, though within a congregation, among other people—facing the Creator. On the Days of Awe, one must stand before the Lord God, before the Divine throne of judgment, the seat of justice and mercy. Throughout all the emotional changes that occur during these days, the one constant feeling is the awareness of standing before the "King, Lord of Hosts" (Isaiah 6:5), "the great, mighty, and awesome" (Deuteronomy 10:17).

Rosh ha-Shanah—The New Year Festival

Rosh ha-Shanah is mentioned several times in the Torah, although not by that name, but simply by an indication of its timing—the first day of the seventh month (see Leviticus 23:24 and Numbers 29:1). It is also called *Zikhron Teru'ah* and *Yom Teru'ah*—a memorial day of fanfare—because of the special commandment to blow the *Shofar** on that day. Although the Torah does not specify the content and significance of this festival, many of its various aspects are revealed through the words of our sages.

The Torah begins counting the months of the year from Nisan (Exodus 12:2). However, the sources indicate that the year begins with the month of Tishrei (Exodus 23:16, 34:22, and Ezekiel 40:1).[99] According to rabbinic tradition, the world was created at this time of year. (At one time, this view stirred up controversy, but it was resolved in early generations; see *Rosh ha-Shanah* 27a). According to this calculation, Rosh ha-Shanah is not the first day of Creation but the sixth day, the day on which man was created. It is also implied in the Bible that this is the Day of Judgment, as it says, "Blow the *Shofar* for the new moon, in the time appointed, on our solemn feast day. For this is a statute for Israel, and a law of the God of Jacob." (Psalm 81:3–4).

All these different meanings complement and support each other, and reveal a simple explanation for blowing the *Shofar* on Rosh ha-Shanah. As we have said, the year is not calculated from the time of the redemption from Egypt (which occurred in Nisan), nor from the Creation of the world (which, according to the accepted opinion, began on the 25th of Elul, five days before Rosh ha-Shanah), but is clearly and specifically calculated from the creation of man, of the human species in general.

The creation of man marks the beginning of God's kingship on earth. Before the existence of humankind there was a world—but it was one without consciousness or choice. In the passive, quiescent world

---

[99] Similarly, in the commonly accepted Gregorian calendar, the names September, October, November, and December seem to indicate that their numerical order should begin from March, but the year is actually calculated from January.

before the creation of man, God was the Creator and Preserver of the world; but only after man begins to exist upon earth can there be any awareness of God's existence, and the possibility of His acknowledgment as the "King of the Universe." The creation of man is, therefore, not only the final act of Creation, but its ultimate goal. It is man, and he alone, who can, if he so desires, make God the "King over the entire Earth" (Zekhariah 14:9), as it says in the Bible (Isaiah 43:7–10),

Every one that is called by My name, I have created him for My glory; I have formed him and made him . . . You are My witnesses, says the Lord, and My servants whom I have chosen; that you may know and believe Me, and understand that I am He; before Me there was no God formed, neither shall there be after Me.

Each return of the time cycle to its human starting point involves not only the "commemoration of the first day,"[100] but a recoronation ceremony for the King—"with trumpets and the sound of the *Shofar* blast before the King, the Lord" (Psalm 98:6). The "day of the *[Shofar]* blast" mentioned in the Torah is the day on which "the blast of the King is among them" (Numbers 23:21), a recoronation ceremony, the essence of which is recalled in the prayer, "And they shall give You a royal crown."

On the other hand, the day also implies a summing up of the past. It is a day to examine to what extent all human beings (as we say in the Rosh ha-Shanah prayers, "all the creatures of the world pass before Him," and on this day "it shall be said of all nations"), and especially the people of Israel ("My servants whom I have chosen"), have managed to fulfill their greatest purpose in life—to acknowledge God as King over the whole world. This obligation "that you may know and believe Me, and understand" (Isaiah 43:10) is not just a one-time declaration but a way of life that expresses and emphasizes these things. Rosh ha-Shanah can accordingly be seen as a "Day of Judgment" in which the whole world is judged by the degree to which it exists for "My glory" (Isaiah 43:7). In Jewish esoteric thought, the existence of the world is seen as conditional. Every year, God grants the world an

---

[100] From the *Musaf** prayer for Rosh ha-Shanah.

extension, one more year to fulfill its mission, to help fulfill that "the Lord shall reign over all the earth" (Zechariah 14:9).

The prayers of the day express various aspects of this central idea. The general tone of the prayers is one of sublimity, and the attitude is essentially one that regards God as the King over the entire world. That is why there is repeated emphasis on God's "Kingship" in every benediction and prayer. Worshippers have a sense of dread lest their conduct during the past year—their misdeeds or nonfulfillment of their obligations—should fail to justify their continued existence as individuals, as groups, as a state. This feeling adds another dimension to the prayers of the day. Yet, the main theme of the prayers is not one of repentance and supplication. Indeed, from the halakhic viewpoint, Rosh ha-Shana is one of the days on which neither *Taḥanun**—"Supplication"—nor *Vidduy**—"Confession of Sins"—is recited. The focus is rather on resolving to do better in the coming year, and the request that God reveal His glory to the world, so as to make it easier for us to fulfill His commands.

The *Minḥah* Service on Rosh ha-Shanah Eve

It is customary to move forward the time of the *Minḥah** service, the last prayer of the outgoing year, in order to be able to draw it out and concentrate upon it more than usual. It is the custom to recite *Hodu** and *Yedid Nefesh** (unless Rosh ha-Shanah falls on Shabbat). Those who fast on Rosh ha-Shanah eve should say *Anenu** in the *Shome'a Tefillah** benediction of the *Amidah** prayer, but the *Shaliaḥ Tzibbur** does not recite this.

The *Ma'ariv* Service

When Rosh ha-Shanah falls on Shabbat, the *Kabbalat Shabbat** service is recited, as on all festival days. In most Jewish communities, the *Piyyut** of *Aḥot Ketanah** is recited before the service.

The general structure of the Rosh ha-Shanah *Ma'ariv* service is similar to the one for the festival days (see Chapter 10), and if it falls on Shabbat, it is comparable to the prayer service for a festival day that falls on Shabbat. Before the *Amidah*, most congregations recite a verse. If it is Shabbat, they say *ve-Shamru.** If it is not Shabbat, they recite, "Blow the *Shofar* at the moon's renewal, at the time appointed for our festive day. For it is a decree for Israel, a Day of Judgment for the God of Jacob" (Psalm 81: 3–4). The *Amidah* prayer follows the basic pattern for individual recitation used on the Days of Awe in *Ma'ariv*, *Shaḥarit*, *Minḥah*, and even *Ne'ilah** (see below). This general pattern is a fixed one, with slight variations between the different prayers according to the festival and the time of day.

The first two benedictions are recited as usual, with special additions for the ten Days of Awe. All versions of the third benediction, the *Kedushah*,* include an ancient *Piyyut* (some attribute it to Rav[@]), which is a fundamental part of the Rosh ha-Shanah and Yom Kippur prayers. The order and contents of this *Piyyut* are the same for all rites, with some linguistic variations.

The fullest version of this *Piyyut* is that of *Nusaḥ** *Sepharad*, in which this prayer-poem is divided into five parts, the first four sections beginning with the word *u-Vekhen*—"and so." There are many commentaries on the use of this word. Literally speaking, it alludes to the verse "And so I will go in unto the king" (Esther 4:16), but there are also more mystical interpretations of this word, and especially for its fourfold repetition. The phrases "And so shall Your Name be sanctified upon Israel, Your people" and "And so instill fear," speak of the revelation of God's awesomeness in His world. "And so grant honor to Your people" speaks of all the good and plenty that will come after such revelation. "And so the righteous will see and be glad" speaks of the great influence it will have upon humanity when the righteous will rejoice and the evil ones will perish. The fifth section begins "Lord our God, You are He who alone will reign over all Your works," and is a prayer for the manifestation of God's sovereign power and glory, because "You are holy and Your Name is awesome." The prayer then concludes (as on all Ten Days of Repentance) with the benediction *ha-Melekh ha-Kadosh*—"the holy King," (unlike the rest of the year, when it concludes "the holy God"). This formulation is generally the same in all rites, but some either abbreviate or elaborate certain sections.

The central benediction, the one for the festival, is constructed along the same pattern as those for the *Amidah* prayer on festival days:

*Attah Beḥartanu** (see Chapter 10), *Ya'aleh ve-Yavo,** and then some special phrases for this particular festival: "Reign upon the entire world in Your glory, be exalted over all the earth in Your splendor," etc. The conclusion is the same as on festival days: "Make us holy with Your commandments . . . ," ending with the benediction "Blessed are You, O Lord, King over the whole earth, who sanctifies Israel and the Day of Remembrance." If the day falls on Shabbat, mention of Shabbat is made within the benediction, as one does in the central benediction for all the other festivals. The *Amidah* prayer then concludes with the three standard final benedictions, with the additions made on the Ten Days of Repentance. After the *Amidah* prayer, if it is Shabbat, they recite *va-Yekhulu** and the *Me'ein Sheva* benediction.*

In accordance with certain mystical books, it is now customary in most versions to recite aloud, and with great solemnity, Psalm 24, which refers to God as the "King of Glory" and is a hymn of salutation to greet the arrival of the King. In most congregations, they open the Ark* and stand while reciting this psalm, with each sentence uttered by the *Shaliaḥ Tzibbur* and then repeated by the congregation. Some also recite a special mystical prayer, because kabbalistic sages say that reciting this prayer can ensure one's livelihood for the whole year.

The service is concluded as on all festival eves. In the Ashkenazic rite, Psalm 27*—"The Lord is my light and my salvation"—is recited, and some also add Psalm 81, "Sing aloud unto God our strength".

At the end of the service, the worshippers greet each other with the words "May you be inscribed and sealed for a life of goodness and peace," or with the shorter version, "May you be inscribed for a good year." The response to this greeting should be not merely "The same to you," but a full repetition of the same formula.

Kiddush and the Festive Meal

In essence, the *Kiddush** for Rosh ha-Shanah is the same as that for festivals. If it is Shabbat, the appropriate additions are made. There are minor variations among the different rites, yet all of them add, just before the conclusion, the phrase "and Your word, O King, is true and enduring forever."

Our sages have said (*Kritot* 6a), that in spite of the prohibition against fortune-telling, one may still use good-luck omens. For this reason, it is appropriate at the beginning of the Rosh ha-Shanah meal to eat foods whose names or characteristics represent some good omen. In the Talmud, they mention *Ruvia* (a kind of bean) and *Silka* (a kind of spinach), as well as dates and leeks. In various places, people add other foods with names that indicate abundance and good fortune. In a number of communities, there are fixed formulations (some of which can be found in the more detailed prayer books), which are pronounced before eating each of the different foods. It is also customary to eat the head of a sheep (as a reminder of the binding of Isaac) or the head of a fish (to signify being the head and not the tail).

In most places, it is the custom to begin the festive meal with a piece of apple dipped in honey, and to recite after the blessing, or after eating the apple, "May it be Your will that the new year be a good and sweet one." It is customary to eat many sweet and rich foods throughout this day, as it is said, "Eat the fat and drink the sweet . . . for this day is holy unto our Lord" (Nehemiah 8:10); and to refrain from eating anything sour, or any food that might cause one to become indisposed for the prayers of the following day. Many other such customs abound (see *Shulḥan Arukh*, *Oraḥ Ḥayyim* 583).

The *Shaḥarit* Service

The *Korbanot** section, and most of the *Pesukei de-Zimrah,** up to *Nishmat,** are essentially the same as on other festival days. In all Ashkenazic rites, the *Shaliaḥ Tzibbur* begins his prayer from his private seat among the congregation by chanting, with a special melody, the words from the last section of *Nishmat,* "O King"; and only he continues with "seated upon a high and sublime throne," after walking to the pulpit. Before beginning *Barekhu,** Ashkenazim recite Psalm 130—"Out of the depths I call to You, O Lord." The *Ḥazzan** then recites the *Kaddish,* and it is customary to recite some of the *Yotzerot**—"O King, girded with might," "His glory is spread out," and also a *Reshut** for *Barekhu.*

In most rites, the benediction of *Yotzer Or** and *Ahavah Rabbah** are recited in the formulation used for festival days. Most Ashkenazim also recite *Yotzerot* within the *Yotzer Or* benediction. In all prayer rites, the *Shema** and *Emet ve-Yatziv** are recited as in the weekday services.

The individual recitation of the *Amidah* prayer is the same as in the Rosh ha-Shanah *Ma'ariv* service. For the *Amidah* repetition,* Ashkenazic communities introduce a large number of *Piyyutim*, beginning with the prayer of the *Shaliaḥ Tzibbur*, who asks permission from the congregation: "I am awestruck as I open my lips with words based upon the teachings of the wise and understanding." This is followed by numerous *Piyyutim* within each of the first three *Amidah* benedictions. There is not complete conformity in the recital of these *Piyyutim*, with some reciting them all and some only a few of the *Piyyutim* in the *Maḥzor.** In the Ashkenazic rite, there is a special series of *Piyyutim* recited when the first day of Rosh ha-Shanah falls on Shabbat.

After the *Amidah* prayer *Avinu Malkenu** is recited according to different customs. In some congregations, the *Shaliaḥ Tzibbur* recites part of it, from "bring us back to You," or "rend the evil [aspect of the] edict," or "inscribe us in the book of good life," to "inscribe us in the book of forgiveness and pardon," with the congregants responding sentence by sentence. Other congregations recite the entire *Avinu Malkenu* without prior recital by the *Shaliaḥ Tzibbur.* There are some who follow the Lurianic* custom of omitting the first sentence, "we have sinned before You," as well as any other sentences that are a form of confession or mention of sin. The Ashkenazim do not recite *Avinu Malkenu* when Rosh ha-Shanah falls on Shabbat.

*Kaddish Titkabbal** is recited after *Avinu Malkenu.* In *Nusaḥ Sepharad*, the Song of the Day* and Psalm 27 are recited.

Torah Readings

Taking out the Torah scrolls is done almost entirely as on all festivals. In addition, in most communities the Thirteen Attributes* are recited, even on Shabbat. They are repeated three times, followed by a special formulation of the prayer *Ribbono Shel Olam**—"Master of the Universe," in which people pray for themselves and their families, asking for life, health, and sustenance during the coming year.

Two Torah scrolls are taken out, and five persons are called up (seven on Shabbat) to read from the first scroll. The readings on Rosh ha-Shanah and Yom Kippur have their own special cantillation melody. The selection is from the story of Isaac's birth and the prayer of Hagar and Ishmael (Genesis 21:1–34), and there are different ways of dividing this Torah portion among the persons called up to read it. Various reasons are given for selecting this Torah reading: it mentions the birth of Isaac, which is proof of God's providence and the fulfillment of His promises to the righteous (according to the sages, Isaac was born on Rosh ha-Shanah); and it includes the prayer of Hagar and Ishmael in the desert, and tells how they were answered with a miracle, to teach us that God hears the prayer of all supplicants.

The *Maftir,** about the *Musaf* sacrifices for Rosh ha-Shanah (Numbers 29:1–6), is read from the second scroll. The *Haftarah** is about the birth of the prophet Samuel (I Samuel 1:1–2:10), which is reminiscent of the story of Isaac's birth. Samuel is also said to have been conceived on Rosh ha-Shanah. It is a widespread custom to call up to a Torah reading the *Ba'al Teki'ah*—the *Shofar** blower (see below), as well as the *Shaliaḥ Tzibbur.* The last benediction for the *Haftarah* concludes with the formulation "King of all the earth, who sanctifies (Shabbat and) Israel and the Day of Remembrance."

The Ashkenazic custom is to insert the phrase "in honor of the Day of Judgment" within the *Mi she-Berakh** formulation. The Torah scrolls are then lifted up in view of the congregants, then rolled up, but they are returned to the Ark only after the *Shofar* blowing.

Teki'ot—The Blowing of the *Shofar*

Blowing the *Shofar* on Rosh ha-Shanah is the special commandment for this festival day. In all prayer rites, it is performed with great ceremony, and the blowing is usually done close to the *Bimah,** while the Torah scrolls are still there.

The Torah gives no explanation for the commandment to blow the *Shofar,* and the sages of every generation have explained this commandment in many different ways. Some of these explanations are mentioned, or alluded to, in the prayers, both those said before the *Shofar* blowing, and in the *Musaf** prayer service and its accompanying

Piyyutim. Maimonides@ [101] sees it as a rousing call to Jews to wake up from their spiritual slumbers and to bestir themselves in the service of their Creator. In many sources, beginning with the very earliest *midrashim*,* the blowing of the *Shofar* is seen as a means of overcoming the forces of evil. As it is said in the benediction of *Shofarot* (see below), the blowing of the *Shofar* alludes to the future redemption, when the spirit of impurity will be entirely banished from the earth. The *Shofar* should be made of a ram's horn, in allusion to and in commemoration of the binding of Isaac, which is referred to in various ways in the prayers for Rosh ha-Shanah. Others have written that the sound of the *Shofar*, which is not a musical sound at all, is the symbolic expression of a person's cry to God, simply voiced, without words or melody, like the outcry of the soul longing for redemption. In mystical literature, beginning with the *Zohar*,# many explanations are offered, even for the different *Shofar* blasts. The blast of the *Shofar* is explained both as a symbolic expression of the creation of the world in general, and of humanity in particular, and as a symbolic shattering of evil and the turning of judgment into mercy.

There are two main divisions in the blowing of the *Shofar*. The first series of *Shofar* blasts, which are sounded before the *Musaf* service, is called *Teki'ot de-Meyushav*—"sounding of the *Shofar* while seated"—because one is not obligated by law to stand then, although in actual practice it is customary to do so. The second series of *Shofar* blasts is called the *Teki'ot de-Me'umad*—"sounding of the *Shofar* while standing"—which occurs during the central benedictions of the *Amidah* prayer in the *Musaf* service, at which time one is required to stand.

Some congregations study a selection from the *Zohar* (Leviticus 98b) before the blowing, and, in some rites, the *Shofar* blower engages in further study in order to increase his *Kavvanah*.* In many communities, the local rabbi or sage addresses the congregation with inspiring words, to awaken the congregants' hearts to the spiritual significance of the *Shofar* blasts.

Many recite *Piyyutim* and biblical verses before sounding the blasts. Psalm 47 is recited seven times in most rites. All traditions include six verses whose first letters form the acronym *KRA' STN* (which means "confound the Devil"). In most liturgies these verses are:

---

[101] *Yad ha-Ḥazakah, Sefer ha-Mada, Hilkhot Teshuvah*, chap. 3, halakhah 4.

Lamentations 3:56 (or Psalm 119:49), and verses 160, 122, 162, 66, and 108 of Psalm 119. Some precede this by reciting "From the depths I called upon the Lord" (Psalm 118:5). All end with the words "God ascends through *Teru'ah** . . ." (Psalm 47:5). In the Ashkenazic rite, the *Shofar* blower recites these aloud, verse by verse, and the congregants respond by repeating them.

In many congregations, the *Shofar* blower makes a supplication in which he prays that he will faithfully represent the congregation in fulfilling the commandment of *Shofar* blowing and its *Kavvanot.*

After all these preparations, the *Shofar* blower recites two blessings. The first is "He who has made us holy with His commandments and commanded us to hear the sound of the *Shofar*" (the actual obligation being to hear the *Shofar,* rather than to blow it). The second is the *she-Heḥeyanu** blessing. The congregation responds Amen* to both blessings, but not *Barukh Hu u-Varukh Shemo** ("May He and His Name be blessed").

In most congregations, the custom is that one person reads aloud the sequence of the *Shofar* blasts, so that the *Shofar* blower does not get confused. Whoever does this should be well versed in the laws of *Shofar* blowing, and able to decide whether the blower should repeat an unsuccessful blast. This custom is a very ancient one, already alluded to in the Mishnah.*

The triadic sequence of *Shofar* blasts is as follows: *Teki'ah** — *Shevarim** — *Teru'ah** — *Teki'ah* / *Teki'ah* — *Shevarim* — *Teki'ah* / *Teki'ah* — *Teru'ah* — *Teki'ah.* These ten blasts are repeated three times, a total of thirty blasts. In many congregations, it is the custom for the *Shofar* blower to pause a little between each of the three sets of ten blasts, and to make a silent confession (though some prohibit this, since it constitutes an interruption—*Hefsek**—between the blasts). In many congregations, the worshippers murmur words of prayer based on a mystical formulation, beseeching that the *Shofar* blasts be graciously received on high.

At the end of this first sequence of *Shofar* blowing, it is customary everywhere to recite a few verses. In some congregations, the *Shofar* blower recites them first and the congregants repeat after him. These verses begin, "Fortunate is the people who knows the sound of the *Shofar* . . ." (Psalm 89:15–17). Most rites also add verse 19. Then *Ashrei** is recited, and the Torah scrolls are returned to the Ark.

The *Musaf* Service

In some places, it is customary to precede the *Musaf* service with special words of prayer. In the Ashkenazic rite, the *Shaliaḥ Tzibbur* recites the prayer *Hineni he-Ani mi-Ma'as*—"Here I am, deficient in meritorious deeds"—in which he juxtaposes his own unworthiness with the high and honorable position of public emissary for the *Musaf* prayer. Some congregations recite four verses whose first letters spell the Tetragrammaton. This is followed by the half *Kaddish*.*

The *Musaf Amidah* for Rosh ha-Shanah is singular among *Musaf* prayers in having nine benedictions instead of the usual seven. In place of the usual one central benediction, there are three: *Malkhuyot*, *Zikhronot*, and *Shofarot* (see below). These three blessings were instituted by the Sages of the Great Assembly, and the Mishnah presents differences of opinion regarding the number and order of the verses mentioned in each blessing. Their final formulation was apparently given by the great *Amora** Rav,@ and for this reason they were called *Teki'ata de-Vei Rav* ("the *Shofar* blasts according to the school of Rav").

These three benedictions, composed in a lofty, eloquent style, express various aspects of God's Kingship. Each consists of ten biblical verses appropriate to the theme, in the following sequence: three verses from the Torah (Pentateuch), followed by three from the *Ketuvim* (Writings), three from the *Nevi'im* (Prophets), then a concluding Torah verse.

The verses in the *Malkhuyot* ("Kingdoms") benediction refer to the Kingship of God and His rule upon earth, and our acceptance of His reign over us. The verses in the *Zikhronot* ("Remembrances") benediction refer to God as the King of the Universe who remembers all deeds and watches over all His creatures, examining, appraising, and passing judgment upon them. The verses here are only those that mention remembering for good and for salvation. In the *Shofarot* benediction, the verses refer to the revelations of God in this world, from the one on Mount Sinai to the revelation that will occur in the future redemption, each accompanied, in some way, by the sounding of the *Shofar*, heralding the appearance of the King. After each of these three *Amidah* benedictions, the *Shofar* is blown in the triadic sequence of ten blasts, as above.

The silent *Amidah* prayer begins with the first three Rosh ha-Shanah benedictions (see above, in the section on *Ma'ariv* for Rosh ha-Shanah). The fourth benediction begins as in the *Musaf* of every festival: *Attah Beḥartanu*—"You have chosen us"—followed by "because of our sins we have been exiled from our land . . ." The Ashkenazim recite the biblical verses about the *Musaf* sacrifices of the day (including the verses for the Shabbat *Musaf* sacrifices, if it is Shabbat). Instead of the phrase for the three pilgrimage festivals, "and we are unable to appear and bow before You," they say, "and we are unable to fulfill our obligations."

This is followed by the *Aleinu** prayer, which here is the beginning of the *Malkhuyot* benediction. The benediction concludes with the same formulation as in the central *Amidah* benediction for all the other Rosh ha-Shanah services, "Reign over the entire world. . . . Blessed are You Lord, King over all the earth, who sanctifies (Shabbat and) Israel and the Day of Remembrance."

In *Nusaḥ Sepharad*, they sound the *Shofar* even during the silent *Amidah* prayer, and blow thirty blasts (three times the triadic sequence). These *Shofar* blasts are sounded without a person reading aloud to direct the *Shofar* blower, although there are some Ḥassidic congregations that allow for this. After the *Shofar* blowing, they generally recite *Hayom Harat Olam*—"Today is the birthday of the world," which is said even if it is Shabbat. This same procedure is followed after the *Zikhronot* and the *Shofarot* benedictions. The final three benedictions of the *Amidah* prayer are recited in the formulation for the Ten Days of Repentance.

In the *Amidah* repetition of the Rosh ha-Shanah *Musaf* service, numerous *Piyyutim* are usually recited, the largest number being those in the Ashkenazic rite. In this rite, the *Shaliaḥ Tzibbur* recites the *Piyyut* of *mi-Sod Ḥakhamim*—"With words based upon the teachings of the wise and the understanding," as well as another *Piyyut* at the end of the first benediction. There are *Piyyutim* within the second benediction, too, and the third benediction also opens with *Piyyutim* (some reciting more of them and some less). After the various *Piyyutim*, which also include refrains *(Pizmonim*)* sung by the *Ḥazzan* and the congregation, many congregations recite *u-Netanneh Tokef.** The *Keter* Kedushah* is then recited, and in some congregations it is greatly extended by inserting even more *Piyyutim* between each of the phrases.

In the Ashkenazic rite, they add further *Piyyutim* and *Pizmonim* (here, too, the number of *Piyyutim* recited varies from one congregation to another). The fourth benediction, *Malkhuyot*, begins, as in the individual *Amidah* prayer, with *Aleinu.* When they reach the words "But we bend the knee and bow down," the entire congregation and the *Ḥazzan* bow down to the ground, either prostrate or only kneeling (see *Keri'ah**).

Some congregations recite *Attah Horeita,** along with other verses, at the same time as the *Ḥazzan.* In most communities, the *Shaliaḥ Tzibbur* recites a short prayer, *Oḥilah la-El*—"I place my hope in God, I entreat His countenance, asking Him to grant me the gift of speech." In the Ashkenazic rite, the *Ḥazzan* precedes this with another prayer: "Inspire the lips of those who have been appointed by Your people, the house of Israel." In some congregations, the *Ḥazzan* says this entire prayer by himself, while in others the congregants recite a part of the prayer: "Let them not stumble with their tongues . . ." Some recite another *Piyyut* after *Oḥilah.* Then the *Ḥazzan* continues with the second part of *Aleinu*, and proceeds until the conclusion of the *Malkhuyot* benediction.

At the end of the benediction, the *Shofar* is blown (in most places, the triadic sequence of ten blasts), and the congregation then says *ha-Yom Harat Olam* (even if it is Shabbat, when the *Shofar* is not blown). In the Ashkenazic rite, if Rosh ha-Shanah falls on a weekday, when the *Shofar* is blown, they also recite *Areshet Sefateinu*—"May the utterance of our lips be pleasing before You . . . and accept with mercy and favor our recitation of [the Scriptural verses of] *Malkhuyot.*"

Some Ashkenazim recite a *Piyyut* as a prelude to the *Zikhronot* benediction, and then, after the *Ḥazzan* recites the benediction, the *Shofar* is sounded as before, and the congregants then recite "*Areshet Sefateinu* . . . and accept . . . our recitation of the *Zikhronot* [verses]". Some Ashkenazim also say an introductory *Piyyut* before the *Shofarot* benediction. Then the *Shofarot* benediction is recited, the *Shofar* is blown, and *ha-Yom Harat Olam* is said, and, among the Ashkenazim, "*Areshet Sefateinu* . . . *Shofarot.*"

In most versions, the *Retzeh** benediction is recited as usual. However, in nearly all Ashkenazic congregations, if there is a *Kohen** in the synagogue, they say, "May our prayer please You as a burnt offering and sacrifice . . ." just before the end of the benediction, as is usually done on festival days. In *Nusaḥ Sepharad*, the *Ḥazzan* concludes the benediction with a different formulation, which was apparently the formulation used in the Temple: "Blessed are You Lord, whom alone we serve with reverence."

The *Modim** benediction is usually recited in the same manner as in all the other Rosh ha-Shanah prayer services. In the Ashkenazic rite, just before the phrase "Inscribe all the children of Your covenant for a good life," the following prayer is inserted: "Our Father, Our King, remember Your compassion and suppress Your wrath, and eradicate pestilence, sword, famine . . . from us."

After the *Modim* benediction, the Priestly Blessing* is done, and in some congregations the *Ḥazzan* chants it in a special melody.

The *Sim Shalom** benediction is recited as usual, and most variants of the liturgy include an extended formulation of the addition made on the Ten Days of Repentance, "And in the book of life . . .". Then the *Piyyut ha-Yom Te'ammetzenu*—"On this day, strengthen us"—is said. The Ashkenazic custom is to recite only the beginning and end of it, but the Ashkenazim add another prayer formulation—"As of this day, bring us, joyous and happy, to the Temple in Jerusalem"—and the *Shaliaḥ Tzibbur* then concludes this last benediction of the *Amidah* prayer.

In the Ashkenazic rite, *Kaddish Titkabbal** is recited immediately, and, just before the word *Titkabbal*, the *Shofar* is blown again. In most congregations, they sound the triadic sequence of blasts. The *Kaddish* is then concluded.

The *Musaf* service closes in the usual manner. The Ashkenazic custom, in those congregations where the *Shofar* is not blown during the silent *Amidah* prayer, is to blow thirty blasts after reciting *Ein ke-Eloheinu*,* and another ten after the *Aleinu* prayer. To this are added the Song of the Day* and Psalm 27.*

After the service ends, it is customary in some communities to greet one another with a different blessing from that of the previous evening, *Gemar Ḥatimah Tovah*—"May you be sealed for a good life."

The *Minḥah* Service

The *Minḥah* service is like that of all other festival days, opening with the *Korbanot*, *Ashrei*, and *u-Va le-Zion Go'el.** If it is Shabbat, there is a Torah reading as on all Shabbat days.

The *Amidah* prayer is the same as for the *Ma'ariv* and *Shaḥarit* services, and no special additions are made in the *Amidah* repetition. After the *Amidah* repetition, *Avinu Malkenu* is recited (though Ashkenazim do not say it if Rosh ha-Shanah falls on Shabbat). Then the *Kaddish Titkabbal* is recited. The service ends with *Aleinu* and Psalm 27.

Tashlikh

The *Tashlikh* ceremony, which is based on kabbalistic lore, is essentially a symbolic act of "casting out" sins and transgressions. Everyone—except those who follow the Vilna Gaon@—goes to a place where there is water (many look for water that has live fish in it) in order to fulfill the biblical verse "And You will cast all sins into the depths of the sea" (Micah 7:19).

There are various set formulations for the petitions and supplications recited, which differ from one rite to another. Many follow the custom of shaking the hems of their clothing over the water, to symbolize discarding and repudiating their sins.

In some customs, the *Tashlikh* ceremony is not performed on Shabbat; so, if the first day of Rosh ha-Shanah falls on Shabbat, the ceremony is carried out on the second day of the festival.

The Second Day of Rosh ha-Shanah

The second day of the festival is, to some extent, similar to the second day of festivals in the Diaspora, because it is basically a repetition of the first day, and because it is celebrated as a result of doubts that existed regarding the actual day on which Rosh ha-Shanah should be celebrated. However, unlike with the festivals, these doubts were not caused by difficulties in transferring information from the Land of Israel to the Diaspora, but are part of the very essence of the day itself.[102] When the festivals were set according to the testimony of eyewitnesses who had seen the first appearance of the new moon, it was usually impossible to know whether the witnesses would indeed arrive to the *Beit Din* (religious court) during this first day to testify that they had seen the new moon on the previous night. For this reason, during Temple times, even the first day was held in doubt until the witnesses finally arrived. To be on the safe side, it was decided that whatever the case might be, Rosh ha-Shanah would be celebrated for two days. Certain generations did rely on astronomical calculations, and only one day was celebrated in the Land of Israel. In time, however, it became the practice, both in Israel and abroad, to celebrate Rosh ha-Shanah for two days. According to halakhic conceptions, the two constitute "extended holiness"—like one day that lasts for two days. The fundamental doubts regarding the second day of Rosh ha-Shanah still remain, and find expression in some of the laws and customs of this day.

There are other aspects, beyond the halakhic reasons, for celebrating two days of Rosh ha-Shanah. These two days are like the double facets of the year's commencement: the signing and sealing of the previous year, and the beginning of the new year. Mystical sources explain that although the two days are days of judgment, the first day is one of severe judgment, while on the second day judgment is tempered with mercy and is not as severe.

According to the Jewish calendar, as it is set nowadays, the second day of Rosh ha-Shanah never falls on Shabbat, but it can fall on a Sunday, a Tuesday, a Wednesday, or a Friday. When it falls on a Sunday, a few minor changes are made in the prayer formulations—to distinguish it from the preceding Shabbat, and because the *Shofar* was not blown on the first day.

---

[102] Rosh ha-Shanah is the only festival that occurs on the first day of the month.

Prayer Services on the Second Day of Rosh ha-Shanah

The *Ma'ariv* service is the same as on the first day of the festival. If it is the conclusion of Shabbat, the prayer *va-Todi'enu** is recited within the fourth benediction of the *Amidah*.

Since it is forbidden to prepare anything from the first day of Rosh ha-Shanah to the second, candles on the second day are lit after the appearance of the stars. As on the first night, two blessings are recited: "to kindle the *Yom Tov* light," and *she-Heḥeyanu.** However, since there is some doubt regarding the *she-Heḥeyanu* blessing, it is customary for some to place new seasonal fruit on the table and to eat it immediately after the *Kiddush*—before the ritual washing of the hands (see *Netilat Yadayyim**) or at the beginning of the festive meal.

The *Kiddush* ceremony is also the same as on the first day, but if it is the conclusion of Shabbat, it is combined with the *Havdalah** ceremony, in the same formulation used for other festivals (see *Yoknehaz**). Some eat foods whose names are favorable signs at this festive meal, as on the first night of Rosh ha-Shanah. Some women light candles on the second night just before the *Kiddush*, so that the *she-Heḥeyanu* blessing over the candles will also apply to the new fruit eaten at that time.

The *Shaḥarit* service is the same as on the first day, except that the Ashkenazim replace the customarily large number of *Piyyutim* with a different selection for the second day of the festival. After the repetition of the *Amidah* prayer, they recite *Avinu Malkenu.* Two Torah scrolls are taken out, as on the first day, and five persons are called up to read from the first scroll. The story of the *Akedah* (Genesis 22:1–24)—the Binding of Isaac—is frequently mentioned in the prayers for Rosh ha-Shanah, for it is an outstanding example of the self-sacrifice and devotion of our Patriarchs, and by its merit we ask for our own salvation and mercy. In the second scroll, they read the same *Maftir* as on the first day, about the *Musaf* festival sacrifices. The *Haftarah* is the words of consolation concerning Israel's redemption, which refer to the idea of remembrance—*Zikhronot* (see above), "Is Ephraim a dear son to me. . . . I remember him still" (Jeremiah 31:1–20). It also mentions the power of repentance and the reward that awaits those who choose the path of God.

The order of *Shofar* blowing is the same as on the first day. In the Ashkenazic rite, the *Shofar* blower recites the *she-Heḥeyanu* blessing on this day as well. It is customary for him to wear a new item of clothing, so that the blessing can also apply to the clothing, thereby eliminating any doubt about the validity of the *she-Heḥeyanu* blessing on the second day of the festival.

The *Musaf* service is the same as on the first day, except that different *Piyyutim* are recited.

The *Minḥah* service is also the same as on the first day, and those who do not perform the *Tashlikh* ceremony on the first day of the festival when it falls on Shabbat, do it now.

If it is a Friday, they recite an abbreviated form of *Kabbalat Shabbat*, as is done on all festivals that occur on Shabbat eve. At the end of the festival, the *Ma'ariv* service is conducted as it is usually done during the Ten Days of Repentance. After this, the *Havdalah* ceremony for the conclusion of a *Yom Tov** is performed.

Yom Kippur—The Day of Atonement

Yom Kippur, the tenth day of Tishrei, is a special day in the year, and in a certain sense, one might say that it is a unique entity, separate from all other days, and cannot be counted among them (see *Yoma* 20a). Although in the Torah Yom Kippur is called *Shabbat Shabbaton*—a Sabbath of complete rest (Leviticus 16:31)—the Halakhah does not consider it the strictest day of rest, and its sanctity and honor are less than that of Shabbat. Nevertheless, everyone recognizes that it is the most exalted of all days. The Talmud tractate that is entirely devoted to the laws for Yom Kippur is called *Yoma*, which means "the Day." Even among simple folk, it is known as "the Holy Day."

As indicated in the Torah, and expressed in prayer, this day is essentially one of atonement and purification from sin. The atonement obtained on this Day of Atonement does not result from one's repentance and self-purification but from its nature as a day of pardon and Divine revelation, emanating from God Himself. The very notion of pardon and atonement contains a conception of reality that transcends the bounds of common rationality. The recognition that there is pardon for sins means that, in some way, the past can be changed, that acts which were done, which existed in reality, may be considered as not having occurred at all.

Furthermore, the concept of crime and punishment is primarily based upon the assumption that they have a cause-and-effect relationship, and that, as the biblical verse says, "Evil shall slay the wicked" (Psalm 34:21). Forgiveness, therefore, is not only a change or reversal of the Supreme Law that defines good and evil but a violation of the laws of causality, an elimination and cancellation of the past. As it is said, "I have carried away your transgressions like a thick cloud, and your sins as a mist" (Isaiah 44:22). The pardoning of sins is not like removing a stain, which leaves a faint mark, but like a wind dispersing the clouds, leaving no sign of their having been there before. Forgiveness becomes, then, the actual creation of a new temporal order in which it is as if the sin never existed. Moreover, it is as though by the very power of repentance "sins have become merits" (*Yoma* 86b), and the past is rewritten according to another scale of values.

The sages say that repentance preceded the creation of the world (see *Midrash Genesis Rabbah*# 1), which means that repentance transports a person above and beyond the realities of the created world, with its order of time, forming, as it were, a new creation. And since Yom Kippur is the day of Divine pardon and forgiveness, it is the revelation of a Supreme Essence that transcends the limits of the whole world. The commentary on the verse "I, I alone, am He who wipes away your transgression for My sake" (Isaiah 43:25) places the words "I, I alone" on a higher level than the "I" with which the Ten Commandments begin (Exodus 20:2). This revelation, which transcends and cuts through the boundaries of the world, is the essence of this day, and its power is defined in the words of the sages as "the very day itself atones" (*Yoma* 87a).

In relation to this aspect of revelation from above, there are two basic things that man must do in order to be prepared for such atonement. When the Temple was in existence, there was a special order of sacrificial service practiced solely on Yom Kippur.[103] This order of service was performed entirely by the High Priest, and included his entry, alone, on that day only, into the Holy of Holies, and sending out the

---

[103] As detailed in Leviticus 16, and in the Mishnah, Tractate *Yoma*.

scapegoat into the wilderness. Now, though Temple services are no longer performed, the Yom Kippur prayers give prominence to the order of services in the Temple in lengthy, poetical formulations (there are a few versions; see *Seder ha-Avodah**). Even the custom of kneeling and prostration, as practiced in the Temple, is followed.

The second means of preparation for atonement is through purification and separating oneself from all profane matters. On Yom Kippur, all work is prohibited, just as on Shabbat (although the punishment is less severe), and it is also a day on which the commandment "and you shall afflict your souls" applies. This is fulfilled by refraining from all the physical pleasures of the world—eating and drinking, bathing, wearing leather shoes, and sexual relations.

Yom Kippur Eve

The eve of Yom Kippur has a special character of its own, because it contains certain customs and prayers in preparation for Yom Kippur itself. This is a twofold preparation. On one hand, there is an obligation to eat and drink on this day. Our sages have said that anyone who eats and drinks on the ninth day of Tishrei (Yom Kippur eve) is considered as one who fasts on both the ninth and tenth (*Berakhot* 8b). This day is one of joy, almost like a festival, and therefore *Taḥanun* is not recited, and in some places it is customary for people to greet each other with a festive blessing. On the other hand, there are also customs practiced on this day that involve atonement, purification, and confession.

The order of *Seliḥot** service is usually very short on this day—some do not recite it at all, though others extend it as on the eve of Rosh ha-Shanah. After *Seliḥot*, the ceremony of *Kapparot** is performed. According to mystical traditions, *Kapparot* should be performed in the early hours of the morning.

The weekday *Amidah* prayers are recited without *Taḥanun*, and some people wear festive clothing for the *Shaḥarit* service. In most rites, worshippers omit Psalm 100—"A psalm of Thanks"—because no thanks offering was brought to the Temple on this day. As for reciting *Avinu Malkenu*, customs differ, with some reciting it and others not. The custom is for all to purify themselves by immersing in a *Mikveh*,* both for the sake of purity, and as a part of the repentance process.

Although it would also be appropriate for all women (from the age of twelve) to immerse, this is not practiced everywhere.

Before *Minḥah*, some people follow the custom of *Malkot.** *Taḥanun* is not recited during the *Minḥah* service; however, at the end of the *Amidah* prayer each individual must offer a *Vidduy*—Confession of Sins. The formulation of the *Vidduy* for Yom Kippur—called *Al Ḥet**—is used, but the *Shaliaḥ Tzibbur* does not recite it. This confession is said considerably before the beginning of Yom Kippur, for fear that one may become fuzzy (due to excessive eating and drinking before the fast), and consequently unable to make the Confession on Yom Kippur itself (*Yoma* 37b).

But beyond the confession of sins before God, it is important for one to make peace with other people, asking for pardon and forgiveness for having sinned against them and having caused them harm, either purposely or by accident. Our sages say that Yom Kippur atones only for sins committed against God; however, there is no atonement from Heaven for sins committed against one's fellow humans (which are also considered sins against God) unless one is forgiven by them (*Yoma* 35b).

Just before the festival begins, a meal is eaten in preparation for the fast. This meal is called the *Se'udah Mafseket*—the concluding meal. In some places, *le-Shem Yiḥud** is recited before the meal, and many conduct the meal like a festive feast, with lit candles on the table. In many communities, there is a variety of *Ḥallah* bread and special foods for this meal. There are also various customs regarding foods that are not to be eaten at this meal, either because they would make the fast more difficult, or for other reasons.

In some communities, it is customary for parents to bless their children before going to the synagogue for *Kol Nidrei.** All ask pardon of each other.

Kol Nidrei

Kol Nidrei, the prelude to all the Yom Kippur prayer services, is a ceremonial custom performed in all Jewish communities and is one of the high points of the Yom Kippur services. A well-known legend claims that this formulation was recited by the Marranos—the forced converts in fifteenth-century Spain, who used to gather secretly, at the risk of their lives, to pray together. For them, this was a festive declaration that they annul all their coerced commitments to their assumed, false faith. In fact, however, the recital of *Kol Nidrei* on Yom Kippur eve is already mentioned in the Responsa of the *Geonim,** centuries before the Expulsion from Spain.

Actually, the point of the recitation of *Kol Nidrei* is halakhic and legalistic: it is a public ceremony for *Hattarat Nedarim**—absolution of vows and prohibitions—an *a priori* cancellation of vows that might be taken in the course of the coming year.[104] Whence, then, the deep emotional significance of *Kol Nidrei*? This significance derives from a wider and more comprehensive context: Yom Kippur is wholly a day of purification, in which God removes the burden of our sins accumulated over the past year. Corresponding to that, we below make a parallel movement of confessing our sins openly and casting them off.

Most of the vows made by a person during the year have little to do with holiness and spiritual elevation; usually they are angry reactions, or attempts to provoke someone. Life is full of aggravated expressions such as "If you do not do this I shall never speak to you again!" or "I shall never set foot in this house again!" Often, such statements are halakhically binding vows. The absolution of vows, and the inner resolution to annul them forever, not only removes obstacles from interpersonal relations but also relieves the spirit of unnecessary burdens, which should be thrown aside, together with all other sins and transgressions.

The phrase "vows and prohibitions" has an even broader meaning. Our inner freedom is curtailed not only by external factors but even more so by psychological patterns and inner constraints, such as wishes or plans that we build up, and "vows" that we make, so to speak, to ourselves, until we become enslaved by them. The release from all vows is therefore a ceremonial act of freeing oneself from these chains and granting one's soul the liberty to stand before God without this cumbersome burden. The *Kol Nidrei* ceremony, then, has a deep and

---

[104] A similar ceremony is performed on Rosh ha-Shanah eve also, and, in certain rites, at two or three other times of the year.

spiritual meaning that gives the worshipper a feeling of elevation of soul and freedom of spirit in preparation for the day of pardon and forgiveness.

Kol Nidrei, like all *Hattarat Nedarim* ceremonies, should begin before the onset of the Holy Day. It is the custom for men to wear a *Tallit** even in those congregations where it is not customary to wear them at this time of the day (see Chapter 16).

In many communities, the worshippers prepare themselves to receive this holy day by reciting words that stir the heart. In some congregations, all those present read set texts, such as certain psalms and accepted *Piyyutim*, *Vidduy* formulations, or prayer texts such as the *Tefillah Zakkah* ("pure prayer").[105]

The Holy Ark is then opened, and three Torah scrolls are taken out[106] and placed on the *Bimah*.[107] The first Torah scroll is given to the *Shaliaḥ Tzibbur*, and the others are given to two leading members of the community.[108] The reason for doing so is that the *Kol Nidrei* formulation contains the release and cancellation of legal prohibitions or bans; and since some of these bans are made over a Torah scroll, their annulment should also be made in this dignified manner. The three persons holding the Torah scrolls are thus like a religious court of law *(Beit Din)*, which is usually composed of three judges, and has the power to annul vows and cancel bans. The custom is for those holding Torah scrolls to walk with them around the *Bimah*, enabling the congregants to kiss the scrolls, and then return to their positions on either side of the *Shaliaḥ Tzibbur*, who is standing before the Ark.

The *Shaliaḥ Tzibbur* then begins by reciting a verse that expresses the spiritual significance of Yom Kippur: "Light is sown for the righteous, and gladness for the upright in heart" (Psalm 97:11). In some congregations, the *Shaliaḥ Tzibbur* repeats this verse several times, and the congregants respond by reciting the verse as well. Then *Kol Nidrei* is

---

[105] A prayer-confession composed by Rabbi Avraham Danzig,@ author of *Ḥayyei Adam.#*

[106] In some congregations, two, and in others only one scroll, the most ornate one, are taken out of the Ark.

[107] This is in accordance with what is written in the book *Peri Etz Ḥayyim.#*

[108] In certain localities it is customary to sell the privilege of taking out and holding the Torah scroll, especially the first scroll, and it is considered an act of great merit, which should be fulfilled in the best possible way.

recited three times, each time in a higher voice, in a traditional tune that stirs the heart deeply.

Having recited that, the *Shaliaḥ Tzibbur* reads the prayer of Moses pleading for Israel: "Please forgive the iniquity of this people, in keeping with the greatness of Your kindness, and as You have forgiven this people since Egypt and until now" (Numbers 14:19). He then adds, "And there it is stated," after which all the congregants recite three times the continuation of the same verse: "And the Lord said, 'I have pardoned in accordance with your words.'" The verse in its entirety is then repeated once again by the *Shaliaḥ Tzibbur*. This statement is not merely a repetition of a pardon that had once been given. Rather, the Holy Congregation is acting as "the Congregation of God"; and it is by this very power of God's holiness within them that they say, as though in God's Name, "I have pardoned in accordance with your words."

After this, the *Shaliaḥ Tzibbur* recites the *she-Heḥeyanu* blessing for the festival day in a loud voice.[109] On all other festival days, this blessing is recited over the *Kiddush* cup of wine; but since Yom Kippur is a fast day, the blessing should be made for the sanctity of the day alone.[110] At the conclusion of this blessing, the Torah scrolls are returned to the Ark and the prayer service is continued.

The *Ma'ariv* Service

If Yom Kippur falls on Shabbat, the *Kabbalat Shabbat* service is recited in the same way as on all festivals which occur on Shabbat.

The *Ma'ariv* service is the same as for all festivals but contains one change in the Reading of the *Shema:* the sentence *Barukh Shem Kevod Malkhuto le-Olam va-Ed**—"Blessed be the name of the glory of His Kingdom for ever and ever"—is recited aloud (as against the rest of the year, during which this phrase is whispered). This is done in all the prayers of Yom Kippur.

---

[109] The congregants should also recite this with him in a lower tone, and try to finish it slightly ahead of him, so as to be able to respond to his blessing with Amen.

[110] Women who lit candles in honor of the festival, and have already recited the *she-Heḥeyanu* blessing over them, do not repeat it here.

In most congregations, before the beginning of the *Amidah*, the verse "For on this day atonement shall be made for you, to cleanse you, that you may be clean from all your sins before the Lord" (Leviticus 16:30) is recited. If it is Shabbat, this is preceded by *ve-Shamru** (Exodus 31:16–17).

In the Yom Kippur *Amidah* prayer, there are seven benedictions. The first three are exactly the same as those for the Rosh ha-Shanah prayer, including all the additions made in the *Kedushah* benediction (see above). The fourth benediction (the central one) is the special benediction for Yom Kippur, which basically resembles the central benediction for *Yom Tov* days in general, and Rosh ha-Shanah in particular.

This central benediction begins with *Attah Beḥartanu* and *Ya'aleh ve-Yavo*, in which the phrase "on this Yom Kippur" is said. After this begins the section of special prayers for this day: "Forgive our wrongdoings on this Day of Atonement. . . . Wipe away and remove our transgressions and sins from before Your eyes, as it is written, 'I, even I alone, am He who wipes away your transgressions' (Isaiah 43:25); 'I have wiped away your transgressions like a thick cloud' (Isaiah 44:22); 'For on this day atonement shall be made for you' (Leviticus 16:30); 'For You are the Pardoner of Israel and the Forgiver of the tribes of Jeshurun.'"

Most rites go on to the conclusion of the benediction: "Blessed are You, Lord, King who pardons and forgives our sins and the sins of His people, the House of Israel, and removes our trespasses each and every year; King over the whole world, who sanctifies (Shabbat), Israel, and Yom Kippur." The last three *Amidah* benedictions are then recited, as on Rosh ha-Shanah.

At the end of the *Amidah* prayer, the *Vidduy* is recited: first *Ashamnu*,* and then *Al Ḥet*, and the *Amidah* is concluded.

When Yom Kippur falls on Shabbat, *va-Yekhulu** and the *Me'ein Sheva** benediction are recited. After that, it is the custom in all Jewish congregations to recite the order of *Seliḥot** services, which are similar to the usual *Seliḥot* recited on fast days, as well as many other supplications and *Piyyutim*. The Thirteen Attributes* are also recited several times, and in many prayer rites they are recited twenty-six times (the numerical value of the Tetragrammaton) in the course of the day.

The prayers, *Piyyutim*, and *Pizmonim* vary from one tradition to another. The Ashkenazic version includes the largest number of them, though not all of them are recited everywhere.

In most rites, the *Vidduy* and *Al Ḥet* are repeated. In the Ashkenazic rite, *Avinu Malkenu* is recited at the end of the *Seliḥot* service, except when Yom Kippur falls on Shabbat.

In most congregations, they recite Psalm 24—"The earth is the Lord's, and all therein," as on the eve of Rosh ha-Shanah, but others recite it at the end of the series of psalms for the day. Most congregations also recite the first four psalms from the Book of Psalms.

It is customary after the *Ma'ariv* prayer for congregants to recite *Piyyutim* that elevate the thoughts and awaken the heart. Most Ashkenazim recite the entire *Shir ha-Yiḥud.** During the night, many study the five chapters of the Mishnah, Tractate *Yoma*, which deal with the laws for Yom Kippur. Some prayer books include a fixed order of study, compiled of texts from the Bible, the Mishnah, and the *Zohar.*

The *Shaḥarit* Service

In general, the *Shaḥarit* service resembles the one for Rosh ha-Shanah, and in most rites they are identical until the *Nishmat* prayer. Some do not recite the blessing "who has provided me with my every need" in the *Birkhot ha-Shaḥar,** because it refers to wearing leather shoes. Some make this blessing at the conclusion of Yom Kippur, while putting on leather shoes again.

In the Ashkenazic rite, there are special *Yotzerot* for Yom Kippur that are recited within the *Yotzer Or* benediction. If it is Shabbat, all make the appropriate additions for that day.

The silent *Amidah* prayer is the same as in the *Ma'ariv* service. In almost all versions of the prayers, *Piyyutim* are recited within the *Amidah* repetition. Each version has its own series of *Piyyutim*, but there is some overlap. The largest number of *Piyyutim* are found in the Ashkenazic rite, but not all are actually recited, even though they are recorded in their *Maḥzor.*

The repetition of the *Amidah* prayer contains the *Vidduy* within the fourth benediction (some recite the version of Rav Nissim Gaon,@

or other forms of the *Vidduy*), as well as *Al Ḥet*, and in certain rites, numerous additional *Piyyutim*. The rest of the prayer is the same as for Rosh ha-Shanah.

After the *Amidah* prayer, *Avinu Malkenu* is recited (the Ashkenazim omit it if it is Shabbat). In *Nusaḥ Sepharad*, they recite the Psalm of the Day and Psalm 27.

Torah Readings

The ceremony for taking the Torah scrolls out of the Ark is the same as for Rosh ha-Shanah: the Thirteen Attributes, the same formulation of the *Ribbono Shel Olam* prayer, and all the additions, as they are made in the different rites. Two scrolls are taken out, and six persons are called up to read from the first one (seven, if it is Shabbat). No additional persons are called up.[111]

The Torah reading is about the Yom Kippur service in the Sanctuary, which is described just after the story of the death of Aaron's sons (Leviticus 16:1–34). This passage describes the holy rituals performed by the High Priest in the inner Sanctuary, especially his entry into the Holy of Holies on Yom Kippur, and about the pardoning of sins on that day. It is written[112] that one should be moved to tears when reading about the death of Aaron's sons. Such sorrow contains an element of pardon and a promise of recompense.

In the second scroll, the *Maftir* is read, which deals with the Yom Kippur *Musaf* sacrifices (Numbers 29:7–11). The *Haftarah* is the selection in which the prophet instructs the people of Israel how to conduct a fast day so that it will be "a day pleasing to the Lord" (Isaiah 57:14 to 58:14). In the blessings after the *Haftarah*, some say "King who pardons and forgives," while others say "And Your word is true and enduring for ever."

After the Torah reading, Ashkenazic congregations (and various

---

[111] Unlike regular Sabbaths, in which it is permitted to call up to a Torah reading more than seven people.

[112] *Magen Avraham*[#] on *Shulḥan Arukh, Oraḥ Ḥayyim*, 621, in the name of the *Zohar*[#] and Rabbi Isaac Luria.[@]

others) commemorate the dead (see *Yizkor**). This is supported by a *midrash* (*Sifrei*,# Deuteronomy 21:8) which says that the dead, too, need atonement. That is why they mention the dead, pledge charity for the sake of uplifting their souls, and pray for rest and peace for their souls.

The Torah scrolls are then returned to the Ark, as is done on Shabbat and all festivals.

The *Musaf* Service

Among Ashkenazim before beginning the silent *Amidah*, the *Ḥazzan* says his personal prayer, *Hineni he-ani mi-Ma'as* ("Here I am, deficient in meritorious deeds"), and some add other prayers to this. The half *Kaddish* is recited in all rites, and the congregants then recite the silent *Amidah*.

The order of benedictions in this prayer is the same as on all festival days; the three first benedictions are as in the *Shaḥarit* service. Some details vary among the different prayer rites in the central benediction. However, they all begin with *Attah Beḥartanu* ("You have chosen us") and *Mipenei Ḥataeinu* ("Because of our sins"). Ashkenazim also recite the verses about the *Musaf* sacrifices for the day (and for Shabbat, if it is Shabbat). Then comes the section "Pardon our iniquities." In all versions, the fourth benediction is concluded as in the *Shaḥarit* service. After the *Amidah* prayer, the *Vidduy* and *Al Ḥet* are recited.

In nearly all versions of the liturgy, *Piyyutim* and other additions are inserted. These *Piyyutim* vary among the different traditions, and the Ashkenazic rite contains a large number of *Piyyutim* (though not all are recited by all). In the Ashkenazic rite, *u-Netanneh Tokef* is recited just before the *Kedushah*.

The *Keter Kedushah* is recited (some interweave a few *Piyyutim* among its phrases), and the third *Amidah* benediction is concluded in the usual way for the Days of Awe. The fourth benediction begins in the same way as in the silent *Amidah* prayer, until the end of the verses about the *Musaf* sacrifices (among those who recite these verses). In most congregations, they say *Aleinu*, and the Ashkenazic custom is to kneel or prostrate oneself when reciting the words "We bend the knee, bow down and praise" (see *Keri'ah**).

In nearly all rites, a poetic rendition of the *Seder ha-Avodah**—the order of sacrificial service in the Temple on Yom Kippur—is now recited. Before he begins this, the *Shaliaḥ Tzibbur* recites introductory *Piyyutim.* In the Ashkenazic rite, it is *Oḥilah* ("I place my hope in God"). The *Seder ha-Avodah* itself, in all rites, is a long *Piyyut,* in alphabetical order, which begins with the creation of the world and ends with a detailed account of various rituals and sacrifices done by the High Priest in the Temple on Yom Kippur. There are variations, according to *Nusaḥ,* in the choice of *Piyyut* (ancient versions had additional *Piyyutim*). In most rites (including *Nusaḥ Sepharad*), they recite the *Piyyut Attah Konanta*—"You established the world"—which is ascribed to Rabbi Yossi ben Yossi.[@] In the Ashkenazic rite, they recite the *Piyyut Amitz Koah ve-Rav Onim*—"Strong in power and great in might"—ascribed to Rabbi Meshullam bar Kalonymus.[@]

In Ashkenazic congregations, and many others, when they reach the place in the *Piyyut* where it says, "And when the *Kohanim** standing in the Temple court read the glorious and awesome Name . . . they would bend their knees, bow down and fall on their faces," the *Ḥazzan* and the entire congregation bow down to the ground three times. A cloth or a piece of paper must be placed between one's head and the floor (not between one's knees and the floor, as many erroneously do), because it is forbidden to bow down on a stone floor, except in the Temple.

At the end of the *Seder ha-Avodah* is the *Piyyut* "How radiant was the High Priest when he came out of the Holy of Holies in peace." Most prayer rites have alphabetically arranged *Piyyutim* that describe and pay homage to the splendid appearance of the High Priest, based on an actual description of the High Priest in the apocryphal book of Ben Sira.[#]

Now come various *Piyyutim* (which vary from one rite to another), that begin, "Fortunate is the eye that saw all these, indeed, when the ear hears of it, our soul grieves." These *Piyyutim* express sorrow for the destruction of the Temple, and hope for its rebuilding, through the merit of our fasting and atonement for our sins.

Ashkenazim then recite some *Seliḥot* that recall the troubles of our nation in its exile. Next is the *Piyyut Eleh Ezkerah* ("These things do I remember"), a midrashic account of the death of Ten Holy Martyrs who were among the great sages of Israel executed by the Romans over the course of a few generations. This commemoration of the Ten Martyrs relates to the services for Yom Kippur in two ways. The *Shaharit* Torah reading, about the death of Aaron's sons "when they drew near before the Lord" (Leviticus 16:1), is analogous to the death of these martyrs. Secondly, our sages have said (see *Mo'ed Katan* 28a) that the deaths of righteous people bring atonement for Israel, especially when they die in public sanctification of the Divine name, as these Ten Holy Martyrs did, as is stated in this *Piyyut*. According to tradition, Rabbi Akiva@, who was one of these martyrs, was executed on Yom Kippur.

Each *Nusah* continues with different *Selihot* and *Piyyutim*, then the *Vidduy* is recited (some recite the Grand Confession), and *Al Het*, followed by more *Selihot* and words of praise, and the fourth benediction is concluded as usual. Finally, the last three benedictions of the *Amidah* prayer are recited in the same formulation as in the *Musaf* service for Rosh ha-Shanah, with all the appropriate additions and changes.

Among Ashkenazim, the *Shaliah Tzibbur* recites *Kaddish Titkabbal** to conclude the *Musaf* service, without reciting *Ein ke-Eloheinu** and *Aleinu.**

Those who do not recite the Song of the Day after the *Shaharit* service, recite it now, after the *Musaf* service. In some congregations, Psalm 24 and a prayer for one's livelihood are recited.

The *Minhah* Service

The *Minhah* service on Yom Kippur has some unique aspects, in that it contains both Torah and *Haftarah* readings (even if it is a weekday), and, because it is so close to the *Ne'ilah* service (see below), certain things are omitted and left to be recited in that latter service. Ashkenazim recite only the *Korbanot* section, and omit *Ashrei** and *u-Va le-Zion Go'el,** which are recited later, in the *Ne'ilah* service. If it is Shabbat, the verse "As for me, may my prayer come to You, Lord, at an acceptable time" (Psalm 69:14) is not said. Neither the Thirteen Attributes* nor *Ribbono Shel Olam** are said while the Torah scroll is being taken out of the Ark, as is done in the *Shaharit* service. Only one scroll is needed, and three persons are called up to read. The Torah selection (Leviticus 18:1–30) is a warning against the abhorrent practices of other nations, and expressly prohibits all sexual perverseness. These readings are meant to arouse the sinners to repentance, and to evoke feelings of remorse among those who have not yet sinned, but who may yet be carried away by the desires of their hearts.

After the Torah reading, the third person called up reads the *Haftarah* for the Yom Kippur *Minḥah* service, which consists of the entire Book of Jonah. It is customary to conclude with the verses from Micah 7:18–20. The purpose of this reading is to illustrate how much can be attained through the power of repentance, both personally and for the entire community, and how merciful God is toward sinners who reform their ways. The blessings for the *Haftarah* are then recited, but in most places only the first four are read (and not all five, as in the *Shaḥarit* service).

The half *Kaddish** is not recited at the end of these readings; the Torah scroll is returned to the Ark, and then the half *Kaddish* is recited before beginning the silent *Amidah* prayer. This *Amidah* is the same as that of the *Ma'ariv* and *Shaḥarit* services, with no changes. In the repetition of the *Amidah*, there are additional *Piyyutim* in most rites, many of which were composed especially for this prayer. There are quite a large number of *Piyyutim* in the Ashkenazic rite.

There is no Priestly Blessing in this *Minḥah* service, in any rite, and instead, the *Shaliaḥ Tzibbur* recites the formulation "Our God . . . bless us with the threefold blessing . . . ," After the *Amidah*, *Avinu Malkenu* is recited, though Ashkenazim do not recite it on Shabbat. In some instances, it is also omitted if it is getting late, and the *Ne'ilah* service might not begin on time.

In most rites, if it is Shabbat, the *Tzidkatekha** verses are recited. It is customary, except among the Ashkenazim, to conclude with *Aleinu*.

The *Ne'ilah* Service

The *Ne'ilah** service is the prayer that concludes the Yom Kippur prayers. In mishnaic and talmudic times, this prayer service was recited also on major public fast days, but in our own times it has become a special prayer, said on Yom Kippur alone.

Our sages differed as to whether the service is called *Ne'ilah*—which means "locking up"—because it is recited at the time for "locking the Temple gates" or at the time for "locking the Heavenly gates" (the end of the day). Certain differences ensue about when to set the exact time for this prayer service. The halakhic ruling is that the time for *Ne'ilah* is at the end of the day, and it should be recited before evening arrives, yet it sometimes happens that the prayer ends after dark. Our sages have said that "the very day itself atones" (*Yoma* 37b) and the culminating point for atonement on this day is at the very end, the hour of the *Ne'ilah* service. For this reason, this prayer contains much supplication, and the Thirteen Attributes are repeated over and over again.

In all versions of the Ashkenazic rite, they begin this prayer service with *Ashrei* and *u-Va le-Zion Go'el* (but not the *Korbanot** section, which was already recited in the *Minḥah* service). The other rites usually include a *Piyyut* that begins *El Nora Alilah*—"O God, awesome in deeds, grant us pardon at this time of the *Ne'ilah*"—and then *Ashrei*. In most congregations the Ark is opened when the *Amidah* repetition begins, and it is left open until after *Kaddish Titkabbal** at the end of the service.

In both the silent and the public *Amidah* prayers of the *Ne'ilah* service, all instances of the words "Inscribe us" are replaced by "Seal us," because this time of prayer is the hour of final judgment, and all are "signed and sealed" by the heavenly court of justice.

The silent *Amidah* prayer is the same as in the *Shaḥarit* service, with one change at the end—the *Vidduy* is recited, but not *Al Ḥet*.

After the *Vidduy* comes a special prayer for *Ne'ilah*, "What shall we say before You, who dwells on High," which is essentially the same in all rites. However, the Ashkenazic version contains a section "You extend a hand to transgressors." This prayer is about man's smallness and insignificance before God, and about how God does not want to punish the sinners or to have them die, but rather desires their repentance, which gives life to the world.

The longer version of the *Keter Kedushah** is recited, as in the *Musaf* service. The fourth benediction includes *Piyyutim* and the

Vidduy. Then the *Seliḥot*, in which the Thirteen Attributes are repeated frequently, are recited (in the Ashkenazic rite, they are recited thirteen times).

The *Shaliaḥ Tzibbur* recites the added prayer "You extend a hand to transgressors" to its end and concludes the fourth benediction in the usual way. He then recites the last three benedictions: *Retzeh** as usual, and *Modim** and *Sim Shalom** in the formulation used in the *Musaf* service. If there is still time (namely, if it is still before sunset), the Priestly Blessing is recited, except by Ashkenazim in the Diaspora. In some places, part of the *Seliḥot* service is recited later, in order to have sufficient time to say the Priestly Blessing properly.

After the *Amidah* repetition for *Ne'ilah*, most congregations recite *Avinu Malkenu* (changing "inscribe us" to "seal us"), even if Yom Kippur falls on Shabbat. Although normally one does not say words of supplication on Shabbat, now it is a question of "If not now, when?" and it is considered a time of emergency in which one must beg and plead, even on Shabbat itself. In the Ashkenazic rite, the *Ḥazzan* and congregants recite this aloud, sentence by sentence.

In most traditions, the *Ne'ilah* prayer is concluded in a special way, yet the actual details differ in each version. Ashkenazim all recite *Shema Yisrael* once, and then *Barukh Shem Kevod** aloud three times. Then the phrase *Ha-Shem Hu ha-Elohim*—"The Lord is God"—is recited seven times.

The *Shaliaḥ Tzibbur* then recites the full *Kaddish*, and before saying *Titkabbal* it is customary in most versions to blow the *Shofar*. Some do so before the *Kaddish*, and some do so afterward. The time set for sounding the *Shofar* is twenty-one minutes after sunset (some make it thirty-three, and some even forty-five minutes after sunset).

There are various meanings given for this sounding of the *Shofar*. Some think that it is meant to indicate to all the people that the fast has ended. (Sometimes the *Shofar* is blown a little earlier, and then it should be announced that the fast must be maintained a little longer.) Others explain that this is in remembrance of the *Shofar* blast blown on Yom Kippur of the Jubilee Year (*Tur*,# *Oraḥ Ḥayyim* 624), when all lands return to their original owners, and slaves are freed from their masters. This also alludes to our release from the yoke of our sins and transgressions. Others yet suggest that it is a sound heralding victory, promising us that we have been fully acquitted in judgment and are inscribed for a good year.

Among the Ashkenazim, *Shofar*-blowing customs differ. Some blow a series of four blasts: *Teki'ah—Shevarim—Teru'ah—Teki'ah;* and some blow only a *Teki'ah Gedolah*—a single, sustained blast. In some communities, someone reads aloud the order of *Shofar* blasts to the *Shofar* blower, but others do not do so.

After the *Shofar* blowing, it is customary among Ashkenazim to call out in a loud voice, and with great emotional awakening, "Next year in Jerusalem." The *Shaliaḥ Tzibbur* then concludes the *Kaddish.*

In some congregations, the *Ma'ariv* service starts immediately. Some recite the *Ketoret* section and *Aleinu.*

Conclusion of the Festival

The *Ma'ariv* service at the conclusion of Yom Kippur is the same as the conclusion for any other festival day, and includes *Attah Ḥonantanu.* When Yom Kippur occurs on Shabbat, one does not recite *vi-Yehi No'am** and *u-Va le-Zion Go'el*, nor *ve-Yitten Lekha.**

After the prayer service, the *Havdalah* ceremony is performed, with blessings over wine and a lit taper. This blessing is made over a candle that had been burning from the eve of Yom Kippur until its conclusion (since it was forbidden to use fire during the day). One who does not have such a candle should at least transfer fire from somebody else's candle that had been burning all day long; and if even that is not possible, then one should not make the blessing over firelight at all. If Yom Kippur occurs on Shabbat, the blessing over spices is also made, as in the *Havdalah* ceremony at the conclusion of Shabbat. However, Sepharadim, and some Ashkenazim, omit this blessing.

Even though it is permissible to do *Kiddush Levanah** ("Sanctification of the New Moon") earlier, it is customary to wait until the conclusion of Yom Kippur. The manifest reason is that it is appropriate to make this blessing in a time of joy, but according to mystic lore, Yom Kippur itself is the rectification of the "moon's waning," so it seems more appropriate to recite it at this particular time.

The day following Yom Kippur is treated as a quasi-festival day. In many congregations, friends bless each other with holiday greetings, and the meal is also conducted in festive style. Among Ashkenazim, this day is known as *Shem ha-Shem*, "God's Name," because one now reverts to the phrase *ha-El ha-Kadosh*, ("the Holy God") instead of *ha-Melekh ha-Kadosh* ("the Holy King") in the third blessing of the *Amidah* prayers.

It is a widespread custom to "link *mitzvah* with *mitzvah*"[113] by starting to build the *Sukkah** immediately after the conclusion of Yom Kippur, or at least to make a small beginning by laying plans for its construction.

---

[113] *Remah*® on *Shulḥan Arukh, Oraḥ Ḥayyim*, end of sec. 624.

CHAPTER TWELVE ❧ *Special Days*

THERE ARE MANY days throughout the year that are in principle ordinary weekdays but which nevertheless have some special significance, indicated among other things by various additions and changes in the regular order of prayer. These days are not all cut from the same cloth; some are linked with the monthly cycle and others with the annual cycle. They include days of joy and of mourning, days of reflection and of remembrance. For each one, there are the appropriate changes in the prayer services and in the Grace After Meals.*

Rosh Ḥodesh—The New Moon

In several places in the Bible, *Rosh Ḥodesh** is mentioned together with Shabbat and festival days: "And in the day of your gladness, and in your solemn days, and in the beginnings of your months" (Numbers 10:10). *Rosh Ḥodesh* is also referred to as a *Mo'ed* ("festival"; *Pesaḥim* 77a). As the first day of the new month, it begins the count of the days of the month and of the festivals. Since earliest times, it was the custom to observe two days of *Rosh Ḥodesh* in some months (see I Samuel 20:27). This was so because *Rosh Ḥodesh* was declared in accordance with the testimony of eyewitnesses who saw the new crescent moon, which often involved delays and other contingencies.

In our day, we use a fixed annual calendar with lunar months of either twenty-nine or thirty days. When the month has thirty days, the last day of that month is designated the first day of *Rosh Ḥodesh*, and the first day of the next month is the second day of *Rosh Ḥodesh;* the rest of the month is calculated from this day. Halakhically speaking, there is no difference between the two days.

The Torah only refers to the days of *Rosh Ḥodesh* in connection with the *Musaf** offering—the special sacrifice that must be offered together with the ordinary daily one (see Numbers 28:11–15). It was the custom in biblical times to observe *Rosh Ḥodesh* as a day of joyful celebration on which people gathered and held various ceremonies (see Isaiah 1:13 and 66:23); festive family meals were held (see I Samuel 20), as were pilgrimage visits to the prophets (see I Kings 4:23). It was also a holiday from work (see Amos 8:5). Most of these customs were dropped by the Second Temple period, and hardly any of them still remain.

As *Rosh Ḥodesh* is a day of joy, we do not fast on it nor say *Taḥanun,** nor can eulogies be made then.[114] There is also a halakhic ruling, which is not always observed, to hold a festive meal on *Rosh Ḥodesh.*[115] Since earliest times, Jewish women have been accustomed to refrain from work on that day.[116] In certain places no work at all was done, and in others only some kinds were forbidden. Men sometimes joined in this prohibition by refraining from heavy labor, while some people simply avoid doing certain things on *Rosh Ḥodesh*, such as having a haircut or paring their nails.

To these customs one may add the special prayers instituted for *Rosh Ḥodesh.* In the three regular *Amidah** prayers, the prayer *Ya'aleh ve-Yavo** is added just before the end of *Retzeh,** with the phrase "on this day of *Rosh Ḥodesh.*" If one forgot to recite this prayer in the *Shaḥarit* or *Minḥah* services (but not in *Ma'ariv*), one must repeat the entire *Amidah. Ya'aleh ve-Yavo* is likewise inserted in the Grace After Meals just before *Boneh Yerushalayim.** If one forgot to recite *Ya'aleh ve-Yavo* in the Grace After Meals, and only remembered to do so from the fourth benediction and onward, one need not go back to the beginning; instead, there is a special formulation to be recited in such an event.[117] *Rosh Ḥodesh* is likewise mentioned in the *Berakha Me'ein Shalosh.**

The *Ma'ariv* service for *Rosh Ḥodesh* is as usual for weekdays, apart from the inclusion of *Ya'aleh ve-Yavo.* In a congregation, it is customary

---

[114] See *Shulḥan Arukh, Oraḥ Ḥayyim,* 418 and 420.

[115] *Ibid.*, 419.

[116] This custom is already mentioned in the Jerusalem Talmud, *Ta'anit* 1:6. See also *Shulḥan Arukh, Oraḥ Ḥayyim* 417.

[117] See *Shulḥan Arukh, Oraḥ Ḥayyim* 188.

to make a public reminder to recite it just before the *Amidah*. This is not considered an interruption, because it is done for the sake of prayer. However, in the *Shaḥarit* service this is forbidden.

Through the *Amidah*, *Shaḥarit* is like the regular weekday service, except for the addition of *Ya'aleh ve-Yavo*. Some also add in the *Korbanot** section the verses prescribing the *Rosh Ḥodesh* sacrifice (Numbers 28:11–15), thereby fulfilling the verse, "so we will render as bullocks the words of our lips" (Hosea 14:3). At the end of the *Amidah*, half *Hallel** is recited. The reason for this is that *Hallel* on *Rosh Ḥodesh* is not required by law but derives from a Babylonian practice dating to the beginning of the talmudic era. As a result, there are also varying customs and texts for the benediction recited before and after reading the *Hallel*. On *Rosh Ḥodesh* Tevet, the full *Hallel* is recited, because that day is part of the Ḥanukkah festival (see below). On *Rosh Ḥodesh* Tishrei, which is also Rosh ha-Shanah, the New Year festival, *Hallel* is not recited at all (see Chapter 11).

Following *Hallel*, *Kaddish Titkabbal** is recited to mark the conclusion of the main part of *Shaḥarit*. In *Nusaḥ Sepharad* this is followed by the Song of the Day,* and some add Psalm 104.* The Torah scrolls are then taken out of the Ark. The Torah portion for the day, Numbers 28:1–15, is then read, for which four people are called up.

Following the Torah reading, the half *Kaddish** is recited. In *Nusaḥ Sepharad*, *Ashrei** and *u-Va le-Zion Go'el** are now said; in the Ashkenazic rite, the Torah scrolls are first returned to the Ark, followed by *Ashrei* and *u-Va le-Zion Go'el*. In either event, Psalm 20* is omitted, as it opens with the words "May the Lord answer you in the day of trouble," and this is a day of joy. The half *Kaddish* is again read, and the *Musaf* prayer for *Rosh Ḥodesh* is recited.

According to kabbalistic teachings, the *Tefillin** should be removed before *Musaf* for *Rosh Ḥodesh*. Some remove it before the half *Kaddish*, as it is the introduction to the *Musaf* service; others do so immediately after it, in order to complete the recital of four *Kaddish* prayers with the *Tefillin*.

The *Amidah* of the *Musaf* service for *Rosh Ḥodesh* is composed, as are most *Musaf* services, of three parts. The first three and last three benedictions are the same as in any other *Amidah*, while the fourth benediction is a special one for *Rosh Ḥodesh*, beginning with the ancient *Piyyut* "New moon festivals You assigned to Your people." This is essentially concerned with the special status of *Rosh Ḥodesh*, recalling the sacrifices offered on that day, followed by a prayer for redemption, for the return of Israel to its land, and for the rebuilding of the Temple and the restoration of the Temple worship. There are minor variations in the wording of this *Piyyut* in the different prayer rites. In almost all of them, the passage concerning the *Rosh Ḥodesh* sacrifices as given in the Torah (Numbers 28:11) and the accompanying meal offerings and libations, is read.

This is followed by a prayer for the coming month, beginning in most rites with the words "Our God and God of our fathers, renew for us . . .". Twelve things are requested, corresponding to the twelve months of the year: "for goodness and blessing, for joy and gladness, for deliverance and consolation, for maintenance and sustenance, for a good life and for peace, for the pardoning of sin and forgiveness of iniquity." In most rites, the words "for atonement of transgression" are added in leap years (which have thirteen months)—sometimes only until the end of the second Adar.[118] *Nusaḥ Sepharad* inserts the petition "May it be Your will that this month will bring the end of all our troubles and the beginning of our souls' redemption," and in all rites the conclusion is as follows: "For You have chosen Your people Israel from all the nations and instituted for them the rules relating to the new moon. Blessed are You, O Lord, who sanctifies Israel and the New Moon festivals."

The essence of this blessing is that Moses and Aaron were commanded to establish the new moons just before the exodus from Egypt (Exodus 12:1–2), and that this is related to the election of Israel as the chosen people. According to oral tradition, it was at that time that Moses received the laws on how to fix the time of each new month. Hence, the sanctity of *Rosh Ḥodesh* does not come automatically with the astronomical reappearance of the moon; rather, it depends on the sanctification of the new months, decreed by the Jewish religious court. Hence, the formulation of the conclusion of the blessing, "who sanctifies Israel and the new moons": He sanctifies Israel, who, in turn, sanctify and decree the new moons.

---

[118] Which is the extra month added in leap years. For a deeper understanding of this concept, a discussion of the Jewish calendar is required, which goes beyond the scope of this book.

After the congregation has recited the *Amidah*, the *Shaliaḥ Tzibbur** repeats it. In all rites, except in the Ashkenzaic rite, he utters a shortened version of the *Kedushah** of Shabbat *Musaf* (known as the *Kedushah* of *Keter**), beginning with the words "A crown of glory is given to You," and continuing with the regular weekday *Kedushah* formulation. Following the repetition of the *Amidah*, the service concludes as usual. In the Ashkenazic rite, the Song of the Day, which was not recited earlier, is now said with the addition of Psalm 104.*

Minḥah for *Rosh Ḥodesh* is identical to the ordinary weekday service, except for the addition of *Ya'aleh ve-Yavo* and the omission of the *Taḥanun* prayer.

When *Rosh Ḥodesh* occurs on Shabbat, there are special prayers and Torah readings that combine Shabbat and *Rosh Ḥodesh* (see Chapter 9).

Ḥol ha-Mo'ed
The Intermediate Days of a Festival

These are the days between the first and last days of the Pesaḥ and Sukkot festivals. The term *Ḥol ha-Mo'ed* is mentioned in the Mishnah* as *Ḥulo Shel Mo'ed* (*Megillah* 4:2) and since then has become the common term. In rabbinic writings, it is often referred to simply as *Mo'ed*,[119] especially when it is mentioned in conjunction with the term *Yom Tov*.[120]

The term *Ḥol ha-Mo'ed*[121] well describes the essential nature of these days. On Pesaḥ and Sukkot, the first day and last day of the festivals (in the Diaspora—the first two days, and the last day plus an additional day) are holy days during which no work is permitted (except for the preparation of food). The intermediate days somewhat resemble weekdays, in that certain kinds of work are permitted on them, while others are forbidden. The uniqueness of these days, as

---

[119] See *Mishnah*, Tractate *Mo'ed Katan*.

[120] *Yom Tov*—literally, "good day,"—is the common term for a festival day.

[121] *Ḥol* means weekday; *Mo'ed* means festival. *Ḥol ha-Mo'ed* is thus literally "festival-weekday."

stated in the Torah, is that on them special *Musaf* sacrifices were offered in the Temple (see Numbers 28:24; 29:17–34).

Halakhically, these days are holy days on which it is forbidden to fast or mourn, as well as to engage in any actual work (even writing). However, in many cases these prohibitions are lifted, mainly to avoid the considerable financial losses that might be caused by them, or because of festival needs or vital public requirements. On the one hand, our sages warned against treating lightly the sanctity of these days, saying, "He who despises the festival days has no share in the world to come" (Mishnah, *Avot* 3:11). But in practice, these days are indeed "the weekdays of the festival": while the main laws of the festival apply (no leaven on Pesaḥ, *Sukkah** and *Arba'ah Minim** on Sukkot), and there is a certain festive atmosphere, they are quite similar to weekdays with regard to work.

The liturgy for these days is likewise a combination of weekdays and festivals. In most congregations in the Land of Israel, *Tefillin* are not worn on *Ḥol ha-Mo'ed*. Most of the Ashkenazim in the Diaspora do wear them, but even they often refrain from saying the usual benedictions, and remove them before reciting *Hallel* and *Musaf*. This issue was once a matter of controversy among the *Rishonim*,* but most congregations today follow the view of the *Zohar*# that *Tefillin* should not be worn on such days, as to do so would detract from the sanctity of the festival as an *Ot*—a sign of the Divine covenant between God and Israel.[122]

In all *Ḥol ha-Mo'ed* prayers, except for *Musaf*, one recites *Ya'aleh ve-Yavo*, alluding to the relevant festival by name—"this day of the Sukkot festival" or "this day of the Feast of Unleavened Bread." If one forgot to recite this prayer, and did not remember until after the end of the *Amidah*, one must repeat it and make good the omission. *Ya'aleh ve-Yavo* is also recited in the Grace After Meals, and the festival day is also referred to briefly in the *Berakhah Me'ein Shalosh*,* albeit if one forgets to do so here there is no need for any repetition.

Minḥah and *Ma'ariv* are the same as on weekdays, with the addition of *Ya'aleh ve-Yavo* and the omission of *Taḥanun*. On Sukkot, Ashkenazim also recite Psalm 27.* *Shaḥarit* is like that for weekdays, except that in most rites the thanksgiving psalm, Psalm 100,* is

---

[122] As the *Tefillin*, too, are called *Ot* ("sign"). See Deuteronomy 6:8.

omitted from *Pesukei de-Zimrah** during *Ḥol ha-Mo'ed* of Pesaḥ.[123] In most Ashkenazic congregations today (including those of *Nusaḥ Sepharad*), and in certain others, it is customary on *Hosha'na Rabbah* (the last day of *Ḥol ha-Mo'ed* of Sukkot, see below) to recite the *Pesukei de-Zimrah* as on Sabbaths and festivals. Neither *Taḥanun* nor Psalm 20 are recited on *Ḥol ha-Mo'ed.*

Following are the differences between *Ḥol ha-Mo'ed* of Pesaḥ and that of Sukkot.

Ḥol ha-Mo'ed of Pesaḥ

Following the repetition of the *Amidah*, half *Hallel* is recited (with the same laws applicable to the benedictions as to *Rosh Ḥodesh*), and then the Song of the Day* (in *Nusaḥ Sepharad*), followed by a Torah reading.

Two Torah scrolls are removed from the Ark, and four persons are called up. The first three read the daily festival portion from the first scroll (each day has a different selection). From the second scroll, the fourth person reads the portion listing the special additional sacrifices for the festival (Numbers 28:16–25). The Torah selections read from the first scroll were selected in early generations.[124] This order is altered only when the first day of Pesaḥ falls on a Thursday. In the Diaspora, the 16th of Nisan is the second day of Pesaḥ, so that festival rules apply (see Chapter 10), whereas in the Land of Israel it is the first day of *Ḥol ha-Mo'ed.*[125]

---

[123] This is so because the thanksgiving offering contained leaven and was not offered in the Temple on that festival.

[124] There is even a mnemonic device for remembering them; see *Megillah* 31a.

[125] Thus, in Israel three persons are called up to the Torah reading on that day—Leviticus 22:27 to 23:44—while the fourth person reads the section of the festival sacrifices from the second scroll; in the Diaspora, the same reading is divided among five people, plus a (slightly different) *Maftir*. On the 17th of Nisan (the second day of *Ḥol ha-Mo'ed* in Israel, the first in the Diaspora), the first three persons read from Exodus 13:1–16 and the fourth reads the portion about the *Musaf* sacrifices, as is done on all the days of *Ḥol ha-Mo'ed*. On the 18th of Nisan, they read from Exodus 22:24 to 23:19; on the 19th of Nisan from Exodus 34:1–26; on the 20th of Nisan from Numbers 9:1–14. When the first day of Pesaḥ falls on a Thursday, the reading for the 19th of Nisan is brought forward

After the Torah reading, the scrolls are returned to the Ark and the festival *Musaf* service is begun. In the *Amidah* section beginning "And You have graciously given us," one inserts "this day of the Feast of Unleavened Bread . . ." and the passage on the *Musaf* offering relevant to *Ḥol ha-Mo'ed* of Pesaḥ. The service is then concluded as usual.

Ḥol ha-Mo'ed of Sukkot

It is customary to pronounce the benediction on the *Lulav** and *Ethrog** following the *Amidah*. However, some people do so early in the morning, before prayers, in the *Sukkah*.* Then comes full *Hallel*, followed, in *Nusaḥ Sepharad* and some Ashkenazim in the Land of Israel, by *Hosha'not** (most versions of the Ashkenazic rite recite the *Hosha'not* after *Musaf*).

Four persons are called up for the Torah reading, according to the description of the additional sacrificial offerings.[126] There is a different reading every day, and there is also a difference in the Torah reading between Israel and the Diaspora. In the Land of Israel, each one of the four called up reads the section for that day, which is repeated four times.[127] In the Diaspora, there is an uncertainty regarding the date of any given day (e.g., whether the third day of the festival, the 17th of Tishrei, is in fact to be regarded halakhically as the second day or the third day); hence, the Ashkenazic custom is for the first person to read the portion of the previous day; the second person to read the one for that day; the third reads the portion for the following day; and the fourth, the verses of that day and of the following day.[128]

---

to Shabbat, which is the 17th, in expanded form (beginning with Exodus 33:12), and the readings for the 17th and 18th are pushed back accordingly.

[126] From Numbers 29:17–35.

[127] E.g., on the first day of *Ḥol ha-Mo'ed*, which is the second day of the Sukkot festival, the section beginning with the words "On the second day" is read (vv. 17–19).

[128] For example, on the first day of *Ḥol ha-Mo'ed* (which is the third day of the Sukkot festival) the first person (the *Kohen**) reads "On the second day"; the second person (the Levite) reads "On the third day"; the third person reads "On the fourth day"; and the fourth reads "On the second day" and "On the third day."

After the Torah reading, *Ashrei* and *u-Va le-Zion Go'el* are recited (but Psalm 20 is omitted). Then the festival *Musaf* service is begun. The *Amidah* of *Musaf* contains mention of the Torah portion for that day (in the Diaspora, for that day and the preceding one). The Ashkenazim also recite Psalm 27. The service is then concluded as usual.

Hosha'na Rabbah

Over the course of generations, many special customs, most of them based on the Kabbalah, have become connected with *Hosha'na Rabbah*—the seventh day of Sukkot and the last day of *Ḥol ha-Mo'ed*—which was a special day already at the Second Temple period.

On Sukkot, the world is judged for rain and for crops; therefore *Hosha'na Rabbah*, which is the last day of Sukkot, is considered the day on which the fate of man and of the world for this year is finally sealed. Hence, it is treated somewhat like Yom Kippur, in terms of prayers and *Teshuvah* (repentance).

Ma'ariv is conducted as on all the other days of *Ḥol ha-Mo'ed*. Afterward, it is customary to stay up and study Torah all night; there are even special texts (*Tikkun** for *Hosha'na Rabbah*) that are recited. In many places, study is preceded by a public reading of the entire book of Deuteronomy from a Torah scroll.

The *Shaḥarit* prayer is as always, except that the Ashkenazim recite the *Pesukei de-Zimrah* of Shabbat (without *Nishmat Kol Ḥai**). In the repetition of the *Amidah* of *Musaf*, the full *Kedushah* of *Keter* is recited in *Nusaḥ Sepharad*. After the *Hallel* (in *Nusaḥ Sepharad*) or after *Musaf* (in *Nusaḥ Ashkenaz*), the *Hosha'not* are recited, as on all the other days of *Ḥol ha-Mo'ed* of Sukkot; in many congregations, various *Piyyutim* and prayers are added.

Moreover, instead of encircling the *Bimah** only once, the congregation encircles it seven times. When the Temple still existed, the altar used to be encircled seven times on this day, and people would hold willow branches in their hands and then hit the ground with them. Today, after encircling the *Bimah* seven times, the *Arba'ah Minim* are put aside, and each person takes five branches of *Aravah** (willow) and hits the ground with it five times. This custom has profound esoteric meanings.

After *Shaḥarit*, some people have a festive meal, and generally, people do even less work than on the other days of *Ḥol ha-Mo'ed.* It is customary to enter the *Sukkah* for the last time late in the afternoon to "bid it farewell" by eating something there, making a blessing over the food, and reciting a short farewell prayer (in the Diaspora, this is done by many at the end of the eighth day). Then, some of the ornaments and utensils that were inside the *Sukkah* throughout the festival are brought back into the house.

Shabbat *Ḥol ha-Mo'ed*

See Chapter 9, on Shabbat prayers.

Ḥanukkah

The Ḥanukkah festival is not mentioned in the Torah. It was instituted by the rabbis during the Second Temple period following Judah the Maccabee's victory over the Greeks and the purification and rededication[129] of the Temple. This rededication, together with the abolition of the anti-Jewish decrees promulgated by Antiochus IV, King of Syria, and the eventual total liberation from Greek rule, have made Ḥanukkah a festival for all time. For many generations, it had been the practice to commemorate certain other happy events that took place during Second Temple times, but none of these remained after the destruction, and certainly not after the failure of the Bar Kokhba revolt,[130] with the single exception of Ḥanukkah. More than a commemoration of a military victory, Ḥanukkah marks the triumph of the spirit of Israel over the forces of assimilation. Moreover, several miracles occurred during those days, such as the little cruse of oil that

---

[129] In Hebrew, *Ḥanukkah*.

[130] Because the failure of this revolt put an end to the hopes for imminent reconstruction of the Temple.

contained oil for one day, but lasted for eight days. Hence, the sages decreed that this festival should be celebrated by all generations to come, even adding that the days of Ḥanukkah "will never be abolished" (Jerusalem Talmud, *Ta'anit* 2:2).

When first instituted, the festival of Ḥanukkah was celebrated with great joy, in a manner analogous to the three pilgrimage festivals. But later it was ruled that these days were to be considered as weekdays, singled out only by certain special commandments and insertions in the prayers and in Torah readings. These being days of joy, it is forbidden to fast or to deliver eulogies, and some people hold festive meals and eat special foods (during the Middle Ages, *Piyyutim* were composed for these occasions). Other joyful customs for these days, which have no halakhic force, are practiced by each Jewish community according to its own traditions.

Even though the festival days are considered weekdays on which any kind of work is formally permitted, women are accustomed to refrain from working as long as the Ḥanukkah lights are burning.[131] In some places the men also used to stop working during that time. In some Oriental communities, women do not work at all on the first and last days of Ḥanukkah.

The characteristic commandment for Ḥanukkah is the lighting of candles in the evenings. There is a special order of benedictions for this with accompanying *Piyyutim*, each community following its own local customs. In many communities, it is customary to recite Psalm 30, which begins "A psalm and song for the dedication of the house of David."

In the *Amidah* for all the services, a special passage—*Al ha-Nissim**—is recited just before the conclusion of the *Modim** benediction; in the Grace After Meals, this is inserted in the second benediction. In either of these cases, should one forget to say it, there is no need to repeat the prayer.

The *Ma'ariv* service is the same as on weekdays, except for the addition of *Al ha-Nissim*. *Shaḥarit*, too, is as it is on weekdays until the repetition of the *Amidah* (with the addition of *Al ha-Nissim*). This is followed by the full *Hallel*, with its benediction. The Torah scroll is then taken out, and three persons are called up to read the portion on

[131] *Shulḥan Arukh, Oraḥ Ḥayyim* 670.

the sacrifices offered by the princes of the twelve tribes of Israel in honor of the dedication of the Tabernacle, and the next few verses that deal with the lighting of the Temple Menorah (which is also related to Ḥanukkah).

The order of Torah readings is as follows: On the first day of Ḥanukkah, the Ashkenazim read Numbers 7:1–17; in *Nusaḥ Sepharad* and others, they begin the reading from Numbers 6:22–7:17, so as to include the Priestly Blessing (Numbers 6:22–23),* as the miracle of the oil was for the priests, the *Kohanim.** During the subsequent days of Ḥanukkah, the Ashkenazim in the Diaspora divide the Torah portion describing the gift of that particular day between two people, while the third person reads the portion for the next day. On the eighth day, the verses read begin from the portion of that day and continue till the end of the Menorah selection (Numbers 7:54 to 8:4), with the first two readers dividing up the portion for that day between them and the third continuing from "on the ninth day" (according to the Ashkenazic custom in the Diaspora) or repeating the portion for the eighth day (as in all other rites). The last day of Ḥanukkah is often known as *Zot Ḥanukkah*, this phrase being mentioned in the Torah reading for that day (see Numbers 7:84).

The Torah reading is followed by the recital of the half *Kaddish*, and the prayer service is concluded as on other weekdays when the *Taḥanun* prayer is omitted. In some rites, Psalm 30 is then recited in addition to, or instead of, the Song of the Day.

The *Minḥah* service is the same as on weekdays, with the addition of *Al ha-Nissim* and the omission of the *Taḥanun* prayer.

On the Friday of Ḥanukkah, those who light the Shabbat candles early do so a little later (but always before sunset), so as to light the candles as close to nighttime as possible. In addition, thicker candles are lit (or more oil used) so that the candles burn for at least half an hour after the appearance of the stars. On *Motza'ei Shabbat,** the *Ma'ariv* prayer is recited a little earlier than usual, so that the candles can be lit on time.

In some congregations, it was customary to read on Ḥanukkah the Scroll of Antiochus, a very ancient work (variously dated at, before, or after the destruction of the Second Temple), apparently originally written in Aramaic and translated into Hebrew, which tells the story of

Ḥanukkah in a very special way, quite independent of any other sources.

Rosh Ḥodesh During Ḥanukkah

Rosh Ḥodesh Tevet always occurs on the sixth day of Ḥanukkah, and in some years on both the sixth and seventh days. Prayers are then basically those for *Rosh Ḥodesh*, which takes precedence both because *Rosh Ḥodesh* is prescribed in the Torah and because it occurs more frequently. However, *Al ha-Nissim* is inserted in all the prayer services.

Shaḥarit is as it is in any regular weekday service (with the additions of both *Ya'aleh ve-Yavo* and *Al ha-Nissim*), followed by full *Hallel* with a blessing (required because of Ḥanukkah; on other *Rosh Ḥodesh* days, one says only half *Hallel*). The Torah reading is divided among four people (as on every *Rosh Ḥodesh*), and done from two scrolls: three people read the regular reading for *Rosh Ḥodesh*, while a fourth is called up for the reading of the portion of that day of Ḥanukkah. Thereafter, one recites *Musaf* for *Rosh Ḥodesh*, with the addition of *Al ha-Nissim*, and the Song of the Day, with the addition or substitution of Psalm 104.

For *Rosh Ḥodesh* Tevet that occurs on Shabbat, see Chapter 9.

Purim

The festival of Purim, which was instituted in remembrance of the abolition of Haman's decree of genocide against the Jewish people, is mentioned in the Bible in the Scroll of Esther. But because it was not ordained in the Torah, it is considered a festival established by the sages. The applicable commandments are all found in the Scroll of Esther itself, "to make them days of feasting and joy, and of sending portions to one another, and gifts to the poor" (Esther 9:22). It is likewise written there "that these days should be remembered and kept throughout every generation" (9:28)—i.e., by reading the *Megillah*, the Scroll of Esther.

The order of prayer services for Purim is as follows: *Ma'ariv* is as for weekdays, with the addition of *Al ha-Nissim* for Purim within the *Modim** benediction in the *Amidah*. Following the *Amidah*, the Ashkenazic communities recite *Kaddish Titkabbal*,* while the Sephardim say the half *Kaddish*, reciting *Kaddish Titkabbal* after *u-Va le-Zion Go'el*. The *Megillah* is then read, and after its completion *ve-Attah Kadosh** is recited, followed by *Kaddish Titkabbal*, and the service concludes with *Aleinu*.*

If Purim falls at the end of Shabbat, it is the custom in most Oriental communities to first recite the blessing over firelight (see *Havdalah**), and after reading the *Megillah* to recite *vi-Yehi No'am** and so on. *Havdalah* is said at the end of *Ma'ariv*.

The *Shaḥarit* service is the same as on weekdays, with the addition of *Al ha-Nissim*. In some Ashkenazic communities, it is customary to add a series of *Piyyutim*, composed by Rabbi Eleazar ha-Kallir,@ within the benedictions in the repetition of the *Amidah*, in order to further glorify the miracle of Purim.

A Torah scroll is then taken out, and the passage concerning the war with Amalek is read (Exodus 17:8–16). Some return the scrolls to the Ark, and others leave them out during the second reading of the *Megillah*. The service is concluded as usual for weekdays, with the omission of *Taḥanun*. Psalm 22 is read in addition to, or instead of, the Song of the Day.

Among the commandments for Purim is *Mishloaḥ Manot**—the sending of gifts consisting of portions of food, at least two dishes to one person. Friends often exchange presents, to increase feelings of amity and joy. Gifts of money are made to a minimum of two poor people *(Mattanot la-Evyonim)*, but it is commendable to give as much, and to as many people, as possible. On Purim, one does not investigate the beneficiary but offers money to whoever requests it.[132]

The *Minḥah* service is the same as on weekdays, except for the inclusion of *Al ha-Nissim* and the omission of the *Taḥanun* prayer. The festive meal (in fulfillment of the command to make Purim "a time for joy and feasting") is generally held after *Minḥah*. There are no special laws regarding it, but large amounts of food and drink are usually

---

[132] Ordinarily, however, one should make sure that the recipient of charity is indeed worthy of it.

provided, and rejoicing often lasts well into the night. If Purim falls on a Friday, the festive meal is held as early as possible, in order not to intrude upon the coming of Shabbat.

On the festival of Purim, one is supposed to celebrate in an excessive manner. In the Talmud, it states, "A man should get drunk on Purim until he cannot tell the difference between 'cursed be Haman' and 'blessed be Mordechai'" (*Megillah* 7b). Not everyone follows this injunction literally (and a variety of interpretations may be found of it in halakhic works), but it clearly implies an obligation to drink more than usual.

In talmudic times, it was customary to make bonfires on which the effigy of Haman was burnt, and it is customary today to play pranks and make jokes. Even the most distinguished masters of halakhic law did not prevent people from doing so.[133] Adults would play games, and in many places a "Purim Rabbi" was appointed to act as a comedian. People also wear fancy disguises or masks. The day is, on the whole, one of great enjoyment and levity. In some places, even the prayer services at the synagogue are not conducted with the usual solemnity and awe and, so long as no actual transgression is involved, almost any kind of behavior is overlooked on Purim.

Shushan Purim

The Scroll of Esther mentions that Purim is celebrated for two days—on the 14th and 15th of Adar. "But the Jews that were in Shushan . . . on the fifteenth day they rested, and made it a day of feasting, and gladness. Therefore, the Jews of the villages, who dwelt in the unwalled towns, made the fourteenth day of the month of Adar a day of gladness and feasting" (Esther 9:18–19). The halakhah defines "unwalled towns" as those that were not surrounded by walls at the time of Joshua, son of Nun, and the conquest of Canaan (see the Book of Joshua). Consequently, all residents of cities that were walled at the time of Joshua celebrate Purim as was done in Shushan, namely, on the

[133] See *Shulḥan Arukh, Oraḥ Ḥayyim* 696:8.

15th of Adar. This day is referred to as Shushan Purim or, in halakhic terminology, as *Purim de-Mukafim* (literally, "the Purim of walled [cities]").

Although many walled cities are mentioned in the Book of Joshua, most of them have since been destroyed and uninhabited for generations, and even their exact location is in doubt. In practice, in our day the only city in which Shushan Purim is celebrated with certainty is Jerusalem (including the entire greater metropolitan area, even far outside the walls). In certain other cities, about which there is some uncertainty regarding their walled status in the days of Joshua, such as Tiberias,[134] Hebron, and Safed, both days of Purim are celebrated.[135]

The term *Purim Meshullash* ("Triple Purim") is used to refer to those rare occasions when the 15th of Adar—Shushan Purim—occurs on a Shabbat. The structure of the fixed annual calendar ensures that Purim (i.e., the 14th of Adar) never falls on Shabbat, but it does occasionally fall on Friday, in which case Shushan Purim occurs on Shabbat. In such cases, due to the rabbinic edict proscribing the reading of the *Megillah* on Shabbat (to avoid the possibility of carrying it in the public domain), Shushan Purim celebrations are extended for three days (Triple Purim): the reading of the *Megillah* and gifts to the poor are advanced to Friday (the 14th of Adar)—thus, all Jews everywhere read the *Megillah* on the same day; on Shabbat (the 15th of Adar), there is a special Torah reading for Purim,[136] and *Al ha-Nissim* is recited in the *Amidah* and in the Grace After Meals; on Sunday (the 16th of Adar), *Mishloaḥ Manot* are sent, and the Purim feast is held.

---

[134] See *Megillah* 5b.

[135] Some people living in ancient cities such as Jaffa and Gaza, which are mentioned in the Book of Joshua, also maintain this custom. There are also some places outside the Land of Israel where it had been customary to celebrate two days because of such doubts (including, among others, Prague). However, most halakhic authorities maintain that there are no European cities of such hoary great antiquity, and that all such communities should celebrate Purim only on the 14th of Adar.

[136] Two Torah scrolls are removed from the Ark: in the first, the regular weekly Torah portion is read; in the second, the usual reading for Purim morning (Exodus 17:8-16) is read as *Maftir*. As *Haftarah*,* the same one as was read for *Parashat Zakhor* is repeated. See Chapter 9, section titled "The *Arba Parshiyyot*."

Fast Days

During the course of the year, there are various days of fasting on which, in addition to the fast itself, there are a number of changes and additions in the order of prayer services. (Yom Kippur, although a day of fasting, is not considered among these, because it is essentially a festival, and the fasting on that day is intended for purification and spiritual elevation; see Chapter II.)

The fast days may be categorized, on the basis of their essence and the customs practiced on them, as follows: (a) Tish'ah be-Av (the Ninth of Av), whose laws, customs, and prayers give it a unique status; (b) fast days held in memory of tragic events: some are mentioned in the Bible; other, later ones, are either recognized by all Jewish communities, or are kept only by particular communities; (c) fixed fast days for atonement and purification; (d) other fixed fasts; (e) fast days declared on the occasion of public calamities, whenever they occur.

The Ninth of Av (Tish'ah be-Av)

Tish'ah be-Av is one of the commemorative days for fasting and mourning. But because of the many terrible catastrophes that occurred on that day, stricter rules were regulated for it than for other fast days. It is both a stricter fast and a day on which we conduct ourselves like mourners.

According to the scriptural record (II Kings 25:8–9), the destruction of the First Temple commenced on the 7th of Av in 586 B.C.E., and the devastation was completed when the Temple was burnt to the ground and the city of Jerusalem utterly demolished on the 9th of Av. In the year 70 C.E., Titus and his Roman forces set fire to the Second Temple and commenced the total destruction of Jerusalem. This is likewise the day on which the city of Beitar fell to Rome and the Bar Kokhba revolt was suppressed (132 B.C.E.). Our sages note a number of other dire events that took place on this day (Mishnah, *Ta'anit* 4:6).

Apart from the actual catastrophe, which disrupted and undermined the entire fabric of Jewish life, the Temple's destruction is the ultimate symbol of desolation and exile, in both the material and the spiritual sense (symbolically called "the exile of the *Shekhinah**"). For this reason, the Ninth of Av was ordained as a long day of strict fasting (with regulations resembling those of Yom Kippur, although it is a day of a very different character). In addition, it has been designated as a day of mourning, with laws similar to those for someone who had lost a close relative. But because, halakhically, Tish'ah be-Av is a fast day established by the sages, unlike Yom Kippur it does not override Shabbat, so that whenever it falls on a Shabbat, it is postponed to Sunday.

Like Yom Kippur, this fast begins at sunset on the preceding evening and continues until the appearance of the stars on the next day. Not only eating and drinking, but also washing, and wearing leather sandals, or any kind of leather shoes, are forbidden (some do not wear shoes at all); sexual relations are likewise proscribed. The strictness of the fast resembles that of Yom Kippur not only in its duration but also in its obligatory nature, so long as one is not ill (except, of course, for those at risk). Even though Tish'ah be-Av is halakhically considered a weekday and there is no actual prohibition against working, it is customary not to engage in any remunerative labor (although there is some leniency about this from midday on); the sages mildly disapproved of those who would work on this day. Similarly, any labor demanding a considerable amount of time should be avoided. Mourning customs are practiced—people do not greet one another, nor study Torah (except for those parts that deal with mourning or other sorrowful issues), because it is said that the words of the Torah "gladden the heart" (Psalm 19:9). One also does not wear any new or elegant clothes nor any clothing that has been freshly washed. In most Jewish communities, the *Tefillin* and *Tallit** are not worn until the time for *Minḥah*.[137] In certain communities (mainly those following the Oriental custom), however, *Tallit* and *Tefillin* are worn for *Shaḥarit* as well. As in private mourning, one is not allowed to sit on an ordinary chair, but either on the floor (though preferably not directly on the bare ground) or on a low stool. There are some people who actually sleep on the ground, or alter their manner of sleeping in some way, and some who even place stones under their heads. In many communities, it is the practice to

[137] This ruling appears in *Shulḥan Arukh, Oraḥ Ḥayyim* 555.

remove the *Parokhet** (curtain) covering the door of the Ark; others suffice with just drawing it aside. It is a widespread custom to visit the cemetery (but not en masse). Some walk among the ruins of Jerusalem and the Temple, reciting *Kinot** over the destruction. Few lights are lit (even in the synagogue), and one tries to avoid any kind of amusement or frivolity, so as to keep one's mind focused on mourning.

From the middle of the day, there is a slight change in the degree of mourning. The *Parokhet* is replaced and certain mourning practices are eased: it is permitted to sit on a regular chair and to engage in necessary work for the day (e.g., cooking). In most communities, the *Tallit* and *Tefillin* are worn, with the appropriate blessings, for *Minḥah*. (Those who wore Rashi's *Tefillin* for *Shaḥarit* only now don *Tefillin* of Rabbenu Tam*). Various prayers omitted in *Shaḥarit* (such as the Song of the Day) are now recited. In general, the hope for redemption is more strongly felt, because after the destruction and mourning comes the time for comfort and hope, as suggested by the midrashic statement that the Messiah is to be born on Tish'ah be-Av.[138] Hence, it is the practice in some communities to wash the floors of the house and to decorate it in expectation of his coming.

Some of the mourning practices for Tish'ah be-Av are introduced even before the actual beginning of the fast. In the last meal before the fast (*Se'udah Mafseket*) one does not eat two cooked dishes (either roasted or broiled). Three persons should not sit down to eat together, so that there not be a *Zimmun**; if they do so, they do not recite the *Zimmun*, as this is a meal of mourners in which there is distress of the soul. At the end of the meal, there are some who eat a cold hard-boiled egg dipped in ashes while sitting on the ground or on a low stool.

Everyone goes to the synagogue for *Ma'ariv* (even those sitting *Shiv'ah** since on Tish'ah be-Av all have the status of mourners). In some communities, the *Shaliaḥ Tzibbur* announces in an emotional voice the number of years that have passed since the destruction of the Temple. Some recite Psalm 137 ("By the rivers of Babylon") before *Barekhu*.* In the Ashkenazic custom, this is a weekday service in all respects. Following the *Amidah*, the *Shaliaḥ Tzibbur* says *Kaddish Titkabbal*, albeit in some places the phrase *Titkabbal* is omitted on

---

[138] Midrash, *Lamentations Rabbah* 1:51.

Tish'ah be-Av,[139] while in other places only half *Kaddish* is said. After this, everyone sits on the ground and recites the Scroll of Lamentations. In some places, people sit on overturned benches—which, besides the halakhic aspect, is reminiscent of the custom of lowering the bed for those mourning a personal bereavement. At the end of the reading of Lamentations, a few *Kinot* are recited, followed by *ve-Attah Kadosh*. In the Ashkenazic versions, the full *Kaddish* is said, with the omission of the *Titkabbal* phrase. The service concludes with *Aleinu*.

If Tish'ah be-Av occurs on (or is postponed to) Sunday, the *Havdalah* service is not recited at the conclusion of Shabbat, but only the blessing on firelight, which it is best to recite before the reading of Lamentations. The passage *Attah Ḥonantanu** (marking the termination of Shabbat) is recited in the *Amidah* as usual. In some congregations, a sermon is preached to the public on the significance of the day and on repentance.

On the following morning, in most communities no blessing is made even on the *Tallit Katan*,* and the *Tallit* and *Tefillin* are not worn. In *Birkhot ha-Shaḥar*,* the blessing "who has provided for all my needs" is omitted, because this refers to wearing shoes, which is forbidden on this day. The Ashkenazic custom is to pray as on weekdays, except that the *Shaliaḥ Tzibbur* recites *Anenu** after the benediction *Go'el Yisrael*. In certain places (where the Ashkenazic custom is followed), some also include *Piyyutim* (*Kerovot**) in the *Amidah*. The *Kohanim** do not bless the people in the *Shaḥarit* service, just as no blessings are offered in a house of mourning.

Most congregations do not say the *Taḥanun* prayer at all on Tish'ah be-Av, finding allusive support for this ruling in the biblical references to this day as *Mo'ed*.[140] But a simpler reason for this omission is that *Taḥanun* is never said in a house of mourning. The Ashkenazic custom is to recite *Kinot* after the Torah reading.

Three persons are called up for the Torah reading, Deuteronomy 4:25–40, which warns of the destruction and exile that will occur if the people of Israel do not keep the commandments of the Torah. The third person also reads the *Maftir* and the *Haftarah*—Jeremiah 8:13 to

---

[139] This phrase is a request that our prayers be accepted; but on that day it says (Lamentations 3:8): "He shuts out my prayers." See *Tur, Oraḥ Ḥayyim* 559.

[140] Lamentations 1:15, and elsewhere.

9:23—which contains lamentations over the destruction of Jerusalem and the Temple.

After returning the Torah scrolls to their place, the Ashkenazic custom is to recite *Kinot*, and some others recite the Book of Lamentations. The service concludes with *u-Va le-Zion Go'el* (omitting the verse *va-Ani Zot Beriti*—"As for me, this is my covenant"—so that it will not seem as though a covenant is being made over the destruction), and *Aleinu*. The Song of the Day and the *Ketoret** sections are omitted. There are Ashkenazim who then observe the custom of reading Lamentations, while the Oriental and Yemenite rites have the custom of reading the entire Book of Job.

For the *Minḥah* service, the *Tallit* and *Tefillin* are worn with the appropriate blessings, and all the sections skipped in *Shaḥarit* are now recited. Then comes *Ashrei*, followed by the Torah reading, as on every public fast day. The Ashkenazic custom is to recite the same *Haftarah* as on other public fast days—namely, Isaiah 55:6 to 56:7, "Seek the Lord while He is to be found."

After returning the scrolls to the Ark, the usual *Amidah* for the weekday *Minḥah* service is recited, and the congregation inserts the *Anenu* and *Naḥem** prayers. Wherever it is customary to pronounce the Priestly Blessing on weekdays, the *Kohanim* do so, and the service is concluded as usual.

There is a custom based on the Kabbalah of reciting *Birkat ha-Levanah**—the blessing on the New Moon—on the night following Tish'ah be-Av, for it alludes to Israel's renewal and restoration of the people to their homeland and former glory, like the moon's renewal.

Memorial Fast Days

Four days in the year are observed throughout the Jewish world as times of mourning in memory of national catastrophes. The Bible (Zechariah 4:19) specifies three of these as fixed fast days, as follows.

The Fast of Gedaliah

The Fast of Gedaliah (referred to in the Bible as the "fast of the seventh month") falls on the 3rd of Tishrei (the seventh month, counting from the month of Nisan). This fast was instituted in memory of Gedaliah ben Aḥikam, the first Jewish governor in the Land of Judah, who was murdered on the festival of Rosh ha-Shanah (see Jeremiah 41). This murder destroyed the last bastion of support for the Jews who still remained in their country after the Babylonian conquest: some went into exile in Egypt, while others survived in a state of helpless abandonment.

The Tenth of Tevet

The Tenth of Tevet (the "fast of the tenth month") is the day on which Nebuchadnezzar's siege of Jerusalem began (see Ezekiel 24:2), ending in the destruction of the city and the First Temple. Other tragic events that occurred around the same time of year are also remembered on this day.

The Seventeenth of Tammuz

The Seventeenth of Tammuz (the "fast of the fourth month") commemorates the day on which the walls of Jerusalem were breached, leading to the destruction of the Second Temple on the Ninth of Av (the breaching of Jerusalem's walls prior to the destruction of the First Temple occurred on the 9th of Tammuz). This date also commemorates other disastrous events that took place on that day (see Mishnah, *Ta'anit* 4:6).

The Fast of Esther

The Fast of Esther, held on the 13th of Adar, is in memory of the fast undertaken by Queen Esther and the Jewish people before the annulment of Haman's decree (see Esther 4:16). This fast, which lasted for three days, was actually held during the month of Nisan, and the 13th of Adar is not mentioned as a fast day in either the Mishnah or the Talmud. Yet the custom to fast just before Purim[141] is an ancient one, based upon a scriptural verse (see Esther 9:31). The Rosh[@] was the first important halakhic authority to mention this fast. Over the genera-

[141] Mentioned in Tractate *Soferim* 21.

tions, a variety of customs developed relating to the Fast of Esther, and it has been officially accepted throughout the Jewish world as a public fast day. Because it did not originate in talmudic law, but by spontaneous custom, there is greater leniency in its observance than there is for other such days.[142]

Laws and Customs of Memorial Fast Days

All these fast days share a common pattern of laws and customs. The fast itself only applies during the daytime (from dawn* till nightfall). When one of these days occurs on Shabbat, it is postponed to Sunday. The Fast of Esther is not postponed till the following day, because that day is Purim; instead, it is brought forward to Thursday, as Friday is also not an appropriate day for fasting (the one exception to this is the Tenth of Tevet, on which we fast even when it falls, as it occasionally does, on a Friday).

The *Ma'ariv* service is conducted as on regular weekdays (since the fast doesn't begin until the following morning).

Shaḥarit, through the *Amidah*, remains the same as on weekdays. The *Shaliaḥ Tzibbur* repeats the *Amidah* as on weekdays, but after *Go'el Yisrael** he adds *Anenu* as a complete benediction, which ends with the words "Blessed are You, O Lord, who answers [His people Israel] in times of distress." In some Ashkenazic congregations, it is customary for the *Shaliaḥ Tzibbur* to intersperse a number of *Seliḥot* Piyyutim** among the benedictions of the *Amidah*. After the repetition of the *Amidah*, most Ashkenazim (as well as *Nusaḥ Sepharad* worshippers) recite special *Seliḥot* for that day, concluding with *Avinu Malkenu** (with slight variations from the formulation recited during the Ten Days of Awe,* because this is not the beginning of the year), and followed by *Taḥanun*.

This is followed by a Torah reading, to which three persons are called up, from the section dealing with God's pardoning the people for the sin of the Golden Calf (Exodus 32:11–14; 34:1–10). In many communities, it is customary for the congregants to recite aloud the verse "Turn from Your wrath . . ." (Exodus 32:13), the Thirteen Attributes* of Mercy, and the phrase "And pardon our iniquity, our sin, and take us

---

[142] See *Shulḥah Arukh, Oraḥ Ḥayyim* 686:2.

for Your inheritance," and for the reader to repeat these words after them. After the Torah reading, the service is concluded as usual for weekdays.

In the Land of Israel, there are those who wear *Tallit* and *Tefillin* at *Minḥah*, especially among the Oriental communities. After *Ashrei*, half *Kaddish* is said, a Torah scroll is taken out, and the same portion is read as in *Shaḥarit*. In Ashkenazic practice, the third person called up reads the *Haftarah*—Isaiah 55:6 to 56:7. In the *Amidah*, the congregation includes *Anenu* in *Shema Kolenu**; this petition is repeated by the *Shaliaḥ Tzibbur* as an independent benediction after *Go'el Yisrael*. In certain places, the *Kohanim** pronounce the Priestly Blessing*; where they do not do so, the *Shaliaḥ Tzibbur* recites these blessings, introduced by the phrase "Our God and God of our fathers, bless us with the threefold blessing . . ."; even the Ashkenazim conclude with *Sim Shalom** instead of the usual *Shalom Rav*. *Avinu Malkenu* is said after the *Amidah*.

The Twentieth of Sivan—A Fast Day of Remembrance

In the same spirit in which the memorial fast days were established, this fast day was instituted among European communities, especially those in Eastern Europe, in the aftermath of the Chmielnicki massacres connected with the Cossack rebellion of 1648, which brought large-scale ruin to the Jews of Greater Poland. The rebellion lasted for a long time, and involved numerous onslaughts on the Jewish communities (1648–49). Still, the Council of Four Lands* selected the date of the 20th of Sivan (1650) to commemorate these terrible events because on that day the first of a series of particularly brutal pogroms was perpetrated against the Jews of the city of Nemirov. There had also been an earlier massacre on that same day in 1171 C.E., during the Second Crusade; moreover, this date never falls on a Shabbat. Special *Seliḥot* were fixed for this day, some of which were composed by contemporaries of the 1171 massacre, including Rabbenu Tam,@ Rabbi Ephraim of Bonn,@ and his brother Rabbi Hillel. Prayers were conducted on it as on all public fast days, and the fast was observed in many communities until almost our own time.

Over the years, other fast days were instituted in other communities to commemorate catastrophic events that took place on various dates. There are still some Siddurim and *Maḥzorim** which contain *Seliḥot* composed for such occasions and for such places, but since most of these were in memory of local disasters, they did not continue to be observed for very long.

Fast Days for Repentance and Atonement

Various days of the year have been instituted as fast days for the purposes of repentance and atonement for sins.

Monday-Thursday-Monday Fasts

Among these days are to be included the Monday, Thursday, and Monday following the Sukkot and Pesaḥ festivals. These days were decreed as fast days because, as stated in the Talmud (*Kiddushin* 81a), the festivals, which are days of joy and leisure, may also result in transgressing the limits of responsible conduct. Consequently, these fasts were supposed to have been held immediately after the festivals, in order to atone for any such laxity. But since the months of Tishrei and Nisan are considered joyful months, and it is customary not to fast during them, the Monday-Thursday-Monday fasts are held during the following months—Ḥeshvan and Iyyar.

There are further reasons for these fasts: during Ḥeshvan one fasts to plead for rain to fall on the newly planted fields, and during Iyyar, so that the harvest should not be ruined by blight or mildew. Ḥeshvan and Iyyar are also periods of seasonal changes in weather; hence, one fasts and prays for physical health.

Since these days were fixed as public fasts (although not everyone observes them), there are special *Seliḥot* for them also, there is a Torah reading in *Minḥah*, and daily prayers are the same as on any other public fast days.

Shovavim Tat

Some people fast on the Thursdays of those weeks during which the first eight portions of the book of Exodus (whose initial letters spell out, in Hebrew, the appelation *Shovavim Tat*) are read. This custom originated among Rabbi Isaac Luria® and his disciples, the point of it being that this period is a propitious time for purifying the soul from sin. The period was also set aside for fast days, since it generally occurs during the months of Tevet, Shevat, and the beginning of Adar, during which there are virtually no days on which it is forbidden to fast (except for the 15th of Shevat; see below). Moreover, these are winter months, during which it is less difficult to fast because the days are cold and short. There are also brief *Seliḥot* for these days, with different selections for each week.

Yom Kippur Katan

The noted Kabbalist Rabbi Moses Cordovero of Safed (1522–1579) ordained that the eve of *Rosh Ḥodesh* be observed as a minor day of atonement—a fast day of repentance and self-purification. Although this custom was not made mandatory, it has been widely accepted among Jewish congregations and is treated as a public fast day. Special *Seliḥot* are recited after *Minḥah*. If the eve of *Rosh Ḥodesh* falls on a Shabbat or Friday, then *Yom Kippur Katan* is brought forward to Thursday.

Rosh ha-Shanah Eve

Some people fast on the eve of Rosh ha-Shanah, because it is a day of grace and it is appropriate that it should be devoted to heavenly matters. This custom is supported by *Midrash Tanḥuma*# and was prevalent among Ashkenazic communities, whence it found its way into halakhic compendia.[143] Those who fast do not read from the Torah and do not complete the fast (i.e., they eat something before nightfall, so as not to enter the holiday in a state of fasting). Since this fast is based solely on custom, considerable leniency is allowed for the frail and sick, as well as where a *Se'udat Mitzvah**—a meal in honor of a religious rite—is held.

[143] *Midrash Tanḥuma, Emor* 22; see *Shulḥan Arukh, Oraḥ Ḥayyim* 681:2.

The Ten Days of Repentance (*Teshuvah*)

Many people used to fast on the weekdays of the Ten Days of Repentance, with the exception of the eve of Yom Kippur, on which it is mandatory to eat (see Chapter 11). These fasts also belong under the rubric of custom rather than law, being observed because the period before Yom Kippur is one of Divine favor and closeness to God, so that one should conduct oneself therein with sanctity. Since these are considered personal fasts, there is no reading of the Torah and no commitment to complete them. This custom is not widely observed.

Other Fixed Fast Days

The 7th of Adar

The seventh day of Adar is traditionally known as the day on which Moses died (and also the day on which he was born). Some people fast on this day, and there is a special *Tikkun** service. It is a widespread custom to visit the graves of righteous sages on that day (in Israel, it is customary to go to the grave of Rabbi Shimon bar Yoḥai in Meron who, according to the Kabbalah, possessed a spark of Moses' soul). Members of the *Hevra Kaddisha*—the Burial Society (literally, Aramaic for the "Holy Commune")—in particular fast on this day, reciting certain prayers and words of admonition to atone for any irreverence they might have unintentionally shown toward the dead.

The Fast of the Firstborn

It is generally the custom for firstborn sons to fast on the eve of Pesaḥ. This practice originated in the Jerusalem Talmud (though there were sages who raised doubts as to the accuracy of the text). The reason given there is that, since on the eve of the original Passover in Egypt all the firstborn of Egypt were slain, while the firstborn of Israel were saved, it is incumbent upon all Jewish firstborn sons to offer special thanks on this day and dedicate it to the service of Heaven.

Although this fast applies to all firstborn sons, customs differ.

There are those parents who are accustomed to fast in the case of a firstborn son who is not yet old enough to fast himself.

Moreover, since this fast day is not mandatory, our sages have written that it is permitted to partake of a *Se'udat Mitzvah*. Thus, it became a widespread custom for firstborns to complete a talmudic tractate on that day, and thereafter hold a small meal after *Shaḥarit* in honor of the occasion, which would constitute a *Se'udat Mitzvah*. One who does not study the tractate himself can participate in the festive meal held by someone else, and thus hardly anyone actually fasts on this day.

Nonfixed Fast Days

Occasional Public Fast Days

It is accepted practice for Jewish communities, in times of trouble and distress, to declare a public fast on a certain day or days, hoping that the power of prayer and charity, fasting and self-purification, will bring heavenly salvation. The Bible refers to this several times, e.g., "Blow the trumpet in Zion, sanctify a fast . . . then will the Lord be jealous for His land and pity His people" (Joel 2:15–18). Among other instances, the people of Israel fasted for salvation from the Philistines (I Samuel 6:6), when their fields were devestated by a plague of locusts during the period of Joel (1:14), and on the three-day fast called in support of Queen Esther's efforts to overturn Haman's decree in the time of King Ahasuerus (see Esther 4:16). The Mishnah declares that this should be done "for any trouble that comes upon the community" (Mishnah, *Ta'anit* 2:8). Tractate *Ta'anit* is devoted to the laws and customs for such fast days.

Fasts held on occasions of public distress may be declared for universal observance, for one country, for one city, or even by one community within a city. There is no clear-cut definition as to what is considered proper cause for a public fast day, the matter resting with the judgment of the local Jewish religious court. Thus, it might sometimes happen that a fast day is declared in one place where the community has been harmed by a particular event, even though the same event may be fortuitous for another community.

There was a fixed sequence of public fasts, of progressively increasing severity, for a scarcity of rainfall, or drought, in the Land of Israel. If the rainy season began and rain did not fall, a series of fasts was held (as many as thirteen, on Mondays and Thursdays of each week), culminating in several as stringent as the fast on Tish'ah be-Av. During Temple times, there was also a special order of *Shofar** blowing, an additional six blessings were inserted into the *Amidah*, and there was even a *Ne'ilah** service (see Chapter 11). Although some of these rulings were recorded in the *Shulḥan Arukh*,[144] in fact, such a series of fasts has not been held for many generations, albeit even today public fasts are occasionally proclaimed because of a lack of rainfall.

On fast days held for public distress, the prayer services are the same as for any other public fast day, including Torah reading in the *Shaḥarit* and *Minḥah* services. There are special *Seliḥot* for a fast declared for lack of rainfall, as well as a special prayer formulation inserted in the *Amidah*. There is likewise a special *Piyyut* for a fast day held because of an epidemic of children's diseases.

There have also been occasions when a public fast was declared, not for reasons of distress but in order to arouse people to repent. Such a fast is mentioned in the Book of Ezra (Chapter 9). Halakhically, it is left for the local authorities to decide whether such a fast is to be treated like a public or a private fast.

Private Fast Days

In each generation, certain individuals have held personal fasts for various reasons. Often this is because they wish to devote themselves to self-purification and prayer, in order to ask that some distress or pain from which they have been suffering cease. Among such fasts should be included *Ta'anit Ḥalom*—a fast undertaken because of a bad dream that evokes fear and dread. Our sages said that in such a case a person should fast in order to avert an evil fate decreed for him (*Shabbat* 11a). Since such a fast is intended for the serenity of the soul, one may even fast on Shabbat; however, to atone for having infringed upon the joy of Shabbat, one must then fast on another day in compensation (*Berakhot* 31b).

---

[144] Especially *Oraḥ Ḥayyim* 575.

Other private fasts are those held in memory of loved ones. This is mentioned in the Talmud, and it has been common practice in many Jewish communities for a person to fast on the day his mother, father, or his religious mentor died (*Yahrzeit**).[145] However, this custom—as well as private fasts in general—was more or less dropped in modern times, due to the influence of the Ḥassidic movement, which generally sought to diminish self-mortification in Jewish observance.

Another kind of private fast is that undertaken for repentance. Such fasts, already mentioned in the Bible and Talmud, sometimes depend entirely upon the individual's feeling that such would be the correct way to atone for some sin or sins one had committed. However, in the course of time, people usually consulted a religious sage for guidance as to how to expiate sin. In addition to various forms of self-mortification, such atonement would include the assignment of a number of fasts, in proportion to the seriousness of the offenses. Such matters are dealt with in many halakhic compendia, as well as in Kabbalah-oriented manuals. The *Tikkunei ha-Teshuvah* ("Rules of Repentance") of Rabbi Isaac Luria@ impose a large number of fast days, both for sins enumerated in the Torah and for sins of moral corruption and unseemly behavior (for example, a large number of fasts for the sin of anger). Certain religious works, such as *Tikkun Karet*, have also been written on this subject.

Another type of private fast is that undertaken for the cleansing of the spirit and the purification of the soul. Such fasts, too, are mentioned in the Talmud (*Bava Metzi'a* 85a), and are naturally practiced by only a select few.

In this category is to be included the fast for a bride and bridegroom (and in some places also of their parents) on their wedding day, provided it is a day on which it is permitted to fast (albeit in some places it is customary for bride and bridegroom to fast even on a *Rosh Ḥodesh*). It is likewise customary for both bride and bridegroom to recite the confessional prayer *Al Ḥet** after *Minḥah*, as is done on the eve of Yom Kippur.

When a person decides on a private fast, he must explicitly verbalize his intention (using a special formulation for such occasions) during the *Minḥah* prayer preceding the day he intends so to do (see

[145] See *Shulḥan Arukh, Oraḥ Ḥayyim* 568.

*Kabbalat Ta'anit**). A fasting individual does not alter the prayer service, except to add the *Anenu* prayer in the *Shema Kolenu* benediction of the *Amidah* (among Ashkenazim, at *Minḥah* only).

In addition to the usual one-day fasts, there were those who wished to do added penance by fasting two or three days in succession (as recorded in the books of Jewish customs from the Middle Ages on). There were even some people who undertook to fast "from Shabbat to Shabbat," ceasing to eat or drink from the conclusion of Shabbat until the beginning of the next Shabbat.

Another type of fast (observed mainly among Sephardim) is *Ta'anit Dibbur*—a "fast" of speech, in which an individual, or sometimes an entire group of people, avoid speaking of secular matters for one or several days.

Similarly, there is also a *Ta'anit Sha'ot*—a fast of hours, from dawn till midday, which is considered a half-day fast.

As inferred earlier, there are contending views in the Talmud and in later works for or against fasting and self-mortification in general. Some sages used to fast year-round, eating only one meal each night;[146] some did so for many years, and even in recent generations certain righteous people have continued this practice. At the same time, there were many who objected to this mortification of the body, notably leaders of the Ḥassidic movement,[147] who instead recommended that one increase acts of charity and the performance of good deeds.

Special Time Periods

The Ten Days of Repentance

These are the first ten days of the year (from Rosh ha-Shanah to Yom Kippur), referred to by the Talmud as a period of exceptional grace, as it says, "Seek the Lord while He may be found, call upon Him while He is near" (Isaiah 55:6). This time is especially suited for repen-

---

[146] See *Pesaḥim* 68b.

[147] See *Iggeret ha-Teshuvah* of Rabbi Schneur Zalman of Lyady.

tance, and one may even endeavor to better the Divine decree made on New Year's Day (see Chapter 11).

On these days, certain additions are made in prayer services, such as the recital of *Seliḥot*, the recitation of *Avinu Malkenu* in the *Shaḥarit* and *Minḥah* services, and other changes and additions in the regular order of prayer, including in the *Amidah*. Some of these are mentioned in the Talmud, and some were introduced later. Many people fast on all or some of these days, taking greater care to fulfill the commandments than during the rest of the year. Even one who is rather lenient in certain matters, regarding which it is permissible to be so, should be more strict in their observance during these days.

The Ten Days of Repentance include Rosh ha-Shanah—the New Year festival, and Yom Kippur—the Day of Atonement (see Chapter 11), as well as *Shabbat Teshuvah* (see Chapter 9). During these days, certain additions are made in the first three and last three *Amidah* blessings (see Chapter 11).

The Month of Nisan

According to the Halakhah, one does not recite *Taḥanun* nor fast throughout the month of Nisan, because besides the festival of Pesaḥ it contains additional days of joy.

It is the general practice everywhere during the first twelve days of Nisan to read the passages concerning the sacrifices offered by the Princes of Israel at the time of the dedication of the Sanctuary (Numbers 7:1–8:4). There is a special, Kabbalah-based prayer to be recited after the reading, and in some places the Torah scroll is removed from the Ark after *Shaḥarit*, the portions of the princely sacrifices being read—one portion for each day—without the usual blessing before and after the reading.

The Counting of the *Omer*

The days of the Counting of the *Omer* extend from the 16th of Nisan to the 5th of Sivan, during which period one is commanded in the

Torah (Leviticus 23:15) to count the forty-nine days separating Pesaḥ* and Shavu'ot.*

Some, or all of the days of the *Omer* are treated as days of mourning, because of various difficult events that happened, throughout the ages, at this period of time. The main customs are not to get married, not to have a haircut, and the like. However, in most rites there are no changes in the usual prayer services, other than the formulation for counting the days, which is added after the *Ma'ariv* service.

The Three Weeks (*Bein ha-Meitzarim*)

This is the accepted term for the days between the Seventeenth of Tammuz and the Ninth of Av. The words *Bein ha-Meitzarim* literally mean "between the straits," and the term is taken from Lamentations 1:3, "all her persecutors overtook her between the straits." This period is also popularly called the "three weeks." Ashkenazim apply some mourning practices throughout this period—no marriages take place, no haircuts are allowed, the *she-Heḥeyanu** blessing is not recited, etc.

The prayer services for these days are the same as on other weekdays, but those who generally recite the *Tikkun Ḥatzot** at midnight now make a special point of doing so at midday as well.

The major change is in the *Haftarot* recited on the three Shabbats during this period: instead of *Haftarot* related to the contents of the weekly portion, there are three *Haftarot* of evil dispensation (in Aramaic: *Telata de-Fur'anuta*). In most communities, stricter mourning regulations are applied for the days between *Rosh Ḥodesh* Av and Tish'ah be-Av, and all communities observe mourning regulations during the week in which Tish'ah be-Av occurs.

The Month of Elul

The month of Elul is called the "month of mercy" or the "month of *Seliḥot*," and is devoted entirely to repentance and preparation for the days of judgment—Rosh ha-Shanah and Yom Kippur.

During this month, it is customary to fulfill the commandments in the most perfect way possible, and everyone tries to make amends for one's misdeeds, to the best of one's ability. Some are accustomed to hold a *Ta'anit Dibbur*, a "fast of speech" (see above) during this period or a part of it, and some fast throughout the entire month, eating only in the evenings.

From the beginning of the month, Ashkenazic communities blow the *Shofar* after the *Shaḥarit* service. This is a custom rather than law and is analogous to the blowing of the *Shofar* mentioned in the Bible, as a cry of warning against the threat of retribution.[148] Some blow a series of four blasts *(Teki'ah*—Shevarim*—Teru'ah*—Teki'ah)* and some blow ten blasts *(Teki'ah—Shevarim—Teru'ah—Teki'ah / Teki'ah—Shevarim—Teki'ah / Teki'ah—Teru'ah—Teki'ah)*. However, the *Shofar* is not blown on the eve of the New Year, in order to draw a distinction between what was merely a custom and the Torah commandment to blow the *Shofar* on Rosh ha-Shanah itself.

The Sephardic and Yemenite custom is to recite *Seliḥot* on weekdays throughout the month of Elul, while Ashkenazim begin reciting them only from the Saturday night preceding Rosh ha-Shanah. However, if Rosh ha-Shanah falls on a Monday or Tuesday, the *Seliḥot* prayers are brought forward for a week, thus allowing a minimum of four days of *Seliḥot* before Rosh ha-Shanah.

It is also customary in all Ashkenazic communities to recite twice daily, in the morning and in the evening, at either *Minḥah* or *Ma'ariv*, Psalm 27, "The Lord is my light and my salvation," which contains words of spiritual awakening inspiring repentance and reverence.[149]

Days of Joy

Megillat Ta'anit—"the Scroll of Fasts"—one of the first halakhic works to be set down in writing, already in Second Temple times, mentions special days during the year that are to be observed as days of joy, and on which one must not fast or eulogize the dead. However, by talmudic times it had already been decided to cancel these days of joy,

---

[148] See Amos 3:6: "Shall a trumpet be blown in the city, and the people not be afraid?"

[149] In Oriental communities, this psalm is recited all year round.

except for Purim and Ḥanukkah. Nevertheless, it has become customary to celebrate other occasions as days of joy, either for the entire Jewish people or for various communities. Although not actual festivals, these days still have a certain special quality that is reflected in the prayer services.

Local Purims

In many, Jewish communities around the world, certain days of the year have been set aside in memory of some miraculous event that took place among them in the past. These days are called "the Purim of such-and-such a community," or by some special name for the event or person associated with it. There were no fixed customs associated with these days, and each community would celebrate its Purim in its own fashion. These generally included the recital of special *Piyyutim* composed in commemoration of the event and a festive meal. In some cases, *Taḥanun* was omitted on that day. There are scores of such Purim days, and they were usually not kept for more than a few generations.

Similarly, certain families appointed such days for themselves and their descendants to commemorate a miraculous event that happened to their ancestors. One of the most famous of such days is the Purim celebrated by the descendants of Rabbi Yom Tov Lippmann Heller,[@] author of *Tosafot Yom Tov*,[#] who was saved from the Inquisition in Prague in 1629.

Lag ba-Omer (the Thirty-third Day of the *Omer* Period)

This day is mentioned as a joyous day in a number of texts of the *Rishonim*, such as *Sefer ha-Manhig*,[#] but there is in fact no clear source regarding the origin of the celebration. Some say that on this day the disciples of Rabbi Akiva stopped dying of the plague,[150] while others say that on this day the manna began to fall in the Sinai desert,[151] and addi-

[150] *Sefer ha-Manhig*, and in the *Minhagei Maharil*.[#]

[151] Exodus 16; and see *Responsa Hatam Sofer*.[#]

tional reasons are given. The main event celebrated on this day is the popular *Hillula* ("festivity") in honor of Rabbi Shimon bar Yoḥai, who died on Lag ba-Omer; he requested that no one should mourn for him, and revealed many mysteries of the Torah on his dying day.[152] The term *Hillula* is usually reserved for a "marriage feast." Its use here implies that the soul of a righteous person, who has left the world of the living, now attains a rest and joy which is like that of a marriage feast.

No changes are made in prayers for this day, except that that the *Taḥanun* prayer is universally omitted; in some places it is omitted throughout the entire fifth week of the *Omer* period.

It is the practice in many Ashkenazic communities to hold marriage ceremonies on this day, and it is a festive occasion on which one is allowed to have a haircut. Sephardim cease mourning observances for the *Omer* period from the thirty-fourth day onward. A variety of customs are observed on this day: children go out to fields and forests, play with bows and arrows, etc. Since the days of Rabbi Isaac Luria,[@] mass celebrations are held at Bar Yohai's burial site in Meron, near Safed, songs are sung in his honor, and a huge bonfire is lit in his memory. The custom to light bonfires has spread throughout the Land of Israel. In Jerusalem, visits are paid to the grave of Simon the Just, one of the great scholars who bridged the transition period from the time of the Great Assembly to the time of Hillel.

In many synagogues, the hymn *Bar Yoḥai** is sung both on this evening and on the preceding Shabbat.

The Day of Independence and Jerusalem Day

In 1948, the Chief Rabbinate of Israel instituted a special prayer service for *Yom Ha'atzmaut*, Israel's Independence Day—the 5th of Iyyar—the day when the State of Israel was proclaimed. (When this date falls on Friday or Shabbat, celebrations are moved forward to Thursday.)

Following the Six-Day War of 1967, *Yom Yerushalayim*—Jerusalem Day, the 28th of Iyyar—was instituted to mark the restoration of all of

---

[152] See *Zohar,*[#] *Idra Rabbah*, and elsewhere.

Jerusalem to Jewish sovereignty. It is not clear whether these days should be considered as national holidays (for the citizens of the State of Israel) or as religious festivals; likewise, they have not been accepted by all Jews, either because of differences in worldview or because of their undefined status. Nevertheless, many prayer books now contain the order of prayers that has been fixed for these days, or similar formulations, including psalms and expressions of thanksgiving. Many communities treat these days as days of joy, on which *Taḥanun* is not recited. Some congregations recite the *Hallel*, with or without the blessing, as the case may be. This practice is largely maintained in Israel, but is also followed by some Diaspora communities.

Other Days When *Taḥanun* Is Not Recited

There are many days during the year that have an aspect of joyfulness, although they do not enjoy the level of the regular festivals, nor do they have any additional prayers to mark them specially. Some of these are simply days on which it is not permitted to fast, on which *Taḥanun* is not recited, and on which certain passages containing an element of confession or supplication are omitted. The list of such days and details of the laws concerning them vary widely, with some adding and some reducing certain days, and there is also some variation regarding the prayers recited on them. When one of these days occurs on Shabbat, the prayer *Av ha-Raḥamim*,* recited in Ashkenazic communities, is omitted. The general rule for most of these days is that, on those days when *Taḥanun* is not recited, it is likewise omitted in the *Minḥah* service on the preceding day (with the exception of the eves of Rosh ha-Shanah and Yom Kippur).

While some of these dates have been mentioned above, we can summarize them, according to most Jewish communities, in chronological order, as follows.

Rosh ha-Shanah Eve

Taḥanun is not recited on Rosh ha-Shanah eve, because this is a special time of grace to be spent in repentance.

The 9th of Tishrei

The 9th of Tishrei (the eve of Yom Kippur) is a day that involves an aspect of joy, and on which there is a commandment to eat and drink. However, on this day each individual (with the exception of the *Shaliaḥ Tzibbur*) recites the confessional prayer *Al Ḥet* at the end of the *Amidah* in the *Minḥah* service.

From the 11th to the End of Tishrei

These are the days from the 11th of Tishrei until the end of the month (in addition to the Sukkot festival, which is fully festive in its own right). Various reasons have been given for not reciting *Taḥanun* on these days. Some congregations begin saying *Taḥanun* after *Isru Ḥag.**

Tu bi-Shevat

On Tu bi-Shevat ("the fifteenth of Shevat"), *Taḥanun* is not recited because it is the New Year of the Trees. It is the custom in many communities to eat some new fruit; others bring a great variety of fruits and recite a special *Tikkun* service, as formulated in the book *Peri Etz Hadar*,# which elaborates their deep kabbalistic meanings.

The 14th and 15th of the First Adar of a Leap Year

In the first Adar, during a leap year, no *Taḥanun* is recited on *Purim Katan*—the "little Purim"—which takes place on the 14th and 15th of the month.

The 14th and 15th of the Second Adar of a Leap Year

On both these dates during the second Adar, *Taḥanun* is also omitted, even though in most places the *Megillah* is read on only one of them.

Nisan

During the entire month of Nisan, *Taḥanun* is omitted (see above).

The 14th and 18th of Iyyar

Taḥanun is not recited on the 14th of Iyyar, as it is Pesaḥ Sheni—the Second Pesaḥ. This was celebrated in Temple times by those who were unable to bring the paschal sacrifice to Jerusalem in time for the Pesaḥ festival and were permitted to do so on this day. Nor is it recited on the 18th of Iyyar, which is Lag ba-Omer (see above).

The Early Part of Sivan

In Sivan, *Taḥanun* is not recited from *Rosh Ḥodesh* until the 13th of the month, and in some places only until *Isru Ḥag* of Shavu'ot. There are a variety of contributing factors here: *Rosh Ḥodesh*, the three "preparatory" days before the receiving of the Torah on Shavu'ot (which, in Hebrew, are called *Sheloshet Yemei Hagbalah*), and the "seven days of the completion of the festival," on which the festival offerings could still be brought to the Temple.

The 15th of Av

On the 15th of Av, no *Taḥanun* is recited because this was a day of exceptional festivity during Temple times, for a number of reasons (see *Ta'anit* 30b–31a).

Other Customs

In addition to these days that are observed throughout Jewry, it is the practice of various communities to institute certain days in commemoration of joyful events (see the section on local "Purim" above). The Ḥassidim, in particular, omit the *Taḥanun* prayer on those days on which the *Tzadikkim* (righteous sages) died, which is their *Hillula*. This is modeled upon Lag ba-Omer, when the traditional *Hillula* of Rabbi Shimon Bar Yohai is celebrated (see above). In other communities, *Taḥanun* was omitted on the days when their local leaders died, and often on the *Yahrzeit** of other significant people as well. It is the custom among Ḥassidic communities to designate as joyful days such dates as the 19th of Kislev (the day on which the Maggid of Mezeritz®

died, also the day on which Rabbi Schneur Zalman of Lyady,[@] the founder of the Ḥabad movement, was released from prison); or the 18th of Elul, the birthday of the Ba'al Shem Tov[@] and of Rabbi Schneur Zalman of Lyady. Similar customs are also practiced among Sephardic communities, who still often hold mass festivities, including visits to the tombs of righteous and sainted leaders, on such days.

CHAPTER THIRTEEN ❧ *Torah Readings*

PUBLIC TORAH READING has its origins in the earliest period of Jewish history. Moses had already read certain portions of the Torah—"the Book of the Covenant"—before the whole congregation of Israel (Exodus 24:7). The Torah itself contains the commandment to read the Torah in the presence of the entire nation—men, women, and children (the commandment of *Hakhel*, or "Assembly")—during the Sukkot festival following a sabbatical year (Deuteronomy 31:10-13). This special reading was conducted with great ceremony in the Temple, with the king of Israel reading portions of the Torah before the entire people. According to rabbinic tradition, already in the time of Moses the prophets instituted regular Torah readings on every Shabbat, and even during the weekdays no more than two days are to go by without a Torah reading. The rules for reading the Torah became formalized during the days of Ezra the Scribe, who set down the general order of readings that apply to this very day (*Bava Kamma* 82a).

Torah reading is therefore a commandment and an instituted practice in itself, and it predates the order of regular prayer services. Its main purpose is to ensure that all the people of Israel would study the Torah and would become familiar with at least the most notable part of it—the Five Books of Moses. Apparently, it was initially customary for people to assemble in a public forum, either in a building set aside for public gatherings[153] or, for special occasions, in the city square, as was the custom ever since mishnaic and talmudic times. However, when regular public prayer services were formally instituted, the Torah readings were integrated within them, and were conducted in close conjunction with the *Amidah*—either before, as in the Shabbat *Minḥah* service, or subsequently, as in the *Shaḥarit* service.

---

[153] As indicated in the term *Beit ha-Knesset*—"synagogue"—"a place of public gathering."

Yet Torah readings have never ceased to be an important means for Torah study, and for many generations it was the general practice to provide a translation into the vernacular, so that even those who did not comprehend the language of the Bible could learn and understand what was being read. This custom continued to be observed in many places until late medieval times.

The Cycle of Torah Readings

A distinction should be made between the fixed cycle of Torah readings, in which the entire Pentateuch is read from beginning to end during the course of the year, and Torah readings held on special days and occasions that are selected to accord with that day or occasion.

In our times, it is the custom in all Jewish communities to begin the cycle of Torah readings with the book of Genesis on the Shabbat immediately following the Sukkot festival (which is therefore called *Shabbat Bereshit* —"the Shabbat of Genesis"), and to complete the cycle with the final Torah portion in Deuteronomy, which is read on Simḥat Torah. Generally speaking, on every Shabbat one of the fifty-four Torah portions *(Sidrah*, or *Parashat ha-Shavu'a)* of the Pentateuch is read. This was the order of Torah readings instituted in Babylonia, while in the Land of Israel the custom was, in ancient times, to have a cycle of approximately three years of Torah readings, with one of 154 or more portions read every Shabbat.[154] The Land of Israel custom was practiced at least until the twelfth century, but lapsed as a result of the small number of Jews living in the country, even though traces of this cycle are still evident in halakhic and aggadic works of Midrash.*

In the Shabbat *Minḥah* service, and in the *Shaḥarit* service on Mondays and Thursdays, the first section of the Torah portion assigned for the following Shabbat is read. However, if a festival happens to fall on that Shabbat, it is not the Torah selection for the festival that is read in the above prayer services, but the first section from the portion in line to be read according to the normal cycle. The division of the Torah into fifty-four portions makes it impossible to actually read one

[154] The number of Torah portions is indicated in most biblical texts, and there are editions in which the books are divided into Torah portions.

portion each Shabbat in a regular year (which, according to the Jewish calendar, consists of an average of 354 days, or about fifty weeks). Therefore, it is necessary, at times, to read two portions on one Shabbat. Even during leap years, which may have as many as 385 days, a number of Torah portions have to be joined together.

The reading of special Torah selections on the festivals entails other changes in the regular order. Since there is an additional day of *Yom Tov** in the Diaspora, when this occurs on Shabbat (i.e., the last day of Pesaḥ or the second day of Shavu'ot), the result is that while the Diaspora congregations read Torah selections relevant to the festival, those in the Land of Israel continue with the regular cycle, thus creating a disparity for several weeks between the Torah portions assigned in Israel and those in the Diaspora. However, during the summer months the readings are brought into alignment once more by an additional combination of Torah portions on one Shabbat in the Diaspora.

There are accepted traditions regarding these combinations of Torah portions: none of those in Genesis are joined; in Exodus the last two portions, *Vayakhel* and *Pekudei*, are sometimes read together; in Leviticus the combined portions are *Tazri'a* and *Metzora*, *Aḥarei Mot* and *Kedoshim*, *Behar* and *Beḥukkotai;* in Numbers, *Ḥukkat* and *Balak* (only in the Diaspora); and in Deuteronomy, *Nitzavim* and *Vayelekh*.

There are also certain customs that result in the combination of Torah portions. The two Torah portions *Beḥukkotai* (in Leviticus) and *Ki Tavo* (in Deuteronomy) both contain an admonition, and it is the custom not to read them on Sabbaths immediately preceding Shavu'ot and Rosh ha-Shanah, but rather at least one Shabbat prior to them.

There are special Torah readings on each festival day and other special occasions during the year, such as *Rosh Ḥodesh*, Ḥanukkah, Purim, and fast days (see Chapter 12), and they are selected to accord with the relevant day or occasion. If one of these falls on Shabbat, one must differentiate between festivals (those specified in the Torah as days of "holy convocation"—with the exception of *Rosh Ḥodesh*) and the other special days. On festivals, the Torah selection for that particular festival replaces the regular weekly Torah portion. But on the other special days, the regular portion is read, and for the *Maftir** a second Torah scroll is taken out from the Ark,* and the relevant Torah selection for that day is read.

It sometimes happens that two special occasions fall on the same

Shabbat (such as *Rosh Ḥodesh* Tevet and Ḥanukkah, or *Rosh Ḥodesh* Adar and Shabbat of the Portion of *Shekalim*). In these cases, three Torah scrolls are needed for the different Torah reading: one for the regular Torah portion, and the other two for the portions pertaining to these two special occasions. Three scrolls are also required on Simḥat Torah, even when the festival falls on a weekday (for further details, see Chapters 9–12).

Taking the Torah Scrolls Out of the Ark

Torah scrolls are removed from or replaced within the Holy Ark in a ceremonial manner, accompanied by prayer and song. The words recited on taking out the scrolls are generally the same for all occasions of Torah reading, but there are certain differences between the texts for Shabbat and festival mornings and those of weekday readings (and to some extent also of the Shabbat *Minḥah* service). In addition to changes in wording, there is far less ceremony, and fewer additional blessings, on weekdays, in order to spare the congregants an additional burden and loss of working time. But on Sabbaths and festivals, when everyone has more leisure, all is carried out with greater composure and stricter attention to ceremonial details.

The following is a description of the customs practiced on weekdays (for Sabbaths, see Chapter 9). Before opening the Ark, the Ashkenazim recite (sometimes sing), "And it came to pass when the Ark set forward, that Moses said: Rise up, O Lord, and let Your enemies be scattered; and let them that hate You flee before You" (Numbers 10:35); and "For out of Zion shall go forth the law, and the word of the Lord from Jerusalem" (Isaiah 2:3), followed by the blessing, "Blessed be He who gave the Torah to His people Israel in this holiness." Then, a prayer from the *Zohar*,# *Berikh Shemeih*,* is recited. The *Zohar* itself recommends that this be done when the Torah scrolls are taken out of the Ark.

One of the congregants is given the honor of opening the Ark and taking out the Torah scroll. This in itself is considered an act of great merit, which is offered to someone of importance among the congregants, or is sold as a special honor. He then hands it over to the *Shaliaḥ*

Tzibbur,* who holds it in his right hand, as is done in all instances when a Torah scroll is carried, in accordance with the verse "from His right hand went a fiery law for them" (Deuteronomy 33:2); and he embraces the scroll in such a way that the upper part of it leans against him. If the scroll is heavy, he may use his left hand to support it.

The *Ḥazzan* then recites the verse "O magnify the Lord with me, and let us exalt His name together" (Psalm 34:3). In some places this is done with ceremony, in which the *Ḥazzan* turns to face the Holy Ark while reciting the first half of this verse, and raising the scroll slightly while reciting the second half. This is in accordance with a rabbinic *midrash* that the entire Torah is God's name.[155]

The congregation responds with the recital of certain relevant verses. In the Ashkenazic custom, they say, "Yours, O Lord, is the greatness, and the power and the glory" (I Chronicles 29:11); "Exalt the Lord our God, and worship at His footstool, for He is holy"; "Exalt the Lord our God, and worship at His holy mount, for the Lord our God is holy" (Psalm 99:5,9).

In the Ashkenazic custom, while the *Ḥazzan* conducts the Torah scroll to the *Bimah*,* the following prayer is said: "May the All-Merciful Father have compassion on the people borne [by Him],[156] and remember the covenant with the mighty ones;[157] may He deliver our souls from evil times (namely, periods of bodily or spiritual failure), and banish the evil impulse from the ones carried by Him [cf. Zechariah 3:2]; may He graciously grant us eternal survival and fulfill our wishes in ample measure for salvation and mercy."

From the time the Torah scroll is removed from the Ark until it is placed on the *Bimah*, all rise in its honor, for the Talmud indicates (*Kiddushin* 33b) that all must stand up in the presence of the Torah scroll and are not permitted to sit until it is laid down in its place. It is customary in some places to approach as closely as possible to the Torah scroll, and whoever is near enough kisses its covering or case. Some touch it with the fringes of their *Tallit** and then kiss these. It is also the custom to accompany the scroll to its place (see Tractate *Soferim*# 14).

---

[155] See Naḥmanides' introduction to the Torah.

[156] A term used for the people of Israel, who are borne by God; cf. Isaiah 46:3.

[157] The term used for the Patriarchs of the nation; cf. *Rosh ha-Shanah* 11a.

The Order of Calling Up to the Torah

The honor of being called up to a public Torah reading is known as *Aliyah la-Torah* (literally, "Ascending to the Torah")—a term from medieval Jewish literature that is now universally accepted. On the most literal level, this is so because the platform *(Bimah)* from which the Torah scroll is read is elevated, and the person called up to the Torah reading has to mount this platform. But there is another, more abstract significance: that Torah reading is an honorary ascent, a spiritual elevation for the reader.

One does not ascend to a Torah reading unless invited, and this invitation is publicly announced by the synagogue warden *(Gabbai*)*, or by whoever is in charge of such matters. Customs differ regarding the manner in which the invitation to Torah reading is made.

In Ashkenazi congregations, the person is called up by his name and that of his father. The *Ḥazzan* (or *Gabbai*) in charge, in continuation of what was recited while taking out the Torah scrolls, says:

And may He help, shield and deliver all who trust in Him, and let us say, Amen. Let all render glory to our God and give honor to the Torah. Let the Kohen* *come forward. Arise . . . [calling out the Hebrew name of the person being called up, and that of his father] the* Kohen. *Blessed is He who in His holiness gave the Torah to His people Israel.*

He then adds the verses "The law of God is perfect . . ." (Psalm 19:7–8), "God will give strength . . ." (*ibid.*, 29:11) and "God is perfect in His ways . . ." (*ibid.*, 18:30). Some do not recite these verses. The response of the congregation is, "And you who cleave to the Lord your God are all alive today" (Deuteronomy 4:4). If there is no *Kohen* in the congregation, they say, "There is no *Kohen* here. Let [the Hebrew name of the person being called up, and his father's name; and if he is a Levite, they add "the Levite"] ascend instead of a *Kohen.*"

In many places, they add a title to the name: if he is a married man, they call him "Rabbi" (or "Rav"); if he is single, they call him, according to local custom, "the young man" or the "bridegroom." In certain places, there is an official title such as "*Ḥaver,*" "Rav," "Our Master," or other such titles. It is the practice to be very precise in stating the name of the person called up and the name of his father—and if he has several names, they are all cited—because this is a public declaration, one of several matters in which precision in naming is important for halakhic reasons. Care is taken to use his Hebrew name, unless he has none. A convert, or someone whose father is unknown, is called "son of Abraham." Whoever is called up to the Torah reading is not permitted to refuse this privilege, because such a refusal is an insult to both the honor of the Torah and that of the congregation. The one called up should demonstrate that it is a pleasure for him to go to the *Bimah*, and he should do so eagerly and by the shortest route. If the routes are equidistant, he should choose the right-hand direction. Once he reaches the *Bimah*, he must wait until the *Gabbai* recites the *Mi she-Berakh** blessing for the person preceding him, and then recite the first blessing on the Torah (see below), and at the end of the reading he recites the final blessing.

It is the custom in most congregations for the next person to be called up as soon as this final blessing is concluded, and only then does the *Gabbai* say *Mi she-Berakh* for the former person.

There are several formulations for the *Mi she-Berakh* blessing, both short and long, and there are variations in the formulation for different days in the year. There is a special one for a sick person (either a family member of the person ascending to the Torah, or any other person). Another formulation is used for one who has a family celebration, and yet another for those whom one wishes to honor publicly. It is customary in most congregations to insert within the *Mi she-Berakh* the phrase "because of his vow," in reference to a donation to the synagogue or to some other charitable or holy cause. Some add the phrase *Beli Neder* (literally, "without a vow," and here, in the sense of "please God"), so that this promised donation is not considered a formal vow (which would make the one who has pledged liable to serious punishment if it is not paid) but merely a voluntary gift. However, it is highly commendable to donate something, both in order to fulfill the obligation to give charity and to show that this honor is appreciated by, and important to, the person called up. Such a donation, however, is not halakhically mandatory; therefore, at weekday Torah readings it is not the usual practice to make one. In some places, no mention is made of a definite amount, but merely of an unspecified "gift" according to the generosity of the giver.

In the Ashkenazic custom, the person called up remains on the *Bimah* during the Torah reading of the person who follows him, and only after the latter has concluded the final blessing does the former descend and return to his place. Among the Ashkenazim, it is customary to greet the person as he returns to his seat with the words *Yishar Koaḥ* ("May strength be increased," in the sense of "Bravo!") as a form of encouragement and in thanks for the blessings he has made on their behalf. In some places, everyone shakes his hand in congratulation.

Such practices are customary mainly on Shabbat and on festivals, but on weekdays there is much less ceremony, and some even curtail the *Mi she-Berakh* and the donation vows.

Blessings for the Torah

The person called up to the Torah reading pronounces blessings before and after the reading. Some sages have said that the blessing before the Torah reading is a Torah commandment, and some say that even the concluding blessing is Torah-based (*Berakhot* 21a). In any case, these blessings are of the highest importance, both in themselves and for the honor they accord the Torah and the congregation. As we know, Ezra the Scribe blessed God before reading from the Torah (Nehemiah 8:6).

First, the rolled-up scroll is opened. In many customs, the person called up kisses the scroll—not directly, because this is prohibited, except in times of distress, but by touching it with the fringes of his *Tallit* (or *Tzitzit**), or with the scroll covering or band (see below), and then kissing these. Some touch the specific section about to be read, while others touch its beginning and its end, so as to define it. Others yet touch the beginning, the end, and again the beginning. Then the blessing is pronounced.

While reciting the blessing, one does not look at the scroll, so that it will not appear as though the blessing were written in the scroll. There are various customs for this; in most cases, the person turns his head aside (some say to the left).

It is an ancient custom for the person called up to grasp the two poles of the scroll (or its case) while making the blessing, and to continue holding one of them throughout the reading. This custom is mentioned by the *Rishonim** and relies on Lurianic Kabbalah.*

Before the actual pronouncement of the blessing, introductory words are said; some are according to local custom, while others are based on halakhic law. In all congregations,[158] the person making the blessing says, "Blessed be the Lord who is blessed"; the congregation responds with "Blessed be the Lord who is blessed for all eternity," and the person blessing repeats this phrase. The formulation of the first blessing is,

Blessed are You, Lord our God, King of the universe, who has chosen us from among all the nations and given us His Torah. Blessed are you, O Lord, who gives the Torah.

This formulation is derived from the Talmud, where it says that this is "the most supreme of all blessings," because it links together the choosing of Israel and the sanctity of the Torah (*Berakhot* 11b).

The concept expressed in the words "who has chosen us from among all the nations," is mentioned throughout the Bible; this particular formulation is based on the biblical verse "the Lord your God has chosen you to be a special people unto Himself, above all other nations" (Deuteronomy 7:6). The words "And given us His Torah" are explained in accordance with the Torah verse "These are the statutes and judgments and laws which the Lord made between Him and the children of Israel on Mount Sinai by the hand of Moses" (Leviticus 26:46). The combination of the election of Israel and the giving of the Torah is in accordance with the passage "He shows His word unto Jacob, His statutes and judgments unto Israel; He has not dealt so with any nation" (Psalm 147:19).

The use of the present tense in this blessing, "Blessed are You Lord, who gives the Torah," refers to what our sages have said, that the voice of God from Mount Sinai has not ceased to be heard, and it continues to speak at all times;[159] and even though we do not merit to hear

---

[158] According to Mishnah, *Berakhot* 7:3, and Talmud, *Berakhot* 50a.

[159] See the Rosh® on Deuteronomy 5:19.

it, He gives the Torah at all times. Others say that the meanings of the Torah, and the new commentaries on it that are being written all the time, are a continuation of the constant revelation of the Torah[160]

At the conclusion of the Torah reading, the person who makes the blessing rolls up the Torah scroll, and it is the practice to kiss the scroll once again before making the final blessing. The formulation of the final blessing is

Blessed are You, Lord our God, King of the universe, who has given us the Torah of truth and planted eternal life within us. Blessed are You Lord, who gives the Torah.

This blessing, which is in praise of the Torah, is said after its reading. The blessing that precedes the reading refers only to the merit and honor in receiving the Torah, while the one after it offers thanks and praise for its contents. The words "the Torah of truth" come from the biblical text "The Torah of truth was in his mouth" (see Malachi 2:6) and are one of the principal terms of praise for the Torah, which is an expression of God's truth, for it is said, "The judgments of the Lord are true and righteous altogether" (Psalm 19:9).

The expression "eternal life" alludes to a number of biblical verses; for instance, "And many of them that sleep in the dust shall wake to eternal life" (Daniel 12:2), or "life for evermore" (Psalm 133:3). Reference can also be made to the Tree of Life in Paradise, which is a symbol of the Torah in general, and of which it is said, "and take of the tree of life, and eat, and live forever" (Genesis 3:22).

The *Tur*# *(Oraḥ Ḥayyim, 139)* interprets the phrase "Torah of truth" as referring mainly to the written law that was given to us on Mount Sinai, while the phrase "and has planted eternal life within us" alludes to the biblical passage "The words of the wise are as goads, and as nails implanted" (Ecclesiastes 12:11). It is also said that "the words of the Torah are fruitful and multiply" (*Ḥagigah* 3b) like saplings, and therefore "plants." For this reason, it is said that this section of the blessing refers especially to the Oral Law. There is an ingenious allusion in *Abudraham*# that the numerical value of the words *Nata'*

[160] *Etz Yosef,*# Commentary to the Siddur, in the book *Otzar ha-Tefillot.*#

be-Tokhenu ("planted within us") is 613—the number of Torah commandments.

Whoever is obliged to recite the *ha-Gomel** blessing on the occasion of recovery from an acute illness or having been spared some ill fate, does so at this juncture, and the congregants respond accordingly. And anyone celebrating his son's Bar Mitzvah* now recites the blessing *Barukh she-Petarani,** in thanks for being relieved of the added legal responsibilities represented by a minor.

Torah-Reading Customs

There is a practice throughout Jewish communities to buy the privilege of, respectively, taking out the Torah scroll, lifting it up and winding it (*Hagbahah** and *Gelilah,** see below), and ascending to Torah readings. The proceeds from these transactions are used mainly for the upkeep of the synagogue or for other charitable causes, as the case may be. Besides the contribution this makes to public funds, the *Rishonim** have said that it demonstrates a sense of affection and respect for the *mitzvah.** Even though the Torah was freely given, and according to Halakhah it should be taught without fee, still, whatever one acquires by payment, one values more and thereby gains greater pride. In certain places, this is done in the manner of a public auction, the privilege being awarded to the highest bidder. Yet, in spite of the fact that it is permissible to speak of monetary matters connected with a *mitzvah* even on Shabbat, there were many who protested at the unsavory aspects of this practice; especially since it sometimes leads to competition between wealthy people, which is not entirely for the sake of Heaven and which prevents others, who are possibly more deserving, from receiving such honors—simply because they cannot afford them. For this reason, such "auctions" have nowadays been largely discontinued, or are carried out on a more modest scale, without public fanfare.

By law, the person who ascends to the Torah should read from the scroll himself. However, in the majority of Jewish congregations, most worshippers are unable to do this adequately, because the text of the Torah scroll is without any punctuation, vowel markings, or musical notations (see below, and in the Glossary: *Ta'amei ha-Mikra**). In order to read correctly, one has to memorize the division into verses and the vowel markings. Also, the lack of uniform spelling, and the occasional omission of vowel-like letters, may often lead to errors in reading. In addition, it is necessary to remember the varying cantillation in order to read the words with the correct melody. In earlier generations, those more practiced in reading were called up, and if it was necessary to call up one not well versed, someone else would assist him or read in his stead. It therefore became the practice in most congregations to have a professional Reader *(Ba'al Keriah*)* of the Torah who reads for all those called up.[161]

It is customary, after the person called up completes the first blessing, for the Reader to say Amen* and to begin reading the Torah portion, and when he finishes, the former pronounces the final blessing. Among the more strictly observant, the person called up repeats the words being read, but softly, so as not to confuse the Reader, and in this way it comes to pass that he indeed reads the Torah himself.

In Ashkenazic congregations, the one who ascends to the Torah is never alone on the *Bimah* (or only with the Torah Reader). There are at least one or two others standing on either side of the Torah scroll. This practice is hinted at in the Midrash (Tractate *Soferim*# 14, and also *Pirkei de-Rabbi Eliezer*# 44) as well as in the books of the *Rishonim.** The reason cited there is that we are reminded of the giving of the Torah, which was transmitted by God through His messenger. It also lends dignity to the Torah to have two persons (who are usually the *Gabba'im* or others serving in some religious capacity) stand like a guard of honor. These functionaries are, in fact, the ones who call up people to Torah readings, pronounce the *Mi she-Berakh* blessings, and serve as prompters for the Reader, by whispering or by sign language, to remind him of something he has forgotten, or to resolve any confusion that might occur. By law, there have to be at least two people near the Torah scroll: the Reader and the person called up to the Torah reading.

It is a pious custom during Torah readings for everyone listening to stand up, a practice supported by both biblical texts and the Talmud (*Megillah* 21a). But because of inconvenience and human weakness, this was not established as mandatory. Even though there are some congregations in which this custom is commonly observed, most congre-

---

[161] This finds support in a custom practiced in the Temple, namely the recitation of the confession during the offering of the first fruits (Mishnah, *Bikkurim* 3:7).

gants tend to sit during the Torah reading. It is appropriate to stand, or at least raise oneself slightly, when the person making the blessing says *Barekhu.** Nevertheless, it is customary for the whole congregation to stand during the reading of specific Torah portions, such as those of the Ten Commandments* or the Song of the Sea,* and it is also the practice to rise for the completion of one of the Five Books of the Pentateuch and to say *Ḥazak.**

On completion of the Torah reading, the half *Kaddish** is recited, generally by the Reader, or sometimes by the person called up, or even by one of the congregants. When two Torah scrolls are taken out, the half *Kaddish* is recited after reading from the first scroll (used for the main portion). However, at the Torah reading during *Minḥah* services, the half *Kaddish* is recited right before the *Amidah*.

Hagbahah ("Raising") and *Gelilah* ("Winding") of the Torah Scroll

The custom of raising the Torah scroll and displaying it to the congregants is mentioned in Tractate *Soferim*, Chapter 14, but there are differences in practice. In the Ashkenazic custom, the scroll is raised after the Torah reading, while in certain Ḥassidic congregations in Israel it is held aloft before the Torah reading.

Hagbahah with a Sephardic Torah scroll (left) and with an Ashkenazic Torah scroll (right)

The raising of the Torah scroll is also carried out in different ways. In the Ashkenazic custom, the person who has been given the honor of *Hagbahah* grasps the two poles, opens the scroll to show three columns, and turns around with it to display it to the congregation. Some make a complete turn from right to left, while others make a half turn to the right and then to the left. According to Rabbi Isaac Luria,@ all the congregants should strive to see the writing in the open Torah scroll.

During the raising of the Torah scroll, it is customary to recite certain verses of the Torah, each prayer version having its own selection of verses. It is also the practice to bow slightly toward the Torah scroll, as is indicated in Tractate *Soferim* (*ibid.*). In many places, one raises a finger in the direction of the scroll while reciting the verses of praise, and some extend a kiss from a distance.

The winding of the Torah scroll after a reading (*Gelilah*) is mentioned in Tractate *Megillah* 32a, where it says that this is an important *mitzvah*, and that the winder of the Torah scroll receives a reward comparable to that of all those who read it.

Among Ashkenazic congregations, the person who raises the Torah scroll sits down with the scroll held open, while the winder tightens up the scroll. In some places, the raiser puts the open scroll down on the *Bimah*, rolls it up, and sits down with the closed scroll, while the task of the winder is to make sure that the scroll is wound up well. The Talmud (*Megillah* 32a) says that the scroll must be wound in such a way that the stitches holding the folio sheets together can be seen. The reason for this is a practical one: to make sure that the scroll is tightened to the right extent, not too loosely, and not so tightly as to tear the seams. It is also necessary to see to it that the scroll is tight on the inside, without loose sheets on the inside while tight ones are only on the outside. This procedure completed, the winder fastens the band of the scroll not with a real knot but with a slip knot or with a fitted clasp, replaces its mantle covering, and hangs the *Yad** (pointer; see below), the breastplate, and the *Rimmonim** (finials) or *Keter** (crown).

Even though scroll winding is an important *mitzvah*, this task is sometimes given to a boy under thirteen years of age, because this is not a *mitzvah* that one performs on behalf of others in order to exempt them.

In some congregations, the raising and winding of the Torah scroll are "sold"; and everywhere, those who perform these functions are called up by name, and the *Mi she-Berakh* blessing is pronounced over them. Generally, the one who raises the scroll continues holding it until the end of the Torah reading (including the *Haftarah** reading, and the rest of the prayers recited before the scroll is returned to the Ark). He may, if he wishes, hand it over to someone else to hold. Sometimes there is a special stand for the scroll.

Returning the Torah Scrolls to the Ark

Before returning the scrolls to the Ark, it is customary in most congregations to say words of prayer. In most Ashkenazic congregations (*Nusaḥ Ashkenaz* and *Sepharad*, but not Ḥabad), they say, "May it be the will of our Father in Heaven . . ." which is found already in the *Siddur of Rav Amram Gaon.*# In *Nusaḥ Sepharad*, they recite here the *Ashrei*,* *la-Menatzeaḥ*,* and *u-Va le-Zion Go'el*,* followed by *Kaddish Titkabbal.**

The *Ḥazzan* lifts up the Torah scroll, and some verses of praise are recited. In the Ashkenazic custom, the *Ḥazzan* begins with "Let them praise the name of the Lord, for His name alone is sublimely exalted" (Psalm 148:13), and the congregants respond with

His radiance is upon the earth and heavens. He shall raise the glory of His people, the praise of all His pious ones, the children of Israel, the people close to Him. Praise the Lord! (ibid., 13–14*)*

Most of the Ashkenazic congregations (including those of the *Nusaḥ Sepharad* version, except for Ḥabad) recite Psalm 24 on all days, except for Shabbat morning. In other customs, other verses of praise are recited. Then most communities (except those that follow Rabbi Isaac Luria,@ such as Ḥabad) recite "And when it rested, he said, Return, O Lord, unto the many thousands of Israel" (Numbers 10:36), as well as other verses from various sources.

While the Torah scroll is being returned to its place, everyone stands until it is placed in the Ark, and during its return—just as when it was being taken out—congregants approach and kiss it. It is customary for the raiser and winder to escort the *Ḥazzan* to the Ark, and for the rest of the congregation to accompany them for a little way. When the *Ḥazzan* reaches the Ark, the person who had taken out the Torah scroll is there, waiting to put it back in. Then the Ark is closed and the prayer services continue.

The People Called Up to the Torah Reading

The Mishnah* determines the number of persons called up to the Torah reading on the various occasions. This number is linked to the sanctity of the day, with additional persons called up according to its degree of sanctity and the laws pertaining to the prohibition of work.

In the *Shaḥarit* service, which includes the main Torah readings, seven persons are called up on Shabbat (eight, counting the *Maftir;* see Chapter 9); on Yom Kippur, six (seven, with the *Maftir;* see Chapter 11); on a festival day, five (six, with the *Maftir;* see Chapter 10); on *Rosh Ḥodesh* and on *Ḥol ha-Mo'ed*, four (see Chapter 12); and for all the rest of the Torah readings—on Mondays and Thursdays, in the *Minḥah* service of Shabbat and Yom Kippur, on Ḥanukkah and Purim, and on fast days—three persons are called up.

In general, it is customary not to have additional persons called up—except for Simḥat Torah (see Chapter 10)—unless there is some special need for it. There are certain congregations where the number is increased at the Shabbat morning service. While in certain customs it is the practice never to have any additional persons called up, others call many additional persons, especially on joyous occasions when they want to honor a larger number of people.

According to the law, it is enough for each person to read only three verses, but there are certain limitations to this. The first, which is talmudic law (*Megillah* 22a-b), is that one must not begin a reading less than three verses from the start of a Torah section in the text *(Parshiyyah*)*, and that one must conclude the reading at least three verses before the end of a section. In addition, it is customary not to conclude the reading at a place where a negative statement or a threat of punishment is made, but to continue reading up to an appropriate point for making a pause. It is also mandatory not to stop in the midst of the Admonition sections (Leviticus 26:14–46; Deuteronomy 28:16–69), but for one person to read each of them in its entirety. In addition, no break is made during the reading of the Ten Commandments and during other special Torah sections.

A certain order was already laid down in the Mishnah for ascensions to the Torah, so as to avoid contention or competition in this regard. Our sages have ruled that the first one to ascend should be a *Kohen*,* the second a Levite, and then all the rest. According to the Talmud (*Gittin* 59a), there is a descending order in the ascensions, with the more important persons being called up first. But nowadays, certain ascensions—the third and the sixth—are considered as special for various reasons (both straightforward and esoteric), and are set aside as greater honors. There are different evaluations in different congregations as to which of the two is of greater importance.

There are also instances in which the importance of the ascension results from its content, such as the reading of the Ten Commandments or the Song of the Sea. On the other hand, there are places in which people refrain from ascending to read the Admonition section.

The order of ascensions prescribed by law is mandatory, so that if there is a *Kohen* present he is called up first, and if there is no Levite present the *Kohen* reads the following section as well. In some congregations, if there is no *Kohen*, they call up a Levite to the first ascension, but in others this practice is not strictly observed. Since the first and second ascensions are to honor the priesthood and the Levites, the order remains unchanged, and the *Kohen* can only be called up to the first ascension (or to the *Maftir*), and the Levite can be called up to the second ascension, or to the first one instead of the *Kohen* (or to the *Maftir*).

It is customary in many congregations that two closely related persons—a father and son, or two brothers—are not called up one after the other, but another person is called up between them. However, this is not so strictly observed when one of them is called up to the *Maftir*. Similarly, a person can be called up to an ascension and can also be called up to the *Maftir* later on.

There is no law that obliges one to ascend to the Torah reading a fixed number of times a year, and the frequency of ascension depends on synagogue arrangements. It is the general usage everywhere, however, to have a certain schedule, and to ensure that every person ascends to the Torah reading at least once a month (or, if that is impossible, at least once a year). In many places, it is the practice for the rabbi of the community or its leader to be called up every Shabbat.

Certain mandatory ascensions have become the standard custom in all Jewish congregations. Even though it is not based on talmudic law, there are those who have an obligation *(Ḥiyyuv*)*, on certain occasions, to ascend to a Torah reading and are given first priority. They are: a boy who has reached Bar Mitzvah age; a bridegroom who is being feted on that Shabbat (for the Ashkenazim it is the Shabbat before the wedding); someone to whom a child has just been born; and also the main participants in a circumcision* (namely, the father, the godfather *[Sandak]*, and the circumciser *[Mohel]*). It is also a *Ḥiyyuv* to ascend to the Torah reading on the Shabbat before the anniversary of a parent's death (see *Yahrzeit**), and—in a lower degree of priority—that of other relatives, as well as on the *Yahrzeit* itself (if there is a Torah reading on that day). There is a certain accepted order of priorities in these matters, partly dependent on local custom, that can be found in various contemporary halakhic works.

The Torah Scroll

The Torah scroll is written on the skin of "pure"[162] animals and beasts. It is permissible to write the scroll on a roll of processed hide called *Gevil*. However, in most communities it is customary to inscribe the Torah on parchment, or *Kelaf*. During mishnaic and talmudic times, the *Kelaf* used to be made by slitting the skin into layers, and it is the inner side of the hide, nearest the flesh, that is called *Kelaf* in Hebrew (the word is based on the verb *KLF*, "to peel," because the skin is peeled off). In our times, the *Kelaf* is made by removing the outer layers on both sides of the hide, leaving the central layer, which is partially transparent.

The skin must be processed especially for this sacred purpose by a Jewish person, and the processing should be done in such a way that the parchment will be long-lasting, smooth, and easy to write upon.

Torah scrolls do not have any fixed size, and some are exceptionally large while others are very small. However, care is taken to arrange

[162] Namely, animals that are permitted for consumption; included are domesticated animals such as cows and sheep, and wild animals such as deer and buffalo; see Deuteronomy 14.

the sheets in such a way that the height and circumference of the book will be the same. Since it is impossible to write the entire Torah on one single sheet of parchment, each scroll is made up of several sheets sewn together. The sewing should be done with the ligaments of pure animals. There are various laws concerning its execution. Although there is no prescribed length for the sheets, care is taken that each sheet contain at least three columns of script, and not more than eight columns.

There are standard measures for the script, with each line long enough to contain thirty letters, in proportion to the size of the letters in the scroll. Different practices apply in regard to the number of lines on each page, and it is customary to have no fewer than forty-two (or forty-eight) lines, and no more than sixty. Halakhically prescribed space is always left both between the lines and between the pages, and fixed rules apply to this empty space (called *Gillayon*) regarding the amount left at the top and bottom of each page and between pages. Before inscribing the scroll, rows are incised (but not drawn) across it, to ensure a uniformity of lettering and line spacing.

Great care is taken for the Torah scroll to be written in an esthetically pleasing manner, and the lines are therefore justified. However, four lines are left blank between one book of the Pentateuch and another. In addition, the Torah is divided into portions, with a blank space left before them. Three blank lines are left before the larger Torah portions (except for the portions *va-Yiggash* and *va-Yeḥi*, at the end of the book of Genesis, between which there is a space of only one letter). There is also a subdivision into smaller portions, which end in an open *(Petuḥah)* or closed *(Setumah)* manner. This division is based on traditions found in the Oral Law, and anyone who changes it invalidates the entire scroll.

In addition, there are two songs in the Torah—the Song of the Sea and the Song of Moses (Deuteronomy 32:1–43)—that are not written in consecutive lines but in a special manner, so that there is an interstice within each line; any change made in this invalidates the scroll. Furthermore, various customs are observed by scribes in writing scrolls, and even though they are not obligatory by halakhic law, this is the way most Torah scrolls are written. For instance, it is the accepted practice to have every page (column), except for six specific pages, begin with the letter *Vav*.

The Torah scroll must be written for its own sake, and it is the

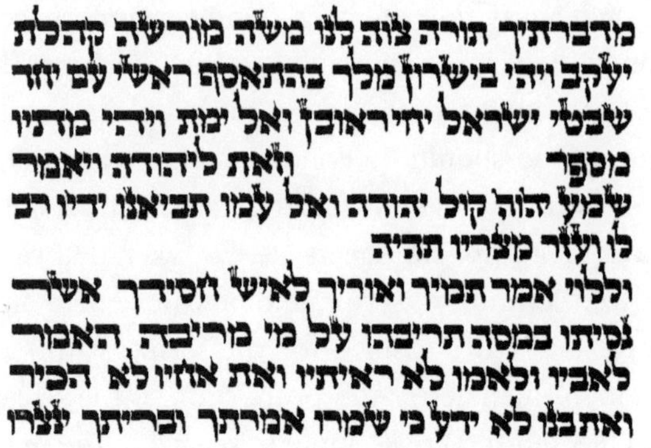
מדברתיך תורה צוה לנו משה מורשה קהלת
יעקב ויהי בישרון מלך בהתאסף ראשי עם יחד
שבטי ישראל יחי ראובן ואל ימת ויהי מתיו
מספר וזאת ליהודה ויאמר
שמע יהוה קול יהודה ואל עמו תביאנו ידיו רב
לו ועזר מצריו תהיה
וללוי אמר תמיך ואוריך לאיש חסידך אשר
נסיתו במסה תריבהו על מי מריבה האמר
לאביו ולאמו לא ראיתיו ואת אחיו לא הכיר
ואת בנו לא ידע כי שמרו אמרתך ובריתך ינצרו

A section from a Torah scroll written in the usual style. Line four shows the *Setumah* ending of one section and the beginning of another. Line six shows the *Petuḥah* ending.

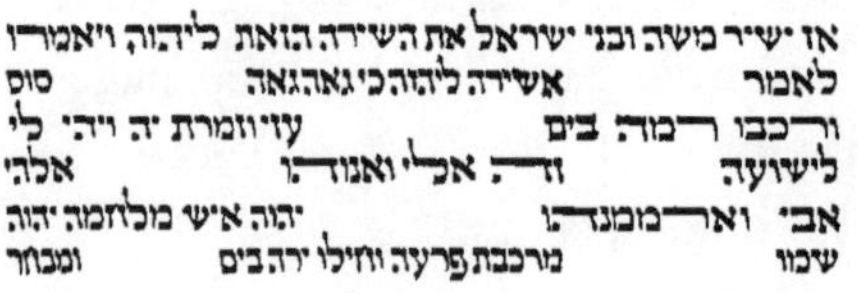
אז ישיר משה ובני ישראל את השירה הזאת ליהוה ויאמרו
לאמר אשירה ליהוה כי גאה גאה סוס
ורכבו רמה בים עזי וזמרת יה ויהי לי
לישועה זה אלי ואנוהו אלהי
אבי וארממנהו יהוה איש מלחמה יהוה
שמו מרכבת פרעה וחילו ירה בים ומבחר

A section showing the special style used for writing the Song of the Sea

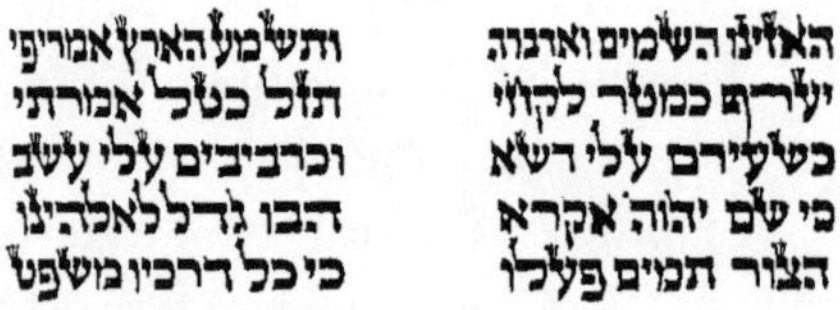
האזינו השמים ואדברה ותשמע הארץ אמרי פי
יערף כמטר לקחי תזל כטל אמרתי
כשעירם עלי דשא וכרביבים עלי עשב
כי שם יהוה אקרא הבו גדל לאלהינו
הצור תמים פעלו כי כל דרכיו משפט

A section showing the special style used for writing the Song of Moses

custom for the scribe to say, before beginning his task, "I am writing this scroll for the sake of the sanctity of the Torah." The scribe should be not only well versed in the laws and customs of scroll writing, and an expert in fine script, but he must also be an honest, God-fearing person. A scroll written by a non-Jew, and (all the more so) by a non-believer, is not valid. The scroll must be written in black ink; any other color invalidates the scroll. In the past, ink made of soot and oil, a sort of India ink, was used. In our times, other kinds of ink are used, but care is taken that it be durable and indelible.

Great precision must be observed in writing the words and letters of the Torah scroll, and there is an extensive and detailed masoretic tradition regarding the exact spelling of every single word in the Torah. Any deviation whatsoever from this invalidates the scroll from the outset. It is also necessary to be precise in writing each letter separately, so that they will all be surrounded by white space ("air") and not run into each other.

The script used in Torah scrolls is unique; in the Talmud it is called "Assyrian script," or *Stam* letters (STM being the acronym, in Hebrew, for the words *Sefarim* [Torah scrolls], *Tefillin,** and *Mezuzot,** in which this script is used). The exact shape and form of these letters are a matter of tradition, which involves many halakhic details. Some explanations and interpretations for the letter formations are given already in the Talmud (see *Shabbat* 104a), and many more can be found in kabbalistic works. There are even some books devoted exclusively to explaining the letter formations and their mystic significance.

The letters are also adorned with decorative stems known as *Tagim,* "crownlets," some having one crownlet and others having three. There are numerous traditions also for the writing of the letters; so, for example, certain letters in certain words are written large or small (there are lists detailing them). Moreover, there are detailed traditions regarding certain letters that should be written in an unusual manner, or given special crownlets. Some early works, such as *Sefer Tagim*—"The Book of Crownlets"—provide a list of such letters. However, in our times, most of the scribes do not use these variant forms (which are a matter of stricter, more enhanced observance), because they are not well versed in these subjects.

Even though the principal laws and customs concerning the formation of the letters are determined by Halakhah, in practice certain differences still exist between the various customs. Mainly, there are three different forms of scribal writing—the Ashkenazic script, the Oriental script, and the Italian script, each having its own precise form of lettering.

These matters concerning the writing of the Torah scroll, with its meticulous division into sections and its precise lettering, are of great importance. They are dealt with in detail not only

Different styles of *Stam* letters. From right to left: the typeset letter, the *Stam* letter in the Ashkenazic style, in the style according to Rabbi Isaac Luria, and in the Sephardic style.

in halakhic works[163] but also by some of the great *Rishonim*,[164] who wrote weighty tomes to explain and clarify them in detail, and there is considerable, and ramified, literature on the subject down to our own times.

Wrappings and Decorations of the Torah Scroll

The early sages explained the phrase "this is my God, and I will adorn Him" (Exodus 15:2) as "adorn yourself before Him in the fulfillment of the *mitzvot:* make . . . a beautiful Torah scroll . . . and wrap it about with beautiful silk" (*Shabbat* 133b, and elsewhere). The cloth coverings of the Torah scroll possess great sanctity, and it is forbidden to use them for any other purpose, even for a holy one (*Megillah* 25b, 27a). It was also pointed out that a special casing was made for the Torah scroll (*Shabbat* 116b).

In our days, there are two different customs concerning the scroll coverings, and these differences also affect the way the scroll is read, rewound, and placed in the Ark. The Ashkenazic custom (which also applies to some of the Moroccan congregations and the Sephardic congregations in Holland, as well as those that originated from there) is for the Torah scroll to be wrapped in a mantle which is a sheath of fabric, while the custom among most of the Oriental congregations, as well as those of the Yemenites, is to place the scroll within a strong casing made of wood or metal. In the Ashkenazic custom, the poles on which the Torah scroll is wound—which are rhetorically called *Etz Ḥayyim** ("tree of life") according to the verse "She [meaning the Torah] is a tree of life to them that lay hold upon her" (Proverbs 3:18)—are constructed in a special manner, so that each pole has a wide circular piece at either end, through which the central handles for winding the scroll and lifting it up are fitted.

---

[163] E.g., Maimonides,® *Yad ha-Ḥazakah,*# *Hilkhot Ketivat Sefer Torah* (The Laws of Writing a Torah Scroll); *Shulḥan Arukh, Oraḥ Ḥayyim, Hilkhot Tefillin*; ibid., *Yoreh De'ah, Hilkhot Ketivat Sefer Torah.*

[164] Such as the Remah®; the author of the talmudic commentary *Meiri*#; and others.

After the Torah scroll is rolled up, it is tied with a special band of cloth, known as a wimple. These bands are made in various styles; some are very long and are wound several times around the scroll. The band is wound over the central section of the scroll, or, as in certain customs, close to the upper third of it. It is not customary to fasten it with a knot, but to make a slip knot (among other reasons, so as not to inadvertently transgress the prohibition to untie a knot on Shabbat). In some places, a metal clasp is sewn at the end of the band, so that there is no need for even a slip knot.

There were some congregations, especially in Germany, in which it was customary for a newborn boy who was about to be circumcised to have a special band on which his name was embroidered, and which was later dedicated to the synagogue to tie the Torah scrolls. This winding and tying of the band is done by the person chosen to rewind the scroll after the Torah reading (see *Gelilah*, above). It is an accepted custom that if a certain invalidation is found in the Torah scroll, this is indicated by first dressing the scroll in its mantle and then winding the band around it.

After winding the scroll and tying it up with a band, it is dressed in a cylindrical mantle made of fabric, usually velvet, in the upper section of which there is a belt to prevent it from slipping off. These mantles are often richly embroidered with silver and gold thread in a variety of designs. Many are dedicated to a departed soul, whose name (and the name of the person dedicating it) is embroidered on the mantle. Since there often are more mantles than Torah scrolls, the custom is to alternate them periodically, either because they wear out, or in honor of the dedicator (e.g., on the anniversary of the departed).

There is no fixed custom regarding the color of the mantle, but in many congregations a white mantle is put on the scrolls during the Days of Awe,* and especially on Yom Kippur (see Chapter 11). In some congregations, all the mantles are made of one color, and there are special ones, with a variety of colors, for Shabbat and festivals.

In most places, ornamental objects called *Rimmonim* are hung over the *Etz Ḥayyim*. These are metal rods, sometimes made of precious metals, with the upper part shaped like a pomegranate, often with bells attached to them. This is a reminder of the High Priest's robe, which had bells and pomegranate-shaped balls attached to its hem (Exodus 28:34).

In well-to-do congregations, a Torah crown *(Keter Torah)* of silver or gold may be placed over the two handles of the scroll's wooden poles in place of the *Rimmonim.* These crowns do not have any specified shape, and are made in accordance with the artist's imagination. However, it is generally the custom to have them constructed of three crowns, one on top of the other, to symbolize the Three Crowns—i.e., the Torah, the Priesthood, and the Monarchy (Mishnah, *Avot* 4:13). A decorated silver breastplate (*Tas*) is placed over the mantle. In certain places, it was customary to decorate the Torah scroll with the *Rimmonim* or crown only on Shabbat and festival days.

The Pointer *(Yad)*

Since it is prohibited to touch the scroll with bare hands (*Megillah* 32a), unless there is some special need to do so, it is the custom in many places to use a *Yad** (literally, a "hand"), a thin wand, with which to indicate the words being read, both so that the Reader will not err and so that the person called up can follow the reading. In many congregations, this *Yad* is indeed shaped at one end like a human hand, with one finger stretched forward. The *Yad* is made of wood or metal, and sometimes even of silver or gold. In many places, there is a chain attached to the *Yad*, and after the Torah reading the *Yad* is hung by this chain on the mantle or the casing of the Torah scroll.

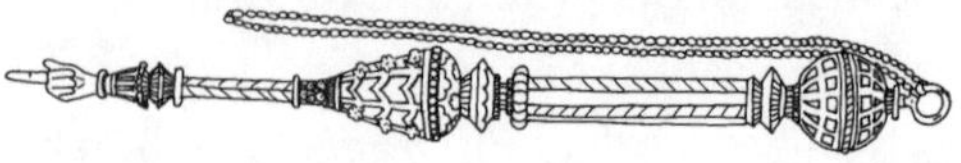

Cantillation of the Torah Reading
(*Ta'amei ha-Mikra*)

When the Torah is read in public, it is chanted according to prescribed cantillation. This should also apply to Torah passages read within the prayer service, such as the *Shema**; however, this latter custom is not very widespread.

The cantillation of the Torah dates back to the beginnings of Oral Law transmission, since it reflects the living tradition of how the words of the Torah are to be read. Our sages have explained the words "and caused them to understand the reading" (Nehemiah 8:8) as referring to the cantillation marks (*Megillah* 3a). These notations indicate not only how every word should be read, but also how to divide up the verse so that its meaning is clear. This is the main sense of the word *Ta'am*, which means "explanation" or "interpretation."

As with the rest of the Oral Law, these cantillation marks were not written down but were transmitted, as a tradition to be learned by heart, by the instructor of little children who taught them Torah (and whose duty it was, among other things, to teach the cantillation; see *Nedarim* 37a). Therefore, these accents are not written into the Torah scroll but appear only in the printed books of the Pentateuch, and the Torah Reader must know the accentuations by heart.

Although the reading of the Torah with its cantillation is mentioned in the Mishnah and Talmud, it seems that only when the Oral Law was being written down did those well versed in the masoretic traditions begin to record the accentuations, to discuss them and to interpret them systematically. In time, the greatest Hebrew grammarians began to deal with this system of cantillation, and most of the older Hebrew grammars devoted considerable space to this. Some contemporary works, too, deal comprehensively with the punctuation aspect of the cantillation system.

The written cantillation signs are uniform throughout the Jewish world, even though their names vary among the different communities. Sources indicate that there were ancient terms for these signs that have changed over the generations, with some still being retained among certain communities, while others are no longer extant. The names used for the accents sometimes explain their significance; e.g., *Sof Pasuk*—"the end of the verse"—namely, full stop; *Etnaḥta*—"pause," i.e., comma. Others refer to the external shape of the cantillation sign, such as *Merkha* (quotation marks), *Karnei Parah* (horns of the cow), or *Mahapakh* (inverted horn), or even indicate the place in the written text, such as *Revi'a* (quarter).

According to a very ancient tradition (which is still followed to some extent today, and in some congregations even systematically so), various hand movements were used to indicate to the Reader how the text should be read.[165] It could be that some of the cantillation symbols are abbreviated graphic representations of these hand movements, and, contrarily, some of these movements may be imitations of the written signs.

In kabbalistic works, from the *Zohar*[#] and onward, there are profound mystic explanations for the cantillation signs and their names, and there is considerable material on varying levels of depth in the homiletic literature throughout the generations.

The accents serve three purposes: (a) the correct reading of the Torah, to determine the stops between the verses and within each individual verse; (b) the accentuation of each word; (c) the melody that accompanies the reading.

The system of cantillation, which according to the Ashkenazic count includes twenty-six accents, determines the correct division of the sentences. Some of them are extremely rare in the Torah text, such as *Karnei Parah*, which occurs only once. For this reason, the accents are divided into two main groups: stop accents that indicate pauses of varying lengths, and servant accents that link words together.

The early grammarians divided the stop accents into three levels, according to the intensity of the pause, and gave them the nicknames of "Emperors," "Kings," and "Ministers" (or "Deputies"). Grammatically speaking, the sentences are divided by the Emperors, and subdivided into sections by the Kings, and these are once more subdivided by the Ministers. The levels in accentuation are of both theoretical and grammatical significance, yet from a melodic viewpoint, it is sometimes the weaker stop accents that are noted and felt more than the stronger

---

[165] Hence the talmudic saying that the right hand is important "because it indicates the accents of the Torah" (*Berakhot* 62a).

ones. The whole complex series of the accents creates a unique punctuation system, one that provides a high degree of precision in the subtle distinctions of meanings, as well as a greater degree of sensitivity toward the inner rhythms of the written text.

The following are explanations for some of the most commonly used accents in the Torah and the Prophets.

Emperor Accents

There are two Emperor accents—the *Sof Pasuk* (full stop) and the *Etnaḥta* (comma). The *Sof Pasuk* indicates the end of the sentence, just as the single dot does in Western punctuation. The *Etnaḥta*, which means "rest" or "pause," is found in nearly every verse of the Torah, and divides the verse into two parts, not always of equal size. This accent is very frequently found in the Torah, because both in its prose literature and in its poetry, sentences are composed of two parts, either parallel and similar to each other, or opposed and contrapuntal. In modern punctuation, there is no sign comparable to the *Etnaḥta*, which may serve as a comma, a semicolon, or a dash. These two accents sometimes have an influence even on the vowels applied to a word, such as changing a short vowel into a long one, and occasionally their effect is to move the stress from the last to the penultimate syllable.

King Accents

All the King accents are lesser pauses, and their degree of disjunction ranges from that of the comma in modern punctuation to stresses in reading that have no comparable modern-day signs.

The *Segol* is the longest of these pauses. It is much more often found in the Prophets than in the Pentateuch, and sometimes, in combination with the *Etnaḥta*, it divides the verse into three equivalent parts.

The *Zakef* (which includes the major form of *Zakef Gadol*, and the more frequently used minor form of the *Zakef Katan*, and is sometimes combined with another accentuation), is a kind of comma.

The *Tippeḥa* is a short disjunctive accent but is more frequently used. It is generally found twice in every verse, just before the *Etnaḥta* and again before the *Sof Pasuk*. It serves to indicate a very brief suspension of breath before completion of the idea being expressed.

The *Revi'a* is a brief interruption, less frequently used than the others, and often serves as a colon.

The *Shalshelet* (which means "chain") is unique for its function not only as a pause but also for the special stress it places upon the word in its particular context.

The *Pesik* may be considered either an accent or merely a calligraphic sign, which generally serves to separate two identical words or to stress the division between two words, each of which must be distinctly emphasized and interpreted.

Minister Accents

Among the Minister accents, the most commonly used are the *Merkha* and the *Munaḥ*, for whose position in every verse there are defined grammatical rules, according to the pause accents that follow. These Minister accents serve to link two or three words into a single sense unit, and there are also accents that serve as deputy ministers to another Minister accent.

Cantillation signs also indicate the correct stress on words, with implications not only for the beauty of the reading but often for the very sense of the phrase. (For example: the word *Ba'ah* has two meanings, in the past tense and the present tense, which are distinguished by the penultimate or the ultimate stress sign; stress may also signify distinction between the verb and noun forms of a word.) The general rule is that the syllable to be stressed is the one that has an accent above or beneath it.

There are two other signs for the accentuation of words—the *Meteg* and the *Makaf*—which are not included in the cantillation system of accent signs and do not possess any melodic value. The *Meteg*, also called *Ga'aya*, is generally found in long multisyllabic words and is placed beneath the syllable of secondary stress. In such instances, besides the major accent that indicates the stress, there is also a lesser stress on another syllable. The *Makaf* serves to combine two words, and sometimes three or four, which are usually short and which should, in terms of their accentuation, be read as one long word. Only one accent is used for such combined words, and it affects the combination as a whole.

The melody for the cantillation differs greatly among the prayer rites, and music researchers have found eight different ways of chanting the accents. The melody used by the Ashkenazic congregations is essentially uniform, although there are differences between that of southern Germany and of Lithuania-Poland, as well as subtler differences within every region.

The melody also varies according to the occasion and to the content of the reading. Thus, there is a special intonation for the Torah reading during the Days of Awe* (see Chapter 11), there are differences between Torah readings and the reading of the *Haftarah*, and different melodies used for reading the Five Scrolls, especially for Lamentations (read on Tish'ah be-Av) and the Book of Esther (read on Purim; see Chapter 12).

Besides all this, since the chanting of the accents is influenced by orally transmitted traditions, musical notation and the human ear can prove that there are differences even within the same prayer rite and between one reader and another. The musical notations should be seen as mere approximations, being too imprecise to record the trills and overtones.

PART FOUR

THE SYNAGOGUE AND COMMUNAL PRAYER

CHAPTER FOURTEEN ❧ *The Synagogue*

Ancient Origins of the Synagogue

We do not know when synagogues were first established. It is evident, however, that since the early years of Jewish nationhood, particular sites were allocated for public gatherings of various types, foremost for prayers and Torah readings. Some of our sages, and later Rashi,@ following in their footsteps, have interpreted the term *Beit ha-Am* ("house of the people") mentioned in Jeremiah (39:8) as indicating a synagogue. This interpretation is somewhat supported by the sages' opposition to the popular use of the term *Beit ha-Am* for the synagogue (*Shabbat* 32a).

In any case, it is certain that by the Second Temple period, synagogues devoted mainly to public prayer were already in existence both in the Land of Israel and in the Diaspora. Evidence of the ancient origins of the synagogue appearing in early rabbinic literature is echoed in accounts given by Philo of Alexandria@ and by Josephus Flavius,@ who lived at the end of the Second Temple period.

The synagogue as a place of prayer has a distinct function of its own, not as a replacement for the Temple but as supplementary to it. For this reason, we find that on the Temple Mount, near the Temple edifice, there was a synagogue intended for public prayer (Mishnah,* *Yoma* 7:1, and elsewhere). The main function of the Temple is to provide a dwelling place for the *Shekhinah*,* and the main service there is the offering of sacrifices. The Temple was also the site of occasional gatherings of the general public to request Divine favor, and anyone could go there to offer a personal, private prayer. Even gentiles were permitted to pray in the Temple.[166] However, the Temple edifice could

---

[166] As described in detail in King Solomon's prayer at the dedication of the First Temple, I Kings 8:29–53.

not accommodate regular public prayer services in which the entire congregation participated together. Thus, although occasional blessings and prayers were recited in the Temple, there was a need for a specially designated place—a synagogue—where people could pray.

According to the Halakhah,* every community with ten or more Jewish men is required to build a permanent synagogue as a place for prayer. This is such a fundamental duty that residents of a town without a synagogue are permitted to compel community members to participate in building one. It was once the custom for Jewish community leaders to impose a tax on all members of the congregation for this purpose. The amounts were calculated according to the economic level of each resident, in relation to the number of family members, or relative to the congregant's assigned seat in the synagogue (e.g., the highest sums were charged for seats placed along the eastern wall of the synagogue).

Ancient Synagogues

Because of religious persecution, most ancient synagogues have been destroyed. We can garner evidence of their existence, however, from written sources, and sometimes also from archeological remains. Besides the testimony recorded by our sages, there are a few traces of synagogue ruins in Jerusalem, and ruins of the synagogue on Masada, as well as in some other places in the Land of Israel, that date back to the Second Temple period.

In Babylonia, there were two very ancient synagogues: one in the city of Neharde'a, nicknamed "the synagogue that moved and settled in Neharde'a" (*Megillah* 29a), and another in the city of Hutzal. The construction of both has been attributed to the first exiles sent to Babylonia during the reign of Jehoiachin in the First Temple period. There are some remaining traces and written evidence of synagogues built in Egypt in the third century B.C.E., and of a magnificent synagogue that once stood in all its massive splendor in the city of Alexandria, only to be destroyed in 115 C.E. [167]

---

[167] Of this synagogue, our sages said: "He who has not seen the double colonnade of Alexandria in Egypt has never seen the glory of Israel" (*Sukkah* 51b).

Evidence from written sources and archeological remains of synagogues were also found in other countries, such as Syria, the Greek islands, Italy, and elsewhere. Sizable portions of ancient synagogues with mosaic floorings and wall sections have been discovered in Israel, mainly in the Galilee region, but also in other parts of the country, such as Na'aran and Ein Gedi. These, however, generally date from the third century C.E. onward—the period of the Jerusalem Talmud or later. The synagogue of Dura-Europos,[168] with its famous wall paintings, also dates from the talmudic era.

Synagogues Outside the City

In many localities, it was customary to build the synagogue outside the city. Among the many reasons for this is that construction of a larger and more magnificent building was easier beyond the city limits.

In the Diaspora, there was the additional reason—that of distancing the synagogue from idolatrous sites, and even from the dwellings of non-Jews. In addition, a synagogue outside the city could also serve as a place of prayer for nearby towns and villages that could participate in the cost of building and maintenance. From various (nonrabbinical) sources, we learn that it was customary to build synagogues near a water source—a sea or a river, considered to be places of greater purity.

The distancing of synagogues from the city is referred to indirectly in a number of ancient halakhic rulings and can be inferred from the liturgy. The *Me'ein Sheva** blessing, for instance, serves to keep most of the worshippers in the synagogue, so that those who are late in finishing their prayers will not have to return to their homes in the city alone at night, through a deserted area.

[168] In northeast Syria, on the banks of the Euphrates.

The Structure of the Synagogue

The characteristic appearance of the synagogue interior was influenced by various factors. The most prominent one is the synagogue being considered a *Mikdash Me'at*—a "little Temple"—and thus, a model, of sorts, of the Holy Temple in Jerusalem. In fact, the general structure of the synagogue actually conforms to that of the Temple.[169]

Corresponding to the Holy of Holies in the Temple, the Holy Ark* is located at the front of the synagogue; and corresponding to the Altar of Sacrifice is the *Bimah*,* positioned at the synagogue's center. In most cases, the synagogue also contains a women's gallery (*Ezrat Nashim*), as was found in the Temple. In most places, it is customary not to have the outside entrance opening directly into the prayer hall, but rather to have an entrance room where one can prepare for prayer—taking off one's outer garments, wrapping oneself in the *Tallit*,* putting on the *Tefillin*,* and the like, as well as reciting some informal prayer. This entrance room corresponds to "the Levites' camp" on the Temple Mount, which surrounded the Temple edifice.

Such a comparison between parts of the synagogue and of the Temple is not limited to the resemblance in formal design. It also has a deeper aspect, having to do with our relationship with those institutions, both halakhically and conceptually.

The Holy Ark in the synagogue, which corresponds to the Holy of Holies and the Ark of the Covenant in the Temple, is the focus of holiness in the synagogue, because it contains the most sanctified object of all—the Torah scroll. For this reason, those who are in the synagogue take great care not to turn their backs to it, so that even when moving away from it, they do so by stepping backward or sideways. In most places, the seating area nearest the Ark is considered a preferred, more honorable location within the sanctuary, and it is given to the more eminent and distinguished members of the congregation.

It is a widespread custom for individuals to enter the synagogue

---

[169] See Maimonides,® *Yad ha-Ḥazakah, Sefer Avodah, Hilkhot Beit ha-Beḥirah*, chaps. 1–2.

when no prayers are being conducted, and to stand as close as possible to the Holy Ark to offer a private prayer for their personal sorrows and tribulations, or to express heartfelt thanks. On special occasions, such as when reciting *Avinu Malkenu** or the *Ne'ilah** prayer, the doors of the Ark are opened to symbolize the revelation of the *Shekhinah*.

In most congregations, there is a curtain over the Ark. This curtain is not merely decorative or used as an additional covering for the Torah scrolls besides the Ark itself, but represents the *Parokhet**—the Ark curtain—which was hung in the Temple to divide the Holy from the Holy of Holies.

The *Bimah*, the raised platform that is the center of synagogue activity, is representative of the sacrificial altar that stood in the Temple courtyard. It is the practice of many congregants to conduct at least some parts of the prayer service, if not all of them, with the *Shaliaḥ Tzibbur** (see below) standing on the *Bimah*. In all congregations, the Torah readings are conducted from the *Bimah*.

The distancing of the *Bimah* from the Ark and its placement at the center of the synagogue is significant in several ways. On one hand, it emphasizes the distinction and distance between the Ark, which symbolizes the hidden, concealed *Shekhinah*, and between God's revelation through words, which is reenacted during the Torah reading. The removal of the Torah scroll from, and returning it to, the Ark, often performed with great ceremony, is reminiscent of the journeyings of the Ark of the Covenant in the desert, as reflected in the verses recited at the beginning and the end of the Torah reading (see Chapter 13). Another point of significance is raised when the *Bimah* is located in the center of the synagogue, among the congregated worshippers. Placing the *Bimah* and the Ark together at the front of the synagogue seems, by comparison, to turn the entire synagogue into a center for rituals, with the congregation watching the proceedings from afar. The placement of the *Bimah* in the center of the synagogue is a statement that prayer is a communal function in which all the worshippers participate, this being the very purpose of public prayer.

The Women's Gallery

In excavations of ancient synagogues, both in Israel and elsewhere, there is clear evidence of a women's gallery—a separate section intended for the women who attended the public prayer services—that in most cases had a separate entrance.

Some synagogues, especially those in Eastern Europe, had no women's gallery, either because very few women attended services, or because it was not officially a public synagogue, but rather a location for men to gather together for prayers (such as the many Ḥassidic Houses in Eastern Europe; see *Shtibel*, below). Women who came to such places would find some kind of temporary arrangement, either in an adjoining room or outside the synagogue itself.

In most communities, both historical and contemporary, however, the synagogue has a women's gallery, although there is no standard structural form for this. In large synagogues, the women's gallery is usually constructed as a raised balcony—apparently similar to what was customary in various ancient synagogues—with the men praying in the hall below. These balconies or galleries are not of one standard pattern. Some are built along three of the four sides of the synagogue, excluding the side where the Holy Ark is located; others consist of a balcony built above the back part of the prayer hall. Other synagogues have a women's section adjoining the men's prayer area, sometimes behind it and sometimes along one or more sides of the building. When a women's gallery is built alongside the prayer hall, it is usually constructed as a separate room with curtained windows, so that women can hear the *Shaliaḥ Tzibbur** and the Torah readings.

Orientation

The synagogue has a specific orientation not dependent upon the points of the compass but always fixed in the direction of the Land of Israel, Jerusalem, and the Temple. This was already alluded to as early as in Solomon's prayer at the dedication of the Temple: "and pray unto You toward their land, which You gave unto their fathers, the city which You have chosen, and the house which I have built for Your Name" (I Kings 8:48).

Synagogues built in Jerusalem are therefore oriented in the direction of the Temple Mount—meaning that the Holy Ark is placed on the side facing the Temple Mount, toward which worshippers lift their faces in prayer. Synagogues in the Land of Israel or in neighboring countries face Jerusalem, while the synagogues in more distant lands face toward the Land of Israel. In addition to what is implied in Solomon's prayer, that ostensibly all prayers pass through the Temple site, there is another implication, mentioned by our sages, that "in this way, all Israel will be turning their hearts towards one place" (*Berakhot* 30a). Every Jew, in private, and even more so in public prayer in the synagogue, becomes united, through his prayers, with the prayers of the entire nation, directed always toward one particular point.

For various reasons, synagogues in many European countries faced toward the east, so that it became common usage for the front of the synagogue to be called the *Mizraḥ*—"East." There are often wall decorations in the synagogue on which the word *Mizraḥ* is inscribed.[170] However, this eastward orientation was only a general direction, not adhered to everywhere, since it was not always possible to construct the building to face the precise direction. Rabbi Schneur Zalman of Lyady[@] writes in his halakhic work (known as *Shulḥan Arukh ha-Rav*[#]) that in order to establish the exact direction it is necessary to use spheric trigonometry.

In fact, however, to the extent that there is, in the Jewish worldview, one particular direction that has an element of sanctity to it, it is not the eastward direction but the westward. It was in this direction that the Tabernacle in the desert faced, as did the Temple.

---

[170] Sometimes, even with the acronym *Mi-Tzad Zeh Ruaḥ Ḥayyim*—"From this side comes the spirit of life."

Synagogue Accessories

The Holy Ark

The Ark, known in rabbinical Hebrew as the *Tevah*, is essentially a closet, intended to contain the Torah scrolls in the synagogue. In ancient synagogues, the Ark was usually kept in a small, guarded room near the synagogue, and was taken into the synagogue during prayer time. In our times, the Ark is assigned a fixed place and is sometimes even incorporated into the synagogue structure.

Arks are constructed in various shapes and forms, according to local conditions and customs. The Ark nearly always has two doors, as can be seen even in ancient drawings, and it is covered with a *Parokhet* (curtain). In some localities, it is built on the same level with the synagogue, while in others it is built above ground level, with steps leading up to its support platform, serving also as the podium on which the *Kohanim** stand while reciting the Priestly Blessing.* In some communities, such as certain communities in North Africa, the Ark is made up of numerous closets that together occupy the entire front wall of the synagogue. In some cases, there are two Arks, one above the other.

A design in the shape of the two tablets of the Law, sometimes flanked by the image of two lions, often decorates the top of the Ark. Other designs, such as the Torah crown, are also used.

The *Parokhet* covering the Ark, often the contribution and handiwork of women, is usually richly adorned with elaborate designs in styles that match local custom. In most cases, the *Parokhet* is also embroidered with the names of those in whose memory the curtain was donated. In synagogues that have several curtains, the custom is to change them on occasion. Some synagogues use special curtains for festival days, most notably white curtains for the Days of Awe.*

The *Bimah*

The indispensable part of the *Bimah* (podium) is the table or lectern on which the Torah scroll is placed during the Torah readings.

In many synagogues throughout the world, it is customary to build an elevated section—sometimes high enough to require several stairs leading up to it—for the *Gabbai** and the Torah Reader* (see below). This section, on which the reading table is placed, may be surrounded by a banister or pillars on all sides.

Wherever the *Bimah* is thus elevated, it contains sufficient space for those called up for Torah readings, for the Reader, and for the *Gabba'im* who stand at opposing sides of the table. Usually, there is also a bench provided for the person who holds the Torah scroll after the reading.

In most communities, it is customary to blow the *Shofar** on the *Bimah* on Rosh ha-Shanah. This is reminiscent of the blowing of trumpets that accompanied the sacrificial offerings on the altar. During the *Hakkafot,** the *Bimah* is also circled both while the *Hosha'not** are being recited and on Simḥat Torah (see Chapter 10).

Ner Tamid—The Eternal Light

Many synagogues have an eternal light—either a candle, lamp, or electric light, which remains lit at all times, recalling the Temple Menorah. In some places, the light is placed in front of the Ark, while in others it is located on the western side of the synagogue.

The Prayer Lectern

In Ashkenazic communities, the *Shaliaḥ Tzibbur** has a special prayer lectern at the front of the synagogue near the Ark. In some places, the *Shaliaḥ Tzibbur*'s standing place is positioned at a spot slightly below floor level, in fulfillment of the verse "Out of the depths I call to You, O Lord" (Psalm 130:1).

A plaque is often placed over the lectern, with the inscription "I have set *(Shivviti)* the Lord always before me" (Psalm 16:8). In many congregations, this plaque—often simply called a *Shivviti**—is decorated with verses inscribed in the shape of a Menorah, and also contains inscriptions of the letters of the ineffable Name (the Tetragrammaton) in various complex combinations.

In many synagogues, it is the practice to place a lamp or lighted candles in front of the *Shaliaḥ Tzibbur* during prayer time, especially when the person leading the prayer is a mourner, or one marking the anniversary of a close relative's death (see *Yahrzeit**). Some light two candles, and those who follow kabbalistic teachings light five candles.

Prayer lecterns have no fixed form but are made according to local custom and the financial means of the synagogue community. Therefore, the lectern is sometimes simply a wooden stand, while in other cases it is a work of elaborate craftsmanship.

Candles and Lamps

According to the Halakhah, a synagogue must have windows and should be amply lit, both for its own dignity and for the benefit of the worshippers praying there. In addition, it is the custom to add extra candles and lights in the synagogue to grace it with greater honor. Additional candles are customarily lit whenever there is a circumcision* ceremony in the synagogue. It is also customary to bring candles on Yom Kippur. This accords with the verse "Glorify the Lord in the fires" (Isaiah 24:15). There is no standard practice in these matters, and all depends on local custom. Some synagogues have many chandeliers, and in some places, synagogue lamps have special typical shapes.

The Basin

It is mandatory to wash the hands ritually before prayer (see *Netilat Yadayyim**), as alluded to in the verse "I will wash my hands in innocency: so will I compass Your altar, O Lord" (Psalm 26:6). Even one whose hands are clean should rinse them symbolically. In addition, there is the ritual handwashing ceremony for the *Kohanim* before they mount the podium to bless the people. For this purpose, there has always been, since ancient times, a basin, either outside the prayer area or in the courtyard—as there once was in the Temple as well.

Seating

Since parts of the prayer service are conducted while sitting, the synagogue contains seats for the worshippers. We know that in early generations, there were synagogues where the congregants sat on mats spread out on the floor, while in other synagogues they sat on stone or wooden benches or on chairs.

Seating is generally arranged in two possible ways. Many synagogues, following ancient custom, have most of their seats ranged on all sides, around the *Bimah*, while in others nearly all of the seats are facing the Holy Ark. From earliest times, it has been the practice to seat the community elders and dignitaries in the front section of the synagogue on either side of the Ark, facing the congregants. In some synagogues, special seats of honor are reserved for the rabbis and congregational leaders.

The Talmud praises the person who sets a fixed place for his prayers (*Berakhot* 6b, 7b); indeed, in well-organized synagogues, each male congregant has his own reserved seat, for which a fee is often charged. Congregants have complete right of possession over this seat, which can even be handed down to heirs after their decease.

In some synagogues, tables are placed in front of the seats for resting Siddurim and other ritual accessories. Other synagogues feature special benches designed with a place for prayer accessories, as well as a flat surface on which to place the Siddur. In yet other congregations, an elevated wooden stand, known in Yiddish as a *Shtender*, is set up in front of the worshippers (or only the dignitaries). The *Shtender* is appropriate for use both while sitting and standing.

Additional Accessories

Besides those items that comprise an essential part of synagogue construction and functioning, synagogues commonly have additional ritual articles, some used for prayer and associated ceremonies, and others for other religious rituals performed in the synagogue.

In many synagogues, there is a special *Tallit* set aside for the use of the *Shaliaḥ Tzibbur*, and many also keep a few "public" prayer shawls on hand for anyone who may arrive without his own. Similarly, some synagogues keep one or more pairs of *Tefillin** for those who do not have any. The synagogue also has a *Shofar*, sometimes several, for use on Rosh ha-Shanah (see Chapter 11) and during the month of Elul (see Chapter 12). Even though in most cases the *Shofar* blower has his own *Shofar* with which he is most practiced, the synagogue *Shofar* is nevertheless used, particularly during the month of Elul, when blowing the *Shofar* is a custom and therefore performed with less stringency than when it is halakhically required.

Synagogues in which it is customary to make *Kiddush** on Shabbat eve have a special *Kiddush* cup for this purpose, and many also have a wine cup and other items needed for the *Havdalah** service. Similarly, it is a widespread custom to light the Ḥanukkah candles in the synagogue, and even though it is not mandatory, there often is a public Ḥanukkah Menorah in the synagogue. In some synagogues, the Menorah is not only larger than the other lamps, but is much more resplendent and richly ornamented. Some synagogues also own a large Purim noisemaker.[171]

Since it is customary to hold wedding ceremonies in the synagogue or nearby, special wedding canopies and support poles are often kept in the synagogue building. Many synagogues also have a special "Elijah's Chair," often large and elaborately carved and ornamented, for use in circumcision ceremonies.

Practically all synagogues have sacred books, at least Siddurim and Pentateuchs—for prayers and Torah readings. This is particularly necessary in communities where one is not allowed to carry objects from place to place on Shabbat because there is no *Eruv*.[172] But even when there is no need to keep books in the synagogue, and most people do have their own private Siddurim and Torah texts (which ordinarily was not the case in previous generations), synagogues still keep additional prayer books available for public use. Some synagogues have a

---

171 Called *Gregger* in Yiddish, and used to drown out the name of the evil Haman during the reading of the Book of Esther; see Chapter 12.

172 A special wire strung around a group of houses, a neighborhood, or an entire settlement, enabling the inhabitants to carry things from one place to another on Shabbat. See *Shulḥan Arukh*, *Oraḥ Ḥayyim*, 366–395.

special prayer book for the use of the prayer leader, and also special *Haftarah** books; some even have parchment scrolls of the Five Scrolls[173] for those days on which the scrolls are publicly read. In synagogues holding regular Torah classes, there are many study texts and reference books, and it is not uncommon for the synagogue library to be the largest in the community.

It is also customary in many synagogues to hang large-print, easily visible copies of certain prayer excerpts (such as *Modim de-Rabbanan,** or *Berikh Shemeih**) recited by the public.

Synagogue Architecture

Halakhic compendiums contain very few directives regarding the general architectural structure of the synagogue. The only clear halakhic ruling is that the synagogue should be built on the most elevated site in the city, in order that it be higher than all other city buildings (*Shabbat* 11b; *Shulḥan Arukh, Oraḥ Ḥayyim* 150), thus fulfilling the verse "To raise the house of our God" (Ezra 9:9). However, this directive can only be followed in cities where most or all of the residents are Jews, or in a country where the Jews enjoy full religious freedom. Since this was not the case for many generations, it was often impossible to build synagogues in this way. In many places, synagogues were thus deliberately built low, so as to be as inconspicuous as possible to the non-Jews. In order to make the interior space high, the floor therefore had to be dug below street level. Some saw this as fulfilling the verse "Out of the depths have I cried unto You, O Lord" (Psalm 130:1). Even these synagogues were not common because in many places Jews were constrained to make very small and poorly built synagogues, due to local conditions and the difficulties of the times.

It was also the rule to have the main entrance to the synagogue on the side opposite to its fronting wall. If, for example, the Land of Israel is west of a given country, and the synagogue therefore faces west, then the entrance is placed on the east side of the building so that the wor-

---

[173] Namely, the Song of Songs (read on the Shabbat of Pesaḥ); the Book of Ruth (read on Shavu'ot); Lamentations (read on Tish'ah be-Av); Ecclesiastes (read on the Shabbat of Sukkot); and the Book of Esther (read on Purim). See Chapters 9, 10, and 12.

shippers can bow toward the Holy Ark as they enter the sanctuary. An additional guideline is to have a hallway that serves as an antechamber so that the worshipper does not enter the synagogue directly. As noted above, this is reminiscent of the structure of the Temple.

Another directive is that the synagogue be well lighted and have windows, preferably twelve in number, some of which face in the direction of Jerusalem (*Shulḥan Arukh*, *Oraḥ Ḥayyim* 90:4), and through which it is possible to see the sky.[174]

These general directives are the only existing indications for synagogue architecture. The laws and customs regarding the interior decoration and layout of the synagogue do dictate, to some extent, its exterior structure, yet they do not in any way necessitate a specifically defined architectural form. Therefore, halakhically speaking, a synagogue may be round in shape, triangular, square or multilateral, symmetrical or asymmetrical, long or wide. There are also no requisite directives regarding the building materials, so that the synagogue can be built of clay or stone, wood or metal.

This liberty in architectural structure, combined with economic and social constraints, has led to the construction of synagogues and prayer houses in many different styles and shapes. At the same time, there is great similarity in the interior layout of the synagogues among different communities and congregations in distant parts of the world. Such conformity exists not only in matters subject to halakhic rulings, but even in other aspects that are not mandatory. It seems, therefore, that besides cross-cultural influences, there was also a certain well-known tradition in regard to synagogue structure which, although not recorded in books, was handed down from generation to generation.

Ornamentation

Worshippers throughout the generations have always wanted to adorn the synagogue—the "little Temple"—also with regard to its exterior aspect. Generally, an effort was made to beautify it as much as

---

[174] "So that one will focus one's attention when fixing his gaze at the sky, and his heart will be humbled." Rashi's® commentary on *Berakhot* 34b.

possible, according to the preferred style of the period and place. However, many of the sages felt uncomfortable with excessive synagogue ornamentation. Sometimes ornamental decorations were problematic from a halakhic viewpoint, because of their form or content, and sometimes there was the more general fear lest the multiplicity of ornaments would cause distraction from prayer. Some sages expressed an even stronger opinion against synagogue decorations, saying that as long as there are members of the community in need of financial support, such as widows, orphans, poor people, or Torah scholars,[175] it is forbidden to expend money on grandiose edifices.

The first type of ornamentation that we know to have been introduced in ancient synagogues, both according to literary sources and through archeological findings, are the floor mosaic designs, such as those found in Jerusalem synagogues of the Second Temple period, in Masada, and throughout the Land of Israel. These mosaic designs are not of a uniform character: some contain only simple geometric patterns, while others have pictorial representations of Temple artifacts and even of biblical figures. A few of the floor mosaics depict the wheel of the zodiac, in some cases containing also inscriptions, mainly the names of synagogue donors. In certain synagogues, such as that found in Ein Gedi, there was a warning inscription against betraying the secrets of the place, and in the Beit She'an valley a very large mosaic was discovered bearing an inscription citing the halakhic rulings regarding tithes and a list of the different regions in the Land of Israel. The artists who made these mosaic floorings were Jews, but there were possibly also some non-Jewish artists, who occasionally introduced pagan symbols. This is apparently the reason why some sages opposed the laying of mosaics. Mosaics continued to be made for synagogues until the period of the Arab conquest, and even slightly later.

Outside the Land of Israel, there was another kind of ornamentation: wall and ceiling decorations. The earliest was found in the ruins of the Dura-Europos synagogue in northeastern Syria, which dates back to the talmudic era. Various techniques were used for wall paintings, including fresco, oil painting, oil paintings on wood, etc., according to local conditions and customs. The Dura-Europos synagogue

---

175 See Jerusalem Talmud, *Shekalim* 5:4, where this opinion is very vehemently expressed.

depicts mainly people and events from the Bible. However, in later generations human portraits no longer appear, and instead we find landscape paintings, mainly imaginary scenes of Jerusalem and the Temple, the Babylonian Exile, and other such subjects. There also were various symbolic drawings, the most common being that of the four creatures—lion, leopard, deer, and eagle—mentioned in the Mishnah, Tractate *Avot** (5:20), sometimes with inscribed citations from the Mishnah. In almost all synagogues, handwritten or engraved inscriptions were made on the walls, with words that inspire prayer (such as "Know before whom you stand!"[176]) or biblical verses.[177]

Since ancient times, it has been customary in many synagogues to have inscriptions or memorial plaques for those donating substantial gifts, both in their own name and in memory of deceased family members. This practice is alluded to in the verse "Even unto them will I give in My house and within My walls a place and a name . . . an everlasting name that shall not be cut off" (Isaiah 56:5). In some locations, memorial tablets are installed for the deceased, sometimes with memorial candles (or, nowadays, tiny electric lights) placed next to them.

An effort has always been made to ornament and beautify the various sections of the synagogue and its accessories. Wherever people could afford it—as can be seen in some ancient synagogues—each of the objects found in the synagogue was a work of art in its own right. In some congregations, certain unique decorative objects that were thought-inducing were kept in view, as, for instance, in the custom of hanging an ostrich egg in the synagogue. In many synagogues, signboards are hung on the walls, with the text of various prayers for those who do not know them by heart.

Small Synagogues

In every well-established Jewish community, the community members strove to build a large and beautiful synagogue for local residents. In smaller towns, community members prayed exclusively in this synagogue; but in the larger cities, it was necessary to construct

---

[176] Midrash, *Tanḥuma*, Judges 7.

[177] This, despite Maimonides'® objection to the practice; see his *Responsa*, 268.

several synagogues, both because it was not possible to have one that could accommodate all the residents, and because for many people, the distance from the main synagogue was too great.

The Talmud (*Ketubot* 105a) relates that Jerusalem, at the time of its destruction, contained hundreds of synagogues. There is also evidence of many other places where there were numerous synagogues. Sometimes the synagogues were neighborhood centers where those residing in that area would pray. But as early as in the mishnaic period, there were also synagogues built for the use of visitors from other cities or countries, who felt more at ease among those who prayed in the same manner as they.

Similarly, from Temple times and until a few generations ago, there were synagogues for members of specific trade guilds, such as the synagogues for blacksmiths or weavers, as mentioned in the Talmud (*Nazir* 52a), or those for tailors and butchers found in East European communities.

As the Diaspora community grew, an additional factor appeared for the multiplication of synagogues. Those immigrating from a certain city or country had their own style of prayer, including various customs, *Piyyutim*,* and special melodies. When entire communities migrated to other lands, they often imported their communal customs into the new environment by means of establishing their own synagogue. In addition, various congregational groupings would occasionally be formed within the same community, such as the different Ḥassidic groups, and each would build a separate synagogue for themselves.

Understandably, most such synagogues were very small, and to some extent, also temporary. Indeed, the Halakhah distinguishes between synagogues that belong to the entire public and those belonging—socially and financially—to specific groupings, and the rulings regarding the latter are more lenient in some matters (e.g., concerning their possible sale) than in the case of permanent synagogue buildings.

Minyanim

In many communities, the need arose for creating a *Minyan**—a small group of people that gathers to pray at a specific place. Often such *Minyanim* (plural for *Minyan)* would be formed for the benefit of a weak or ill eminent personage, to whose home people would come to enable him to pray in public. Sometimes, such groups would be formed because it suited the convenience of their members. Temporary *Minyanim*, such as the *Minyan* created for prayers in the home of mourners, are very commonplace, and synagogue rulings do not apply to them at all. However, sometimes *Minyanim* that began with a room or building designated for prayer services, gradually became more permanent and grew into small synagogues.

Formerly, many communities were opposed, for various reasons, to the creation of such *Minyanim*, and even prohibited praying with them; but given the proliferation of synagogues, both large and small, opposition was lessened. In practice, many synagogues have indeed originated with the organization of small special-interest groups (such as synagogues for younger people, or groups created as a result of ideological or personal rifts) that led to the formation of established synagogues.

The *Shtibel*

Among the various *Minyanim*, special mention must be paid to the *Shtibel*—the Ḥassidic synagogue. The word *Shtibel* comes from the Yiddish, meaning a "small house" or a "small room." The early Ḥassidic *Minyanim* had to convene in places of their own, separate from the local community synagogue, whether because they wished to pray in their own manner or because they were barred from praying elsewhere. Because of the nature of the Ḥassidic movement, the Ḥassidic *Shtibel* was more informal than the usual synagogue. Though less orderly, it was, on the other hand, a place where prayer was conducted with devotion, personal commitment, and a close sense of congregational fellowship. When such Ḥassidic *Minyanim* became permanent, they would often serve as "Ḥassidic Houses," that is, places not only for prayer and Torah study, but also for social gatherings and friendly encounters. Generally, even when Ḥassidic *Minyanim* grew larger, they remained informal in character, both because of their temporary quarters and because of the greater freedom given to each worshipper to express himself through his prayers.

Many synagogues that follow the Sepharad rite are *Shtibel*-like in character, but they do not always retain all of the *Shtibel*'s original positive aspects.

Synagogue Laws

The synagogue is a hallowed place, and one is expected to conduct oneself therein with all due reverence and holiness.[178] The sanctity of the synagogue and its accessories is comparable to that of objects consecrated for Temple use, which may not be utilized or sold, except under very specific conditions.

One should conduct oneself in the synagogue with utmost dignity; levity, laughter, jesting, or idle chatter are inappropriate, even when services are not being conducted. One should not draw up accounts, eat, drink, or sleep there. The synagogue should not be entered except for the purpose of prayer or Torah study; and if one enters it for some other purpose, such as calling a friend who is inside, one should first sit down briefly and read or recite some passage from the Torah; a person who does not know how to read should ask one of those present to read for him. It is also forbidden to use the synagogue as a shortcut to another destination.

These prohibitions hold under all conditions, except when the activity in question has an aspect of religious obligation, such as drawing up accounts for the sake of observing a commandment, eating a festive meal associated with some religious obligation (see *Se'udat Mitzvah**), or sleeping in the synagogue on Yom Kippur night (see Chapter 11). If one enters a synagogue that has two entrances, one should exit it from a different entrance than that used for entering, as was customary in the Temple.[179]

The honor of the synagogue demands that it be kept clean and its floors well washed. Some of the great sages, regardless of how well

---

[178] A comprehensive rendering of the laws pertaining to the synagogue can be found in Maimonides, *Mishneh Torah*,# *Hilkhot Tefillah* 11; and in *Shulḥan Arukh*, *Oraḥ Ḥayyim* 150–154.

[179] See *Shulḥan Arukh*, *Oraḥ Ḥayyim* 151:1, and *Mishnah Berurah*,# ibid. This is based on the Mishnah, Tractate *Middot* 2:2; see also Tractate *Megillah* 29a, which is according to Ezekiel 46:9.

respected they were, used to clean the synagogue themselves in order to emphasize its great holiness. One should not enter the synagogue with shoes that will dirty its floors, and it is preferable not to come to the synagogue with muddied or dirty clothes. While it is permitted to enter the synagogue with shoes on, in Oriental countries worshippers used to take off their shoes at the entrance, or near their seats. One may not enter a synagogue bareheaded, and certainly not in immodest dress. Many sages forbade entry with an exposed weapon, unless security or other reasons necessitate carrying arms at all times. Although spitting in the synagogue is not forbidden if the soiled spot is cleaned immediately, Rabbi Isaac Luria[@] forbade it. Spitting in the synagogue is to be considered all the more unconscionable in our times, when it is not the practice to spit even in private homes.

It is doubtful if one may even use the attic of an established synagogue for other purposes, and one definitely cannot use the space above the synagogue, and especially the area above the Holy Ark, for unseemly purposes such as a toilet or bedroom. Although according to some opinions this prohibition applies only to permanently established synagogues for the wide public, it is advised to adhere to it in all synagogues.

Even the ruins of a destroyed synagogue should be treated with reverence, and activities prohibited in existing synagogues are forbidden in synagogue ruins as well.

As a matter of course, no synagogue may be sold, except for some higher holy purpose, such as to purchase a Torah scroll. If a synagogue has nevertheless been sold, it should not be given over for unseemly uses. It is, however, permitted to stipulate from the outset that the synagogue be consecrated in such a way as to enable its eventual sale. One may not demolish a synagogue, not even in order to build another in its place; rather, the new synagogue must be built first, and only then may the original edifice be destroyed. Wood and timber that were in the synagogue—even if they were never used, but only put aside for holy use—are also imbued with the status of holiness.

All this applies to permanent synagogues that serve the entire public. Private synagogues may be sold, so long as they are not converted to use for unseemly purposes. The leaders of the community—the "seven city elders" —are permitted to sell the synagogue in the presence of all the residents, but it is preferable that they do so without indicating the purpose of the sale.

The accessories for the sacred Torah scrolls carry a higher level of sanctity than other synagogue items. The general rule is that the closer an item is to the Torah scroll, and the more specific it is for Torah scroll requirements, the higher its level of holiness. Therefore, the *Bimah* used for Torah readings has a special sanctity, and initially one may not use it for any other purpose (although it is customary to stipulate in advance that one may lean over it, or place various items on it). On a higher level of sanctity is the cloth on which the Torah scroll is placed, and yet higher is the level of the Holy Ark and the wrappings and veils of the scroll itself. Most sacred of all is the Torah scroll used for public readings. Torah scrolls cannot be sold, except in extreme circumstances (e.g., in order to redeem captives). Even a privately owned Torah scroll must not be sold, except for sacred purposes.

The Synagogue and the *Beit Midrash* ("House of Study")

The sanctity of the *Beit Midrash*, the house of study, is greater than that of the synagogue, and it is preferable to pray there, in the place set aside for one's studies, than in the synagogue. The sages have nevertheless permitted use of the *Beit Midrash* for purposes such as eating and sleeping, since it was built from the start for the needs of those studying there, and serves as their home. It can therefore be used for such normal human needs as food and sleep. In our times, it is quite common for the synagogue to be initially designated as a *Beit Midrash*, in order that, among other reasons, it not become liable to any prohibitions against inappropriate activities that might inadvertently take place there.

Official Functions and Appointments

Although the synagogue is a "little Temple" and shares many similarities with the Temple, it differs from the Temple in that its operation does not require that certain people fulfill specific functions, such as the *Kohanim** and Levites did in the Temple. In principle, the synagogue can be managed by all members of the "Congregation of God" who pray there, since in prayer all are equal in God's sight, and everyone may share in carrying out the duties imposed on the worshippers. However, in practice, for a number of reasons, set functions and appointments have been instituted in the synagogue.

In spite of the fact that every Jew may fulfill any of the roles in the synagogue, such as prayer leader or Torah reader, not everyone is actually capable of doing so. In addition, the congregation of worshippers, as any other group of people working together, is in need of a guiding and organizing cadre of leaders who can arrange and supervise the performance of necessary tasks and see that they are carried out properly. This applies even to small synagogues with few worshippers, and it becomes a real necessity in large synagogues attended by many worshippers.

As a result, we find that, since early times, persons were assigned well-defined functions in the synagogue, and over the eras, a kind of tradition developed regarding these appointments. In many locations, most of those appointed would serve in those roles both because they were necessary, and because of the honor that they bestowed. In certain localities, there are salaried synagogue functionaries. None of the synagogue functions and appointments is halakhically mandatory, and there are congregations in which synagogue affairs are conducted in good order despite the fact that almost no such formal offices exist.

Head of the Synagogue *(Rosh ha-Knesset)*

During Temple times, at the Synagogue on the Temple Mount, a person was appointed as *Rosh ha-Knesset*—"Head of the Synagogue." In synagogues of that period where it was necessary to use the Greek language, the person charged with this function was called the Archisynagogos.[180]

We do not know the procedure for appointment to this office, but it seems that there was a certain election process. The position was most probably honorary, and also included supervision of the synagogue arrangements and responsibility for handling synagogue funds. The Archisynagogos was in charge of maintaining and safeguarding the building, and of assigning the different functions and honors to be granted during the prayer services throughout the year.

The Head of the Synagogue was given special honors within the synagogue itself—e.g., in regard to his seat in the synagogue, in being called up for Torah readings (see Chapter 13), and the like. In large congregations, the Head of the Synagogue had deputies and assistants to help him fulfill his functions, and it is likely that from early on, in some places, the Head of the Synagogue was an honorary title, while the actual functions were fulfilled by others.

Although the title of *Rosh ha-Knesset* has not been retained, the same function in synagogue management has remained—under a different name.

Parnas

This title was already in use in mishnaic times, and for many generations after, in numerous localities, for the person or persons appointed to conduct communal affairs in general, both in material matters—such as providing for the poor—and in administering congregational arrangements. The *Parnas* was elected by public consensus, but once appointed, he was called upon to act in a high-handed manner. In most cases, the *Parnas* was a wealthy man and diligent public activist, so it was quite often the head of the community who would naturally become the leading member of the synagogue as well.

Large communities, more likely to have many synagogues, often had a more well-defined assignment of functions, and people were specifically selected to head the different synagogues. In some congregations, the title of *Parnas* is still retained. In others, however, it

---

[180] The Greek translation of the same title.

has been replaced by other titles, from the traditional *Gabbai* (see below) to the more modern "synagogue president" and other similar appellations.

Gabbai

THE ORIGINAL MEANING of this term is "fund collector," whether in a governmental capacity or otherwise. Volunteers who collected donations—either money, food, or other items— from the public, and distributed them to those in need of charity, or for various public uses, were distinguished by the title *Gabbai Tzedakah*—"charity collector." In this latter sense, the term *Gabbai* is still employed for charity collectors of all kinds, but it has also become accepted as a title for those functionaries who manage synagogue affairs.

There is always a need for funds for synagogue maintenance and repairs, and sometimes also for the salaries of synagogue functionaries. These are collected by the *Gabba'im* through the contributions and donations of individuals, or through the regular payment of dues or community taxes. The charity collectors, usually volunteer public functionaries, were generally also those who allotted the funds for the intended purposes. In time, they were also charged with the the general management of the synagogue.

In large synagogues, and in places that have a regular and orderly system of management, there are usually several *Gabba'im* functioning as a sort of managing committee for the synagogue. The *Gabbai Rishon*—"Chief *Gabbai*"—serves as Head of the Synagogue, while other *Gabba'im* take charge of various tasks, such as collecting monies, organizing seating arrangements, administering the list of those to be called up for Torah honors, keeping watch over general order and quiet, maintaining the building, and other such matters.

In many localities, the *Gabba'im* are chosen annually on a specified day of the year, at a grand election ceremony, with all the members of the congregation attending and voting by ballot or other methods. In some cases, the position of *Gabbai*—in practice, if not by its formal definition—remains in the hands of one person, or of members of one family, for a protracted period.

In the course of many generations, in locations where Torah

scholars were well established and financially independent (due either to ownership of profitable businesses or possession of private means), the rabbi of the community was often also the head of the synagogue and its *Parnas*. But even then, there were those who maintained that Torah scholars should devote themselves solely to Torah study and teaching, and not overinvolve themselves in extraneous public affairs (see *Kiddushin* 76b and elsewhere).

In later times, when most rabbis received a salary from public funds, there was nearly always a division of labor, sometimes leading to undesirable consequences such as an "uneducated *Parnas* reigning over the public." However, in respectable communities it was ensured that the rabbi of the congregation would be in charge of the spiritual matters and halakhic problems that often arise in the synagogue, while the *Gabba'im* would deal with the synagogue's day-to-day affairs and material needs.

Ḥazzan—Cantor

In early times, it was the practice for anyone who knew how to pray to lead the prayer as the *Shaliaḥ Tzibbur;* only for special festive days would attempts be made to find a more worthy and better-qualified prayer leader. As prayer melodies gradually became more complex, and there was increasing public demand regarding the musical aspects of prayer, the position of a professional *Ḥazzan*, or "cantor," who was well versed in the prayers and their melodies, and who had an especially good singing voice, was gradually created. Even in congregations in which there was no regular *Ḥazzan* during most of the year, a special *Ḥazzan* (usually salaried) was employed to conduct prayer services during the Days of Awe (see Chapter 15).

Shammash

For the practical, ongoing management of the synagogue, it was necessary to find people to take care of a multitude of tasks, ranging from basic responsibilities such as cleaning the synagogue and keeping it in good order, or running the various errands in connection with the synagogue and the prayer services, to maintaining peace and quiet during prayers.

Those who were directly in charge of such arrangements were known in mishnaic times as *Ḥazzan ha-Knesset* (*Yoma* 65b and elsewhere). Later, when the title of *Ḥazzan* was given to the regular *Shaliaḥ Tzibbur*, the person who performed these basic functions of synagogue maintenance came to be known as the *Shammash*.

Large synagogues sometimes had different levels of *Shammash*. The senior *Shammash* was in charge of general synagogue responsibilities, while a subordinate *Shammash*—one or several—carried out necessary tasks. In a few congregations, one of the functions of the *Shammash* was to summon worshippers to the synagogue to assure a *Minyan* was assembled at the hour set for morning prayers, especially on the days when *Seliḥot** services were conducted.

In some congregations, the *Shammash* is the only fixed appointment, unlike other officeholders, who are appointed for a limited period of time. As a result, the *Shammash* is not only the acting manager of all the ordinary synagogue affairs, but he is also responsible for the preservation of community traditions and customs. Indeed, some such functionaries, who were also scholars, recorded for posterity the customs prevailing in their congregation. In some old documents, such as those of the *Va'ad Arba Aratzot*,* the term *Shammash ve-Ne'eman* ("*Shammash* and Trustee") of a specific congregation indicates the officer in charge of the synagogue or communal funds, or the person appointed as regional *Shammash* (*Shammash ha-Galil*), in charge of administrating an entire district.

Ba'al Keriah—Torah Reader

In most Jewish congregations, not all members can read the Torah themselves. It therefore became the practice that not all those who are called up to the Torah actually read their assigned portion themselves, but rather, a person well versed in the Torah text, its vocalization, and its cantillations reads the Torah for the public (for more, see Chapter 13).

In order to read the Torah text correctly, the Reader usually has to prepare himself, and often he must repeat the Torah portion several times so as to remember everything exactly. Of course, one who reads the Torah for the public over a long period of time comes to know it by heart and needs less preparation. But "professional" Torah Readers are usually conscientious enough not to read from the Torah scroll without prior preparation.

In many communities, there is usually one or more persons who volunteer for this service in spite of the effort involved. But in some communities it is necessary to hire Torah Readers.

Meturgeman—Interpreter

During mishnaic and talmudic times, and in many localities also for many generations after, the Torah was translated into the local vernacular, mostly into Aramaic. Since the translation was rendered orally, the translator had to be a Torah scholar who understood the text very well. Even so, in any translation there are inherent difficulties that must be guarded against especially when reading the Torah, since any error may lead listeners astray, in matters of either faith or practice.

Our sages have remarked on the twofold difficulty in translation. On one hand, "whoever translates a verse according to its literal sense, fabricates lies"; on the other, "[whoever] adds thereto, is a blasphemer and a libeler" (*Kiddushin* 49a). They therefore required that one should use only the translations of great men who wrote them with the fullest understanding of the text (e.g., *Targum Onkelos*# for the Torah, *Targum Yonatan*# for the Prophets, and in most localities where they translated into Greek, the accepted, available version of the Septuagint#). Nevertheless, according to Geonic* tradition, interpreters in the Land of Israel continued to take liberties with translation, introducing changes and additions, and this became the basis for the Land of Israel translation (which has been mistakenly called *Targum Yonatan for the Torah*).

At any rate, the interpreter had to be wise and well versed, with a voice that could be heard in the entire synagogue. In the course of time, the Aramaic translation ceased to be understood, and the function of interpreter became obsolete. Only in Yemen did communities continue to translate, and even to provide a double translation—*Targum Onkelos* into Aramaic, and the translation of Rav Sa'adia Gaon® into Arabic.

The Ten *Batlanim*

During talmudic times, synagogues in the larger cities had "ten *Batlanim*." These were ten men of upright and honorable character who had retired from their private business dealings, either because of old age or because they were well off and their affairs were handled by others, and who now devoted themselves to being constantly present in the synagogue in order to serve the public in all matters. These men were volunteer public functionaries, but if necessary, they received salaries from public funds. One of their functions was their very presence in the synagogue, in order to ensure that there was a *Minyan* whenever needed, and that congregants would not have to wait for late-coming worshippers before beginning prayer services.

The presence of these ten men was seen as one of the identifying characteristics of a "big city," as opposed to a town or village. Although in the course of time this specially defined status of the "ten *Batlanim*" ceased to exist, many congregations take pride in the fact that their synagogues are never closed, and that a constant presence of people in the synagogue ensures that help is always available to anyone who may need it.

Rabbi

The function of rabbi is not connected with the synagogue and prayer services, and public prayer is not dependent upon it at all.[181] Nonetheless, the main synagogue in every city usually assigns a special seat for the rabbi of that city, and pays him great honor. Even smaller-synagogues often have a "synagogue rabbi," who is the rabbi of the

---

181 See the discussion on this issue in *Berakhot* 30a and elsewhere.

neighborhood or of the congregational group that prays there. But with the increasing proliferation of small synagogues, it was not always possible to have a rabbi connected with every single synagogue.

Although the presence of a rabbi is not necessary in order to pray, a rabbi fulfills a great social and educational need. It is important that the rabbi—unlike the *Parnas* and the *Gabbai*, who are elected or given authority by public consent to serve in their capacity but are not necessarily Torah scholars—be a Torah scholar whose opinion is valued, so that he can lead the prayer services and the synagogue in the proper direction, impart his spirit onto those present, and answer halakhic queries that often arise during prayer services.

In many cases, the rabbi of a synagogue, besides functioning as a teacher and preacher, also serves as an intermediary or arbitrator in various personal problems that arise in the synagogue—e.g., between the *Gabba'im* and the congregants, or among the *Gabba'im* themselves.

Other Uses of the Synagogue

In every Jewish community or congregation, the synagogue is the heart and center of communal life. Even the poorest congregation, one that has no funds to set up public buildings for other needs, must have a synagogue. Therefore, there has always been in every congregation some structure, or at least a room, designated for this purpose. Large and wealthy congregations could afford the construction of additional buildings for other public needs; but even in such places, there was a tendency to group all the other structures or rooms used for religious purposes in the vicinity of the synagogue. Still, in many localities the synagogue was the only building available for general public use. Moreover, since the synagogue itself is actually used only during prayer time, and is left empty for most hours of the day, it has become common practice for nearly every community since mishnaic and talmudic times to use the synagogue for other purposes as well.

Talmud Torah — Torah Study School for Children

Since the combination of prayer and study is most natural and appropriate for the synagogue, the main additional purpose of the synagogue, since early times, is as a place of Torah study.

It is a commonly accepted practice to designate the synagogue as a *Beit Midrash* ("house of study")—a place where scholars can sit throughout the day and engage in Torah study. This use of the synagogue prevailed throughout the Diaspora already in the Second Temple period. Moreover, there were not always, and surely not in every location, large and well-established *Yeshivot*,* and most of the great Torah scholars of past generations acquired their learning in these houses of study.

Another institutional use was to turn the synagogue, during hours when there were no prayer services, into a *Talmud Torah*—a Torah school for children. In fact, this was one of the purposes of the synagogue as early as in Temple times.[182] In many Jewish communities throughout the ages, schools were adjacent to synagogues, either in adjoining buildings or in rooms within the synagogue structure itself.

In addition to this use of the synagogue by institutions of Torah learning, a variety of Torah study sessions were regularly held there. During mishnaic and talmudic times, the synagogue was the place where the sages delivered their expositions before public audiences. Generally, these were not delivered during prayer services but were held at their own set times.[183] From mishnaic times on, it was the custom for people to gather every Shabbat afternoon in the synagogue to hear the homilies of the sages, delivered in a language and style that could be understood by all. There often was an interpreter who would hear the main points of the exposition from the sage, and then transmit it aloud, adding lengthy explanations in the vernacular. These

---

[182] "There were four hundred and eighty synagogues in Jerusalem, and each had a school and a Talmud house. The school was for the [study of] Torah and the Talmud house for the [study of] Mishnah" (Jerusalem Talmud, *Megillah* 3:1).

[183] The sermons preached by synagogue rabbis every Shabbat in the middle of the prayer services are a fairly recent custom, partially in imitation of non-Jews.

Torah study sessions were given on a regular basis, and were so important that halakhic rulings were enacted to ensure that no disturbance occur while they were being conducted, or to prevent any other activity from interfering with them. Similar lecture sessions were also held on Shabbat eves.

In many communities, there was the fixed function of expositor (*Darshan*—or *Maggid*, as he was known in European communities), who was one of the regular, official position-bearers in the city. There were also itinerant *Darshanim* who wandered from city to city, delivering sermons on various topics. In addition, special sermons were (and still are) given from time to time, such as those on *Shabbat ha-Gadol* (the Shabbat before Pesaḥ) and *Shabbat Shuvah* (the Shabbat between Rosh ha-Shanah and Yom Kippur; see Chapter 9), in which the rabbi gives an exposition on the significance of this special day. Occasional sermons were also given by visiting rabbis, such as emissaries from the Land of Israel who traveled to Jewish communities in the Diaspora in order to collect charity donations for settlements in the Land of Israel. These emissaries usually were important rabbis who were invited to deliver to the public a learned exposition on the Torah.

Besides these sermons addressed to the general public, in every synagogue Torah classes at different levels are held. The people of each locality assemble, sometimes in the early morning before the workday begins, but more often in the evening hours, and form groups for study either among themselves or with a teacher. The various classes range from the most primary level of a *Ḥevrat Tehillim* ("Psalms group"), which simply recites psalms together, through the study of the *Ein Ya'akov* collection of Talmud legends, to high-level Talmud study. In many Jewish communities throughout the world, special study groups have been formed, such as the *Tiferet Baḥurim*, a group of young bachelors, or *Po'alei Tzedek*, for various groups of artisans.

Communal Meetings

In addition to providing space for Torah study, the synagogue also serves as a public meeting place. Occasionally, members of the community have to decide on matters relating to the community as a whole, whether routine activities such as the election of functionaries, or the laying down of regulations for the various needs of the population. At times, there were also urgent matters, such as consultations about ways and means of confronting decrees by the ruling authorities, or other dangerous exigencies. These are clearly reflected in many community records, as well as in records of synagogues that belonged to special groups or fellowships. Indeed, another name for the synagogue is *Beit Va'ad*—"House of Convention," after the various meetings (of rabbis, community functionaries, or the community at large) that were held there for the sake of the entire public.

Weddings and Circumcision Ceremonies

Halakhically speaking, weddings and circumcision ceremonies can be held anywhere; however, in many congregations they are held in the synagogue. In all Oriental communities, the prevailing custom is for the wedding ceremony to be held in the synagogue itself, a practice followed in many other Jewish communities and congregations as well. Even in Ashkenazic congregations, where the custom is to hold the wedding ceremony under an open sky, it is often held in the synagogue courtyard, in a specified area designated for weddings. Similarly, in most communities, circumcision ceremonies are held in the synagogue building.

Beit Din—Religious Court

It was the custom in many communities since early times to use the synagogue as the seat of a *Beit Din*, a "court of law." The city *Dayyanim* (religious judges) would do their work at the synagogue, to which litigants would arrive to present their cases. It therefore often occurred that the person referred to by the sages as the *Sofer* ("scribe") served both as a schoolteacher and as a court clerk who wrote out various legal documents (such as financial documents, divorce bills, etc). The *Sofer*'s double function was related to the fact that the court of law often convened in a room adjoining the *Talmud Torah*, both of which were either inside or adjoining the synagogue building.

Guest House

Because of the great importance of the commandment to provide hospitality, community members would strive to invite guests to dine with them in their own homes. Only in well-established and relatively well-to-do communities would there be a special guest house, or a *Hekdesh* (a hostel for the poor), for housing old, sick, and lonely people. But even when a poor guest was invited to dine, there would often be no place for him to sleep at the home of his hosts. Therefore, the synagogue—and especially the women's gallery, or other adjacent rooms dedicated for the purpose—served as sleeping accommodations for poor guests arriving in the city. Sometimes people who had resigned from all their worldly affairs and devoted themselves to Torah study made the synagogue their permanent sleeping quarters.

For the sake of accommodating such guests, it became the custom to hold a *Kiddush** ceremony in the synagogue on Shabbat eve after the prayer service,[184] in order to enable guests to fulfill their religious obligation of making *Kiddush* over wine. This custom is still observed in many localities, especially among those following the Ashkenazic rite, even though guests no longer eat or sleep in the synagogue.

---

[184] See *Shulḥan Arkukh*, *Oraḥ Ḥayyim* 269; see Chapter 9 of this book, the section on the *Kiddush*.

CHAPTER FIFTEEN

The Shaliaḥ Tzibbur

The Role of the *Shaliaḥ Tzibbur* and Its Origins

Initially, the function of the *Shaliaḥ Tzibbur**[185] in public prayer services was created by reason of practical necessity. Since the prayers had not yet been written down and many people did not know them by heart, there was a need for someone well versed in the prayer formulations. This person was to intone them in a strong voice, so that others could repeat them after him, or could listen and respond with Amen* at the end of every benediction,[186] thus fulfilling their obligation to pray. Even when the number of people familiar with the prayers grew, every congregation still had some individuals in need of a *Shaliaḥ Tzibbur*. For this reason, it was ruled that after the congregants conclude the silent recitation of the *Amidah*,* the *Shaliaḥ Tzibbur* would repeat it aloud, thus enabling the general public to fulfill its prayer obligations. This is what is called *Ḥazarat ha-Shatz*—the repetition* of the *Amidah* prayer by the *Shaliaḥ Tzibbur*, which is an integral part of public prayer to this day (*Shatz* comes from the initials of the words *SHAliaḥ TZibbur*).

The repetition of the *Amidah* was of particular importance on festival days, and even more so on Rosh ha-Shanah and Yom Kippur (see Chapter 12), whose special prayers were not remembered accurately by most of the worshippers, and certainly could not be fluently recited by all (see *Rosh ha-Shanah* 34b, 35a).

However, in time, as the prayers were written down and compiled

---

[185] Prayer leader. Literally, the term means "public emissary" because, as explained below, by reading the prayer aloud, the *Shaliaḥ Tzibbur* would enable the entire congregation to fulfill the obligation to pray.

[186] There are a few congregations that still do so today.

into books that were taught even to little children who had just learned to read, and the prayer formulations became familiar to all, the repetition of the *Amidah* continued merely as a traditional practice, not as an actual necessity. Indeed, Maimonides[@] in his day ruled that this repetition should be abolished, since everyone had already recited the *Amidah* in a befitting manner; as a result, people would converse during its repetition by the *Shaliaḥ Tzibbur*, or engage in other activities, demonstrating disrespect for the prayer and the synagogue, which could be considered a form of desecration. However, this ruling of Maimonides was adhered to by only a limited number of communities, mainly in Egypt, and perhaps also in some neighboring countries where he was considered the indisputable authority of his day. A few centuries later, the *Amidah* repetition was reinstated even in these communities, as in Jewish communities everywhere else. The reason was that, beyond being a traditional custom, the *Amidah* repetition had acquired additional significance by complementing and elevating public prayer.

The *Ḥazzan*

Since the *Shaliaḥ Tzibbur* originally functioned only in a pragmatic role, his position in the community was not considered a steady one. In fact, whenever a *Minyan** gathered to pray, its constituents would select from among themselves one capable to serve as their *Shaliaḥ Tzibbur*. Given the differences in human nature, there would always be some eager to serve in that role, while others would rather refrain. The Talmud already outlines the proper procedure for inviting a person to conduct the prayers, to what extent the person asked should initially appear reluctant, not too eager, and under what conditions he should immediately go forward and lead the prayers. This custom is still extant in many synagogues—generally in the smaller ones—during most of the year, when there is no officially appointed *Shaliaḥ Tzibbur*. In such circumstances, the prayer leader is someone who either volunteers to undertake this task (perhaps he enjoys it or has a special halakhic obligation—*Ḥiyyuv**) or performs it because the congregants plead with him to conduct the prayers.

Such was apparently the general practice in past times, when there was no particular person holding the position of *Shaliaḥ Tzibbur*. In actual fact, however, the prayer leader was usually the *Ḥazzan*. The term *Ḥazzan* was originally applied to the person who served as *Shammash*, a minor functionary charged with keeping order in the synagogue, who also performed various services such as teaching children in the synagogue school, assisting the *Beit Din* (religious court), and other public functions (see Chapter 14). Since the *Ḥazzan* spent a great deal of time in the synagogue and gradually became familiar with the order of prayer services, it was very convenient to have him serve also as *Shaliaḥ Tzibbur.*

But precisely because the halakhic need for a *Shaliaḥ Tzibbur* was gradually diminishing, due to the growing number of worshippers who could pray from the Siddur and had become increasingly familiar with the order of prayer services, the function of the *Shaliaḥ Tzibbur* took on a new aspect. Since the repetition of the *Amidah* was no longer required to enable the public to fulfill its prayer obligations but, rather, had become a matter of tradition and ceremony, it became desirable for the *Shaliaḥ Tzibbur* to add new features to this repetition that were not part of the individual's prayer recitation.

In terms of the general prayer order, this led to the creation of *Piyyutim** (liturgical poems, see Chapter 6). Indeed, there were times when the prayer leaders were also the composers of these new prayers. Many ancient *Piyyutim* still in use today were composed by sages serving as prayer leaders in their local communities.

However, in regard to the personality of the *Shaliaḥ Tzibbur*, there occurred two developments that were not mutually exclusive but which called for different requirements. On the one hand, it was increasingly expected of the *Shaliaḥ Tzibbur* that he have a pleasant voice, so that in those cases when the repetition of the *Amidah* was identical with its silent recitation there was the bonus of a musical experience. On the other hand, an effort would always be made to find prayer leaders who were outstanding, God-fearing Torah scholars able to inspire the congregants to reach a higher level of prayer.

As said, although these two requirements do not necessarily contradict each other, they do differ. Consequently, the role of the *Ḥazzan* became, in the course of time, that of a regular *Shaliaḥ Tzibbur* (who in many cases received for his services a salary that constituted his main source of income) and evolved into a specialized profession. In most congregations, the musical aspect of *Ḥazzanut* ("cantorship") acquired increasing emphasis, with the *Ḥazzan* serving alternately (depending on the different prayer services) as the conductor and leader of congregational singing or as one chanting the prayers in a melodious voice for the edification of the congregants, and introducing new prayer tunes.

Large congregations used to hire *Ḥazzanim* to serve as prayer leaders on Shabbat and festivals, and even made it a rule that only the appointed *Ḥazzan* would conduct the services on those days, while those who had a *Ḥiyyuv* to pray would be limited to reciting the *Kaddish** or to being called up to a Torah reading. Small congregations and *Minyanim* that could not afford to employ a year-round *Ḥazzan* would try at least to engage a professional *Ḥazzan* for the festival days, and in particular for the Days of Awe.*

The *Shaliaḥ Tzibbur* as Emissary to God

An increasingly prominent aspect of the transition to more ceremonious public prayer was the quest for an eminent personage worthy of the position of *Shaliaḥ Tzibbur*.

Even in ancient times (as is evident from the Mishnah and Talmud), we see how the function of the *Shaliaḥ Tzibbur* expanded and became more profound. He no longer served in the purely technical capacity of enabling the congregants to hear the prayer texts, but rather as one whose own supplications would more perfectly express the prayers of the entire congregation. Such a man is not a *Shaliaḥ Tzibbur* merely because he is the official, halakhic representative of the public, reciting the correct formulations at the designated moment. Rather, he plays a far more elevated part, because in a sense he serves as the congregants' emissary to God. The *Shaliaḥ Tzibbur* thus takes on the role of "ambassador"[187] sent by the congregation of worshippers to represent it before God. This is expressed in some of the *Piyyutim*

[187] As is indeed expressed in some of the *Piyyutim** that are to be recited by the *Shaliaḥ Tzibbur* alone.

composed for recitation by the *Ḥazzan*. Consequently, his authority, like that of any ambassador, derives from two sources: on one hand, from his being the representative and speaker for the entire congregation; and on the other, because of his character and personal qualities—such as eloquence, wisdom, piety, and righteousness—which enable him to succeed in his mission.

This concept that a pious and wise person can be an emissary in offering invocations, and can plead not only for himself but on behalf of others, is already found in the Bible. It is said of the Patriarch Abraham, "for he is a prophet, and he shall pray for you, and you shall live" (Genesis 20:7). Likewise, the Prophet Samuel says, "God forbid that I should sin against the Lord in ceasing to pray for you" (I Samuel 12:23). Many similar instances can be found in the Bible.

Moreover, another aspect of the role of *Shaliaḥ Tzibbur* is that he not only prays for the congregation but also leads it and guides it in its observances. He is not merely the medium through which the public finds expression but also one who influences it and who draws the entire congregation upward with him. While the silent recitation of the *Amidah* by the congregants is the private prayer of each individual, it is the task of the *Shaliaḥ Tzibbur* to bind all these individual prayers together into a common, unified worship that represents the congregation as a whole.

Furthermore, beyond being a more perfect expression of the "prayers of the many," the prayer of the *Shaliaḥ Tzibbur* must also elevate the congregation, both as individuals and as a group, to a higher level than each of them could have reached by himself. In this sphere, the personality of the *Shaliaḥ Tzibbur* plays a decisive part. The more he is accepted and loved by the congregants, and the stronger his influence over them, the greater his power to bring them to a higher and more impeccable degree of worship. And the more he excels in moral virtues and conduct, the greater his ability to prevail upon the public and to elevate its members spiritually.

It is, of course, not always possible to find a *Shaliaḥ Tzibbur* with all the requisite qualities, and even in mishnaic and talmudic times the prayer leader on ordinary days was simply one of the congregants who knew how to pray. But on special days of the year, when the need was felt to offer prayers on a higher level of devotion, a more qualified person was sought—one who could fulfill this function to greater perfection. This is how the Talmud describes the person deemed most suitable to serve as *Shaliaḥ Tzibbur* during a public fast day:[188] "One having a large family but who has no means of support, who draws his subsistence from [the produce of] the field, and whose house is empty, whose youth was unblemished, who is meek and acceptable to the people; who is skilled in chanting, has a pleasant voice, and possesses a thorough knowledge of the Torah, the Prophets and the Writings, of the halakhic and aggadic Midrash* and of all the Benedictions" (*Ta'anit* 16a).

Included in the list of qualities required of the *Shaliaḥ Tzibbur*[189] are certain spiritual virtues of which he, as *Ḥazzan*, should be possessed, such as an ability to form relationships with members of the public and exert an influence upon those for whom he prays with all his heart—besides those special requirements for public fast days indicated above ("many children and no sustenance") that move him, personally, to pray with all his heart. Therefore, Jewish leaders in all generations have always sought out the most eminent figures to serve as prayer leaders. Indeed, the greatest Jewish sages, such as the mishnaic sages Rabbi Eliezer the Great@ and Rabbi Akiva,@ served in the capacity of *Shaliaḥ Tzibbur* on major prayer occasions, and thus it has been with the most important sages of each generation, and even more so, the first Ḥassidic masters (as well as some of their followers), who have been wont to serve as prayer leaders: sometimes even every Shabbat, but mainly on festival days, and most of all on the Days of Awe.

In some rites, there are certain prayers such as "Here I am, deficient in meritorious deeds," or "I have come to beseech You with a torn and burning heart," which the *Shaliaḥ Tzibbur* recites as a prelude to special prayers, especially those on the Days of Awe. These prayers (which in some places are whispered silently by the *Shaliaḥ Tzibbur* and in others are intoned loudly for all the congregants to hear, to let them

---

[188] Days singled out because of some catastrophic event that affected the entire public, on which everyone fasts and prays for it to be averted; see Chapter 9.

[189] Some of these are mentioned as halakhic requirements in the *Shulḥan Arukh*, *Oraḥ Ḥayyim* 54, which defines the things demanded from the *Shaliaḥ Tzibbur* at all times.

share his sense of dread and awe and his innermost thoughts) provide a profound spiritual explanation of the function of the *Shaliaḥ Tzibbur* as one appointed to be the public emissary on high, whose prayers must supplement what is lacking in those of the congregants.

Various Demands on the *Shaliaḥ Tzibbur*

The combination of the above-mentioned qualities—a melodious voice and a moral, pious, and scholarly personality—is difficult to find. Often, in choosing a person for the task from among various candidates, the community had to decide which of these attributes it valued most.

For generations, there was a general tendency to select a *Shaliaḥ Tzibbur* solely on the basis of his musical qualifications and melodious voice, without taking his other attributes into account. In many localities, the *Ḥazzan* became a kind of singer whose only function was to give esthetic pleasure to his listeners and whose prayers were merely musical performances. Such *Ḥazzanim*, who were simply hollow instruments emitting sounds, not only became the butt of pointed popular jokes but were also subjected to serious and severe criticism by the sages of every generation, as far back as the talmudic era. The talmudic sages (*Ta'anit* 16b) interpreted the verse "she cries out against Me; therefore have I hated her" (Jeremiah 12:8) as referring to an unworthy prayer leader. Yet even when the *Ḥazzan* was not really an "unworthy" person but simply someone possessed of a melodious voice and musical talents, the congregation could usually pride itself on members with loftier spiritual values, albeit of less artistic ability.

In general, the higher the religious level of a community, the more pronounced was the tendency to give preference to a prayer leader with spiritual virtues. In some localities, especially on the Days of Awe, the *Ḥazzan* would always be a man of stature, a leading member of the congregation, whose heartfelt fear of God found expression through prayer, even though his musical attainments left something to be desired. Thus, if a person was known to function as a *Ḥazzan* in a certain community, particularly on the Days of Awe, this was considered a very important distinction, attained only by a man of stature. On the other hand, wherever prayer became more a matter of public ceremony than of profound religious experience, the preference was for a professional *Ḥazzan* of musical ability who could perform (and sometimes even create) musical compositions.

No hard-and-fast ruling was ever set down in this matter (save in a very few localities, but this was exceptional). It was generally realized that even if the *Ḥazzan* had an exceptionally beautiful voice, he was not worthy of praying in front of the congregation if he were just singing a ceremonial text that had no relevance for him and was not in accord with his character, conduct, and beliefs. One who deliberately commits transgressions, and whose prayers are without sincerity, is unfit to be a *Ḥazzan.* Yet even where people recognized the importance of character in a *Shaliaḥ Tzibbur,* they knew that the musical aspect was not merely one of embellishment, but a valuable device that would arouse and uplift the worshippers emotionally; therefore, a person with a pleasing voice could contribute not only to the formal aspects of prayer but also to its content and depth.

The Choir

The performance by a sanctified choir was not entirely discontinued after the destruction of the Temple, when the Levites could no longer sing there.

This kind of singing has apparently always existed. In various ceremonial services—whether at weddings or funerals—there were singers who aired their melodies before an audience, with the latter responding in kind (as in refrains, for instance). It is also known that this vocalization was often accompanied by various musical instruments, which were considered essential to these ceremonies. This was much more prevalent in totally secular singing, and there is even mention of localities where men and women sang together in mixed choirs, much to the chagrin of our sages (*Sotah* 48a).

Choral singing and the like, however, took place even during the prayer services themselves. The Talmud already refers to synagogue practices reminiscent of choir performances. Thus, in some parts of the prayer service it was customary, as it still is today, for certain phrases to be intoned by the *Ḥazzan* and then to be repeated by the congregation. In other instances, the *Shaliaḥ Tzibbur* recites several words and the congregants respond as would a choir. Or else the prayer leader recites half a verse, and the congregation plays its part by completing it (see *Sotah* 30b and elsewhere).

More broadly speaking, one might say that every blessing and prayer that is followed by a response, such as *Barukh Hu u-Varukh Shemo** or Amen, is in itself a prayer uttered in chorus. This applies even more so to blessings and prayers in which certain words are pronounced by one person, with the congregants responding, such as *Barekhu,** *Zimmun,** or *Kedushah.** Moreover, many *Piyyutim* were specifically composed to be sung in this manner, either by the recital of various verses—as in *Shir ha-Kavod** and *Shir ha-Yiḥud**—or by responding with a refrain, as in the *Pizmon.** In order to differentiate between what is to be said by the *Shaliaḥ Tzibbur* and what should be recited by the congregation, instructions appear in many Siddurim before each recited section, such as "*Ḥazzan*" and "Congregation." In practice, however, the songs have not always been retained in this form. Frequently, the *Ḥazzan* desired to chant parts of the song intended for the congregants' response, or the congregation, on its part, wished to participate in reciting (or rather, in singing) sections intended only for the *Ḥazzan*. In the course of time, this led to a blurring of the original form, and new ways of singing the texts were introduced, some of which seriously violate the structure and meaning of the song.[190]

These forms of choir singing are not professional performances but part of the accepted ways of praying. Toward the end of the Middle Ages, we often find that the *Ḥazzan* (who by then had been assigned a unique, specialized role) was accompanied by a small choir, whose members were called *Meshorerim* ("singers"). This kind of choral singing became an accepted practice, especially on festival days (and even more so during the Days of Awe), and it was conducted in various ways. Usually, the *Ḥazzan* would sing the main segments of the prayer assigned to him, and the singers would complement his performance, often by humming, either at the end of the verses or while he was singing. The choir thus served in lieu of an orchestra, since it is forbidden to use musical instruments on Shabbat or festival days. Sometimes, however, the *Meshorerim* were given permission to sing by

---

[190] One example of this is the way in which some of the *Piyyutim** for the Days of Awe—e.g., *ve-Khol Ma'aminim*—are sung in most Ashkenazic congregations.

themselves, and there were even solo parts for singers with especially mellifluous voices. Since the choir was intended mainly as an accompaniment, the singers were often children with soprano voices. However, there were also instances when the *Ḥazzan*, usually a tenor or a baritone, would be accompanied by someone with a deeper voice.[191]

It seems that, at first, *Ḥazzanim* would perform alone, or be accompanied by only two or three singers, and sometimes just one. It was only in the nineteenth century that large and well-organized choirs were formed, either in synagogues or to accompany well-known, itinerant *Ḥazzanim*. These choirs became so well established in the course of time that eventually there were synagogues with choirs led by conductors (who were often also composers), which drew on a regular, prescribed repertoire, while the *Ḥazzan* became merely the leading singer, who, too, followed the directions of the choir conductor. This type of choir could be found not only in urban synagogues (which were sometimes under the influence of somewhat assimilationist trends), but also in the "courts" of several Ḥassidic masters, where stress was placed on this musical aspect. Except in certain cases, such as the last-mentioned, this practice led to a diminution of the religious and spiritual aspects of synagogue singing and to an overemphasis on the purely musical side. In such places, many people would come to the synagogue mainly to enjoy the performance, and only to a far smaller extent in order to pray.

The formation of organized choirs was apparently the result of European cultural influences, since this phenomenon is hardly found among Eastern congregations. In these latter communities, the closest parallel to the role of a *Meshorer* is that of a functionary called a *Somekh*, a man (usually much younger and with a melodious voice) who stands next to the *Shaliaḥ Tzibbur* and recites some of the *Piyyutim* in the prayers for the Days of Awe. Although the *Somekh* carries out a musical assignment, his main purpose is to provide relief to the *Shaliaḥ Tzibbur* from the onerous task of continuous singing placed on him during those days.

---

[191] The seventeenth-century author and bibliographer who wrote the book *Sefat Hakhamim* was also a synagogue singer, and is referred to in various books as Rabbi Shabtai Meshorer ("Rabbi Shabtai the Singer"), and sometimes even as Rabbi Shabtai Bass.

Ḥazzan versus *Ba'al Tefillah*

When *Ḥazzanut* (synagogal music) became an art in its own right, a distinction was made between two kinds of *Shaliaḥ Tzibbur:* the *Ḥazzan*, who served as a professional (on either a permanent or an occasional basis), and the *Ba'al Tefillah* ("prayer leader"), who conducted the services, even though they were not *Ḥazzanim* in the narrow sense of the term.

This distinction was not characterized as a means of determining the level of musical talent, or to differentiate between professional and amateur, since there were regular *Ba'alei Tefillah* ("prayer masters"—some of whom even received a salary from the congregation) who were also outstanding artists. Rather, it refers mainly to the musical characteristics of their performance.

The prayer leader, even when he chants in the course of his prayers, usually avails himself of the traditional melodies and makes no innovations. It is understood, of course, that the individual personality of the prayer leader finds expression even when he uses the traditional tunes, by accentuation of some words, emphasis on certain phrases, and introduction of pauses.

The *Ḥazzan*, on the other hand, usually enters innovations in prayer melodies, and does so in various ways. Some *Ḥazzanim* are also composers, talented enough to create new melodies for the prayers, while others use familiar tunes (composed by other cantors or derived from different sources), and adapt them to the words of the prayer. Even when the *Ḥazzan* prays using a well-known melody, he might be expected to introduce his own musical variations. To a given tune (even a well-known traditional one), *Ḥazzanim* habitually add something original of their own—trills, minor variations, and so forth. One of the criteria for a good *Ḥazzan* is not only the quality of his voice and his control over it but also his ability to improvise and add something new. Thus, two different cantors, singing the same prayer, will never produce an identical musical effect.

In other words, the prayer leader sees himself as a performer who conveys his own, personal interpretation of the traditional tunes, while the *Ḥazzan* (like musicians of various types, both ancient and modern) is an improviser who constantly revises the melody. In this way, the *Ba'al Tefillah*, faithful to the traditional, well-known melodies, can strongly encourage the worshippers (who are very familiar with them) to join him in song, whereas the number of congregants who can participate in the prayers sung by the *Ḥazzan* is relatively small.

The innovations and musical creativity of the *Ḥazzan* may cause various practical and halakhic problems. The melody may sometimes induce certain changes in the accentuation of words, in different phrasing of a sentence, in splitting a word into two parts, or in combining separated words. It often happens that a melody, however beautiful and perfectly suited to the contents of a given prayer, can change and even distort the meaning of its words.

An even more serious halakhic problem occurs when, occasionally, for the sake of the melody, the *Ḥazzan* repeats a word, or words, in a biblical verse. This practice, which is always undesirable, can become a veritable transgression of a prohibition, where a verse contains the Name of God, because of the possibility that the incorrect quotation of the Name may be considered as "taking God's Name in vain" (Exodus 20:7). Therefore, distinguished cantors, who are also Torah scholars to some extent, usually take care not to alter any verse containing God's Name, and certainly do not repeat the Name itself just to suit the melody.

Undoubtedly, the most esteemed *Ḥazzanim* are those who succeed in adapting the melody to the prayer, so that the tunes they compose or modify are not only appropriate to the words but also add significance and sensitivity that will enhance the prayer. *Ḥazzanut*, thus, must not be merely a musical performance but rather a creative activity that provides prayer with an added dimension of depth and feeling.

The *Kavvanah* of the *Shaliaḥ Tzibbur*

When a person takes upon himself to serve as a *Shaliaḥ Tzibbur*, certain things are expected of him. It is unrealistic to hope that every *Ḥazzan* may attain the stature of the most eminent scholars of the past, who in their prayers reached to the loftiest spiritual heights, or even of those who imbued each word of their supplications with manifold layers of meaning. Yet the greatest prayer leaders, in all generations, are the exemplary models of what a *Shaliaḥ Tzibbur* should aspire to be, and he should do his utmost to emulate them and to try and reach their level.

One may understand the main role played by the *Shaliaḥ Tzibbur* from the Ba'al Shem Tov,@ who compares communal prayer to a human ladder, made up of all the members of the congregation, with its foot placed on earth and its top reaching to the heavens (cf. Genesis 28:12). Each worshipper creates a rung in this ladder, with each serving as the basis for the next; and when all are thus attached to one another, one above the other, combined and united, the prayer leader may reach unto Heaven. The successful creation of such a congregation, whose success is based on its unity (like rungs of a ladder, which must be securely joined together), is not entirely within the power of the *Shaliaḥ Tzibbur;* however, the role he plays in it is a significant one. And whenever communal prayer does indeed attain this form, it fulfills its designated function.

There are also a number of technical matters demanded of a *Ḥazzan*. The *Shaliaḥ Tzibbur* must first and foremost be very well versed in the words of the prayers, so that "his tongue does not falter."[192] Even individuals praying alone are required by halakhah to peruse infrequently recited prayer texts before uttering them. This applies all the more to the *Shaliaḥ Tzibbur,* who familiarizes himself with the prayer service before beginning his prayers. By preparing for prayer, he prevents slips of the tongue, and by trying to fully understand the meaning of the prayers—even at their most basic, literal level—he avoids committing errors through an incorrect linking and combining of words.

The preparation of mind and body is relevant in this connection. In many localities, it is customary on Rosh ha-Shanah for the *Ḥazzan*—as well as the *Shofar** blower and other public functionaries—to immerse himself ritually before prayer, in order to attain a higher level of purity. Some prayer books contain special study texts and prayer formulations for the *Shaliaḥ Tzibbur,* to help him prepare himself spiritually.

---

[192] From the prayers of the Days of Awe.

The *Ḥazzan* should feel that he is indeed a *Shaliaḥ Tzibbur*—an emissary representing the public—who prays for the entire congregation. It is therefore advisable, even from a halakhic viewpoint, that the prayer leader be a person well liked by the public, so that everyone can identify with him and feel there is no barrier between him and them because of dispute or hatred.

The *Shaliaḥ Tzibbur* should also empathize with the public, and try to make the congregation participate in his prayer and join in his chanting. A prayer leader whose sole intention is to demonstrate his musical skills is definitely not a suitable *Shaliaḥ Tzibbur*. Yet even one whose intentions are holy should be aware of the community's emotions. When there is too wide a gap between the *Shaliaḥ Tzibbur* and the congregants, i.e., when the *Ḥazzan* overextends his prayers, or cuts them short in disregard of acceptable limits, he detaches himself from the very people he is supposed to represent.

Although the *Ḥazzan* must surely direct his heart toward God, he must still remember that his prayers are not those of an individual (who prays to the best of his ability and with his heart's devotion) but those of the community in general. It is therefore his task to carry the public along with him, no matter whether he is singing a melody in which the congregants join him, or whether he alone is reciting and chanting the words.

Generally speaking, the *Shaliaḥ Tzibbur* is the leader of communal prayer, and he is responsible for uniting all the individual members into a single congregation, to accompany it and to lead it upward. In a sense, the task of the *Shaliaḥ Tzibbur* resembles that of the High Priest on Yom Kippur (see Chapter 11), of whom it is said that he makes "an atonement for himself, and for his household, and for all the congregation of Israel" (Leviticus 16:17). And, like the High Priest, he should know that his position of authority derives from the fact that he is delegated to act on behalf of the entire congregation, and that this is what enables him to transcend his personal limitations and to represent not only himself but the entire community.

CHAPTER SIXTEEN
Prayer Accessories

Prayer Garments

All prayer, particularly communal prayer, is like an audience before the King, Sovereign of the World. Prayer is also a form of service, or sacrifice, offered in a holy place. Both these aspects demand considerable preparation from the person about to enter the royal hall, the "little Temple."[193]

Hence, one needs to prepare for prayer, not only in heart and mind, but also in body, and by wearing suitable garments. Since this preparation is for prayer as such, it must be done even when one prays by oneself, in private. However, one worshipping in a synagogue must take even greater care, as there it is a matter of showing respect not only for prayer but also for the congregation and for the place of prayer. The *Shaliaḥ Tzibbur* must take special care in his dress, for he leads the prayer as representative of the entire congregation.

The general rule is that a person must dress for prayer as he would if he were going to a meeting with a prominent personage: a king or an eminent minister. For that reason, there are no specific directives regarding the type of clothing to be worn, as custom and fashion change from place to place and from one period to another. One should, however, wear garments that are considered dignified in one's period and locality. Therefore, one must not come to the synagogue in torn clothes or in clothing that exposes parts of the body (Mishnah, *Megillah* 4:6), and certainly not in immodest attire. Many people are careful not to pray with exposed arms[194] even if, generally speaking, this is not considered indecent. The leading *Tannaim** and *Amoraim** used to wear their best clothes while attending prayers—a rule that has been

[193] An appellation for the synagogue; see Chapter 14.

[194] As indicated in various books, especially kabbalistic ones.

codified in the Halakhah.* It has thus been deduced, for example, that only if it is accepted practice in a given place to appear barefoot before important people is one permitted to come barefooted to the synagogue as well[195]—and the same goes for analogous matters.

The regulations regarding the garments appropriate to prayer apply to the regular clothing worn by people, as customary in a particular time and place. In addition to these, there are various special garments for prayer and for sacred functions. Even though these are not intended exclusively for prayer, it is considered an obligation (or a greater obligation) to wear them during prayer time.

Many sages throughout the ages used to put on formal attire before prayers, and some even had a complete outfit that they used only for worship. In many communities, people had special clothing and hats that they used only for attending the synagogue and for other sacred events; such is still the practice in many locations, particularly for Shabbat prayers. In many Jewish communities, it is customary to wear white clothes on Yom Kippur; among the Ashkenazim, there is even a special garment for that day, called a *Kittel*,* which is a simple white robe used for special prayers and religious ceremonies.[196]

Head Coverings

According to Jewish tradition, covering one's head signifies acceptance of the Divine yoke, as well as being a sign of modesty, whereas a bare head is seen as an expression of brashness. The Aramaic expression *Reish Galei*—"a bared head"—is used to translate the biblical expression *Yad Ramah*—"a high hand"[197]—meaning freedom, release from all subjugation.

Head covering as a mandatory custom for Jewish men at all

---

[195] *Shulḥan Arukh, Oraḥ Ḥayyim* 91.

[196] See note *(Haggahah)* on *Shulḥan Arukh, Oraḥ Ḥayyim* 610:4. Some wear it on Rosh ha-Shanah as well (see Chapter 11), and some even do so on *Hosha'na Rabbah* (see Chapter 12). Many are accustomed to wear it on *Seder** night (see Chapter 10), and the *Shaliaḥ Tzibbur* wears it during the Prayer for Rain or the Prayer for Dew *(ibid.)*.

[197] In Exodus 14:8, which describes the exodus from Egypt: "and the children of Israel went out with a high hand." See the Aramaic translations to this verse.

times is fairly recent. From the Talmud (*Nedarim* 30b), it seems that formerly, Jewish men did not cover their heads at all times, although even then head covering was considered to be both expressive of and conducive to the fear of God (*Shabbat* 156b). Accordingly, halakhic compendiums prohibit one from walking four cubits with a bared head,[198] although this is in essence a custom of supererogatory piety. However, the custom of wearing a head covering has spread throughout the Jewish world and has been accepted as normative. In our times, in which it has even become a kind of symbol for religious observance, people are more strict about it, arguing that, since it has been accepted as standard practice, whoever does not conform to it is considered a transgressor. In certain localities it is so strictly observed that a head covering is worn not only in public and during the daytime, but even at night while sleeping.

In any event, even in localities or among individuals that did not have the custom of wearing head covering at all times, it was undisputed that one does not enter a holy place, nor recite sacred texts, and certainly not mention the Name of God, while bareheaded.[199] An allusion to this practice may even be found in the Torah, in that the *Kohanim** serving in the Temple must wear a headdress or miter as part of their official garb.

Thus, head covering in the synagogue, especially during prayer services, is a mandatory element of prayer. However, as it is not included in talmudic law nor as a normative practice mentioned in the literature of the *Rishonim*,* there are no fixed specifications as to the size, color, or nature of the head covering. The only halakhic ruling in this matter is that covering one's head with one's hand is not considered a head covering, while another person's hand is. In practice, the type of head covering depends primarily on the custom of the locality or even of the synagogue, subject to the general rules regarding proper clothing to be worn in the synagogue (namely, that it be a dignified kind of head covering that one would wear elsewhere. Thus, makeshift headgear—e.g., those made of cardboard, or a tied handkerchief—although halakhically considered head coverings, are not, if better

---

[198] *Shulḥan Arukh, Oraḥ Ḥayyim* 2:6.

[199] *Shulḥan Arukh, Oraḥ Ḥayyim* 91:3, and commentaries there.

options are available, considered proper synagogue wear. In practice, it is customary to wear at least a small head-covering that should cover the major part of the skull—the *Kippah* ("skullcap"). Its shape, color, and the type of cloth used, however, vary from one place to another. Many sages maintained that the *Kippah* is only suitable for use in the home, but that during prayer—and particularly when worshipping in the synagogue—one should wear a hat suitable to the dignity of the place. Some follow the Kabbalah-based custom of covering the head during prayer with two head coverings, on top of one another—i.e., a *Kippah* covered by a larger hat or by a *Tallit*.*

A far weightier obligation than that incumbent upon men is the requirement for women to wear a head covering. This obligation stems from a completely different halakhic source, and thus is governed by a different set of laws. The basic rule—which according to most halakhic authorities is Torah-based—is that a married woman must cover her head, among other things, so as to indicate publicly that she is married. A married woman who does not cover her head is considered as if she were exposing one of the parts of her body that ought to be covered.[200] However, with the exception of the Yemenites,[201] it is not customary for women who have never been married to cover their hair.[202] While it is considered a proper, pious custom for married women to cover their hair entirely, the minimum halakhic rule is that they at least cover most of it.[203]

As mentioned above, women's obligation to cover their hair does not specifically apply to the synagogue; however, even those women

---

[200] This ruling has further halakhic implications; e.g., it is forbidden to pronounce sacred words while facing such a woman, and it also bars such women from entering a holy place.

[201] In the Yemenite custom, a girl past early childhood had to wear a head covering; almost no other Jewish community, however, ever practiced this. In a few Sephardic communities, it was the custom for unmarried girls to cover their heads at least during the *Amidah** prayer and when reciting Grace After Meals.*

[202] Widows and divorced women, although single, are also obligated to cover their heads.

[203] With regard to covering the hair with a wig, opinions differ. Some allow it even if better options for covering the hair are available, while others maintain that it does not satisfy the requirement for head covering. Most communities follow the more lenient opinion, but the matter has not been definitely settled.

who do not ordinarily cover their heads are accustomed to do so when they come to the synagogue, and this is certainly appropriate behavior.

The *Tallit*

In ancient times, the *Tallit* was the regular, everyday outer garment worn by Jewish men. This garment, which consisted of a large, rectangular piece of woolen cloth, was wrapped around the body whenever one went out to work, or to public places.

In form and use, the *Tallit* is similar to garments commonly worn in those days among other Mediterranean peoples—the Greek himation or the Roman toga. This type of garment is very practical and well suited to the climate in countries in which there are constant variations in temperature, not only between the different seasons but even between the different times of the day, albeit without great extremes of hot or cold. During the cold season or in the night hours, it is possible to enwrap the entire body with the *Tallit*, while when it is hot, it can be folded back to hang loosely over the shoulders without being too much of a burden. This garment is also very practical for different occasions: it can be easily removed when one needs to perform hard physical work, it can serve as a kind of blanket while one is sleeping, and it can also be wrapped elegantly around oneself when going out to attend a ceremony or some public place.

The Torah commandment to attach *Tzitzit*,* "fringes," to one's garments refers specifically to this kind of outer garment, as in the verse "You shall make fringes upon the four quarters of your vesture, wherewith you cover yourself" (Deuteronomy 22:12). According to the oral tradition handed down to the sages, any garment that does not have four corners does not require *Tzitzit*.

With the passage of time, and following the dispersion of the Jews to distant lands, the style of clothing also changed. The *Tallit* was no longer a garment used in daily life, and the clothes worn by Jews did not ordinarily have four corners. As a result, the commandment to wear *Tzitzit* could no longer be fulfilled. True, this commandment is not one that is incumbent upon the individual as such, but rather one that applies only to the wearing of a specific kind of garment. Nonetheless, the result was that this much-cherished and beloved commandment seemed likely to lapse (*Menahot* 41a). In order to prevent this from happening, the custom was adopted throughout the Jewish world to retain the use of this ancient national garment, which also involved the fulfillment of a Torah commandment, at least during prayer periods.[204] In general, the synagogue is considered a special domain, detached to some degree from the dimensions of time and space, where one may, so to speak, reexperience being in another place and time—in the Temple, rebuilt and reestablished on its site.

The *Tallit* was thus transformed from an everyday garment into a sacred one used for holy purposes, i.e., for prayer and for various ceremonial rites, thereby emphasizing its festive aspect. The basic form of the *Tallit* has never changed; moreover, there are even certain details in the making of the *Tallit* which, although not mandatory from the halakhic viewpoint, have been retained by many Jewish communities, and which have unwittingly helped preserve its original form.

When and by Whom the *Tallit* Is to Be Worn

Once the *Tallit* became a special, sacred garment used for prayer, certain fixed customs took shape regarding the times for wearing it and those who should wear it.

The *Tallit* is worn in all Jewish communities at the *Shaḥarit** and *Musaf** services; although there is no halakhic reason to not wear it during *Minḥah** as well, this is hardly ever done. As the *Ma'ariv** service is at night the *Tallit* is not usually worn, since the commandment of *Tzitzit* only applies during the daytime.[205]

It is a widespread custom to wear the *Tallit* throughout the prayer services of Yom Kippur (see Chapter 11), and in many loca-

[204] Some people even wear the *Tallit* before leaving home for the synagogue, or at least put it on before entering it.

[205] As it says in the verses pertaining to this commandment: "that you may see it," and "seeing" can be done only at daytime (*Menaḥot* 43a); see also *Shulḥan Arukh*, *Oraḥ Ḥayyim* 18:1.

tions the *Tallit* is donned in the late afternoon, before the fast day begins, and is left on throughout the *Ma'ariv* service on Yom Kippur eve.

The *Tallit* is likewise worn on special ceremonial occasions, or when performing special functions. Thus, in many localities the *Shaliaḥ Tzibbur* wears it even during the *Minḥah* service, and in some places during the *Ma'ariv* service as well. It is likewise customary for him to wear it during the *Seliḥot** prayers. A person who reads the Torah, and the one called up to the Torah reading, in all cases wear a *Tallit*,[206] although there are those who do not do so where it is not generally worn. The *Kohanim** wear a *Tallit* during the Priestly Blessing.* At times, the *Tallit* is worn in place of an outer garment, to show respect for the public and for the prayer service.

It is customary for the *Ba'alei Berit**—i.e., the child's father, the *Sandak* (godfather), and the *Mohel* (circumciser)—to wear the *Tallit* during the circumcision* ceremony. In Oriental (as well as in German-Jewish) communities, it is customary for the bridegroom to wear a *Tallit* during the wedding ceremony.

There are different customs regarding who should wear the *Tallit*. In Oriental and Yemenite communities, it is customary, in accordance with what is said in the Talmud (*Arakhin* 2a), that a child start wearing a *Tallit* during prayer as soon as he knows how to wrap himself in it—or, at the latest, upon reaching Bar Mitzvah* age.[207] This is likewise the custom among some Ashkenazim, specifically those of German or Central European origin, albeit young men do not cover their head with the *Tallit*. Among the majority of Ashkenazim (i.e., those of East European provenance), however, the custom is that the *Tallit* is worn only by a married man; thus, a bachelor only wears one when serving as a *Shaliaḥ Tzibbur* or in some other official function. However, even those who do not wear a *Tallit* still fulfill the commandment of the *Tzitzit* by wearing the *Tallit Katan*.*

---

[206] Except for some locations, where this is not practiced when not all the congregants wear a *Tallit*.

[207] In some Ashkenazic communities, too, children begin wearing the *Tallit* when they reach Bar Mitzvah age; however, they do not cover their heads with it until marriage.

SIGNIFICANCE OF THE *TALLIT* AND ITS BLESSING

EVEN IN THOSE days when the *Tallit* served as the ordinary, everyday garment, the commandment of *Tzitzit* was seen as having a significance beyond being merely a commandment applying to a specific type of clothing. The Torah says of this commandment, "and you shall look upon them, and remember all the commandments of the Lord, and fulfill them; and you will not follow after your heart and after your eyes" (Numbers 15:39). Hence, the commandment of *Tzitzit* is a general reminder of all the other commandments, and a way of guarding its wearer from temptations and transgressions. Moreover, our sages (*Nedarim* 25a) say that "the precept of fringes (*Tzitzit*) is equivalent to all the [other] precepts of the Torah." This is among the reasons why the passage regarding *Tzitzit* is included in the reading of the *Shema**: because the commandment is of such wide significance, including the bettering of both one's actions and one's soul.

Once the *Tallit* began to be used exclusively as a garment for prayer and for other sacred purposes, the ceremonial and spiritual significance of wearing the *Tallit* became more explicit. The four corners of the *Tallit* have long since become a symbol for the entire universe (see especially Job 38:13). But beyond that, the *Tallit* also serves as a symbol for God's protection. Thus, we read in the devotional psalms, "Hide me under the shadow of Your wings" (Psalm 17:8); "I will trust in the covert of Your wings" (*ibid.*, 61:5); "In the shadow of Your wings will I rejoice" (*ibid.*, 63:8).[208]

Wrapping oneself in the *Tallit*, one thus performs an act that has two complementary meanings. On the one hand, it is a symbolic expression of becoming united with the totality of reality. Our sages have said that the commandment of *Tzitzit* includes all other commandments (the numerical value of the letters of the word *Tzitzit*, together with its eight threads and five knots, amount to 613—the number of commandments in the Torah),[209] so that by wearing the *Tallit* one

---

[208] The Hebrew word *Kanaf*, translated here as "wings," can also mean "corner of garment."

[209] See Rashi's® commentary on Numbers 15:39.

enwraps himself in a "garment of light" containing all the commandments within it. On the other hand, the *Tallit* also symbolizes God's raiment of light, under whose wings man finds refuge.

All these meanings are reflected in the various customs practiced by Jewish communities when wrapping oneself in the *Tallit*. It is customary, before wearing the *Tallit*, to check the condition of the fringes on the folded *Tallit* to assure that they were not torn or damaged on the previous day, and to unravel any knots that might have been formed by the threads. While making this inspection, the following verses are recited: "My soul, bless the Lord! Lord my God, You are greatly exalted; You have garbed Yourself with majesty and splendor, You enwrap [Yourself] with light as with a garment; You spread the heavens as a curtain" (Psalm 104:1–2). In many communities a *Yehi Ratzon** formulation, concerning the *Kavvanah** of performing this commandment,[210] is recited, followed by the blessing, "who has sanctified us with His commandments, and commanded us to enwrap ourselves with *Tzitzit*." One then wraps oneself in the *Tallit* so that the head, as well as the upper part of the body, are covered.[211] This wrapping while reciting the blessing should be like the "wrapping of the Ishmaelites"—the way the desert Arabs wrap both their head and their face—namely, one should cover not only the head, but even the face, with the *Tallit*. According to a custom of the Kabbalists, one first holds the *Tallit* above one's head with both hands while making the blessing, and then places it over the head.[212] One then takes the four corners of the *Tallit* in one hand—some take only the two corners on the right side—places them over the left shoulder, and stands wrapped this way for a little while.[213] During this time, it is customary to recite four verses (8–11) from Psalm 36:

---

[210] Derived from the book *Sha'arei Zion*.#

[211] See *Tur*,# *Oraḥ Ḥayyim* 8.

[212] The custom among many of the Ashkenazim is to cover their faces with the *Tallit* from the top down to the mouth. Although this custom is apparently based on a misunderstanding of halakhic directives, it is nevertheless a traditional practice that ought not to be annulled.

[213] At least the time it takes to walk four cubits. See *Shulḥan Arukh*, *Oraḥ Ḥayyim* 8:3.

How precious is Your kindness, O God! The children of men take refuge in the shadow of Your wings. They shall be satiated with the delight of Your House, and You will give them to drink from the river of Your bliss. For with You is the source of life; in Your light we see light. Bestow Your kindness upon those who know You, and Your righteousness on the upright in heart.

These devotional verses, selected for kabbalistic reasons and recited by the Ashkenazim, express the feeling that wrapping oneself in the *Tallit* is indeed like entering under the shadow of God's wings, with the profound delight stemming from this sense of closeness, created by wearing a garment that corresponds to God's raiment of light, and from which His loving-kindness and righteousness flow.

The *Tzitzit*

Although the *Tallit* itself has acquired a certain sanctity, the Torah commandment essentially refers to the *Tzitzit*—the fringes. This commandment is intended as a permanent reminder to observe all the Torah commandments and to refrain from any transgression resulting from what the heart desires or what the eyes see.

In the simplest sense, the very obligation to wear fringes on a garment, with their special colors,[214] in itself serves as a reminder. Their very singularity reminds the wearer of his Jewishness, as a kind of symbol of his unique existence, so that every time he sees the fringes he is reminded, consciously or unconsciously, that he is obliged to conduct himself in Jewish ways.

Our sages of old explained the various details of this commandment. Thus, "The blue [*Tekhelet* thread] resembles the color of the sea, and the sea resembles the color of the sky, and the sky resembles the color of a sapphire, and a sapphire resembles the color of the Throne of Glory" (*Ḥulin* 89a). They likewise stressed additional aspects, beginning with the fact that the blue color is reminiscent of the heavens which, as the Psalmist says, "declare the glory of God" (Psalm 19:2), and going on to more profound spiritual levels. Thus, the color blue—in

[214] According to the Torah, each *Tzitzit* should have a blue *(Tekhelet)* thread in it; see the section "The Blue Thread *(Tekhelet)*" later in this chapter.

this case, a very deep blue—is an allusion to the *Sefirah** of *Malkhut* (Kingship), which symbolizes the Throne of Glory, the presence of God's *Shekhinah** in the world; moreover, blue is the "essence" of all the colors.[215] There is also a connection between the white and the blue of the fringes, which corresponds to the relationship between the Name of God as it is written and as it is uttered,[216] as well as to that between the attribute of Loving-kindness (symbolized by the white color) and Justice (symbolized by blue).

Besides the general aspect of color, there are the various details of the making of the fringes, involving the long thread tied around the others a specified number of twists, and the number of knots, which, taken together, form a sort of code, whose numbers and combinations allude to various meanings. Thus, the five knots and eight threads of each fringe add up to thirteen, which is the numerical value of the word *Eḥad*—"one." Likewise, the total number of turns according to one custom amounts to twenty-six, which is the numerical value of the Tetragrammaton, while according to another custom they amount to thirty-nine, the numerical value of the words *ha-Shem Eḥad*—"the Lord is One."

The total configuration of colors and forms in the *Tzitzit* thus creates more than merely a symbol. It carries within it a well-defined message—an allusion to God's presence in His world, and to the ways in which He reveals Himself—namely, through mercy and justice. This message is carried by means of an allusion, which is understood by the person who wears the *Tallit*, thereby making it possible to fulfill the verse "and you shall look upon them and remember all the commandments of the Lord" (Numbers 15:39).

Laws and Customs of the *Tzitzit*

Customs differ with regard to covering the head with the *Tallit* during prayers. On the one hand, covering one's head is a way of expressing seriousness and dignity—since whoever is engaged in a matter of importance would also cover his head—as well as being an

[215] See Naḥmanides'® commentary to Numbers 15:38.

[216] For it is forbidden to utter the Tetragrammaton as it is written.

expression of submission resulting from the fear of God (as head covering is generally; see above). There are also kabbalistic reasons for doing so, especially when a person is wearing only a *Kippah* while praying, rather than a hat that is worn when going about in a dignified manner. In some communities, everyone covers their heads with the *Tallit* during prayer time, while in others, unmarried men only cover their heads during the *Amidah** prayer. In certain communities, only the leaders of the congregation—e.g., the rabbi—cover their heads with a *Tallit.*

It is customary, for kabbalistic reasons, to hold the two front fringes of the *Tzitzit* in one's hand during the recital of *Barukh she-Amar** and to kiss them upon completing this blessing. Similarly, it is the practice to gather all four fringes of the *Tallit* in one hand just before the reading of *Shema.*[217] This is done upon reciting the phrase "bring us in peace [*or:* bring upon us blessing and peace] from the four corners of the earth," for the *Tallit* symbolizes the entire world. Thus, the gathering together of its four fringes symbolizes the ingathering of the exiles, or the bringing of blessing and peace. While reciting the third section of the *Shema*, which refers to the commandment of *Tzitzit*, some hold the fringes in front of their eyes and gaze at them throughout the recital of this portion, in order to observe the commandment "and you shall look upon them" in its fullest sense. There is a widespread custom of kissing the fringes each time the word *Tzitzit* is mentioned, while some also pass them across their eyes. According to the Kabbalah, one should continue holding the fringes in his hand until reaching the words "and pleasant, forever" in the benediction of *Emet ve-Yatziv*,* at which one again kisses them and releases them from his hand.

Although there is a special blessing formulation for the *Tallit Katan*,* "Who has sanctified us . . . concerning the commandment of *Tzitzit*," the sages of the Halakhah say that the blessing made for wearing the *Tallit* covers the blessing for the *Tallit Katan* as well. The blessing applies to the entire period of time during which the *Tallit* is being

---

[217] According to the Kabbalah, between the little finger and the middle finger of the left hand. Those who follow the Vilna Gaon® and others hold only the two front fringes and do not kiss them.

worn, even if it is removed for a brief interval. But if it is removed without one intending to put it on again soon afterward, and then is worn once more, one must make the blessing again. In case the *Tallit* inadvertently slips off of one's shoulders, the custom is to repeat the blessing before wearing it again, because there was no conscious intention of removing it.

The custom in Oriental congregations is for the bridegroom to wear a new *Tallit* for the wedding ceremony and pronounce the *she-Heḥeyanu** blessing over it, applying the blessing to the commandment to marry as well. It is a widespread custom among Ashkenazim for the bride to give the bridegroom a new *Tallit* as a wedding gift.

The *Tallit* and *Tzitzit* are "accessories of a commandment," which strictly speaking are considered as sacred objects only while being used in fulfillment of the commandment; once they become torn or worn out, one may do with them as one wishes. However, it has become a general practice not to throw them away disrespectfully but to use them for some other religious purpose or to put them aside in some corner. For the same reason, it is customary to treat the *Tallit* with respect; since it has become a special garment for prayer, it ought not to be worn when entering unclean or impure places, such as a lavatory, but should be taken off before doing so.

Making the *Tzitzit*

The commandment of *Tzitzit* appears in two different places in the Torah: the main passage is the section included in the *Shema** (Numbers 15:37–41), while later there is also another brief mention (Deuteronomy 22:12). The details as to how the fringes should be made were, however, given through oral tradition, and it is this tradition that is always followed.

There are many detailed laws for making the fringes,[218] together with certain differences in custom on various points. But the essentials are as follows: the strings used in tying them are usually made of wool or, at times, from the same material as the *Tallit*. They must be espe-

[218] All of which are to be found in *Shulḥan Arukh, Oraḥ Ḥayyim* 9–16.

cially spun for this purpose, and are formed by interlacing together at least two threads (some interlace them from eight threads). The fringes are made from four strings, each of which is doubled over, forming eight in all. There is no fixed length, but they should be at least "twelve thumb lengths" (which, in most opinions, is either 24 cm or 29 cm—i.e., just under either 10 or 12 inches). It is sometimes necessary in practice to add to this length, either because the threads are thicker, or for esthetic reasons, so that they may suit the length of the *Tallit*. Each bunch of four strings is threaded through one of the holes made in each of the four corners of the *Tallit*.[219] These holes are made about 4 to 6 cm (1½–2½ inches) from the edge of the *Tallit* (some make it as much as 7 cm, or 3 inches, away). The ends of the strings are then evened with one another, and the strings are tied together (four strings with four strings) into a double knot, just below the edge of the *Tallit*. One of the threads, known as the *Shammash* ("servant")—which is deliberately made slightly longer than the others and which, when the law of *Tekhelet* was observed, was the one that was dyed blue—is wound around the others several times (see below), so that the strings form a single strand; another double knot is then tied, and the *Shammash* is again wound around the other strings. This process is repeated until there is a strand with five double knots on it, with the unbound remainders of the threads left loosely hanging. The ideal proportions for *Tzitzit* are considered those in which the unbound threads are twice as long as the bound strand.

Tzitzit fringes on the corner of the *Tallit*

There are different customs regarding the number of times the

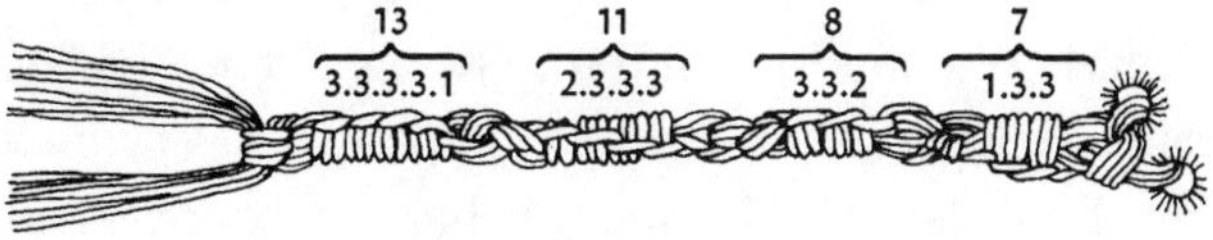

One way of tying the *Tzitzit* knots

[219] In some communities, it is customary, for both halakhic and kabbalistic reasons, to make two adjacent holes in each corner.

Shammash is to be wound around the other strings in the section between the double knots. In most communities, it is wound seven times, then eight, then eleven, and then thirteen times, making a total of thirty-nine times, corresponding to the numerical value of the Hebrew words *ha-Shem Eḥad*—"the Lord is One." In some places, however, the custom is to wind the *Shammash* ten, five, six, and five times—corresponding to the numerical value of the letters of the Tetragrammaton. There are other customs as well.

Making the *Tallit*

The *Tallit* is made of a rectangular piece of cloth, large enough for a man to wrap it around a part of his head and most of his body. Thus, the small neck scarves that are used sometimes as a substitute for the *Tallit* are not only of insufficient size, but the way in which they are worn also negates their value as a *Tallit*.

Under Torah law, the commandment to place fringes applies to a garment made of sheep's wool or linen alone. However, by rabbinical law *Tzitzit* must also be placed on any four-cornered garment, no matter what the fabric from which it is made. Thus, one may also fulfill this obligation with a *Tallit* made, for example, of silk, using fringes of the same material or—as is the more usual custom—of wool. Indeed, one can find *Tallitot* made of all kinds of material; however, those who are strict in their observance use a woolen *Tallit*, which is indisputably subject to the commandment of *Tzitzit*.

Halakhically, there is no particular requirement of color for the *Tallit*, and one may use a *Tallit* of any shade he wishes (if he makes a point of observing the commandments in as ideal a manner as possible, he should make the fringes of the same color as the *Tallit*). In most communities, however, the *Tallit* is white: either entirely so, as in the Sephardic custom, or decorated with black or blue stripes, as in the Ashkenazic custom. In addition to being a general symbol of purity, well-suited for prayer times, the color white also symbolizes, according to the Kabbalah, the Divine attribute of loving-kindness. The priestly garments in the Temple were also predominantly white; similarly, the angelic beings are described as garbed in white (e.g., "the man clothed in linen," Ezekiel 9:11). In the Talmud (*Shabbat* 153a), the verse "Let your garments be always white" (Ecclesiastes 8:9) is also interpreted as referring to the *Tzitzit*.

There is certainly no obligatory form to the decorative stripes on the *Tallit;* nevertheless, in various communities and congregations there developed fixed patterns. These patterns are essentially a remembrance (albeit not always conscious) of the way in which the *Tallit* was made in the Second Temple period, with a variety of decorative stripes. Similarly, the custom to leave the material on two sides of the *Tallit* with rough, unwoven edges, and to tie the loose threads into strands, is also a reminder of the ancient manner of Israelite dress. The general feeling that the *Tallit* is the national garment of the Jewish people led to the designing of the flag of the State of Israel in accordance with the basic pattern of the *Tallit*—i.e., white fabric with narrow blue stripes.

The *Tallit* Band (*Atarah*)

It is customary in many places to mark the upper edge of the *Tallit*, which covers the head, in some special manner. This practice has a halakhic basis, as it is intended to indicate the location for which the different sides of the *Tallit* are to be placed on the body of the one wearing it, so as not to diminish from the importance of the respective sides of the garment. In some communities, an ornamented band (either in the same color as the *Tallit* or in a different color) is attached to that place, and in some cases it is also interlaced with woven or embroidered designs. Others stitch on an embroidered or woven verse from the Torah relating to *Tzitzit;* wealthy people often have this done with silver or gold thread, or by attaching ornaments made of small, thin silver plates. At times, the *Tallit* band may be a work of complex artistry.

The custom of making *Tallit* bands is mainly prevalent in Ashkenazic communities; even among them, there are those who do not practice it, for various reasons, while in all other communities it is hardly ever found.

The *Tallit* Bag

Out of affection and respect for this commandment, rather than because of any requirement of the law, it is customary in many congregations to make a special bag in which to place the *Tallit*. Sometimes the *Tefillin* and Siddur are also placed in it. In many cases, the bag may be decorated with embroidered designs or verses from the Torah, or with the owner's name or initials. It is a widespread custom for the bride to embroider a *Tallit* bag for the bridegroom.

The Blue Thread (*Tekhelet*)

The "thread of blue" mentioned in the Torah (*Petil Tekhelet;* Numbers 15:38) is a woolen thread dyed with a special shade of blue, called *Tekhelet*. From ancient sources, we know that this blue color was extracted from a type of shellfish, known in Hebrew as *Ḥillazon*, which has not been clearly identified. This dye was used for some of the priestly garments worn in the Temple, particularly those of the High Priest (whose robe was all blue), as well as for the *Tzitzit*. This type of crustacean was already quite rare in mishnaic times, and there were doubtless secret professional methods for extracting the color and dyeing the wool. The authentic dye was therefore extremely expensive, leading to the production of counterfeit dyes that were not always easy to detect. By the end of the talmudic era, this dye seems to have been almost completely unknown, and in the course of time the identity of this particular type of shellfish was forgotten, along with the proper methods for extracting the dye and of dyeing the wool. However, since halakhically the absence of a "thread of blue" does not bar one from fulfilling the commandment of *Tzitzit*, throughout the generations Jews continued to make fringes without it.

Around 1880 C.E., the Ḥassidic Rabbi of Radzin, Gershon Ḥanokh Leiner, who was also a renowned halakhic authority, announced that he had managed to identify the shellfish required for the *Tekhelet*—a member of the squid family—and to extract from it the authentic true blue dye. This stirred up a storm of polemic; even though it was not proven that it is forbidden to wear a *Tzitzit* dyed with this blue coloring, it was asserted that the identification was incorrect and that the accepted traditions must be maintained. To date, the Radzin Ḥassidic group, and a small number of other Ḥassidic groups, as well as scattered individuals here and there, continue to use this kind of blue thread in their *Tzitzit*.

More recently, certain sages have suggested identifying this shellfish with one of the various types of similar animals found in the Mediterranean Sea. Most of these scholars think that it is of the type called *Murex trunculus*, but other types have also been suggested.

Tefillin

The commandment to wear *Tefillin* is mentioned in four passages in the Torah: *Shema* (Deuteronomy 6:4–9); *ve-Hayah Im Shamoa* (Deuteronomy 11:13–21); *Kaddesh* (Exodus 13:1–10); and *ve-Hayah Ki Yevi-akha* (Exodus 13:11–16). These passages are written on parchment slips and inserted in the *Tefillin* boxes. The Torah text does not, however, indicate exactly how the *Tefillin* should be made, so that the great majority of the rules regarding their form and structure, and the way they are to be worn, are derived from the oral tradition, as it was given to Moses at Sinai and handed down to us.

According to this tradition, categorized as *Halakhah le-Moshe mi-Sinai* (Sinaitic *halakhah*),* only men are commanded to wear the *Tefillin*. *Tefillin* are to be worn only during the daylight hours of weekdays, but not on Shabbat and festival days (according to some opinions, on those days it is in fact prohibited to put them on). According to the Kabbalah—and such is the predominant practice in most Jewish congregations nowadays—they are also not to be worn during *Ḥol ha-Mo'ed** (see Chapter 12).

The commandment to wear *Tefillin* stands on its own right, and has no inherent connection with prayer. Ideally, one should wear the *Tefillin* all day: at home and while walking in the street, at rest or at work. It would appear that this was the general practice in earliest times. But in a later period, already during the mishnaic and talmudic times, very few people wore the *Tefillin* all day long, for a number of reasons. First, there were a few periods of religious persecution during which anyone found wearing *Tefillin* would be summarily put to death; this obviously led to a certain degree of weakening in the fulfillment of this commandment, at least outside the synagogue.

Another, more significant and ongoing reason was that, because of the sacredness of the *Tefillin*, one needs to take special care regarding their sanctity. They may not be worn in defiled places, and the one wearing them must avoid all forms of evil, both in action and thought, and keep his body and mind pure. The prevailing custom was thus fixed that one wears *Tefillin* regularly only during prayer times, as part of the activities surrounding prayer. The reason why *Tefillin* are worn specifically during the *Shaḥarit** service is that our sages called it improper for a person to mention the commandment of *Tefillin* in the reading of the *Shema*[220] without wearing them at the same time—to do so would be to bear false witness against oneself. For that reason, people have never been too strict about wearing *Tefillin* during the *Minḥah* services, which does not include the reading of the *Shema.*

The name *Tefillin*—from the word *Tefillah*, prayer—apparently derived from this custom of wearing them during prayer services. In the Torah, they are known by the unique term *Totafot*, as well as by the more general words for "sign" and "reminder." Some *Rishonim** and *Aḥaronim** have offered different explanations for the term *Tefillin:* i.e., as being derived either from the root *TFL*, meaning "combination" and "connection," or from the root *PLL*, which means "sign" or "testimony." Other suggestions have also been offered.

Due to the Torah passages placed in the boxes of the *Tefillin*, and because the straps themselves are tied in the shape of letters forming one of God's Holy Names, the *Tefillin* are considered sacred objects: the Torah passages and the *Tefillin* boxes possess a sanctity of their own, while the straps and cases are sacred accessories that must be handled with special care.[221] *Tefillin* that are worn out and can no longer be used must be put away in a respectful and sacred manner. While wearing the *Tefillin*, one is not permitted to sleep, or even to eat a regular meal.

Because of its importance, great care is taken to observe this com-

---

[220] As it says there, "You shall bind them as a sign upon your hand, and they shall be for a reminder between your eyes" (Deuteronomy 6:8).

[221] It is therefore customary that a person whose *Tefillin* fall to the ground must fast for the sake of atonement. See the section on fasts in Chapter 12.

mandment in as ideal a way as possible. The perfectly square shape and black color of the *Tefillin* boxes are mandatory, being *Halakhah le-Moshe mi-Sinai*, and therefore much effort is expended in shaping them to perfection. In addition to precision, there are other embellishments and refinements, some of which have become common practice, such as having each of the boxes made of a single piece of leather rather than of many little pieces stuck together; the size of the *Tefillin;* but, above all, that of wearing two pairs of *Tefillin*—according to Rashi[@] and according to Rabbenu Tam[@] (see below), in order to be freed of all doubt.

The commandment of *Tefillin* requires that one wear two *Tefillin* (or, more properly, a pair)—one on the arm, in fulfillment of "You shall bind them as a sign upon your hand" (Deuteronomy 6:8), and one on the head, to fulfill "and they shall be for a reminder between your eyes" *(ibid.)*. However, the two *Tefillin* are two separate, independent commandments. Thus, so that if for some reason one cannot wear both of them at the same time, he may wear either of them separately, reciting the appropriate blessing(s): for the arm, the blessing is "to lay *Tefillin*," while for the head, some say only the one blessing, "concerning the *mitzvah* of *Tefillin*," and some make both blessings.

Making the *Tefillin*

Each of the *Tefillin* is composed of a box (in Hebrew: *Bayit*, literally, "house"; plural, *Batim*) in which the biblical passages are inserted, and of straps with which to bind the *Tefillin*. Although the boxes and straps of the *Tefillin* serve a practical function, they are integral elements of the commandment. Just as one would not fulfill the commandment were one to wear the *Batim* without the biblical passages, so is the case were one to attach the biblical passages without the boxes and straps. As for the actual making of the *Tefillin*, there are many details that are mandatory, being *Halakhah le-Moshe mi-Sinai;* if any alteration is made, the *Tefillin* are considered invalid.

All parts of the *Tefillin* are made of leather, taken from the hide of various pure animals (in practice, cattle and sheep, and only infrequently from kosher game). The boxes are made from a harder leather, so as to retain their precise shape, while the straps are made from thinner leather. The biblical passages are written on parchment, while the stitching together of the different parts of the *Tefillin* and the tying of the Torah portions are done with the hair and sinews of a pure animal.

Halakhically, there is no standard size for the *Batim* of the *Tefillin* (apart from the *Tefillin de-Shimmusha Rabbah*),[222] and they come in different sizes, ranging from tiny *Tefillin* boxes of less than 1 cm (2/5 inch) in width to large ones of 4 cm (about 1 1/2 inches) wide or more. The straps are made in corresponding width. In the Ashkenazic custom, the *Tefillin* are generally of a larger size, while in the Sephardic custom they are usually much smaller (among other reasons, because according to this custom, some wear two pairs of *Tefillin* simultaneously; see below); however, there is no fixed tradition for this.

The *Tefillin* of the arm consists of one box which, according to *Halakhah le-Moshe mi-Sinai*, should be square, of equal width and length. There is, however, no ruling as to its height; hence, some make the *Bayit* in the shape of a perfect cube, while others make it higher than its length. Within the box are placed the four biblical passages written on a single parchment, which is rolled up and tied with hair threads, preferably those of a calf. It is the practice to then wrap this in a piece of parchment that is also tied with hair threads (on the order of writing the biblical passages, see below.)

The *Tefillin* box itself is constructed as a hollow square container with an open bottom, beneath which another piece of leather is placed in order to close this opening. This base piece is called in the Talmud the *Tittura*, or "bridge"; it too must be square, and larger than the *Bayit*. The seam within the *Tittura*, which goes all around the *Bayit*, must also be square. The *Tittura* is hollowed in one side, and this hollow is called the *Ma'abarta*—"passageway"—through which the strap for tying the *Tefillin* is inserted. Although not all authorities concur that dyeing the *Tefillin* boxes black is a mandatory *halakhah*, it is considered meritorious to do so, and such is the accepted practice.

The *Tefillin* strap for the arm should be long enough to be fastened over the arm, with a loop especially made for this purpose, and then to be wrapped around the forearm at least seven times, and then wound over the palm and the middle finger of the hand. The strap is

---

[222] A special kind of *Tefillin*, used only by a select few.

usually made to fit the size of an average man's hand or longer because, according to some opinions, if a strap of the proper length is obtainable, it is not permitted to sew or glue together a strap that is not long enough. The straps for the arm and for the head should be at least 1 cm.(2/5 inch) in width.

According to *Halakhah le-Moshe mi-Sinai*, the *Tefillin* straps should be painted on the outer side in jet black. The inner side may be painted in any other color, except red, but the general practice is to leave the leather in its original state. At the upper end of the strap, which is attached to the *Ma'abarta*, a knot is made in the form of the Hebrew letter *Yod* (י). This, too, is *Halakhah le-Moshe mi-Sinai.*

The structure of the *Tefillin* box for the head is more complex. According to the Halakhah, it must be made up of four adjoining compartments; those who are meticulous about the performance of the commandments take care to ensure that this is made of a single piece of leather. These four compartments are then pressed together to form a perfect square (at least in length and width, if not in height; see above). The four biblical passages are written on separate pieces of parchment, each placed in one of the compartments. The order in which they are placed (in the *Tefillin* box of the head), and of their writing (on the single parchment in the *Tefillin* of the hand) is the subject of an ancient dispute, which later came to be known as the contrary views of Rashi and of his grandson, Rabbenu Tam. The view of Rashi (which was apparently the generally followed custom in the Land of Israel) has been accepted halakhically. According to this view, the *Kaddesh* passage is placed in the extreme left compartment (from the wearer's viewpoint), followed by *ve-Hayah Ki Yeviakha*, the *Shema* passage in the third compartment, and *ve-Hayah Im Shamoa* in the extreme right one. According to Rabbenu Tam, the passages in the third and fourth compartments are to be placed in the reverse order.

Another Sinaitic *halakhah* requires that the Hebrew letter *Shin* (ש) be embossed in relief on the *Tefillin* box of the head. This is done on both sides of the box; but whereas the letter *Shin* placed on the right side of the *Bayit* (from the wearer's perspective) is made in its normal three-pronged form, the one on the left is made in a special manner, with four prongs.

The *Tefillin* box of the head likewise has a *Tittura* and a *Ma'abarta* for the strap that binds it. The strap is inserted in the *Ma'abarta*, making with it a circle the size of the wearer's head, which is then tied with a knot in the form of the Hebrew letter *Dalet* (ד).

This "*Tefillin* knot" is not made in the same manner everywhere. In Ashkenazic custom, a very complicated knot is made, which eventually takes on the semblance of this letter, while in the Sephardic custom the knot is made to form a double *Dalet*, which looks like a final *Mem* (ם). After the knot is tied, the two ends of the strap are not of equal length, that of the right-hand side being longer.[223] If one does not have long straps, it is sufficient if they are 20 cm (about 8 inches) in length.

The Content of the Commandment of *Tefillin*

The commandment of wearing *Tefillin* involves two aspects: the contents and meaning of the biblical passages written and deposited therein, and the *Tefillin* boxes and straps.

The biblical passages embody several of the basic essentials of the Jewish faith: the belief in God, love of God to the point of self-sacrifice, reward and punishment, the exodus from Egypt, the election of the people of Israel, and their inheritance of the Land of Israel. Alongside these, several central positive commandments (see *mitzvah**) are mentioned: the Passover, Torah study, *Tefillin*, and *Mezuzah*.* The sages have even found there allusions to all the Ten Commandments. In that sense, this commandment fulfills the words in the *Kaddesh* passage, "And it shall be for a sign unto you upon your hand, and for a memorial between your eyes, that the Lord's law may be in your mouth" (Exodus 13:9). The *Tefillin* thus contain the essential principles of God's law, together with the injunction to continue studying it, and to preserve and observe it. Hence, this commandment is a "remembrance" and a "reminder," for through its passages we are reminded of our true essence and calling.

The distinctive aspect of this commandment, however, lies in the *Tefillin* themselves. The *Tefillin* of the arm are usually referred to in the Torah as *Ot*—"a sign"—while the *Tefillin* of the head are called *Totafot*—"a reminder." Although the word *Totafot* is mentioned in the

---

[223] Some make the right-hand strap end reach to the navel, and the left-hand one to the chest; others make the right-hand strap reach the thigh, and the left-hand one the navel.

Mishnah as referring to a kind of ornament placed on the forehead, the exact meaning and etymology of the word are not clear. There is no identifiable root in either Hebrew or any cognate language, and even the sages saw it as a foreign word (*Sanhedrin* 4b). But even without understanding its meaning, the very structure of the *Tefillin* and the way in which they are worn indicate their significance—namely, as emblems of royalty. The *Tefillin* of the head is like a royal diadem, and the *Tefillin* of the arm is a symbol of royal sovereignty.

Unlike the imposing crowns worn by kings at grand ceremonies, a royal coronet or diadem is a single circlet worn around the head, bearing on its front the symbol of majesty. Such is the *Tefillin* of the head, which in many ways corresponds to the golden crown of the High Priest (*Tzitz*) on which the Name of God was engraved, and which is referred to as "the frontlet of the holy diadem" (Exodus 39:30). On the same place where the *Tefillin* of the arm is bound, a Torah scroll used to be bound on the arm of the King of Israel, as one of the symbols of his kingship.

The halakhic statement that "all Israel are princes" (*Shabbat* 111a) is based on the verse "You shall be a peculiar treasure unto Me above all people: for all the earth is Mine. And you shall be unto Me a kingdom of priests and a holy nation" (Exodus 19:5–6). Because the people of Israel are like members of a royal nobility, related and bound to the King of Kings, therefore it says, "And kings shall be your nursing fathers . . . they shall bow down to you with their face toward the earth" (Isaiah 49:23). This is likewise the point of the sages' midrashic interpretation of the verse "And all the people of the earth shall see that the name of the Lord is called upon you; and they shall be afraid of you" (Deuteronomy 28:10) as referring to the *Tefillin* of the head (*Berakhot* 6a). The *Tefillin* themselves are a symbol of our connection with the Supreme King, "For I am a great King . . . and My Name is awesome among the heathen" (Malachi 1:14). This is also the way our sages have understood the verse "put on your turban" (Hebrew: *Pe'erkha*—"your glory"; Ezekiel 24:17) as indicating the *Tefillin* (*Mo'ed Katan* 15a). They also explain the blessing[224] "who crowns [the people of] Israel with glory" as referring to the *Tefillin*. Since the *Tefillin* bear numerous symbolic features, analogous to symbols of royalty, it is most

[224] Recited at the very beginning of the *Shaḥarit* service; see *Birkhot ha-Shaḥar*.

important to observe all the detailed instructions for making and donning them—their form and color, their precise placement on the body, and the way they should be bound.

There is yet another aspect to the *Tefillin.* The crown of *Tefillin* acts as a corporeal symbolic pattern, representing the supernal reality of the upper worlds. Our sages say that "God wears *Tefillin*" (*Berakhot* 6a), and that when God told Moses, "you shall see my back parts" (Exodus 33:23), He showed him the knot of the *Tefillin* (*Berakhot* 7a). That is, just as the Supreme King is crowned with a royal coronet, so, too, do we also crown ourselves with coronets. The *Zohar*# offers a similar interpretation: "Whenever one places the *Tefillin* on his head and arm, a voice goes forth every day to all the creatures of the Holy Chariot, and to all the Ofanim, Seraphim and the angels in charge of our prayers: Give honor to the image of the King" (*Tikkunei Zohar*# 47). This mutual relationship is described in *Shir ha-Kavod** in the words "His splendor is upon me, and my splendor is upon Him."

While the *Tefillin* of the head represents the crown and coronet, the *Tefillin* of the arm represents the bond of love and intimacy expressed by the binding of the straps upon our bodies. These are called "strong bands of love,"[225] binding together the "bridegroom and bride"—God and *Knesset Yisrael.** Our sages have expounded the verse "Set me . . . as a seal upon your arm" (Song of Songs 8:6) as similarly indicating the *Tefillin* of the arm.

The description of *Tefillin* in terms of the verse "the name of the Lord . . . called upon you" is not only understood in the metaphorical sense of our being "royal sons": it is also true in the most literal sense, as the letters of the *Tefillin—Shin* embossed on the *Tefillin* of the head, *Dalet* on the knot at the back of the head, and *Yod* in the *Tefillin* straps of the arm—together form the Holy Name, שדי, *Shaddai*, indicating God's unbounded lordship and sovereignty. The biblical passages inside the *Tefillin*, containing a royal declaration concerning Israel as the chosen people and the perpetual bond between God and Israel, likewise support this meaning.

Alongside these aspects of greatness and glory, the *Tefillin* also represent submission to the Divine yoke and acceptance of heavenly authority. In a certain sense, these two aspects are interrelated: who-

---

[225] As in one of the *le-Shem Yiḥud** formulations recited before wearing the *Tefillin.*

ever carries such a royal symbol is obliged to behave in the appropriate manner. Just as the coronet conveys honor to its bearer, it also requires that the bearer honor it, behaving with great care and dignity while wearing it. Many of the halakhic rules regarding the *Tefillin* express the same sentiment found, in another context, in the verse "he shall be holy . . . because the crown of his God is upon his head" (Numbers 6:7). Hence, any act of disrespect, or any form of pollution, whether of body or of mind, displays scorn and contempt for this diadem.

There is yet another aspect to all this. When a person dons the symbols of Divine sovereignty, he himself submits to the authority of the Kingdom of Heaven. He thereby acknowledges and reminds himself of his commitment and his duty to minister and serve. The *Rishonim** have explained[226] that, by placing the *Tefillin* on the head and against the heart,[227] one subjugates one's mind and heart to God. Just as tying the *Tefillin* binds one up above, so does it also bind one below, by connecting one's powers of thought, the feelings of the heart, and the power of action, which from now on are no longer in a state of lawlessness, as one is now bound to perform the will of the Ruler of the World.

This combination of crown and chains is, in fact, mentioned in the biblical passages in the *Tefillin* boxes. The exodus from Egypt[228] represents, on the one hand, the release of the people of Israel from slavery, but at the same time it also brings them into the servitude of God, "For unto Me the children of Israel are servants; they are My servants whom I brought forth out of the land of Egypt" (Leviticus 25:55). The status of "God's servant" includes both the total and absolute commitment toward Him, and the greatness of being God's elect: "Fear not, O Jacob, My servant; and you Jeshurun whom I have chosen" (Isaiah 44:2); "Behold, My servant shall deal prudently, he shall be exalted and extolled, and be very high" (*ibid.*, 52:13). As against this bond of Divine election and service, which is a bond of understanding and wisdom, there is also an element of love and fear. Love, with all of one's

---

[226] See Naḥmanides' commentary to the portion of *ve-Hayah Ki Yeviakha*.

[227] The *Tefillin* of the arm is placed against one's heart; and the *Yod* knot of the *Tefillin* faces the heart.

[228] Mentioned in the portions of *Kaddesh* and *ve-Hayah Ki Yeviakha*.

heart, soul, and might; and the fear that comes with any deviation from it: "Take care lest your heart be lured away" (Deuteronomy 11:16). This glorious combination of crown and chains thus ties together our complete, total relationship as both sons and servants to our Father and King.

The Manner of Donning *Tefillin*

ALTHOUGH THE COMMANDMENT of wearing *Tefillin* is germane throughout the daylight hours, they should be put on as early as possible. They may even be donned before sunrise* but, according to most opinions, no more than sixty minutes before that. The *Tallit* must be put on first, and immediately thereafter the *Tefillin*, following the general rule of "ascending in holiness." The *Tefillin* of the arm is donned first, followed by the *Tefillin* of the head, and they are removed in the reverse order, so that one is never wearing the *Tefillin* of the head without the *Tefillin* of the hand.

Our sages have received, as *Halakhah le-Moshe mi-Sinai*, that the *Tefillin* should be placed on the left arm.[229] Sages of old have already noted that in the Bible, the right hand is always called *Yamin*—"the right"—while the left hand is called simply *Yad*—"hand."[230] For that reason, left-handed people should put the *Tefillin* on the right arm, which is the weaker one for them. In *Tefillin* made specifically for the right hand, the *Yod* knot is placed on the opposite side, so that it is close to the body.

Unlike the *Tefillin* of the head (see below), the *Tefillin* of the arm need not be visible, because the commandment says that "it shall be for a sign unto you," which is interpreted to mean "for you alone, and not for others." Some sages understand this as meaning that one may cover it with the sleeve if he wishes. Others, however, interpret these words as implying that covering the *Tefillin* of the arm is mandatory—and this has indeed become generally practiced custom.

The *Tefillin* of the arm is placed on the upper arm, where the

---

[229] This is based on a particular interpretation of the peculiar spelling of the word *Yadekhah*—"your hand" (in Exodus 13:16)—as "the weaker hand"; see *Menaḥot* 37a.

[230] See, for instance, Judges 5:26.

muscle bulges. The method of donning it is to place the loop made by the strap around the arm, hold the *Tefillin* box in place, pronounce the blessing "to lay *Tefillin*," and then tighten the loop. Thereafter, the strap is wound several times around the forearm and the hand. These windings are not mandatory by law but are a matter of custom, which is observed in different ways. Some wind the strap three times over the upper arm.[231] In all customs, the strap is then wound seven times around the forearm, between the elbow and the wrist. There are, however, variant customs for doing this: in the Ashkenazic rite, it is wound toward the body, while all others wind it away from the body. The strap must not be wound under the *Tittura*, because to do so would separate the *Tefillin* box from the arm.

At this point, it is customary not to complete the additional windings of the strap around the palm of the hand; rather, with the end of the strap wound loosely over the hand, the *Tefillin* of the head are donned, and only after that are the windings of the strap around the hand completed. Some place the *Tefillin* of the head even before making the seven windings around the forearm.

The *Tefillin* of the head is placed in the middle of the head, above the forehead, just over the spot where the hairline begins, the place determined by the tradition of the sages as being "between your eyes" (Deuteronomy 6:8).[232] The *Tefillin* must be in the very center of the head, to fulfill the words, "for a memorial between your eyes." The *Tefillin* knot at the back of the head should be placed in such a way as to rest on the upper edge of the hollow behind the skull. The straps of the *Tefillin* of the head are brought to the front of the body, one on the right and one on the left.

The straps should be well tightened, so that the *Tefillin* boxes do not move from their places throughout the course of prayer, as the commandment stipulates that the *Tefillin* be on those specific parts of

[231] In a few congregations, the strap is also wound once over the brim of the *Tefillin*.

[232] Our sages bring further proof for this interpretation from the verse "You shall not . . . make any baldness between your eyes" (Deuteronomy 14:1), in which it is clear that the baldness is made in the place where the hair grows.

the body. It is common according to Sephardic custom, and among a few individuals in other customs, that those who wear *Tefillin* of Rabbenu Tam (see below) as well, wear both pairs of *Tefillin* simultaneously, one on top of the other; however, the practice is to hide the *Tefillin* of Rabbenu Tam under the head covering.

The *Tefillin* of the head should be visible according to the verse "And all people of the earth shall see that you are called by the name of the Lord" (Deuteronomy 28:19), which, according to our sages, refers to the *Tefillin* of the head. For this reason, even those who cover their heads with the *Tallit* during the prayer do not cover the place of the *Tefillin*. According to Rabbi Isaac Luria,[@] however, one should cover it with the *Tallit*.

After this is done, the winding of the *Tefillin* around the hand is completed. The method of winding the strap over the palm differs from one custom to another. In many congregations, it is wound in such a way as to resemble the Hebrew letter *Dalet* (ד). In order to do so, the strap is first wound three times around the middle finger of the hand, and then the winding is completed over the back of the hand. In some customs, the straps are wound in such a way as to form both the letter *Dalet* and the letter *Shin* (ש) which, together with the *Yod* (י) knot of the *Tefillin* of the arm, completes the formation of one of the Holy Names (שדי, see above). If there remains some part of the strap that is still loose, it may be wound over the palm for the sake of convenience.

The *Tefillin* should be left in that position, and should be touched every now and then (there are accepted customs as to the proper times for doing so), so that one's attention will not be diverted from them, and especially in order to assure that they remain in their proper place, and to tighten them if necessary. Care should be taken that the black side of the straps faces outward, and to adjust them should they become reversed. *Kohanim*, who must wash their hands prior to blessing the people, or one who needs to free his hand in order to hold the Torah scroll, may undo the strap windings on the palm and wind them temporarily over the wrist, and later rewind the strap as before.

The *Tefillin* should be removed in the reverse order from which they were put on. One first undoes the windings over the hands, then removes and folds up the *Tefillin* of the head, and only then removes the *Tefillin* of the arm.

Blessings and Recitations

In most Jewish communities, it is customary to recite *le-Shem Yiḥud** before performing commandments; similarly, there is a *le-Shem Yiḥud* formula to be recited before putting on the *Tefillin*. The precise text of this formula differs from custom to custom: the Sephardic one is brief, while the Ashkenazic one is considerably longer, containing a reflection upon the meaning of the commandment of *Tefillin*, to the effect that it is meant to remind us of God and His commandments, that the *Tefillin* are placed on the arm, opposite the heart, and on the head, opposite the mind, in order to subject all these organs to the service of God. There is yet another version[233] in which the more mystical aspects are stressed—i.e., the meaning and intention of each of the details of this commandment, emphasizing the aspect of God's sovereignty over the world.

It is the custom of most Ashkenazim to make the blessing for the *Tefillin* and to put them on while standing. In the Sephardic custom, based on the Kabbalah, the blessing on the *Tefillin* of the arm and the act of donning it are specifically performed while sitting, whereas the *Tefillin* of the head are put on while standing.[234]

The blessing for the *Tefillin* is recited after placing the *Tefillin* over the arm, but before tightening the strap (by which one fulfills the commandment to "bind" them; Deuteronomy 6:8). The blessing recited is "Blessed are You, Lord our God, King of the universe, who has sanctified us with His commandments, and commanded us to lay *Tefillin*." The verb *le-Haniah* ("to lay" or "to put on") conveys in one word what is said about both the *Tefillin* of the hand and the *Tefillin* of the head: *ve-Hayu*—"and they shall be" (Deuteronomy 6:8; 11:18)—that is, that the

---

[233] Taken from the book *Sha'arei Zion*.#

[234] Some sages (Rabbi Schneur Zalman of Lyady® in his *Shulḥan Arukh ha-Rav*,# 25, and others) have suggested a way of fulfilling this commandment to accord with all the different opinions—namely, to recite the *Tefillin* blessing while standing, as with all the blessings recited over commandments, and to then don the *Tefillin* while sitting. However, only few do so in practice.

Tefillin be placed in their proper places as a "sign . . . and a memorial" (Exodus 13:9).

Most Ashkenazim—both those following the Ashkenazic and Sepharad rites, except for Ḥabad and some few individuals—follow the opinion according to which a separate blessing should be made over the *Tefillin* of the head as well. In other prayer rites, however, this latter blessing is only recited when there is a verbal interruption—*Hefsek**—between putting on the *Tefillin* of the arm and of the head.[235] The wording of this latter blessing is more general, referring to the completion of the act of this commandment, "who has sanctified us with His commandments, and commanded us concerning the commandment of *Tefillin*." This blessing too, is recited after the *Tefillin* have been placed on the head, and before tightening the *Bayit* on its place. However, even those Ashkenazim who regularly say this blessing also take into consideration the view that this blessing is superfluous, and therefore add, immediately after tightening the straps, the words *Barukh Shem Kevod Malkhuto le-Olam va-Ed.**[236] When the blessing for the *Tefillin* of the head becomes mandatory, as after an interruption, as mentioned above, this phrase is not added.

After putting in place the *Tefillin* of the head, many have the custom of reciting a brief prayer, of mystical significance:

From Your wisdom, O supreme God, may You imbue me; from Your understanding give me understanding; with Your kindness do greatly with me; with Your power cut down my foes and rebels. [May] You pour goodly oil upon the seven arms of the Menorah, to cause Your good to flow to Your creatures; [May You] "open Your hand and satisfy the desire of every living thing." (Psalm 145:16)

This prayer alludes to the four compartments in the *Tefillin* of the head, and to various aspects of the *Tefillin* of the arm, which have profound mystical meanings.

Following this, while the strap is wound around the middle finger, the following verse is recited: "I will betroth you to Me for ever; and I will betroth you to Me with righteousness, justice, kindness, and mercy. I will betroth you to Me with fidelity, and you shall know the

---

[235] I.e., by speaking on matters not related to the fulfillment of this commandment.

[236] As is usually done whenever there is fear of having made a blessing in vain.

Lord" (Hosea 2:21–22). The winding of the strap around the finger forms a ring, symbolizing the ring of betrothal—the betrothal between God and the people of Israel, as expressed in this verse. The strap is wound three times around the finger, forming three separate rings, corresponding to the three times in which the word "betroth" is mentioned in these verses.

After completing the donning of the *Tefillin*, it is customary to recite those two biblical passages contained within the *Tefillin* that are not included in the regular order of prayers: *Kaddesh* (Exodus 13:1–10) and *ve-Hayah Ki Yeviakha* (*ibid*., vv. 11–16). Whoever cannot manage to say them then, should recite them at the end of the prayer service, before removing the *Tefillin.*

Tefillin of Rabbenu Tam

As mentioned, there is a very ancient difference of opinion regarding the proper sequence in which the four biblical passages are to be placed within the *Tefillin* of the head. This difference of opinion has never been theoretically resolved; moreover, each view relies upon ancient custom, the kabbalists even claiming that the *Tefillin* of Rabbenu Tam@ is the main one. It has therefore become the custom—practiced mainly by Ḥassidim who follow the Sephardic rite, as well as by some who follow the Oriental rite—to wear two sets of *Tefillin*.

The *Tefillin* of Rabbenu Tam are donned without making a blessing, and it is customary to recite all, or some, of the passages of the *Tefillin* while putting on each of these two sets of *Tefillin*. A very small number of pious individuals wear another two pairs of *Tefillin* (known as *Shimmusha Rabbah* (see above,) and the *Tefillin* according to the opinion of the Ravad@). There are those who set aside special times, or special activities, for putting on the additional *Tefillin* (e.g., the *Minḥah* service, or a special study session).

Some Laws and Customs of *Tefillin*

The commandment of *Tefillin* is considered of especially high value, and the sages define the phrase "Jewish transgressors with their bodies" (*Rosh ha-Shanah* 17a) as alluding to "the cranium which does not put on the *Tefillin*." For this reason—particularly according to that reading of this dictum that sees it as referring to "one who has never worn *Tefillin*"—there are those who attempt to have all Jews put on *Tefillin*.

Because the *Tefillin* are called "[an adornment of] glory," mourners do not wear *Tefillin* on the first day of mourning.[237] For the same reason, it is customary in most communities not to wear *Tefillin* on the morning of Tish'ah be-Av (see Chapter 12). *Tefillin* are also not worn on Shabbat and festival days; those who follow the Sephardic rite throughout the world, and people of all communities in the Land of Israel, also do not wear them during *Ḥol ha-Mo'ed* as well (see Chapter 12).

The sanctity of the *Tefillin* is very great, for which reason one must guard their holiness with utmost care. Hence, the sages ruled that a child may not begin wearing *Tefillin* until he knows how to keep his body in a proper state of cleanliness. In practice, it is the custom throughout the Jewish world that a boy starts wearing *Tefillin* only when he reaches Bar Mitzvah* age, and is trained in the execution of this *mitzvah* a few months before this.

While wearing the *Tefillin*, one must be very scrupulous about both bodily and spiritual cleanliness. In terms of bodily purity, one must take care that there is nothing either filthy or foul-smelling about one's body. If one is unable to keep one's body clean because of illness, it is preferable not to wear *Tefillin*, or to do so only for that short period of time during which one can remain clean. One should also be careful while wearing the *Tefillin* to keep one's mind from thoughts about sexual or other desires; concerning this matter as well, there are those who have written that he who is unable to prevent himself from indulging in such thoughts should preferably not wear *Tefillin*. Although in our times, due to the decline of the generations,[238] people are not as strict about these matters, one must at least try to purify his body and heart from anything evil.

The *Tefillin* is halakhically defined as a sacred object, and therefore

---

[237] This is learned from Ezekiel 24:17. See also *Mo'ed Katan* 15a.

[238] This concept reflects the accepted notion that, generally speaking, in ancient times people were better than they are today, and that each generation is of lesser stature and quality than the former one.

one may not enter the lavatory or bathhouse with it. It is also forbidden to have sexual intercourse in a room where they are kept. In those places where it was customary to take an oath over a sacred object, the *Tefillin* were often used for this purpose. *Tefillin* that have become worn out or defective must be stored away in a holy place, like all other sacred objects. One should also show respect for the *Tefillin;* thus, for instance, they must not be hung up (unless placed in a bag), and one should not sleep while wearing the *Tefillin.*

It is customary to store the *Tefillin* in a bag, and to place them there in a predetermined order, so that one does not take the *Tefillin* of the head out of the bag first.[239] One who has two pairs of *Tefillin* should mark them so as not to confuse them with each other. It is also generally the custom to embroider the bags with various kinds of ornamentation.

In recent generations, it is also customary among many people to use special boxes for storing the *Tefillin* and protecting their exact square shape and color. Some also make a special small box to cover the *Tefillin* box for the arm which, being often covered by a sleeve, is liable to be eroded.

While these protective boxes and bags are not inherently sacred, if they have been made specially for this purpose, they become ritual articles that must be treated appropriately.

The Prayer Sash

The Talmud (*Shabbat* 10a) indicates that one should wear a sash while praying, because this is a sign of dignity and respect, as well as a way of fulfilling the verse "prepare to meet your God, O Israel" (Amos 4:12). Indeed, it is a halakhic ruling to do so (*Shulḥan Arukh, Oraḥ Ḥayyim* 91b). Wearing a sash has an additional halakhic significance, in that it makes a separation between the heart and the genitals of the worshipper, when wearing a robe or cloak.

Now that the style of dress has changed in most Jewish communities, there is no longer a need for a sash as a divider. Moreover, halakhic

---

[239] For this would result in "putting a commandment aside," since the *Tefillin* of the arm is worn first. See *Shulḥan Arukh, Oraḥ Ḥayyim* 25:6.

authorities have ruled that one who does not wear a belt for adornment and style on other occasions is not obliged to do so during prayers. Nevertheless, the custom of wearing a sash, known in Yiddish as a *Gartel*, during every prayer (as well as in major ceremonies) has become a widely adopted custom among Ḥassidic congregations following the Sepharad prayer rite. In some communities, the sash is worn from Bar Mitzvah age on, while in others it is only customary after marriage. There were also some prominent figures who, although not Ḥassidic, wished to fulfill this halakhic ruling literally, and wore a sash during their prayers.

Although there are no halakhic specifications for the sash, there is a standard custom, accepted by all Ḥassidim, whereby the sash should be made of real or artificial silk and should be black in color (in some communities, particularly when worn together with a *Kittel*,* it may also be white). The sash is generally made of several thick strands twisted together; however, there are differences in their number (due to geographical reasons or individual tastes), and sashes may be woven from three, seven, sixteen or more thick strands, with loose threads at the ends. The sash is generally long enough to be wound several times around the waist, with the two ends hanging at the sides of the body.

Hand-Held Objects

According to talmudic law, as well as later halakhic rulings,[240] while praying, one may not hold any object in one's hands that one would be anxious not to drop, especially during the *Amidah* prayer. The reason for this ruling is both that it is a sign of disrespect and that it causes one's attention to be partially diverted rather than concentrating fully upon prayer.

However, it is permitted, or even meritorious, to hold certain things in one's hand, because they are either related to prayer or of assistance to it. Some of these objects are mentioned in the Mishnah, while others appear in later halakhic compendiums.

---

[240] *Shulḥan Arukh, Oraḥ Ḥayyim* 96.

The Siddur

Prayer books were only introduced long after the institution of prayer services, and even of regular communal prayers. During mishnaic and talmudic times, care was taken not to put prayer formulations into writing at all. Even in later generations, when prayers and prayer books began to be written down, these texts were not widely used, for technical reasons: writing materials were very expensive, and a well-executed copy of a manuscript was extremely costly. In those days, only prayer leaders, or those few who could afford it, owned prayer books. Only after the invention of printing and the production of cheap paper did books in general, and prayer books in particular, become available to everyone, so that the prayer book eventually became the book most widely distributed among the Jewish people.

Because in ancient times Siddurim (in manuscript form) were scarce, halakhic authorities had to rule that it is nevertheless permissible to hold a Siddur during prayer time, and there should be no worry that doing so would distract the person holding the book from his prayer, because the Siddur actually helps him pray.[241]

There has never been a standard model for a prayer book, either in structure and size or in range of the material included therein. Yet beyond considerations of cost and personal taste, there were some general factors that led to the acceptance of certain types of Siddurim. One example is the quite prevailing division between Siddur and *Maḥzor*. Whereas the Siddur is generally used for the regular prayer services, namely, those of the weekdays and of Shabbat, the *Maḥzor* is intended for the festival prayers, especially the prayers for the Days of Awe. This division was necessitated by the large number of *Piyyutim** written for the prayers of those days, which are often longer than the entire regular prayer service.

As with all sacred accessories, there is special merit in the external adornment of the prayer book as well. Those who could afford to do so embellished them with rich and ornate bindings, and at times, espe-

---

241 See *Shulḥan Arukh, Oraḥ Ḥayyim* 96b.

cially during the Middle Ages, manuscript prayer books were adorned with numerous illuminations and illustrations.

In some communities, where it was customary for unmarried women not to attend the synagogue, a Siddur would be given to the bride by the bridegroom as a wedding gift.

Although the Siddur was always written in Hebrew, it would often contain halakhic instructions and remarks in the vernacular. In many cases, a full translation of the prayers would also be added for the benefit of those who did not know Hebrew, so that they would be able to understand the prayers they were reciting.

As the Siddur was to be found in every Jewish home, and was carefully preserved because it was a holy book, people often wrote memoranda or made notes on its flyleaf (and sometimes on that of other holy books) to indicate their children's birth dates, or the anniversaries of the deaths of their parents or of other relatives.

Because, over the course of time, most worshippers learn the texts of the regular prayer services by heart, some are in the habit of reciting certain prayers, such as the *Amidah*, with their eyes closed and without using a prayer book. On the other hand, there are some authorities who think that one who prays with a Siddur is not only less likely to make a mistake but will also be less distracted from his prayers. One who almost automatically recites familiar prayers by heart may easily find his thoughts straying to other matters while his lips are uttering the words. For this reason, it was urged that one should always pray from a Siddur, and some took care to do so even for short and oft-recited blessings. There is, however, no definite halakhic ruling on this point, and it depends partly on local custom, and partly on the personal feelings of each worshipper.

The *Arba'ah Minim* ("Four Species")

The Talmud (*Sukkah* 41b) highly praises the Jerusalemites of the Temple period who, during the festival of Sukkot (see Chapter 10), used to hold the *Arba'ah Minim** in their hands all day long. Whenever leaving their homes or going anyplace, they used to hold in their hands the *Lulav** and the other three species, even while praying or reciting the *Shema*. Thus, while generally speaking it is considered undesirable to hold an object in one's hands while praying, this case is seen as a manner of expressing special affection for observing a certain commandment. Hence, during Sukkot, the *Arba'ah Minim* are not regarded as objects unrelated to the prayers, but rather as deeply connected with the prayers of these days. This is no longer the practice today (except among a very few individuals), and the *Arba'ah Minim* are laid aside during prayer time, except for the recital of the *Hallel** and the *Hosha'not,** when it is the general custom to hold them.

In addition, the *Lulav* is shaken while reciting certain verses of the *Hallel.* At that time, one holds it as is done while pronouncing the blessing on it—i.e., grasping the *Lulav* and the two accompanying species in the right hand, and the *Ethrog** in the left. During the recital of the rest of the *Hallel* and the *Hosha'not,* however, they may be held as is convenient. In our times, it is also the custom, at the end of the recitation of the *Hosha'not* of *Hosha'na Rabbah,** to hold the willow branches in one's hand. All these customs are observed today for the same reason they were observed in those ancient times in Jerusalem—as a sign of affection for the commandment, which both accords with prayer and enhances it.

CHAPTER SEVENTEEN

The Music of Prayer

Music and Prayer

Since earliest times, music has universally been a part of God's creatures' worship of their Creator. From the very beginning of our national existence, the worship of God with prayer and sacrifice has been accompanied by music (see Exodus 15:1, 20), and music played an important part in the Temple service as well.

Music adds a further emotional dimension to man's Divine service in two ways. On the one hand, the very presence of music lends a fundamental quality of splendor and dignity to a ceremony. Just as music fulfills this function in royal palaces and in state ceremonies, so does it function in this manner in the Temple of God, as well as in every "little Temple"—the synagogue. On the other hand, there is special music for particular matters or occasions, which can deepen the emotions relevant to them, be they times of sorrow or joy, or times devoted to spiritual meditation and repentance, or to Torah study.

Music in the Temple

Temple music, too, served these two functions. In the Temple's holy service, which is the model for communal prayer in the synagogue, music—both instrumental and choral—was an integral part of the service. Whenever public sacrifices were offered, especially during the festivals and on *Rosh Ḥodesh,** they were accompanied by a ceremonial blowing of trumpets by the priests (see Numbers 10:10); similarly, trumpets were blown on all festive occasions in the Temple (see Mishnah, *Sukkah* 5:5).

In addition, there was the vocal music, sung by the choir of Levites standing on the rostrum. From various sources, it appears that the music of this choral singing was modified to suit different times and occasions, and was meant to deepen the emotional-experiential aspect of Temple service. This choir sang the Song of the Day,* accompanied by an orchestra of many instruments, some of which are mentioned in Psalm 150:

Praise Him with the call of the Shofar; *praise Him with harp and lyre. Praise Him with the timbrel and dance; praise Him with stringed instruments and flute. Praise Him with resounding cymbals; praise Him with clanging cymbals.*

Though we know the names of the musical instruments used during the First and Second Temple periods, and some of them have actually been identified, we have no definite knowledge about the melodies that were played and sung. It seems that the singing was mainly voices at different tonal heights joining together, including the soprano tones of the young Levites. The choristers apparently sang the same melody in unison, and even the orchestra, with its many sounds, simply joined the uniform melody.[242]

Some psalms—as we learn both from their structure and from biblical allusions—were antiphonic choral songs, in which various parts were sung by different people. Sometimes one person would sing the main lines, and the choir would respond (as in Psalm 136, for instance), and sometimes each group of singers sang a specific part of the song.[243]

Moreover, it is obvious that various melodies were played on different occasions, and as accompaniment to certain psalms. This is indicated by the titles at the head of many psalms that give various directions "to the Chief Musician" (*la-Menatzeaḥ*). Some believe that the names given to various psalms, such as *Mizmor*, *Mikhtam*, *Edut*, *Maskil*, *Shiggayon*,[244] and others, represent different musical forms.

---

[242] This seems to be supported by the verse "The trumpeters and singers were as one, to make one sound to be heard in praising and thanking the Lord" (II Chronicles 5:13).

[243] Already in the Talmud, there is a discussion on the subject of ancient song. See *Sotah* 30b.

[244] *Mizmor* ("Psalm"; e.g., in Psalm 24); *Mikhtam* (as in Psalm 16); *Edut* (as in Psalm 60); *Maskil* (as in Psalm 32); *Shiggayon* (as in Psalm 7).

Also, many biblical commentators explain the word *Selah*, which appears only in psalms, as a specific musical term. Other commentators understand certain titles in the psalms[245] as indicating to the conductor which well-known melody of those days should be used for the specific text. This is similar to the practice followed even today, by which specific melodies or tunes, to be sung for various poems and songs, are indicated in writing.

The Loss of Ancient Music

Despite all this testimony regarding music in the Temple, nothing has actually remained except documentary evidence. Although in Temple days, and even many generations before, there were already various types of musical notation, we do not possess any notations for Temple music. There are cantillation signs for the entire Bible, common to all Jewish communities, that signify stresses and pauses in the text, but the melodies associated with these signs differ from one community to another. This is especially evident with regard to the Book of Psalms, on which a large portion of our prayers is based. The cantillation signs for the books of Psalms, Proverbs, and Job follow a completely different system, which proves that a different musical tradition existed for poetry; however, most congregations have no traditional melody for these signs, and whenever they are read in the synagogue, it is mostly in a traditional recitative, which often ignores the cantillation signs altogether. For this reason, even if certain of our ancient musical notations have been preserved, they can tell us only very little about Temple music.

In the course of time, and with the dispersion of Jewish communities to many far and distant lands, the original music was forgotten. Musicologists have raised various theories in their attempts to reconstruct the music played in the Temple and the original music of the Jewish people. Some think that certain traditional prayer melodies,

---

[245] Such as *Al Shoshanim*, Psalms 45:1; *Al Alamot*, Psalms 46:1; and *Al Mut la-Ben*, Psalms 9:1. The meaning of all these terms is uncertain, but they could possibly be translated as "upon roses," "upon maidens," and "upon the death of the son."

especially those of the Ashkenazim, are of very ancient origin, rooted in Temple music. This theory is based on the fact that these melodies differ greatly from the music of surrounding cultures, and some of them are based on Oriental musical scales. In addition, there are a few melodies—such as the traditional tune for Psalm 144—common to many Jewish congregations, with only slight variations, which may point to one ancient origin that existed before the exile and dispersion of the Jews.

Some believe that the Gregorian chant of the early church borrowed its main motifs from the one source that served as the church's model of perfection—Temple music—as evidenced by the elements or traces of original Jewish music present in the Gregorian tradition.

Evolution of Prayer Music

As the memory of ancient music slowly subsided, until it was completely forgotten (even though vestiges perhaps still remain in certain prayer melodies), new forms and other styles of prayer music gradually developed.

Because prayer melodies, unlike Torah readings, are not grounded in mandatory halakhic rulings, and due to the constant desire for new melodies to accompany the prayers, this music was always, and everywhere, very much influenced by the environment. Musical styles of the surrounding nations, their popular and classical secular music, and even their religious music, provided patterns for imitation and adaptation. There has always been constant tension between two contradictory trends: the conscious or unconscious influence of local music, and the desire to emphasize the differences, in order not to reach the point of cultural assimilation even in this sphere. Traditional prayer music is, apparently, a fusion of these two factors, which continue to constantly affect the creation of new melodies. It is the extent and quality of outside musical influences that have led to the creation of the various prayer melodies and tunes of the different Jewish communities.

By the Middle Ages, Jewish music could already be divided according to the different countries in which Jews had settled. We have no real knowledge of the melodies that were current among the Jewish communities in these countries, since they were not written down.

However, it is clear that even then there were noticeable differences between the musical styles of the different communities.

Overshadowing the many subdivisions that existed during the Middle Ages, even before the time of Rashi® in the tenth century C.E., was a more general division—which exists to this day—between the musical style of Jews living in Islamic countries (in Asia and North Africa) and that of Jews living under Christian rule (in most of the European countries). This division generally corresponds to, but is not identical with, the division between Ashkenazim and Sephardim, which started becoming noticeable during this same period. At that time, and for many generations to follow, there were several large Jewish communities that did not entirely fall into either category, both in general cultural terms, and particularly regarding the musical forms adopted for their prayers (e.g., the Jews of Provence, and later, the Jews of Christian Spain). But over time, and with the increasing number of expulsions and migrations, this overall division became more marked, and although there still are many musical differences among various congregations, they are far less prominent than the elements that divide the two main communal groupings—the Ashkenazim and the Sephardim.

In terms of prayer texts, the differences between these two main groups are often as minor as variations between prayer formulations of different congregations or even individual synagogues serving the same. However, it is the differences in melodies that exert the greatest emotional influence on the worshipper. In various locations, and especially in Israel, when different congregations are in closer proximity to each other, there is an interchange of influence even in prayer music; nevertheless, the fundamental difference between the two major groupings is still very great.

Melodies of Oriental Congregations

The Jewish communities under Islamic rule had a closer relationship with the local culture than did European Jewry. In nearly all Oriental countries, Jews conversed in the local vernacular even among themselves (and this is true even in those places where a local Jewish jargon developed, and even among the Jews of Spain, despite the fact that among themselves they also conversed in Ladino).[246] This led, over the centuries, to the creation of an enormous body of Jewish literary works in Arabic (in many cases, written in Hebrew characters), and also generated closer contact with the surrounding culture. For all these reasons, the music of these countries had a much greater influence on Oriental Jewry than Christian music had on the Jews of Europe.

Cultural-linguistic influences were not the only reason for the reduced opposition to adapting Arabic melodies. First and foremost is the religious aspect: Judaism has never considered Islam as a form of idolatry, and therefore, the precautions against using any symbol or concept produced by Islam were never too rigorous.[247] But there was also a musical reason: the character of original Jewish music, which most probably was Oriental in nature,[248] must have facilitated the assimilation of other Oriental musical influences.

Indeed, certain characteristics, which presumably existed in original Jewish music (and which are still evident even in the melodies of congregations living in Europe), merged well with Arabic music—e.g., the division of tones and half tones into smaller units, and the use of trills. Not only quarter tones, but other subdivisions, which have no corresponding marks in Western musical notation, such as thirds of a tone, are frequently employed in this music. This phenomenon combines well with trills, which form an integral part of cantorial music in Eastern and Western countries alike. The trill is always a form of improvisation, of extemporizing, and depends on the skills and talent of the *Ḥazzan,** as well as the community's understanding of and appreciation for this type of music.

Oriental cantorial music, like Arabic vocal music, is based not on any definite tonal structure, nor on scales, but rather on the *Maqam*, a cluster of notes that forms a single, indivisible musical unit. A *Maqam* is defined not by the individual tones that it contains but as a whole unit, in a manner similar to the melodies of each of the Bible cantillation signs. The *Maqam* can be a brief musical phrase that is

---

[246] A form of Old Spanish, mixed with Hebrew words and idioms.

[247] See Maimonides' *Iggeret ha-Shemad* ("Letter on Assimilation").

[248] As indicated, for instance, by the tendency to sing in unison.

repeated again and again in the course of the singing, or it can have a longer, more complex structure. By its very nature, the *Maqam* cannot be recorded in Western musical notation, because it is grasped as a whole, and the person who sings it is constantly introducing variations such as trills, stresses, and changing tonal gaps, according to the theme or to the ability and preferences of the singer. More complex forms of singing are created by a sequence of several *Maqams*, in which the musical talent of the cantor is demonstrated by his ability to shift from one *Maqam* to the next, and by the ways in which he combines them with each other.

In addition to the traditional melodies made up of various *Maqam* forms, Oriental communities have also borrowed melodies from other cultures, which in time have become part of the traditional prayer music. Such melodies, especially for the *Zemirot** and *Piyyutim,** are often indicated as "such-and-such melody," in order for the singer to know which melody is suited for each particular text.

Since the Sephardim were dispersed across many countries—in some of the European countries as well as Asia and Africa—their prayer music has absorbed many motifs from these countries, which created the differences among the various congregations. The musical styles of the Sephardim in Western countries (such as Holland, and the Sephardic communities that migrated from Holland to other countries) were always far more influenced by European (mainly Spanish) music, and are a musical genre of their own, different from the special musical styles of the Sephardim in Balkan countries, such as Bulgaria and Greece. In contrast to these, the music of the Jews in Arab countries is quite unified, although among them, too, there are marked differences. Thus, for instance, the Yemenite prayer rite is clearly defined as unique in terms of prayer customs; yet from the melodic aspect, it is classed as belonging to the Sephardic music of the Oriental communities.

Ashkenazic Cantorial Music

The Ashkenazic Jews of Europe developed their own traditions and styles of prayer music. We have substantial knowledge regarding ways in which this prayer music was created. For a number of generations, there was an increasing influence of local folk music, mainly in France and Germany, and also, indirectly, of Christian religious music, with cantors introducing more and more "gentile songs" into the prayers. The Maharil@ vehemently opposed this trend. Not only did he voice his objection to foreign music, but also, being one of the great prayer leaders of his time, he traveled from one community to another, reestablishing the traditional prayer melodies. By virtue of his great authority, the Maharil succeeded in laying the foundations for the prayer rite accepted by all Ashkenazic communities, mainly the *Nusaḥ** for Shabbat, festival days, and the Days of Awe.* Although in the course of time Ashkenazic Jewry broke up into many disparate and distant communities, this prayer rite remained the basis for all Ashkenazic communities, in spite of the differences in emphasis and the additions made.

The Ashkenazic *Nusaḥ* comprises four different modes, named after the prayers in which they are used: *Yishtabbaḥ,** *Yekum Purkan,** *Mi she-Berakh,** and *Ahavah Rabbah.** The first three are constructed mainly according to an established musical scale, but they differ from the melodies of the other nations in being based upon a combination of several musical scales in the same melody. For example, the *Yishtabbaḥ* mode is a combination of the Aeolian and the Phrygian scales; the ancient *Yekum Purkan* mode is also a combination of various scales; and the *Mi she-Berakh* mode is made up of various musical scales, believed by some musicologists to contain the rudiments of a unique musical scale. The *Ahavah Rabbah* mode is not based on a European musical scale but is essentially an Oriental *Maqam*, known as *Maqam Ḥejaz*, which is frequently used in East European cantorial music.

Besides the special melodies used mainly for the prayers of the Days of Awe, there are differences between the basic chants of the prayers for weekdays and Shabbat, for the Days of Awe, and for special prayers (such as the Prayers for Rain* and for Dew*). Each of these has a melodic style of its own either for the entire prayer, or for the major parts of it, used also for other sections of the prayer service, such as the *Kaddish** which precedes them.

The Ashkenazic rite, like the Sephardic, broke down into the various styles developed in the different countries to which this Jewry dispersed: Germany, Bohemia, Lithuania and Poland, Rumania and

Hungary. Yet in spite of various outside influences and the addition of special tunes and melodies for various prayers, it has largely retained its basic, uniform character.

New Melodies

Besides the traditional prayer melodies that derive from ancient sources and are common to many congregations, new melodies have also been composed over the generations. Most were ad hoc, created for a specific prayer or by a particular cantor. But there were also some melodies that came to be used regularly in a certain synagogue or by a specific community, and some even spread to other localities and eventually became an integral part of the traditional prayer service. In the main, just as the creation of new prayers has never ceased—whether in the form of *Piyyutim*, new prayer formulations, or *Yehi Ratzon** formulations—so has there always been an ongoing creation of new prayer melodies.

Although little material on prayer music in early generations has survived, there is evidence that it was very common for Jewish communities and cantors to introduce outside melodies into the prayer service, and that certain sages strove to counter this tendency by reviving and strengthening the status of the older melodies. And of course, there were also new musical compositions created by prayer leaders or other composers. These were generally used in the singing of *Piyyutim* and *Zemirot* within the prayer service. For a few centuries, there was, mainly in Italy, multifaceted creativity in the sphere of religious music; some of the compositions of this period are known to us through literary references, and some have even been preserved in musical notation. Besides prayer melodies, these works include choral songs and even complete oratorios. At times, eminent sages engaged in composing such works, and some even had them printed. For example, the great scholar of Jewish law and esoteric wisdom Emmanuel Ḥai Ricchi[249] printed some musical notations of prayer melodies that he composed at the end of his commentary on the Mishnah.

---

[249] Italy, 1688–1743.

A particularly large amount of new prayer melodies has been created in the past few centuries among the Ashkenazim in Europe. These melodies had two different sources, which were sometimes in opposition to each other, and sometimes merged. In Western countries—or, more precisely, in Germany—a trend developed of creating standardized prayer melodies which, from the start, were strongly influenced by modern European music. This musical approach, called by some of its adherents "arranged music"—as opposed to the "emotional music" of cantors and traditional prayer leaders—was influenced to a great degree by Christian ritual. Thus, even when the basic melody was an ancient tune, it would take on a Western form, both in the addition of harmonies and in the way it was sung (by a professional, polyphonic choir, and in houses of prayer that drifted away from Jewish tradition, to the point that they even included orchestral accompaniment). In addition, various non-Jewish musical forms, such as the fugue, were introduced into the prayers.

On the other hand, there was the strong influence of Ḥassidic melodies. Ḥassidism introduced into the world of religious music a wealth of new melodies that originally were not necessarily meant to be part of prayer. Ḥassidic melody, in itself, was religious music, a way of serving God with the aid of, and through, music. These melodies were first sung in the meeting places of the Ḥassidim, at meals connected with the performance of a commandment *(Se'udat Mitzvah*)* and at other events. Many of them were wordless tunes, or melodies to which words were adapted—from prayers, *Zemirot*, or *Piyyutim*. Ḥassidic music often drew, consciously or unconsciously, from its surroundings. A large number of melodies were intentionally adapted from folk songs and melodies of the people who lived in the area, mainly from the Ukrainians and the Wallachian-Rumanian peoples. Even original compositions were influenced by the rhythms and musical styles of those peoples. The use of such melodies was considered by the Ḥassidic teachers as a way of "raising the sparks," or locating and underscoring the point of holiness within the profane, and was based on the view that, although people may sing and chant for personal reasons, the melody invariably contains yearning and prayer for the source of all goodness in the world, for God's *Shekhinah.**

In general, these melodies underwent various processes of change as they were transformed to melodies of holiness and prayer. Parts of them were suppressed and others emphasized, and thus they took on a new character. In time, melodies from more Western sources, which had been transmitted to Eastern Europe in various ways, were also introduced.

Those melodies sung without words, or along with words that differed entirely from the original text, were also introduced into prayer music. In some localities, this new type of singing, with or without words, became a significant part of the prayers recited by the *Shaliaḥ Tzibbur** (see Chapter 15). Furthermore, there was an urge to compose more and more new melodies of this kind. At times, this trend became so dominant that the traditional prayer melodies, even for the Days of Awe, became secondary and receded to a sort of background music. But even in places where most of the prayers were still sung to traditional melodies, some parts of the prayer were sung with special melodies that gradually became a tradition in themselves (albeit only of a specific congregation or locality). These two types of melodies are often distinguished from one another by their appellation: the basic traditional melodies of prayer are called *Nusaḥ** ("rite" or "version"), while new melodies adapted to special sections of the prayer are referred to as *Niggun* ("tune").

In our times, there is a merging between the new melodies derived from both of these musical trends, because even melodies from distinctively West European origins have been introduced into the accepted order of prayer services, although they are not always sung in the exact manner in which they were originally composed.

The infiltration of new melodies into the prayer services in our day is not always properly controlled. In the past, important personages devoted attention to the quality of new melodies, choosing those that were the best and most appropriate. Nowadays, however, there are cantors—whether professional or amateur—who introduce melodies that not only derive from foreign sources but are also not connected either with the contents of the prayers or with the required concentration of mind *(Kavvanah*)*. At the same time, however, there is a process of selection that is not always conscious but is based upon healthy popular instincts, whereby inferior tunes are gradually ejected, and only worthwhile melodies are retained.

Styles of Prayer Music

In nearly all Jewish communities, prayer music consists of two components. The first is that of the regular prayers, which have no actual melody but are intoned as a recitative that differs from congregation to congregation. In most Ashkenazic communities, the *Shaliaḥ Tzibbur* does not recite aloud every word—except for the repetition* of the *Amidah** and certain other prayers—but pronounces aloud only the final verses or lines of each section. In those parts of the prayer that he recites in full, he places a special stress on the end of each section (e.g., at the end of each of the *Amidah* benedictions). In Sephardic communities, on the other hand, the *Shaliaḥ Tzibbur* recites the entire prayer aloud, and in many communities the entire congregation, too, chants the prayers aloud, to the same tune as the *Shaliaḥ Tzibbur.*

Prayer that is recited aloud is chanted uniformly, paying heed mainly to the punctuation signs, with no other special stresses except at ends of sections (e.g., a biblical passage or a specific prayer). At these instances, the chant becomes more strongly emphasized, so that everyone will notice that there is a pause.

This is the case with the regular weekday prayers; but even then, there are various sections in which the recitative is replaced by a proper melody, which in most cases is the traditional melody for that particular prayer. On Shabbat, however—and more so on festival days, especially during the Days of Awe*—the musical part of the prayer becomes much more pronounced and predominant. The festive, traditional *Nusaḥ* takes pride of place in the prayers, and many prayers are recited in their special, traditional melodic chant. Also, since worshippers have more leisure on these days, an ever-growing number of new prayer tunes are composed, and the congregants, too, participate to a greater extent in singing the prayers.

Musical Expression in Prayer

The musical aspect of prayer is expressed in many different ways. The most prominent is through the singing of the *Ḥazzan*. Besides the sections that the *Ḥazzan* recites aloud in the accepted recitative form, there are various prayers, such as the repetition of the *Amidah* and other prayers recited only by the *Ḥazzan*, in which he sings long sections of prayer either in the traditional melodies or the newer ones. Generally, it is the *Ḥazzan* who determines the prayer music, not only in what he sings himself, but also in directing those parts in which the congregants participate.

In this manner, the personality of the *Ḥazzan* is of crucial importance, because it is not only the quality of his voice that is significant here but his overall personality and the spiritual and religious image that he projects. The way he conducts the prayer music can have an enormous influence, either positive or negative, on the quality and essence of the communal prayer.

In various sections of the prayer service, depending to a large extent on local custom, the entire congregation sings the words of the prayer. This is accepted practice for those sections of prayer that were initially intended for public response and which often have traditional melodies. It is also general practice that at certain points in the prayers, such as the end of prayer sections or of biblical verses, the entire congregation acts as an accompanying chorus, humming a melody without words.

A person praying individually—be it when he is present in the synagogue with the congregation yet is deeply absorbed in his own private prayers, or when praying alone—may also chant the prayers. Sometimes one chants to oneself a quiet repetition of the traditional prayer melodies, and sometimes one uses other tunes that arouse one to pray. This is more frequently the case among the Ḥassidim. They employ many melodies sung by individuals that are intended to arouse devotion or spiritual awareness, and are sung either with the words of prayer or as wordless melodies designed to bring about spiritual awakening. At times, however, the process may work the other way around, when a person in prayer suddenly finds expression for his feelings by creating a melody that he himself, or those who have heard him, may later use and disseminate among others. In the treasury of Jewish music, there are many melodies that have been composed in this way, not as intentionally created musical pieces but as expressions of emotional experiences that assumed a musical form.

APPENDICES

GLOSSARY OF TERMS

Adon Olam—A hymn of praise to God, recited before the *Shaḥarit** service.

Afikoman—The piece of *Matzah** eaten at the end of the *Seder** night meal.

Aggadah—A genre of Jewish literature that abounds in the Talmud and in the Midrash. Aggadah includes stories and comments about biblical heroes and other Jewish historical figures, parables, aphorisms, and homilies.

Aḥaronim—Jewish sages from the sixteenth century onward. See also *Rishonim.**

Ahavah Rabbah—The second blessing before the reading of *Shema** in the morning.

Ahavat Olam—The second blessing that precedes *Keriat Shema** in the *Ma'ariv** prayer. It is parallel to the second blessing recited before *Keriat Shema* in the *Shaḥarit** prayer, but shorter.

Aḥot Ketanah—A *Piyyut** recited in most rites before the *Ma'ariv** prayer of the first day of Rosh ha-Shanah.*

Akdamut—An Aramaic *Piyyut** recited prior to the Torah reading on the festival of Shavu'ot,* praising the Almighty and describing the various worlds.

Al ha-Nissim—A special prayer recited in the *Amidah** and the Grace After Meals* on Ḥanukkah and Purim.

Al Ḥet—A detailed confession formulation recited in the Yom Kippur* prayers.

Aleinu—A prayer usually recited at the end of prayer services. Its main content is a splendid declaration of the acceptance of the heavenly yoke by us and by the entire world.

Aliyah—(literally, "going up" or "ascent") The honor of being called up to recite the blessings over (and, in some cases, to read) one of the sections of the Torah reading. See Chapter 13.

Amen—The response recited upon hearing someone else recite a blessing;

it is derived from the same root as the Hebrew words for "faith" and "truth."

Amidah—The core prayer in the prayer service; also known as *Shemoneh Esreh.**

Amidah repetition—The recitation aloud of the *Amidah** prayer by the *Shaliaḥ Tzibbur,** after the congregants have finished their silent, individual recitation.

Amora (pl., *Amoraim)*—Term used to refer to talmudic sages from after the tannaitic period until the final redaction of the Talmud* (220-500 C.E.). The *Amoraim* interpreted the statements of the *Tannaim** and expanded upon them.

Ana be-Khoaḥ—A prayer of entreaty to God to help the Jews. Written in mishnaic times, the first letters of its words are an acrostic for one of the Holy Names.

Anenu—A blessing added to the *Amidah* prayer on fast days (except Yom Kippur*).

Aravah—Willow branches, one of the *Arba'ah Minim** of the festival of Sukkot.* There is also a custom (based on Kabbalah) to strike the ground with willow branches on *Hosha'na Rabbah.**

Arba Parshiyyot—Four Torah portions read by the *Maftir** on the Sabbaths of the month of Adar. See Chapter 9.

Arba'ah Minim—Four kinds of plants waved and blessed during the Sukkot festival. The four kinds are: *Ethrog** (citron), *Lulav** (palm), *Hadas* (myrtle branch), and *Aravah** (willow branch). See Chapter 10.

Ark—A special cabinet or container in the synagogue in which the Torah scrolls are kept.

Arvit—Another name for *Ma'ariv,** the Evening Prayer Service.

Ashamnu—The first word of the short *Vidduy.**

Ashrei—The common appellation for Psalm 145, a psalm of major importance recited several times during the course of the daily prayer services.

astronomical high noon—Midday, exactly six astronomical hours* after sunrise*.

astronomical hours—The talmudic method of

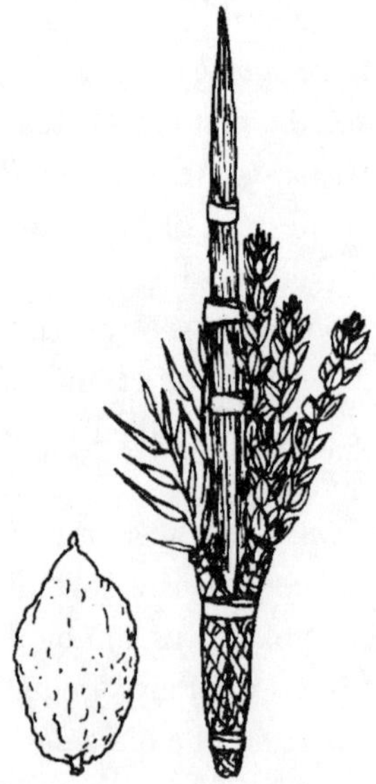

From left to right: *Ethrog*, *Aravah*, *Lulav*, and *Hadas*

dividing the day and night into twelve hours each, the precise length of each "hour" changing daily according to the times of sunrise and sunset.

Atarah—"Crown," the appellation for the ornamented upper part of the *Tallit.** See Chapter 16.

Attah Beḥartanu—"You have chosen us," the beginning of the middle *Amidah** blessing recited on all festivals.

Attah Ḥonantanu—The *Havdalah** formulation added to the fourth *Amidah** blessing at the conclusion of Shabbat and festival days.

Attah Horeita—A formulation recited upon taking the Torah scroll out of the Ark* on various occasions.

Av ha-Raḥamim—A prayer for the souls of communities and individuals killed for the Sanctification of God's Name. Composed during the Crusades.

Avinu Malkenu—"Our Father, Our King." A very ancient prayer composed of many verses, all of which begin with "Our Father, Our King." Recited during the Ten Days of Repentance* and in public fasts.

Avot—A tractate of the Mishnah* that contains aphorisms and practical and moral guidance from our sages.

Ba'al Keriah—"Torah Reader," the person who reads the Torah in public. See Chapter 13.

Ba'alei Berit—All those who have a major role in a circumcision* ceremony—namely, the father of the baby, the circumciser *(Mohel)*, and the godfather (*Sandak)*.

ba-Meh Madlikin—The second chapter of Tractate *Shabbat*, dealing with the laws of candlelighting. Many recite it every Shabbat eve.

Bakkashot—Hymns sung in Oriental communities on Shabbat dawn, mainly during the winter months.

Bar Mitzvah (for a girl: Bat Mitzvah)—(a) One who has reached legal majority, the age at which one is obligated to fulfill all of the *mitzvot* (thirteen years for a boy, twelve years for a girl); (b) the ceremony marking this occasion.

Bar Yoḥai—A poem, recited or sung on various occasions, praising the great *Tanna,** Rabbi Shimon bar Yoḥai (to whom the *Zohar*# is attributed). Composed in the sixteenth century by Rabbi Shimon Lavi.

Barekhu—A formulation of call-and-reply (of the *Ḥazzan** and the congregants) recited on various occasions—e.g., before the *Shema** blessings in the *Shaḥarit** and *Ma'ariv** prayers, or before a Torah reading.

Barukh ha-Shem le-Olam—A collection of verses and entreaties recited, in some rites, after the *Hashkivenu** blessing in the weekday *Ma'ariv** prayer.

Barukh Hu u-Varukh Shemo—"Blessed be He and blessed be His Name." A formulation recited at certain times upon hearing God's Name mentioned within a blessing.

Barukh she-Amar—The opening blessing of *Pesukei de-Zimrah*.*

Barukh she-Petarani—". . . who has released me for being punishable [for this boy]." The blessing recited by a father on his son's first *Aliyah** to the Torah upon becoming Bar Mitzvah.*

Barukh Shem Kevod Malkhuto le-Olam va-Ed—"Blessed be the name of the glory of His kingdom forever and ever." A formulation recited after the first verse of the *Shema** reading, and after mentioning God's Name unnecessarily.

Bein ha-Meitzarim—The appellation for the three weeks between the 17th of Tammuz and the Ninth of Av (see Chapter 12), which is a period of mourning for the destruction of the Temple.

Beit Hillel—The disciples of Hillel the Elder, around the end of the Second Temple period, whose overall approach to the Halakhah was more lenient than that of their rivals, the disciples of Shammai *(Beit Shammai).*

Berakhah Me'ein Shalosh—The final blessing, recited after having consumed cake, wine, or the special fruits of the Land of Israel (grape, fig, pomegranate, olive, and date); it is a lengthy formulation, which is a sort of summary of the first three blessings of the Grace After Meals.*

Berikh Shemeih—An excerpt from the *Zohar*,# recited while the Torah scroll is being taken out of the Ark.*

Bimah—The central podium in the synagogue. The Torah scrolls are read from this raised platform.

Birkat ha-Gomel—A blessing of thanksgiving, recited in the presence of a *Minyan** by a person delivered from danger.

Birkat ha-Ḥodesh—A prayer formulation recited on the last Shabbat of every month in which the day or days of the coming *Rosh Ḥodesh** are announced.

Birkat ha-Levanah—See *Kiddush Levanah*.

Birkat ha-Shanim—The ninth blessing of the *Amidah** prayer of weekdays. A request for abundant rains and good livelihood.

Birkat ha-Shir—A blessing recited during the course of reading the Passover *Haggadah*.*

Birkat ha-Torah—A mandatory blessing recited (a) at the beginning of the *Shaḥarit** service, in anticipation of the Torah study to be done in the course of the coming day; (b) before each portion of the Torah reading in the synagogue.

Birkhot ha-Mitzvot—Blessings recited before the performance of numerous commandments. Normally recited while standing.

Birkhot ha-Nehenin—Blessings made before and after various physical pleasures, such as eating, drinking, and the like.

Birkhot ha-Re'ah—Blessings recited over pleasant scents.

Birkhot ha-Shaḥar—A series of fixed blessings recited before the *Shaḥarit** service, expressing thanks to God for various routine things, such as waking up, rising, seeing, etc.

Boneh Yerushalayim—The appellation for two blessings that speak of the rebuilding of Jerusalem: (a) the fourteenth blessing of the *Amidah**; (b) the third blessing of the Grace After Meals.*

circumcision (Hebrew, *Berit Milah*)—The rite of cutting off the prepuce, performed on all Jewish males at the age of eight days.

Council of Four Lands (Hebrew, *Va'ad Arba Aratzot*)—The umbrella institution of self-government of the Jewish communities under the rule of the Polish crown from the middle of the sixteenth century C.E. until 1764.

Counting of the *Omer*—The counting of the forty-nine days between Pesaḥ* and Shavu'ot.* The counting ("Today is X days, which is Y weeks and Z days of the *Omer*") is preceded by a blessing; in most rites, some psalms and requests are added, both before and after the counting.

dawn (Hebrew, *Alot ha-Shaḥar*)—Halakhically, the time at which light begins to appear in the morning, before sunrise.*

Days of Awe—The appellation for Rosh ha-Shanah* (the New Year Festival) and Yom Kippur* (the Day of Atonement). See Chapter 11.

Ein ke-Eloheinu—"There is none like our God." A short *Piyyut** recited close to the end of the *Shaḥarit** service.

El Adon—An ancient *Piyyut** recited in the *Yotzer Or** blessing in *Shaḥarit** of Shabbat.

El Erekh Appayim—(a) An opening to the recitation of the Thirteen Attributes of Divine Mercy*; (b) a short entreaty recited at the end of the longer *Taḥanun** section recited on Mondays and Thursdays.*

Elohai Netzor—A prayer formulation recited upon concluding the *Amidah.**

Emet ve-Emunah—The first blessing after the *Shema** recitation in the *Ma'ariv** service. The *Emet ve-Emunah* blessing deals with redemption.

Emet ve-Yatziv—The blessing on redemption recited after the *Shema** recitation in the *Shaḥarit** service.

Eshet Ḥayil—"Woman of Valor." The final section of the last chapter of the book of Proverbs (31:10-31). A song of praise for the homemaker and for the *Sefirah** of *Malkhut* ("Kingdom"). See Chapter 9.

Ethrog—Citron, one of the *Arba'ah Minim** of the festival of Sukkot.*

Etz Ḥayyim—(literally, "tree of life") The appellation for the poles around which the Torah scroll is wound.

Gabbai (pl., *Gabba'im*)—Formerly, a tax and charity collector; presently, the person in charge of synagogue affairs and finances. See Chapter 14.

Gelilah—The act of rolling the Torah scroll after its reading in public. The one honored with performing this act is called the *Golel*. See Chapter 13.

Gemara—Another name for the Talmud.*

Geonic period—589–1038 C.E.; more than 450 years during which the *Geonim*, the heads of the Babylonian *Yeshivot** in Sura and Pumbedita, served as the supreme halakhic authorities in the Jewish world.

Geonim (sing., *Gaon*)—See Geonic period.

Geulah—(a) The appellation for the blessing that follows the recitation of the *Shema**; (b) the appellation for the seventh blessing of the weekday *Amidah*,* concerning redemption.

Geulot—A type of *Piyyut*.*

Go'el Yisrael—The seventh blessing in the weekday *Amidah** prayer. A request for redemption.

Grace After Meals—The blessing recited after eating a meal in which bread was consumed. A mandatory Torah commandment, it is composed of four blessings and some additional recitations.

Grand *Hallel* or Great *Hallel* (Hebrew, *Hallel ha-Gadol*)—The talmudic appellation for Psalms 135–136. Recited within the *Pesukei de-Zimrah** of Shabbat, and as part of the Passover *Haggadah*.*

ha-Aderet veha-Emunah—A poem of praise, with stanzas that appear in alphabetical order, that is recited by some before *Barukh she-Amar*.* This poem is found in the ancient book *Pirkei Heikhalot Rabbati* (chapter 26:7), and the sages say that it is recited by the angels. Major Ashkenazic rabbis have said that because of the extreme sanctity of this poem, it must be recited only in public, and only on Yom Kippur (see Chapter 11). However, the disciples of Rabbi Isaac Luria@ ruled that it be recited daily. Some of those who follow the Sepharad rite recite it daily; others do so only on Shabbat. In other rites, it is found in the prayers of the Days of Awe* (see Chapter 11) and of other festivals.

ha-Gomel—See *Birkat ha-Gomel.*

ha-Ma'ariv Aravim—The first of the two blessings that precede *Keriat Shema** in the *Ma'ariv** prayer.

ha-Mappil—The main blessing of the *Shema* Upon Retiring to Bed.* Primarily a prayer for restful sleep and for waking up the following morning. See Chapter 8.

Haftarah—The reading of a portion from the Prophets, supplementary to the Torah readings, on Sabbaths and festivals.

Hagbahah—The custom of raising the Torah scroll immediately before or after the public Torah reading and displaying the writing on the parchment to the whole congregation. See Chapter 13.

Haggadah—The text read during the Passover night *Seder.**

Hakkafot—The custom of joyously encircling the *Bimah** with the Torah scrolls seven times on the festival of Simḥat Torah.*

Halakhah—The legal part of the Torah (both Written and Oral) that defines actual practice. Its origins are Divine. Its principles are written in the Torah (the Five Books of Moses) and greatly expanded in the Mishnah,* the Talmud,* and later codes. Specific rulings are called *halakhot.*

Halakhah le-Moshe mi-Sinai (Sinaitic *halakhah*)—A law which, while not written in the Torah, is viewed as an integral part of the Sinaitic revelation, having been given orally to Moses. Although considered part of the Oral Torah, such *halakhot* enjoy an authority tantamount to that of (written) Torah law.

half *Hallel*—See *Hallel.*

half *Kaddish*—A short version of the *Kaddish** recited in a number of places in the prayer services.

Hallel—Psalms 113–118, recited during festival days. The full *Hallel* is recited during all of Sukkot,* the first day (or, in the Diaspora, two days) of Pesaḥ,* Shavu'ot*, and all of Ḥanukkah. The half *Hallel* (in which certain sections are skipped) is read during the rest of Pesaḥ and on *Rosh Ḥodesh.**

Ḥanukkah—The festival of lights, celebrated for eight days in the month of Kislev, commemorating the Maccabees' victory over their Greek oppressors and the restoration of the Temple service.

Hashkavah—Prayer for the dead.

Hashkivenu—The second blessing after the *Shema** recitation in the *Ma'ariv** service. Its main content is a plea for a peaceful night.

Ḥatan Bereshit—The appellation for the person honored with being called up to the Torah to read the beginning of the first portion of Genesis (*Bereshit*) on Simḥat Torah.*

Ḥatan Torah—The appellation for the person honored with being called up to the Torah to read the last portion of the Torah on Simḥat Torah.*

Hatavat Ḥalom—A ceremony performed for one who has had a troubling bad dream.

Hattarat Nedarim—Absolution of vows, usually done on the eve of Rosh ha-Shanah (see Chapter 11) and, by some, also on a few other occasions.

Havdalah—A ceremony marking the end of a Shabbat or festival day. See Chapter 9.

Ḥazak—The call customarily recited by the entire congregation upon terminating the public reading of each of the Five Books of the Torah.

Ḥazzan—Cantor or prayer leader. See Chapter 15.

Hefsek—An interruption in the midst of a prayer caused by saying various things.

Ḥiyyuv—The obligation of a certain person either to recite *Kaddish** for someone or to be called up to a particular Torah reading.*

Hodu—A hymn of prayer recited during the *Shaḥarit** service, compiled of verses from a number of biblical sources.

Ḥok le-Yisrael—A book containing verses from the Torah, the Prophets, and the Writings, as well as from the Talmud,* the *Zohar*,# and other books. These verses are organized according to the days of the week and the weekly Torah portions. Many people follow the custom of reading from it daily after the *Shaḥarit* prayer. The book was compiled by Rabbi Ḥayyim Vital.@

Ḥol ha-Mo'ed—The intermediate days of the festivals of Sukkot* and Pesaḥ,* namely, the days between the first and the last days of those festivals. These days are festive in nature; however, certain types of labor are permitted. See Chapter 12.

Ḥonen ha-Da'at—The fourth blessing in the *Amidah** prayer for weekdays, which is a plea for wisdom.

Hosha'na Rabbah—The seventh day of the festival of Sukkot,* and the last day of *Ḥol ha-Mo'ed** of Sukkot, which has special status and special customs, mainly the custom of beating the ground with willow branches. See Chapter 12.

Hosha'not—(a) *Piyyutim** recited during the *Shaḥarit** services throughout the Sukkot festival; (b) the willow branches used for beating the ground on *Hosha'na Rabbah*.* See Chapters 10 and 12.

Isru Ḥag—The day following each one of the three pilgrimage festivals (see Chapter 10), on which there are certain elements of festivity.

Kabbalah—Jewish mystical thought, and the literature and tradition in which it is embodied. Nowadays, this refers mostly to the *Zohar*# and to Lurianic Kabbalah.*

Kabbalat Shabbat—A series of psalms and *Piyyutim** customarily recited before the *Ma'ariv** service on Shabbat eve.

Kabbalat Ta'anit—A formulation whereby a person who intends to have a private fast on a certain day makes a commitment to fast at the end of the *Minḥah** prayer of the previous day.

Kaddish—A prayer of major importance, composed in the Aramaic language. It is recited only in a *Minyan*,* at various points within the various prayer services, as well as at a variety of ceremonies and important occasions.

Kaddish de-Rabbanan—An extended version of the *Kaddish*, recited in a *Minyan** after participants have studied a section of the Oral Law.

Kaddish Titkabbal—The *Kaddish** formulation recited after the conclusion of the public recitation of an *Amidah** prayer.

Kaddish Yatom—"The Orphan's *Kaddish*." A *Kaddish* formulation slightly longer than the half *Kaddish*,* recited in several places in the prayer services and in most places by mourners.

Kapparot—A custom practiced close to Yom Kippur,* in which a hen, fish, or money is taken, and after a certain formulation is recited, is given for charity, in expiation for one's sins.

Kavvanah (pl., *Kavvanot*)—The understanding and inner intention of the worshipper regarding words uttered in prayer or motivation in the performance of the commandments. See Chapter 5.

Kedushah—A prayer formulation describing the angels' threefold utterance of the word "holy" *(Kadosh)*. It is a fundamental component of the public recitation of the *Amidah** prayer.

Kegavna—An excerpt from the *Zohar*# recited in the Ḥassidic (Sephardic) rite on Shabbat eve prior to the *Ma'ariv** prayer service. *Kegavna* speaks of the holiness of Shabbat.

Keri'ah—Bowing down, as an expression of giving honor, done regularly in a few places in the *Amidah** prayer. On the Days of Awe,* it involves actual prostration on the floor.

Keri'ah during daily prayer

Keri'ah on the Days of Awe

Keriat ha-Torah—The public reading of the Torah. See Chapter 13.

Kerovot— A series of *Piyyutim** recited in the first three blessings of the *Amidah** prayer on Shabbat or festival mornings.

Keter—"Crown." In most prayer rites, this is the opening word of a special, long *Kedushah** formulation recited in the repetition* of the *Musaf** *Amidah*,* as well as in some other special prayer services.

Keter Torah—"Torah Crown." A crown-shaped ornament, usually made of silver, placed on the Torah scroll upon removing it from and returning it to the Ark.*

Ketoret—See *Parashat ha-Ketoret.**

Kiddush—A ceremony whereby the Shabbat or festival day is sanctified through blessings on wine and on the sanctity of the day. The term ordinarily refers to the ceremony held on the eve of the Shabbat or festival.

Kiddush Levanah—The order of prayers and blessings recited upon the appearance of the new moon at the beginning of every month.

Kiddusha Rabbah—The *Kiddush** ceremony held on the morning of the Shabbat or festival day.

Kinot—Dirges over the destruction of the Temple, the exile, and other catastrophes that befell the Jews. Read on the Ninth of Av.

Kittel—A special white robe, worn in Ashkenazic communities at major ceremonies—e.g., for the prayers of the Days of Awe.*

Knesset Yisrael—The overall entity of the Jewish people, the inner foundation of which is the *Shekhinah.**

Kohen (pl., *Kohanim*)—"Priest." A senior member of the tribe of Levi, descendant of Aaron (Moses' brother). When the Temple stood, the *Kohanim* were in charge of holy worship, sacrifices, etc.

Kol ha-Ne'arim—The appellation for a special *Aliyah** to the Torah on Simḥat Torah,* in which all the children under Bar Mitzvah* age are called up. See Chapter 10.

Kol Nidrei—A formulation of absolution of vows recited with solemn ceremony at the beginning of the Yom Kippur* prayers, before the *Ma'ariv** service.

Korbanot—"Sacrifices." The common appellation for the first section of the *Shaḥarit** service, which includes various sections about the Temple sacrifices.

la-El Asher Shavat—A short yet important *Piyyut** for the Shabbat day, recited immediately after *El Adon.**

la-Menatzeaḥ—An appellation for Psalm 20,* recited at the weekday *Shaḥarit** service.

le-Olam Yehe Adam—A prayer recited during *Shaḥarit,** before *Pesukei de-Zimrah.** The origin of this prayer is in the *midrash** *Tanna de-Vei Eliyahu Rabbah* (chapter 21)..

le-Shem Yiḥud—A formulation recited prior to the performance of a commandment, immediately before reciting the blessing on that commandment.

Lekhah Dodi—A *Piyyut** for *Kabbalat Shabbat,** recited by Jews throughout the world. See Chapter 9.

Levite—A member of the tribe of Levi, but not a descendant of Aaron (see *Kohen**). Levites were charged with secondary worship tasks in the Temple (singing, and keeping the Temple gates), as well as with teaching Torah throughout the Jewish people.

Lulav—Palm branch, one of the *Arba'ah Minim** of the Sukkot* festival. See Chapter 10.

Lurianic Kabbalah—The Kabbalah* according to Rabbi Isaac Luria.@

Ma'amadot—Selections from the Torah, Prophets, Writings, Mishnah*, and Talmud* that are usually recited daily after the *Shaḥarit** prayer. There is a different selection for each day of the week. The custom of reciting the *Ma'amadot* was established during the Geonic period.* It was based on the practice, during the Second Temple period, of dividing the Jewish people for special prayer and Torah readings into twenty-four parts *(ma'amdot)* that paralleled the twenty-four groups into which the *Kohanim* were divided to rotate their Temple service.

Ma'ariv—The Evening Prayer Service (also called *Arvit*). See Chapter 8.

Maftir—(a) The person reading the *Haftarah**; (b) a small part from the Torah read prior to the *Haftarah* reading by the same person who is called to read the *Haftarah*. See Chapter 13.

Maḥzor (pl., *Maḥzorim*)—Prayer books for the festivals.

Malkhuyot—"Kingdoms." The first of the three central blessings in the *Musaf** prayer of Rosh ha-Shanah.* See Chapter 11.

Malkot—An ancient custom, practiced after the *Minḥah** prayer on Yom Kippur* eve (see Chapter 11), in which people receive thirty-nine symbolic lashes to atone for those transgressions which, according to the Halakhah,* are punishable by flogging.

Mashiv ha-Ruaḥ—The reference to rains in the winter season in the second *Amidah** blessing.

Matzah—The unleavened bread eaten throughout the festival of Pesaḥ.* See Chapter 10.

Me'ein Sheva—"Sevenfold Blessing." The formulation recited by the *Shaliaḥ Tzibbur** after *Amidah** of the *Ma'ariv** prayer on Shabbat eve. The Sevenfold Blessing contains a summary of all the seven blessings of that *Amidah*. See Chapter 9.

Meḥayeh ha-Metim—The second *Amidah** blessing. *Meḥayeh ha-Metim* speaks of the resurrection of the dead.

Melaveh Malkah—A common appellation for the meal held at the conclusion of Shabbat, which serves as a way of escorting the departing Shabbat Queen.

Mezuzah—Parchment on which the first two portions of the *Shema** are written by a scribe, rolled up and placed on the doorposts of every Jewish home. Usually, the *Mezuzah* is placed inside a *Mezuzah* case.

Mi she-Berakh—A blessing made for those who have been called up to a Torah reading, and at times, on the same occasion, for the sick and for women who have given birth.

Midrash—An exegetic part of the Oral Law that explains the Written Torah by means of parables, homilies, and the like. The Midrash includes various collections of such teachings by our sages. There are two main types of Midrash: halakhic Midrash, which is mainly legal in content, and aggadic Midrash, which is usually narrative. Some of the major *midrashim* are: aggadic *midrashim*—*Midrash Rabbah*, *Midrash Tanḥuma*, *Tanna de-Vei Eliyahu;* halakhic *midrashim*—*Mekhilta* (on Exodus), *Sifra* (on Leviticus), *Sifrei* (on Numbers and Deuteronomy).

Mikveh—A reservoir of natural water (i.e., water that has not been drawn artificially) large enough that an adult can immerse his or her entire body in it. Immersion in a *Mikveh* is a means for attaining purification for various halakhic purposes. Nowadays it is the custom (mainly among Ḥassidim) to go to the *Mikveh* daily before the *Shaḥarit** service in preparation for prayer. In addition, it is a normative halakhic requirement for women following menstruation and before resuming marital relations.

Minḥah—The Afternoon Prayer Service. See Chapter 8.

Minḥah Gedolah, *Minḥah Ketanah*—Terms used for various times for reciting the *Minḥah** prayer. *Minḥah Gedolah* is half an hour after astronomical high noon,* or midday; *Minḥah Ketanah* is from three-and-a-half astronomical hours* after midday till sunset.

Minyan—A quorum of ten Jewish men, the minimal number required for the recitation of certain prayers, performance of certain ceremonies, and other halakhic issues.

Mishloaḥ Manot—A present containing two kinds of food, which every Jew is obligated to give to at least one other Jew on the occasion of the festival of Purim.* See Chapter 12.

Mishnah—The first and most fundamental collection of Halakhah* of the Oral Torah. The Mishnah was first committed to writing by Rabbi Yehudah (Judah) the Prince. It is divided into six volumes (*sedarim*), each volume (*seder*) is divided into tractates, each tractate into chapters, and each chapter into *mishnayot* (sing., *mishnah*). The six *sedarim* are: *Zera'im* (Agricultural Laws), *Mo'ed* (Holy Days), *Nashim* (Family Laws), *Nezikin* (Civil Law), *Koddashim* (Temple-related Law), and *Taharot* (Laws of Ritual Purity).

mitzvah (pl., *mitzvot*)—"Commandment" or "injunction." A command either explicitly written in the Torah or later ruled by the sages. *Mitzvot* are of two general kinds: positive commandments, which involve an action; and negative commandments, which involve refraining from doing certain things.

Modeh Ani (fem., *Modah Ani*)—"I Thank You." The first words to be uttered upon waking in the morning.

Modim—The next-to-last blessing in the *Amidah** prayer. *Modim* is an expression of gratitude for all of God's mercies and for our very existence and closeness to Him.

Modim de-Rabbanan—A formulation recited by the entire congregation while the *Shaliaḥ Tzibbur** recites the *Modim** blessing in the repetition* of the *Amidah** prayer.

Mondays and Thursdays—Two days on which, even when no holidays are being celebrated, there are in any case some additions in the daily prayers: Torah readings and longer *Taḥanun** sections. These additions were instituted because in ancient times these were days when many people would come to the cities from the surrounding villages to buy and sell goods at the market, to attend the courts of law, etc.

Morid ha-Tal—A formulation regarding the fall of dew, recited by some in the second *Amidah** blessing during the summer season.

Motza'ei Shabbat—The conclusion of Shabbat.

Musaf—A prayer in addition to the three usual daily prayers, recited on those days on which an additional sacrifice used to be offered in the Temple, namely, Sabbaths, festivals, and *Rosh Ḥodesh*.*

Naḥem—A special prayer added onto the *Amidah** on the Ninth of Av. See Chapter 12.

Ne'ilah—The fifth and last prayer service, recited at twilight. Nowadays it is recited only on Yom Kippur*; in former days it was also recited during major public fasts.

Nefilat Appayyim—The custom of resting one's face on one's arm while reciting certain parts of the *Taḥanun*.*

negative commandments—See *mitzvah*.*

Netilat Yadayyim—Ritual washing of the hands, which is mandatory (a) upon waking up in the morning; (b) after going to the bathroom; (c) before prayer; (d) for *Kohanim*,* before reciting the Priestly Blessing*; (e) before eating bread.

Nishmat Kol Ḥai—A special prayer, recited on the morning of Shabbat and festival days, right before the *Yishtabbaḥ** blessing.

Nusaḥ (pl., *Nusaḥim*)—Prayer rite (or version). See Chapter 7.

Ofanim—A type of *Piyyut** recited in some congregations within the blessing of *Yotzer Or** on Shabbat mornings.

Parashat ha-Ketoret (also called *Pittum ha-Ketoret*)—Verses from the Torah (Exodus 30:34–37, and 7–8), with related sayings of our sages, dealing with incense offerings at the Temple. This segment is recited in several places in the prayer services.

Parashat ha-Man—Exodus 16:4–36, which speaks of the manna that rained down from the heavens. Some recite it daily after the *Shaḥarit** prayer, because it stresses the faith in God's providence, and God's ability to nurture all the world's creatures.

Parashat ha-Tamid—Numbers 28: 1–8, which speaks of the daily secrifices in the Tabernacle (and later, in the Temple). This portion is read within the *Korbanot** section of the *Shaḥarit** prayer, as well as before the *Minḥah** prayer. Some recite a short prayer about the restoration of Temple worship, before and after reading it, and ask that our reciting these verses be considered as if we have offered an actual sacrifice.

Parashat ha-Teshuvah—Deuteronomy 30:1–10, which speaks of the *Teshuvah* (repentance; see Chapter 11) of the Jewish people at the end of days. Some recite it after the *Shaḥarit** prayer.

Parashat ha-Yir'ah—Deuteronomy 10:12–11:9, which speaks of man's duty to fear God and love Him for all the miracles and favors He confers upon us. Some recite it after the *Shaḥarit** prayer.

Parokhet—The curtain over the Ark.* See Chapter 13.

Parshiyyah—A small biblical portion, based on a very ancient division. See Chapter 13.

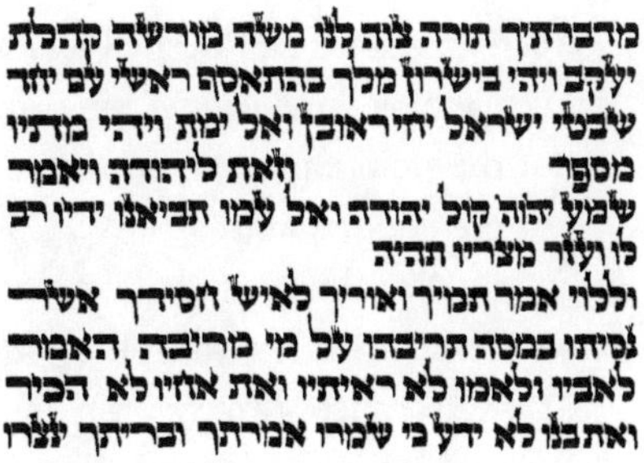
מדברתיך תורה צוה לנו משה מורשה קהלת
יעקב ויהי בישרון מלך בהתאסף ראשי עם יחד
שבטי ישראל יחי ראובן ואל ימת ויהי מתיו
מספר וזאת ליהודה ויאמר
שמע יהוה קול יהודה ואל עמו תביאנו ידיו רב
לו ועזר מצריו תהיה
וללוי אמר תמיך ואוריך לאיש חסידך אשר
נסיתו במסה תריבהו על מי מריבה האמר
לאביו ולאמו לא ראיתיו ואת אחיו לא הכיר
ואת בנו לא ידע כי שמרו אמרתך ובריתך ינצרו

Pataḥ Eliyahu—An excerpt of major importance from the introduction to one of the books of the *Zohar*# *(Tikkunei Zohar* 17a), which includes a general description of the world according to the Kabbalah. Some recite it daily as part of the prayer service; others recite it only on Shabbat.

Pelag ha-Minḥah—One and a quarter astronomical hours* before sunset.* This period of time has halakhic significance in regard to prayers. (For instance, whoever prays *Ma'ariv** before sunset must take care not to pray *Minḥah** later than *Pelag ha-Minḥah;* see *Berakhot* 26b.

Pesaḥ—The festival of Passover. Along with Sukkot* and Shavu'ot,* one of the Shalosh Regalim,* the three pilgrimage festivals. See Chapter 10.

Pesukei de-Zimrah—Various biblical passages, mostly psalms, recited in the *Shaḥarit** service before the *Shema** blessings.

Pirkei Avot—A tractate of the Mishnah* containing aphorisms and practical and moral guidance from our sages. Also commonly referred to as *Avot.**

Piyyut (pl., *Piyyutim*)—Liturgical poems that are not part of the ordinary order of prayers, and which have been inserted in various places in the prayer services. See Chapter 6.

Pizmon (pl., *Pizmonim*)—A prayer-song, especially one containing a refrain.

positive commandments—See *mitzvah*.*

Prayer for Dew (Hebrew, *Tefillat Tal*)—A prayer recited before, after, or during the *Musaf** prayer on the first day of Pesaḥ,* which is the first prayer service in which rains are no longer mentioned in the second *Amidah** blessing.

Prayer for Rain (Hebrew, *Tefillat Geshem*)—A prayer recited before, after, or during the *Musaf** prayer on Shemini Atzeret,* which is the first prayer service in which rain begins to be mentioned in the second *Amidah** blessing.

Priestly Blessing (Hebrew, *Birkat Kohanim*)—A blessing, commanded in the Torah (Numbers 6:22–26). The Priestly Blessing is made by the *Kohanim*,* in some of the public prayers, to the rest of the congregants.

The center of this medieval seal of the printer Shalom ha-Cohen Propes of Amsterdam shows the position of the *Kohen*'s hands during *Birkat Kohanim*.

Psalm 20—A psalm recited daily, since ancient times, within the *Shaḥarit** service (except for most days on which *Taḥanun** is not recited). Psalm 20 speaks of delivery in times of war and trouble.

Psalm 23—A psalm recited a number of times during Shabbat that speaks of the serenity of the soul basking in God's bounty.

Psalm 27—"The Lord is my light and my salvation." A psalm recited twice daily from the first day of the month of Elul until Shemini Atzeret.* Psalm 27 alludes to the Days of Awe* and to Sukkot.*

Psalm 92—"A Psalm, a Song for the Shabbat day." A psalm recited several times during the course of the Shabbat prayers.

Psalm 93—"The Lord is King; He has garbed Himself with grandeur." A psalm recited a few times during the Shabbat prayers.

Psalm 100—"A psalm for the thanksgiving-offering." Psalm 100 is recited within the weekday *Shaḥarit** prayer service.

Psalm 104—"My soul! Bless the Lord." A psalm recited on *Rosh Ḥodesh*.*

Purim—The festival commemorating the deliverance of the Jews from the decrees of Haman as described in the Book of Esther. See Chapter 12.

repetition of the *Amidah*—See *Amidah* repetition.*

Reshut—A type of *Piyyut** that serves as an introduction to a prayer, a blessing, or a ceremony.

Retzeh—The third-to-last blessing in the *Amidah** prayer. *Retzeh* speaks of the restoration of Temple service.

Retzeh ve-Haḥalitzenu—A section added to the third blessing of the Grace After Meals* on Shabbat.

Ribbono Shel Olam—"Master of the Universe." An opening formulation employed in various prayers.

Rimmonim—(literally, "pomegranates") The appellation for various ornaments used to adorn Torah scrolls. *Rimmonim* are usually made of precious metals, often in bell or pomegranate shapes.

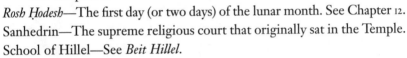

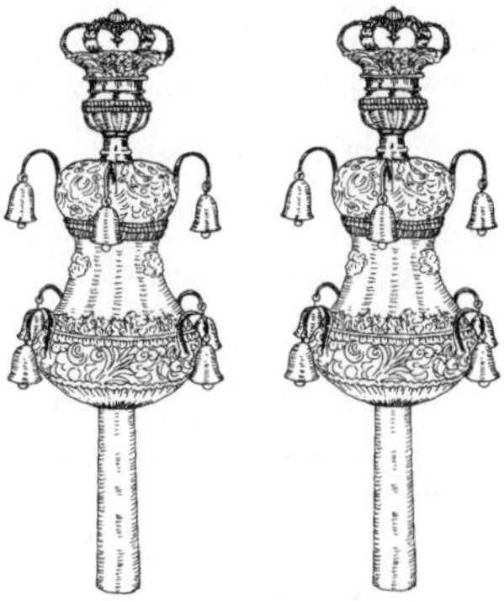

Rishonim—Jewish sages from after the Geonic period* until the sixteenth century C.E.. See also *Aḥaronim.**

Rosh ha-Shanah—The New Year's festival. See Chapter 11.

Rosh Ḥodesh—The first day (or two days) of the lunar month. See Chapter 12.

Sanhedrin—The supreme religious court that originally sat in the Temple.

School of Hillel—See *Beit Hillel.*

Se'udah Shelishit—The third Shabbat meal, eaten in the afternoon hours. Considered a time of special favor.

Se'udat Mitzvah—A festive meal connected with the performance of a commandment—e.g., after a circumcision, after a wedding, upon finishing the study of a tractate of Talmud. and the like.

Seder—The appellation for the festive ceremony and meal on the eve of Pesaḥ, during which the *Haggadah** is read.

Seder ha-Avodah—A central section of the repetition* of the *Amidah** prayer in the *Musaf** service of Yom Kippur, describing the Temple worship on that day as it used to be performed by the High Priest.

Sefirah (pl., *Sefirot)*—Each one of the ten Divine manifestations in this world, to which the various spiritual powers of man correspond. For a detailed discussion of this, see, for instance, *The Thirteen Petalled Rose* by Adin Steinsaltz.

Seliḥot—Orders of prayers and *Piyyutim** recited before and during the Ten Days of Repentance,* in all the prayer services of Yom Kippur,* and in public fasts.

Shaḥarit—The Morning Prayer Service. See Chapter 8.

Shaliaḥ Tzibbur—The prayer leader, considered an emissary to God on behalf of the entire congregation.

Shalom Aleikhem—A *Piyyut** recited or sung upon returning home from the synagogue on Shabbat eve. *Shalom Aleikhem* greets the angels that accompany one home.

Shalosh Regalim—The three pilgrimage festivals: Pesaḥ,* Shavu'ot,* and Sukkot.* See Chapter 10.

Shavu'ot—The Festival of Weeks, also known as the Festival of the Giving of the Torah, celebrated seven weeks after Pesaḥ.* Along with Pesaḥ* and Sukkot,* one of the *Shalosh Regalim*,* the three pilgrimage festivals. See Chapter 10.

she-Heḥeyanu—"Who has granted us life . . ." A blessing recited on various occasions—e.g., on festivals, upon performing certain periodically required commandments, and for various other things that cause special joy.

Shekhinah—God's manifestation in the world.

Shema—(literally, "Hear!") The recitation of three Torah portions: Deuteronomy 6:4–9, Deuteronomy 11:13–21, and Numbers 15:-37–41. The first verse is "Hear, O Israel, the Lord is our God, the Lord is One." The *Shema* is recited daily in the *Shaḥarit** and *Ma'ariv** services, and before retiring to bed, as well as on other occasions. It contains the main principles of Jewish faith and forms the basis of our individual and collective relationship with the Almighty.

Shema Kolenu—The sixteenth blessing of the weekday *Amidah** prayer. A plea for the prayers to be accepted.

Shema Upon Retiring to Bed—The *Shema** portions, along with other blessings, psalms, and entreaties, recited prior to going to sleep.

Shemini Atzeret—The eighth day of the Sukkot* festival, which is a festival in its own right. See Chapter 10.

Shemoneh Esreh—The most central prayer in the order of prayers, also called *Amidah*.* See Chapter 8.

Shevarim—One of the sounds made by the *Shofar*.* A combination of three rather short blasts.

Shir ha-Kavod—A deeply devotional poem, attributed to Rabbi Yehudah ha-Ḥassid (Judah the Pious). *Shir ha-Kavod* is usually recited during or after the Shabbat Morning Prayer Service.

Shir ha-Yiḥud—A long poem, consisting of seven sections, speaking of God's unity and greatness, probably composed in the twelfth century C.E., and usually recited on the night of Yom Kippur,* after the *Ma'ariv** service.

Shiv'ah—The first seven days of mourning.

Shivviti—A page or board containing the verse "I have set the Lord always before me" (Psalm 16:8), together with other verses and adornments. A *Shivviti* is often placed where the *Shaliaḥ Tzibbur** can readily see and be inspired by it.

Shofar—A ram's horn, cleaned and processed in specified ways. The *Shofar* is blown on Rosh ha-Shanah* as a Torah commandment and, customarily, on certain other occasions as well. See Chapters 11 and 12.

Shofarot—The last of the three central blessings of the Rosh ha-Shanah* *Musaf** prayer. *Shofarot* speaks about various aspects of Divine revelation. See Chapter 11.

Shome'a Tefillah—See *Shema Kolenu.**

Shovavim Tat—Appellation for the weeks during which the first eight portions of the book of Exodus are read. These weeks are particularly conducive for repentance.

Sim Shalom—A prayer for peace, which is the last of the *Amidah** blessings.

Simḥat Beit ha-Shoevah—Joyful celebrations, held since Temple times during *Ḥol ha-Mo'ed** of the Sukkot* festival.

Simḥat Torah—The day on which the yearly cycle of Torah reading is concluded and started again. In the Land of Israel, it is held on Shemini Atzeret,* while outside Israel it is celebrated on the following day, the second *Yom Tov** of Shemini Atzeret.

Song of Songs—One of the Five Scrolls in the Bible, customarily read every Shabbat eve and on the morning of the Shabbat within the festival of Pesaḥ.*

Song of the Day—The psalm recited for each day of the week. Originally, sung by the Levites in the Temple.

Song of the Sea—The song recited by Moses and the children of Israel after the parting and crossing of the Red Sea (Exodus 15:1–19).

Songs of Ascents—Fifteen psalms (Psalms 120–134), corresponding to the fifteen steps in the Temple, recited (all or in part) in different points during various prayer services.

Sukkah—A temporary booth or hut that Jews are commanded to build and to live in for the seven (or, in the Diaspora, eight) days of the festival of Sukkot.* See Chapter 10.

Sukkot—The Festival of Booths. Along with Pesaḥ* and Shavu'ot,* one of the *Shalosh Regalim,** the three pilgrimage festivals. See Chapter 10.

sunrise—The moment at which the sun begins to shine, which has halakhic significance for a variety of matters.

Ta'amei ha-Mikra—Cantillation, the system of signs that determine both the punctuation of biblical verses and the melody to which they are to be read. See Chapter 13.

Taḥanun—A series of entreaties recited on weekdays after the *Amidah** prayer of the *Shaḥarit** and *Minḥah** services.

Tallit (pl., *Tallitot*)—Prayer shawl. See Chapter 16.

Tallit Katan—A four-cornered garment with *Tzitzit*,* worn by men under their shirts.

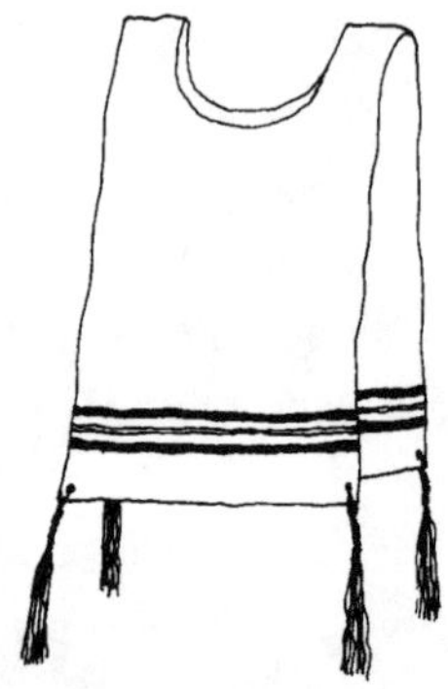

Talmud—The most important book in the history and culture of the Jewish people. It includes the Mishnah, and was created over the course of some thousand years, both in the Land of Israel and in Babylonia. There are, in fact, two Talmuds: (a) The Babylonian Talmud, compiled in Babylonia and finalized in the beginning of the sixth century C.E.; (b) the Jerusalem Talmud, composed by the *Amoraim** of the Land of Israel, especially in the city of Tiberias, and finalized some 150 years before the Babylonian Talmud.

Tanna (pl., *Tannaim*)—Term used for a sage or sages during and after the Second Temple period, from Shimon ha-Tzaddik (the end of the third century B.C.E.) to the students of Rabbi Judah the Prince (the beginning of the third century C.E.). The *Tannaim* created the Mishnah, the Tosefta, the Midrash, and more.

Tefillin—Phylacteries. It is a Torah commandment to wear *Tefillin* on the head and on the arm. See Chapter 16.

Tefillin of Rabbenu Tam—A pair of *Tefillin** in which the order of the portion is slightly different. Customarily worn by many people as an additional pair of *Tefillin*. See Chapter 16.

Teḥinnot (sing., *Teḥinnah*)—Various kinds of prayer entreaties.

Teki'ah—One of the sounds produced by the *Shofar*.* It consists of one long blast.

Ten Commandments—Exodus 20:1–14. Some people recite them daily after the *Shaḥarit** service. It is customary to stand whenever they are read publicly.

Ten Days of Repentance—The first ten days of the Jewish year, starting on Rosh ha-Shanah* and ending on Yom Kippur.* These days are considered days of special Divine favor, especially conducive to repentance and mending one's ways.

Teru'ah—One of the sounds produced by the *Shofar.** It consists of a series of very short blasts.

Third Meal—See *Se'udah Shelishit.**

Thirteen Attributes (of Divine Mercy)—The thirteen aspects of mercy with which God reveals Himself to the world, as they are detailed in Exodus 34:6–7. They are recited as part of the *Taḥanun*,* the *Seliḥot*,* and other services.

Tikkun—In the context of prayer, a series of psalms and prayers, or a study sequence, recited or studied at night. See *Tikkun Hatzot** and *Tikkun Leil Shavu'ot.**

Tikkun Ḥatzot—A series of psalms, biblical verses, *Piyyutim*,* and entreaties, customarily recited after midnight. See Chapter 8.

Tikkun Leil Shavu'ot—The order of Torah study customarily recited on Shavu'ot.* Also, the custom to remain awake all that night and study Torah. See Chapter 10.

Tikkunei Shabbat—Certain parts of the Mishnah,* Tractate *Shabbat*, customarily studied in conjunction with each of the three Shabbat meals. See Chapter 9.

Torah Reader—See *Ba'al Keri'ah.**

Torah reading—Each time, within a prayer service, when a part of the Torah is read from a Torah scroll. See Chapter 13.

Torah reading, being called up to—Inviting one of the congregants to the *Bimah** to read a part of a Torah reading.* See *Aliyah.**

Tosafot—Commentaries, criticism, and new interpretations to the Talmud added to Rashi's@ commentary on the Babylonian Talmud by Rashi's grandchildren and other rabbis.

Tzidkatekha—Three verses from Psalms, all starting with this word, recited near the end of the Shabbat *Minḥah** service.

Tzitzit—(a) The Torah commandment to wear fringes on the four corners of specific garments; (b) the fringes themselves. See Chapter 16.

u-Netanneh Tokef—A *Piyyut** recited on the Days of Awe* before the recitation of the *Kedushah*,* describing in lofty language the holiness of the day and the process of Divine judgment.

u-Va le-Zion Go'el—A series of verses and prayers recited daily after the *Amidah** prayer.

Ushpizin—The "seven pastors"—Abraham, Isaac, Jacob, Moses, Aaron, Joseph, and David—who, according to tradition, come to every *Sukkah** as spiritual guests on each of the nights of the Sukkot* festival. See Chapter 10.

Va'ad Arba Aratzot—See Council of Four Lands.

va-Todi'enu—A *Havdalah** formulation recited in the *Ma'ariv** prayer of a festival that falls on *Motza'ei Shabbat.**

va-Yehi bi-Nesoa ha-Aron—Verses and prayers recited upon opening the Ark* and taking out the Torah scrolls. See Chapter 13.

va-Yekhulu—Genesis 2:1–3. Verses that speak of the origin of the Shabbat day. These verses are considered a testimony and are read three times on Shabbat eve. See Chapter 9.

ve-Attah Kadosh—The beginning of the *Kedushah** formulation, recited within *u-Va le-Zion Go'el.**

ve-Hu Raḥum—Psalm 78:38. A verse recited daily before the *Ma'ariv** prayer service on weekdays, as well as on some other occasions.

ve-Shamru—The opening word of the verses of Exodus 31:16–17, customarily recited at the end of the *Hashkivenu** blessing, prior to the *Amidah** prayer of the *Ma'ariv** of Shabbat.

ve-Yitten Lekha—Collected verses of blessing, success, and peace, customarily recited on *Motza'ei Shabbat.** See Chapter 9.

vi-Yehi No'am—Psalm 91, preceded with the last verse of Psalm 90. Recited (except for a few exceptions) on *Motza'ei Shabbat.**

Vidduy—"Confession [of sins]." The *Vidduy* is recited daily within the order of *Nefilat Appayim** in the *Shaḥarit** and *Minḥah** prayers and in the recitation of the *Shema* Upon Retiring to Bed.* It is recited on other occasions as well, such as during the *Seliḥot.**

Weekly Portion (Hebrew, *Parashat ha-Shavu'a*)—The part of the Torah read on each of the Sabbaths of the year. The Torah is divided in such a way that the entire Pentateuch is read during the course of one year. See Chapter 13.

Ya'aleh ve-Yavo—The common appellation for a special prayer recited on festival days, on *Ḥol ha-Mo'ed,** on the Days of Awe,* and on *Rosh Ḥodesh.** It is recited both within the *Amidah** prayer and the Grace After Meals.*

Yad—(literally, "hand") One of the accessories of the Torah scroll; a kind of pointer used by the *Ba'al Keriah** for indicating the exact part of the Torah that is being read. See Chapter 13.

Yahrzeit—The anniversary of the death of a close relative, to which some special rules pertain.

Yamin Tovin—See *Yom Tov.*

Yedid Nefesh—A profound devotional *Piyyut** written by Rabbi Eliezer

Azkari of Safed (d. 1600 B.C.E.). The acrostic of its four verses makes up the Tetragrammaton.

Yehi Khevod—Collected verses (mainly from the Book of Psalms) that speak of God's grandeur and His rule over the world. Recited in the *Shaḥarit** service before *Ashrei.**

Yehi Ratzon—"May it be Your will." The opening words of many prayers.

Yekum Purkan—Two blessing formulations, in Aramaic, recited by Ashkenazim after the Torah reading* on Shabbat mornings.

Yeshivah (pl., *Yeshivot*)—A house for the study of Mishnah* and Talmud.*

Yigdal—A *Piyyut** by an anonymous writer in which Maimonides'@ Thirteen Principles of Faith are written in poetic language. Often recited at the end of prayer services.

Yishtabbaḥ—The blessing that concludes the order of *Pesukei de-Zimrah** every morning. In many ways, it is parallel to the blessing of *Barukh she-Amar.**

Yizkor—The custom of mentioning and recalling the souls of the departed and of making a commitment to charity in their memory. Customarily recited on Yom Kippur* and on the last days of the *Shalosh Regalim*,* the three pilgrimage festivals.

Yoknehaz—An ancient mnemonic for the special *Kiddush**-*Havdalah** order for a festival day that falls on *Motza'ei Shabbat.** See Chapter 10.

Yom Kippur—The Day of Atonement. See Chapter 11.

Yom Kippur Katan—A day of fasting and repentance observed by some on every eve of *Rosh Ḥodesh.**

Yom Tov (pl., *Yamim Tovim*)—(literally, "good day[s]") An appellation for festival days. See Chapter 10.

Yotzer Or—The first of the *Shema** blessings, recited every morning.

Yotzerot—An appellation for various kinds of *Piyyutim.**

Zemirot—The appellation for various songs sung in honor of the Shabbat, either during or after the Shabbat meals.

Zikhronot—The second of the three middle blessings of the *Amidah** of the *Musaf** prayer of Rosh ha-Shanah. See Chapter 11.

Zimmun—An introductory blessing to the Grace After Meals,* recited whenever at least three people eat together (either three men or three women; but in a mixed group, only when there are three or more men).

BIOGRAPHIES

Ba'al Shem Tov (Rabbi Israel Ba'al Shem Tov)—(Ukraine, 1698–1760) Founder of the Ḥassidic movement.

Ba'alei ha-Tosafot (Tosaphists)—(France and Franco-Germany, twelfth and thirteenth centuries C.E.) Talmudic commentators, descendants, and disciples of Rashi.@ The Tosaphists authored brief discourses (known as *Tosafot*, "additions") on individual talmudic passages, some of which are included on the main pages of the talmudic text with other major commentaries. Their work is based largely on the commentary of their teacher, Rashi.

Ezra the Scribe—(late fifth to early fourth centuries B.C.E.) Leader of the second wave of the return of the Jews from Persia at the beginning of the Second Temple era (see the biblical book of Ezra). Ezra laid the foundations of Judaism for all coming generations. Among other rulings, he instituted public Torah reading on Monday and Thursday mornings and as part of the Shabbat *Minḥah** prayer. See Chapter 13.

Josephus Flavius—(b. Jerusalem, 37 C.E.; d. Rome, ca. 100 C.E.) *Kohen;** military commander of the Jewish army in the wars before and during the destruction of the Second Temple; renegade and historian. The writings of Josephus (especially *The Jewish War* and *The Antiquities of the Jews*) are nearly the sole source of historical information on that period.

The Maggid of Mezeritz (Rabbi Dov Baer)—(1704–1772) Student and successor of the Ba'al Shem Tov, he was the primary organizer and theoretician of the Ḥassidic movement.

Maharil (Rabbi Ya'akov ben Moshe Halevi Molin)—(c. 1360–1427 C.E.) One of the greatest Ashkenazic sages of his time, who served as Rabbi of Ashkenaz (Franco-Germany) and the surrounding countries, as well as halakhic decisor and head of a *Yeshivah*. His halakhic rulings, along with many of the customs he established, are observed by Ashkenazim to this day.

Maharsha (Rabbi Shmuel Eideles)—(Poland, 1555–1631) One of the greatest

Talmud* commentators of all generations, he is renowned particularly for his commentaries on the aggadic sections of the Talmud.

Maimonides (Rabbi Moshe ben Maimon)—(1138–1204) Generally considered the greatest medieval Jewish sage and one of the greatest sages of all generations. Maimonides was a halakhic decisor, philosopher, commentator, physician, and scientist. He was the author of many works; outstanding among them was the code of laws called *Mishneh Torah* ("Repetition of the Torah") which, because it consisted of fourteen volumes (the number fourteen being expressed in Hebrew by the letters of the word *Yad*—"hand") also came to be known as the *Yad ha-Ḥazakah* ("The Strong Hand"); *The Guide for the Perplexed;* a commentary on the Mishnah; several major epistles; and numerous other works.

Naḥmanides (Rabbi Moshe ben Naḥman)—(b. Spain, 1194; d. Acre, 1270) One of the greatest medieval Jewish sages, halakhic authority, philosopher, mystic, Bible commentator, poet, and doctor. Participated and was victorious in numerous polemics with church leaders.

Philo of Alexandria—(Egypt, 20 B.C.E.–50 C.E.) Important Hellenistic Jewish philosopher.

Rabbenu Gershom Meor ha-Golah—(Western Europe, 965–1028) The greatest halakhic authority of his day, he decreed a number of rulings followed by all to this day. He also composed several *Seliḥot.**

Rabbenu Tam (Rabbi Yaakov ben Meir Tam)—(France, ca. 1100–1171) A grandson of Rashi,@ he was the leading halakhic authority of his day, the central figure among the *Ba'alei ha-Tosafot,*@ and author of *Sefer ha-Yashar.*

Rabbi Akiva—(c. 50–135 C.E.) The central figure in the third generation of *Tannaim,** he laid the foundations for the compilation of the Mishnah.*

Rabbi Avraham Danzig—(Vilna, eighteenth to nineteeth century). Author of the books *Ḥayyei Adam*# and *Ḥokhmat Adam.*

Rabbi Avraham David of Buczacz—(1771–1840) Ḥassidic rabbi and author of a number of books of Halakhah* and Ḥassidic thought.

Rabbi Avraham ibn Ezra—(Spain, 1089–1164) Poet, grammarian, Bible commentator, philosopher, astronomer, and physician.

Rabbi Eleazar ha-Kallir—(Land of Israel, sixth to seventh century C.E.) One of the greatest religious poets of all generations, his *Piyyutim** and *Seliḥot** occupy a central place in the Ashkenazic liturgy.

Rabbi Eliezer the Great (Rabbi Eliezer ben Hyrkanus)—One of the great sages of the Mishnah.* For a detailed biography, see Steinsaltz, *Talmudic Images* (Fort Lee, N.J.: Jason Aronson, 1997).

Rabbi Ephraim of Bonn—(1133–1196) Halakhic authority and author of *Piyyutim*,* he lived during the Crusades.

Rabbi Ḥayyim Vital—(Safed, 1543–1620) Studied with the greatest sages of Safed. He was the closest disciple of Rabbi Isaac Luria,@ and eventually committed all of Luria's teachings to writing.

Rabbi Isaac Abravanel—(1473–1508) One of the leaders of the Jews expelled from Portugal in the sixteenth century. Wrote a major commentary to the Bible and other books of Jewish philosophy.

Rabbi Isaac Luria—(b. Jerusalem, 1534; d. Safed, 1572) One of the greatest Jewish mystics of all times; founder of Lurianic Kabbalah.* Known as "the Saintly Ari" (acronym for Ashkenazi Rabbi Isaac).

Rabbi Meshullam bar Kalonymus—(tenth to eleventh century) Italian-Jewish sage and poet.

Rabbi Moshe ibn Ezra—(1055–1135) One of the greatest of the Spanish-Jewish poets.

Rabbi Moshe Sofer—(1762–1839) One of the major halakhic decisors of the nineteenth century; leader of Orthodox opposition to Reform movements in Germany and, later, in Hungary.

Rabbi Schneur Zalman of Lyady—(b. Belorussia, 1745; d. Ukraine, 1813) Among the first great Ḥassidic leaders, founder of Ḥabad Ḥassidism. He wrote numerous books, among them the *Tanya*, a new version of the *Shulḥan Arukh*, and a Siddur.

Rabbi Shalom Shabbazi—(1619–1680) The greatest Yemenite Jewish poet.

Rabbi Solomon ibn Gabirol—(Spain, 1021–1050) Prominent philosopher who was also one of the greatest Spanish-Jewish poets.

Rabbi Yehudah Halevi—(b. Spain, 1075; d. Egypt or Israel, ca. 1140) Outstanding Spanish-Jewish poet and philosopher; author of the *Kuzari*, a polemic dialogue in defense of Judaism.

Rabbi Yom Tov Lippmann Heller—(Prague, 1579–1654) One of the greatest rabbis of his generation; author of the Mishnah commentary *Tosafot Yom Tov.*

Rabbi Yosef Ḥayyim of Baghdad (Ben Ish Ḥai)—(Iraq, 1833 [or 1835]–1909) Torah scholar and mystic, the greatest halakhic authority of Iraqi Jewry, author of numerous books and prayers.

Rabbi Yosef Karo—Author of *Shulḥan Arukh.** Born in Spain, he was, as a child, among the Jews expelled in 1492; lived most of his adult life in Safed. Among his other famous books: *Kesef Mishneh*—his commentary on Maimonides'@ *Yad ha-Ḥazakah,*# and *Beit Yosef*—his commentary on the *Tur.*#

Rabbi Yossi ben Yossi—(Land of Israel, fourth or fifth century C.E.) The first known author of *Piyyutim.** His *Piyyutim** excel in the beauty of their language and in their poetic inspiration.

Rashi (Rabbi Shlomo Yitzhaki)—(France, 1040–1105) The greatest Torah and Talmud commentator of all times. Rashi wrote Responsa and composed numerous *Piyyutim.**

Rav (Rabbi Abba bar Aivu)—(second century C.E.) One of the greatest sages of the first generation of Babylonian *Amoraim.**

Rav Hai Gaon—(939–1038) One of the major *Geonim,** son of Rav Sherira Gaon,@ head of the Pumbedita *Yeshivah** in Babylonia, and among those who laid the foundations of the Halakhah* for future generations.

Rav Nissim Gaon—(Egypt, ca. 950–1062) One of the greatest Torah sages and leaders of North African Jewry.

Rav Sa'adiah Gaon—(b. Egypt, 882; d. Babylonia, 942) The central figure of the Geonic period,* father of rabbinic literature. He was also a philosopher, grammarian, poet, and translator of the Bible.

Rav Sherira Gaon—(906–1006) One of the *Geonim,** head of the Pumbedita *Yeshivah** in Babylonia, author of many Responsa and of an important *Iggeret* ("Epistle") giving a history of the transmission of the tradition of Oral Torah.

Ravad (Rabbi Avraham ben David of Pousquières)—(1120–1198) Among the greatest talmudic sages of all generations. He was renowned for his glosses on Maimonides' halakhic work, as well as for his own important halakhic works.

Rema (Rabbi Moshe Isserles)—(Poland, 1525?–1572) One of the greatest halakhic authorities of all generations, and a major commentator on the *Shulḥan Arukh.*

Remah (Rabbi Meir Halevi)—(second half of the fourteenth century) One of the greatest sages of Franco-German Jewry.

The Rosh (Rabbi Asher ben Yeḥiel)—(b. Franco-Germany, 1250; d. Spain, 1327) One of the greatest *Rishonim,** studied under the *Ba'alei ha-Tosafot.*@

Tosafot—See *Ba'alei ha-Tosafot.*@

The Vilna Gaon (Rabbi Eliyahu ben Shlomo Zalman of Vilna)—(1720–1797) Among the greatest Torah scholars of all times, he wrote many important and influential works on a great variety of topics, among them many commentaries to the Talmud and other books, as well as commentaries on sections of the *Zohar.*# He was considered the greatest halakhic authority of his day. A special prayer rite, created on the basis of his rulings, is followed by his disciples to this day.

Yonatan ben Uzziel—(first century B.C.E.–first century C.E.) Considered the greatest disciple of Hillel the Elder; the Aramaic translation of the Prophets is attributed to him.

BIBLIOGRAPHICAL NOTES

Abudraham—The most important commentary on the Siddur, composed in the fourteenth century by Rabbi David Abudraham of Spain.

Ben Sira—Apocryphal book of wisdom literature written by a man named Ben Sira in Jerusalem in the second century B.C.E. Though very highly acclaimed by the Jewish sages, the book was not included in the final codification of the Bible.

Etz Yosef—A nineteenth-century commentary on the aggadic *Midrash Rabbah** by Rabbi Ḥanokh Zundel bar Yosef.

Ḥayyei Adam—A book by Rabbi Avraham Danzig,@ in which he sums up the laws of *Shulḥan Arukh*, *Oraḥ Ḥayyim*.

Kuzari—A theological-apologetic book originally written in Arabic by Rabbi Yehudah Halevi,@ recounting the story of the conversion of the king of Khazar to the Jewish faith (completed shortly before Halevi's death, ca. 1140).

Levush—One of a series of books by Rabbi Mordechai Gimpel Yaffe (Poland, sixteenth century), whose titles all begin with the word *Levush*, "garment." The specific book referred to here is his commentary on *Shulḥan Arukh*, *Oraḥ Ḥayyim*.

Ma'avar Yabbok—A book of laws related to visiting the sick, comportment with the deceased, and comforting mourners, written by Rabbi Aharon Berekhiah of Modena (d. 1639).

Magen Avraham—Major commentary on the *Oraḥ Ḥayyim* section of the *Shulḥan Arukh*, written by Rabbi Avraham Gombiner (Poland, 1637–1683).

Maḥzor Vitry—A comprehensive Siddur for the entire yearly cycle that also contains many *Piyyutim** and numerous laws and customs. This *Maḥzor* was composed in the eleventh century by Rabbi Simḥah of Vitry, a disciple of Rashi.@

Meiri—The common appellation for the encyclopedic Talmud* commentary *Beit ha-Beḥirah*, written by Rabbi Menaḥem bar Shelomo ha-Meiri (Provence, 1249–1316).

Mekhilta—See Midrash.*

Midrash Genesis Rabbah—An aggadic *midrash** on the book of Genesis.

Midrash Numbers Rabbah—An aggadic *midrash** on the book of Numbers.*

Midrash Tanḥuma—A *midrash** on the Torah based on the triennial Torah reading cycle (see Chapter 13), ascribed to the *Tanna** Rabbi Tanḥuma bar Abba of the Land of Israel (end of the fourth century B.C.E.).

Minhagei Maharil—Collection of the customs of Rabbi Yaakov Molin (known as Maharil; Germany, fifteenth century), who established the Ashkenazic rite. The major Ashkenazic melodies are attributed to him.

Mishnah Berurah—Major commentary on the *Shulḥan Arukh*, *Oraḥ Ḥayyim* by Rabbi Israel Meir ha-Cohen of Radin (Poland, nineteenth to twentieth century), known as the *Ḥafetz Ḥayyim*.

Mishneh Torah (also called *Yad ha-Ḥazakah*)—The monumental halakhic work of Maimonides@; the only book of Halakhah* that encompasses all areas of Jewish life, including those customs no longer in practice.

Otzar ha-Tefillot—A Siddur published approximately 100 years ago that contains many commentaries on prayers, as well as clarifications of prayer versions and the origins of prayers.

Peri Etz Hadar—Sometimes attributed to and possibly based on the work of Nathan of Gaza (1643/4–1680), the *Peri Etz Hadar* comprises a liturgy and study order for Tu bi-Shevat (see Chapter 12). It is based on kabbalistic sources.

Peri Etz Ḥayyim—The main teachings of Rabbi Isaac Luria@ as committed to writing by his major disciple, Rabbi Ḥayyim Vital.@

Pesikta Zutrati—Midrash and commentary on Leviticus, Numbers, and Deuteronomy composed by Rabbi Tuviah ben Rabbi Eleazar (sixteenth century).

Pirkei de-Rabbi Eliezer—An aggadic *midrash** ascribed to the *Tanna** Rabbi Eliezer the Great.

Responsa Ḥatam Sofer—Books of Responsa of Rabbi Moshe Sofer.@ These Responsa are considered highly authoritative.

Sefer ha-Ḥinukh—Commentary on the 613 Torah commandments, arranged in the order in which they appear in the Torah, ascribed to Rabbi Aaron Halevi of Barcelona (ca. 1235–1300).

Sefer ha-Manhig—A compendium of prayer laws and customs and the order of prayer by Rabbi Avraham bar Nathan ha-Yarḥi (Lunel, Provence, France, ca. 1155–1215).

Sefer ha-Rokeaḥ—A book on repentance, awe, and reverence for God, and laws in various spheres of Jewish life, by Rabbi Eleazar bar Yehudah of Worms (sixteenth century).

Septuagint—The first translation of the Bible into Greek, said to have been accomplished by seventy sages in only seventy-two days (first half of the third century B.C.E).

Sha'ar ha-Kavvanot—One of the eight "gates" (books) on Kabbalah written by Rabbi Ḥayyim Vital.@

Sha'arei Zion—A highly influential book of prayers and penitence rites by Rabbi Nathan Neta Hanover, based on the writings of Rabbi Isaac Luria@ (first published in Prague, 1662).

Shelah (*Shenei Luḥot ha-Berit*)—The most important and influential book by the great rabbi and mystic Rabbi Isaiah Hurwitz (b. Prague, 1560; d. Tiberias, 1630),who was called "the Holy Shelah" after the title of his book. The book contains instruction and guidance in all spheres of Jewish life. The Shelah also wrote an important commentary to the Siddur.

Shenei Luḥot ha-Berit—See *Shelah*.

Shulḥan Arukh—A summary of the halakhic laws and rulings in the four parts of the *Tur*,# written by Rabbi Yosef Karo@ (Safed, sixteenth century). The *Shulḥan Arukh* is the fundamental halakhic code still in use today.

Shulḥan Arukh ha-Rav—The *Shulḥan Arukh*,# as revised, rewritten, and commented upon by Schneur Zalman of Lyady (1745–1813), founder of Ḥabad Ḥassidism.

Siddur Beit Ya'akov—See *Siddur of Ya'avetz*.

Siddur of Maimonides—This Siddur, not written as an independent book, is included within the *Mishneh Torah*.# It greatly influenced Jewish prayer rites in Israel and in Egypt, and its influence continues to be felt to this day in the Yemenite rite.

Siddur of Rashi—Probably written by the disciples of Rashi,@ this Siddur contains laws and customs of prayer based on Rashi's teachings.

Siddur of Rav Amram Gaon—The earliest known Siddur, written by Rav Amram ben Sheshna Gaon in Babylonia in reply to a request from the Jewish community in Spain (ca. 860 C.E.). See Chapter 6.

Siddur of Rav Sa'adiah Gaon—Written by Rav Sa'adiah Gaon@ about one hundred years after the *Siddur of Rav Amram Gaon*.# This Siddur includes, in addition to the regular prayers, many *Piyyutim** composed by Rav Sa'adiah himself.

Siddur of Ya'avetz—(also called *Siddur Beit Ya'akov*) A comprehensive and highly influential prayer book written in Germany by Rabbi Yaakov Emden (1698–1776), known by his initials as Ya'avetz. His Siddur includes introductions and essays on Halakhah and philosophy.

Sifrei—A halakhic *midrash** on Numbers and Deuteronomy attributed to the great *Amora** Rav.@

Tanna de-Vei Eliyahu—An aggadic *midrash** which, unlike most midrashic works, is not a collection of homilies but rather a unified, highly personal work. The work is divided into two parts: *Tanna de-Vei Eliyahu Rabbah* and *Tanna de-Vei Eliyahu Zuta.* The date of its composition is unknown, but it was probably written in the Land of Israel sometime between the third and tenth centuries C.E..

Targum Onkelos—The most authoritative, predominantly literal Aramaic translation of the Torah, based on the teachings of the great *Tannaim** Rabbi Yehoshua and Rabbi Eliezer, and ascribed to the proselyte Onkelos (second century C.E.).

Targum Yerushalmi—An Aramaic translation of the Torah that employs great midrashic freedom. Erroneously called *Targum Yonatan;* there are two versions of this translation: one of the entire Torah (except for fifteen verses), and the other, of which there are only 850 verses.

Targum Yonatan—The authorized Aramaic translation of the Prophets. Composed in the Land of Israel and ascribed to the great *Tanna** Yonatan ben Uzziel.@

Tosafot Yom Tov—A fundamental commentary on the Mishnah by Rabbi Yom Tov Lippmann Heller.@

Tractate *Soferim*—One of the "minor" or, rather, external Talmud tractates, written by the *Geonim.** A comprehensive collection of laws regarding Torah scrolls and how they are to be written and read.

Tur—A comprehensive collection, arranged by topic, of all the halakhic rulings from the Talmud and the *Rishonim**; compiled by Rabbi Yaacov bar Asher (Ashkenaz, 1270–1343).

Yad ha-Ḥazakah—See *Mishneh Torah*.

Yalkut Reuveni—Collected essays, arranged by topics, with commentary on the Torah portions. Based on kabbalistic sources, the *Yalkut Reuveni* was written by Rabbi Avraham Reuven Hashki Katz and first published in 1681.

Zohar—The fundamental work of Jewish kabbalistic (mystical) thought. The *Zohar* comprises many books and is made up of midrashic sections. Its origins are attributed to the *Tanna** Rabbi Shimon bar Yoḥai.

THE JEWISH MONTHS
And the Festivals and Special Days That Occur in Each of Them

(The dates in the month are given in parentheses. As for the special days themselves, see the Glossary of Terms.)

Tishrei—(1–2) Rosh ha-Shanah; (3) Fast of Gedaliah; (3–9) *Shabbat Shuvah;* (10) Yom Kippur; (15–21; in the Diaspora, 15–22) Sukkot; (22; in the Diaspora, 22–23) Shemini Atzeret and Simḥat Torah.

Ḥeshvan (also called Marḥeshvan)—No special days.

Kislev—(25–2 or 3 Tevet) Ḥanukkah.

Tevet:—(10) Fast day in commemoration of the beginning of the Babylonian siege of Jerusalem.

Shevat—(15) Tu bi-Shevat.

Adar—(13) Fast of Esther; (14) Purim; (15) Shushan Purim. In leap years, there are two months of Adar; in that case, the 14–15 of the first Adar are called *Purim Katan* ("little Purim") and the actual Fast of Esther and Purim festival are celebrated during the second Adar.

Nisan—(15–21) Pesaḥ.

Iyyar—(5) Israel's Independence Day; (15) Pesaḥ Sheni ("the second Pesaḥ"); (18) Lag ba-Omer; (28) Jerusalem Day.

Sivan—(6; in the Diaspora, 6–7) Shavu'ot.

Tammuz—(17) Fast day in commemoration of the breaching of Jerusalem's walls by the Babylonians.

Av—(9) Tish'ah be-Av, fast day in commemoration of the destruction of the First and Second Temples; (15) Tu be-Av.

Elul—No special days; however, the entire month is devoted to preparation for the Days of Awe.*

INDEX